CONSUMER PSYCHOLOGY

ROBERT E. SMITH

strive4growth, llc

Professor Emeritus of Marketing
Indiana University

Copyright © 2015 Robert E. Smith

PUBLISHER	*strive4growth Publishing*
PRINTING & BINDING	*MagCloud*
DESIGN	*James Rosen*
EDITING	*Laura Buchholz & Robert Smith*

CONSUMER PSYCHOLOGY

Copyright © 2015 Robert E. Smith
All rights reserved.

ISBN-13: 978-1-4211-5388-2

The materials in this textbook are subject to copyright. They are provided solely for the student's personal and educational use and may not be further used, reproduced, or distributed, except in compliance with U.S. copyright laws.

Printed in the United States of America.

VIDEOS, ELABORATIVE QUESTIONS, CUSTOM FEEDBACK, AND GROWTH EXPERIMENTS RELATED TO THE CONCEPTS IN THE TEXT ARE AVAILABLE AT STRIVE4GROWTH.COM

CONSUMER PSYCHOLOGY
CONTENTS OF BOOK

CHAPTER 1	-	CONSUMER BEHAVIOR AND KEY ACCOUNTS
CHAPTER 2	-	THE INTERNAL MODEL
CHAPTER 3	-	THE STRUCTURE OF MEMORY
CHAPTER 4	-	MEMORY OPERATIONS, STUDYING, AND LEARNING
CHAPTER 5	-	COMPONENTS OF THE INTERNAL MODEL: BELIEFS AND VALUES
CHAPTER 6	-	COGNITIVE CONSISTENCY
CHAPTER 7	-	SELECTIVE DEFENSE MECHANISMS
CHAPTER 8	-	CONSUMER INVOLVEMENT
CHAPTER 9	-	MOTIVATION I: THE PRECONDITIONS TO NEED SATISFACTION
CHAPTER 10	-	MOTIVATION II: DEFICIENCY NEEDS AND NEUROTIC NEEDS
CHAPTER 11	-	MOTIVATION III: GROWTH NEEDS
CHAPTER 12	-	MOTIVATION IV: SUBCONSCIOUS MOTIVATION
CHAPTER 13	-	FEELINGS I: EXPECTED-VALUE
CHAPTER 14	-	FEELINGS II: EMOTIONS
CHAPTER 15	-	FEELINGS III: ATTITUDES AND ATTITUDE CHANGE
CHAPTER 16	-	CONSUMER DECISION MAKING
CHAPTER 17	-	NONDECISION MAKING I: THINKING SHORTCUTS
CHAPTER 18	-	NONDECISION MAKING II: FEELING SHORTCUTS
CHAPTER 19	-	RELATIONSHIP MARKETING AND CONFLICT RESOLUTION
CHAPTER 20	-	SELF-IMPORTANCE AND SELF-WORTH
CHAPTER 21	-	INTIMACY, LOVE AND TOLERANCE IN SUCCESSFUL RELATIONSHIPS
CHAPTER 22	-	CONSUMER SATISFACTION, DISSATISFACTION, AND QUALITY OF LIFE
CHAPTER 23	-	CUSTOMER LOYALTY AND DISLOYALTY

CHAPTER 1
CONSUMER BEHAVIOR AND KEY ACCOUNTS

INTRODUCTION	1.1
WHY STUDY CONSUMER BEHAVIOR	1.2
TYPES OF BEHAVIOR	1.3
Overt Behavior	1.3
Verbal Behavior	1.3
Cognitive Behavior	1.4
MODELS OF BEHAVIOR	1.4
THE SCIENTIFIC METHOD	1.6
CONSUMER CONSTITUENCIES	1.7
Professional Consumer Constituencies	1.7
External Consumer Constituencies	1.7
Internal Consumer Constituencies	1.7
Personal Consumer Constituencies	1.8
Key Accounts	1.8
Key Account Summary	1.9
CONCLUSION	1.9
**EXPERIMENT 1.1	KEY ACCOUNT MARKETING**	1.9
ELABORATION QUESTIONS	1.10

GUIDING QUESTIONS

- What is marketing?
- What is consumer behavior?
- Why study consumer behavior?
- What are the major types of behavior?
- Why are models of behavior important?
- What is the scientific method?
- Why are we using the scientific method to study consumer behavior?
- Who are your most important consumers?
  - In the professional environment?
  - In the personal environment?

INTRODUCTION

The study of consumer behavior has developed within the scientific discipline of marketing. Marketing deals with human exchange behavior where one person(s) sells or trades something to another person(s). People involved in marketing have a keen interest in understanding why and how buyers go about purchasing and using products and services. In fact, the most common definition of consumer behavior is: **the activities involved in purchasing and using goods and services.**

CONSUMER BEHAVIOR

Figure 1

Several important aspects of this definition warrant further elaboration. First, note that both the buyer and the user are identified in the definition. In some cases, like gift giving, the person who buys the product (or service) is not the person who actually uses it. However, this distinction is normally ignored, and most books concentrate on the decision-maker since s/he makes the purchase.

Second, there are three different types of "activity" referred to in the definition: (1) physical (the overt actions people perform), (2) verbal (what people say and write), and (3) mental. Mental activity refers to the psychological processes that determine how and why people act, and thus, is the most important aspect of studying consumers behavior. If we want to understand and influence other people's overt behavior (and we often do), we must understand the underlying mental processes. To understand these mental activities we must turn to psychology, economics, sociology, and anthropology (i.e., the behavioral sciences). Since mental activities are the most central component of consumer behavior, the psychological aspects usually play a much greater role. Indeed, in the most practical sense, the study of consumer behavior is really an area of **applied social psychology.**

A third important aspect of the definition is the distinction between products and services. In the past, consumer behavior concentrated on tangible products. However, increasing attention is being paid to service marketing as the world economy becomes more service oriented. Examples of services include insurance, politicians, museums, banks, charities, and education. Moreover, the scope of marketing and consumer behavior has been further broadened by the recognition that "purchase" does not always mean money for products. Indeed, many of the important exchanges you make do not involve the transfer of money for products but involve an exchange of service for service (e.g., you do a favor for a friend and they do one for you).

Fourth, it is important to note that marketing involves the **exchange of value** between two parties. These relationships are, therefore, typified by **give and take.** That is to say, each party to the exchange gives and takes something of value. Moreover, these give-and-take relationships exist in different environments. For example, commercial exchanges usually involve trading money for products and services. However, your professional environment (i.e., your career) will involve the exchange of money (i.e., your salary) from your employer for physical and verbal behaviors from you (e.g., calling on accounts, asking questions, etc.). In your personal environments (i.e., with family and friends) the exchange is normally service for service (e.g., an exchange of favors).

WHY STUDY CONSUMER BEHAVIOR

Studying consumer behavior is popular for several reasons. First, it is obviously important for marketing professionals to have a thorough understanding of what makes consumers decide to buy certain products. We can serve consumers better if we know more about them. As the consumer orientation of the "marketing concept" suggests, the consumer is king. That means we must allocate substantial resources to gain a better grasp of the consumer's decision making process.

This knowledge about consumers should help us provide our services more efficiently - a major concern for future managers. For example, it is well known that many promotional dollars are wasted. A clearer conception of what makes the consumer buy should help marketers design more effective

EXCHANGE BEHAVIORS

Commercial Exchange
Job Interview Exchange
Personal Exchange
Informational Exchange ← classroom

Figure 2

Advertising Strategy is based on Consumer Psychology

advertisements and personal sales presentations. Similarly, a college graduate searching for an entry level position in marketing should be able to design a much better sales strategy (i.e., job interview) if s/he knows what features the consumer (i.e., company representative) is looking for in the interview. Thus, a true understanding of consumer behavior should help you better manage both commercial transactions (money for goods or services) and personal transactions (service for service). However, before we get to this type of material, it will be useful to obtain a better understanding of some background issues. Since we will be building a model of human exchange behavior, it is important to agree on the definitions of several key terms.

TYPES OF BEHAVIOR

OVERT BEHAVIOR

This represents the actual physical behavior that people display. It can be easily observed simply by watching other people. When we notice other peoples' facial expressions, gestures, study habits, athletic skills, posture, etc., we are observing their overt behaviors. It is important to note that all overt behavior requires some amount of energy (ranging from very low to very high) to operate the physical apparatus of the individual. Consequently, the individual must perceive some reason (motivation) for engaging in the behavior.

Generally, the strength of an individual's motivation to perform an act is determined by the equation:

$$\text{MOTIVATION} = (\text{EXPECTED BENEFITS} - \text{EXPECTED COSTS})$$

The more the benefits outweigh the costs, the more motivated the individual is to perform the behavior. Obviously, the energy expended is a major component of the individual's calculation of expected costs. For example, most people would be more likely to perform an effortful behavior for a friend (from whom they could reasonably expect future benefits) than for a stranger (whom they may never see again). Thus, overt behaviors represent physical actions that require some amount of effort and motivation to perform.

VERBAL BEHAVIOR

This category includes all word oriented communications (i.e., speaking and writing) that people perform. It includes such subtleties as voice inflections, vocabulary, word choice, syntax, etc. Clearly, verbal behavior requires some physical activity and therefore qualifies as "overt." However, it is useful to make a distinction between what people say (or write) and what they actually do. This distinction between verbal and overt behavior is important because people often do not actually do what they say they will. For example, it is much easier to say you will get a high GPA. or help your friends move than it is to perform the overt behaviors. In fact, the actual correlations between verbal predictions and actual behavior are often quite low (r ≈ .30).

COGNITIVE BEHAVIOR

In addition to discussing how people act, we will also be interested in how people think. Recall that before a person performs an overt behavior, s/he must be sufficiently motivated in terms of expected benefits. Therefore, any study of human behavior should not only look at which acts are performed but also at why these acts were displayed. Only by knowing why people act as they do, can we accurately predict how they will act next. Therefore, the internal mental process that determines motivation or expected benefits is crucial to our understanding of human behavior. This internal "thinking" will be referred to as cognitive (mental) activity. Notice that unlike overt behaviors, we cannot directly observe how another person thinks or feels. Because cognitive activity is internal, the only person who has direct access to it is the person doing the thinking. The closest approximation others can make is to ask the person to report key thoughts and feelings (verbal behaviors) or observe what the person actually does (overt behaviors). summarizes the types of behavior we will consider in this book.

MODELS OF BEHAVIOR

Models are frequently used to make a complex process easier to understand, usually by reducing the complex process to a more simplified form. For example, it is not necessary for an automobile manufacturer to produce an entire new car to find out if consumers like its proposed styling. Drawings (graphic models) or small mock ups (iconic models) could easily be substituted with only minor loss of detail. Thus, models simplify by revealing the basic structure or organization of the process they represent.

The earliest models of human behavior may seem bizarre by today's standards, yet each represented the "state of the art" during its time. These early efforts were heavily influenced by superstitions, myths, and rituals. In most of these models, humans were regarded as little more than puppets under the control

BEHAVIOR CLASSIFICATIONS SUMMARY

BEHAVIOR	DOMAIN	OBSERVABILITY	DESCRIPTION
Overt	Physical Actions (External)	By Individuals and Others	What You Do
Verbal	Spoken or Written Words (External)	By Individual and Others	What You Say or Write
Cognitive	Mental Thoughts (Internal)	By Individual Alone	How You Decide What to Do and Say

Table 1

Mythological Goddesses in Greek Architecture

of spirits, gods, and evil forces. These superhuman entities acted according to personalities that were beyond the full comprehension of mere mortals. Over time, lore and myth built up around each of the major players, and the relationships described in mythologies represented some of the first behavioral models. In Greek mythology for example, Aphrodite represented love, Athena was wisdom, and Apollo was light and music.

Ancient Greek Philosopher, Plato

The major achievement of these myths and superstitions was their recognition that human behavior was directed in some way by organized forces. Their organizing devices (i.e., gods, demons, etc.) were simple to be sure, but that is usually true of new efforts. The major problem with the early models was their low predictive ability, which resulted largely from inaccuracies in their assumptions. In addition, the belief that human behavior was controlled by alien forces provided little motivation for people to accept responsibility for their own actions. Under these conditions, people find it easy to fall into self-defeating behaviors (e.g., sacrificing a loved one to appease gods that did not exist!). Ultimately, the uncertainty and minimal adaptive value of mythologies caused them to decline in popularity. After many years, they could no longer compete with new and exciting models that were being developed and proposed.

These new models were typically based on philosophy (Socrates, Aristotle, Plato) or religion (Christianity, Islam, Hinduism, Buddhism, Judaism). An important achievement of the religious models was their prosocial character. They revealed rules based upon self sacrifice for group benefit. As an example, some of the Ten Commandments are normative statements that restrict self serving behaviors (e.g., lies, theft,

The Scientific Method

adultery, etc.) to improve social interactions. Without question, these newer models produced a giant step forward in the social adaptiveness and well being of our ancestors.

The major drawback to the religious and philosophical models is their limited scope. They are great for social and spiritual guidance but do not effectively address many important issues like how to cure sick and injured people, how to advance technology, or why people commit crimes. While these problems do not detract from the social adaptiveness of these models, they caused a movement about 500 years ago that resulted in a scientific renaissance.

THE SCIENTIFIC METHOD

A major problem with early models of human behavior was their lack of objectivity, people often placed interpretations on events that were self serving or otherwise biased. Such bias is a fatal error in attempts to predict accurately because it causes the individual's interpretation to differ from reality. Ideally, it would be best to have a point of view that is **completely objective.** If this could be accomplished, then little or no bias should exist to influence our interpretation of observed behavior. To be completely objective, an observer should have a completely open mind about the events under investigation. That is, the observer should have no vested interest in the results of the behavior.

Unfortunately, most people are not inclined to carefully inspect behaviors or events in which they have no interest. Instead, we typically pay attention to behaviors that are related in some way to our lives. This means we normally have a significant vested interest in what we pay attention to, and thus, we frequently interpret behavior in a biased fashion. Within this scenario, it is not difficult to see why there are so many arguments and differences of opinion between people (who usually have competing vested interests).

In an effort to eliminate the biases introduced by most perspectives, researchers have developed the "scientific method" over time. The most fundamental goal of science is objective observation and investigation. Normally, principles, laws, rules, etc. are added to the "body of science" only after they have been subjected to rigorous objective tests. This criterion means that any person who correctly performs a similar test should obtain similar results. That is, people can find out for themselves if the body of science is correct or incorrect. Whereas clergymen from different religions cannot agree on the origin or destination of human beings, and while politicians cannot agree on territorial rights, scientists from all religions and all countries generally agree that the universe is expanding and that water boils at 100 degrees centigrade (STP). When disagreements do occur in science an objective test usually can be developed to settle the issue.

Thus, in general terms, we can think of the scientific method as an approach to studying behavior that stresses objectivity. Because this approach is least likely to introduce personal biases into the observation and interpretation of behavior, it will be the point of view adopted in this book. As noted above, the goal of the scientific method is objectivity in the observation and interpretation of behavior. To accomplish this goal, scientists apply five steps to their research:

1. Examine existing knowledge.
2. Develop a testable hypothesis.
3. Collect objective observations (data).
4. Analyze data.
5. Draw conclusions and report findings.

CONSUMER CONSTITUENCIES

Achieving success in your career will normally require successful exchanges with both professional consumer constituencies and personal consumer constituencies.

PROFESSIONAL CONSUMER CONSTITUENCIES → focus on end users

Professional consumer constituencies are your customers at work. Normally, consumer behavior textbooks consider end users as the consumers of most interest. While this is often true, there are also many other important consumers at work. These consumers can be external to the firm you work for, or internal to the firm.

EXTERNAL CONSUMER CONSTITUENCIES

If you work in marketing for a company, the following consumers would be external to your firm:

1. **End users** - the people who actually use or consume the product/service. They are normally the focus of consumer behavior classes.

2. **Retailers** - the stores or vendors that sell the product/service to end users. These may be a physical store or a website. *(clothing stores)*

3. **Wholesalers** - the companies that sell the product/service to retailers

4. **Advertising Agencies** - the company that creates ads for end users or trade show displays for retailers and wholesalers.

5. **Government Agencies** - organizations that regulate or control important aspects of the marketing of the product/service.

6. **Media** - television, radio, newspapers, websites, etc. that carry important information about your company or product/service to end users.

INTERNAL CONSUMER CONSTITUENCIES → essential for success

These are people who work in the same company with you and "consume" your physical and verbal behaviors.

1. **Supervisors** - Every company has a "chain of command," a formally specified organization of authority and responsibility. As you enter the workplace you will usually be in the lower echelons and therefore, have a variety of supervisors (i.e., people ahead of you in the chain). You will need to be very careful how you "market" yourself to these supervisors. Indeed, inability to understand and get along with supervisors probably causes more career failures than an inability to sell to end-users!

2. **Peers** - These are your co-workers, that is, people at the same level in the

Professional Key Accounts

1.7

company hierarchy. This is a delicate exchange relationship because you both cooperate with these people (e.g., work on a project together) and compete with them (e.g., for promotions and raises).

3. **Subordinates** - These are the people you supervise (e.g., below you in the hierarchy). Your ability to effectively market yourself to these consumers reflects your leadership abilities.

4. **Staff** - These are the support workers (e.g., secretaries, receptionists, etc.) who often play an important role in how successful you are in your career.

PERSONAL CONSUMER CONSTITUENCIES

These are people who consume your physical and verbal behaviors outside of the workplace. Thus, your family and friends also consume and react to your behaviors. These accounts are usually very important to your self-concept and often play a major role in your success at work. For example, it is harder to succeed at work if your personal exchanges produce significant conflict.

KEY ACCOUNTS

A key account is any consumer constituency that determines a significant amount of the rewards or punishments that you receive. In the professional environment, your immediate supervisor will probably play the greatest role in determining your reinforcement and therefore, will be a key account, as would be any co-worker you often rely on for help. Similarly, any external end user that buys a lot of product/service from you will be a key account. In the personal environment, your parents, siblings, girl/boy friend, spouse, in-laws, and best friends will be some of your key accounts.

It is very important to your professional and personal success to be able to identify your key accounts and give them your best efforts. Surprisingly, forces exist that often make this very difficult (e.g., we often take our parents and spouses for granted and give little effort to marketing ourselves to them). As an example, advertising texts usually stress how the end users are the key accounts for ad agencies – that unless they buy the product the client will take their business to a different ad agency. I found this often not to be

KEY ACCOUNT SUMMARY

KEY ACCOUNT	% OF TOTAL REINFORCEMENT	% OF TOTAL PUNISHMENT
1. Father	10%	15%
2. Mother	15%	10%
3. Girl/Boyfriend	35%	30%
4. Brother	10%	5%
5. Roommate 1	10%	0%
6. Roommate 2	1%	10%
7. Friend 1	5%	2%
8. Classmates	2%	2%
9. Recruiters	5%	8%
Total Accounted for	**93%**	**92%**

→ major marketing partners/challenges

Table 2

true. Instead, the real key accounts were the clients themselves – if we had a good relationship with them, they continued to do business with us (up to a point).

KEY ACCOUNT SUMMARY

List your current key accounts and identify how much of your reinforcement and punishment each contributes. For example your personal key accounts probably include many of the people shown in Table 2.

1.
2.
3.
4.
5.
6.
7.
8.
9.
10.

CONCLUSION

You may not have thought about it in these terms, but during your life, you have developed some specific ideas about what makes people act in certain ways - your own personal model of behavior. If you are like most people, your model contains the remnants of your experiences, education, and early training. The accuracy of your model is what we are concerned with in this book. As we develop our scientific model, you should compare it with your own model. When disagreements occur, feel free to raise them in class.

For important conflicts, we can construct objective tests to see which model works best. During this experience, you should find occasions where your current model is insufficient or inaccurate, and this will also be true of the scientific model. These inadequacies will provide further opportunities for improving our models. This is important because increasing your ability to accurately predict behavior will improve your chances for success. Therefore, improving the accuracy of your internal model is a goal worthy of pursuit, even though it is not without its difficulties.

EXPERIMENT 1.1
KEY ACCOUNT MARKETING

1. Who are your most important personal key accounts?

2. Who will be your most important professional key accounts in your entry level job?

3. Find two college graduates (any age) working in a marketing position. Explain the idea of key accounts and ask them to identify their major professional key accounts (at least 3 each for Internal and External accounts) and the amount of professional reward and punishment they get from each. Make sure to get the job title that the key accounts hold.

4. Next, ask them to order their key accounts in terms of their importance to their professional success.

5. Summarize the results and make some interesting observations regarding the key accounts that will be most important in your own career.

6. Summarize your philosophy regarding "marketing yourself to your key accounts."

ELABORATION QUESTIONS

- Do expected-benefits always have to exceed expected-costs for each exchange?

- To what extend does your verbal behavior accurately predict your overt behavior?

- What happens to you if your verbal behavior does not predict your overt behavior?

CHAPTER 2
THE INTERNAL MODEL

INTRODUCTION	**2.1**
THE ENVIRONMENT	**2.1**
Sub-Environments	2.1
REQUIREMENTS FOR SURVIVAL	**2.2**
Nourishment	2.2
Protection	2.2
Reproduction	2.2
INSTINCTUAL EVALUATIONS	**2.3**
Introduction	2.3
Definition of Instincts	2.3
INSTINCTS ARE POWERFUL MOTIVATORS	**2.3**
Instincts are Nonverbal	2.4
Instincts are Fixed for Life	2.4
MODELS OF BEHAVIOR	**2.4**
The Instinctual Model	2.4
The Cognitive Model	2.4
THE INTERNAL MODEL	**2.5**
SCHEDULE OF REINFORCEMENT	**2.5**
MALADAPTIVE BEHAVIORS	**2.6**
Instinctual Failure	2.6
Perceptual Failure	2.6
Learning Failure	2.6
CONFLICTS BETWEEN THE INTERNAL MODEL AND THE ENVIRONMENT	**2.7**
Responses to Punishment	2.7
**EXPERIMENT 2.1	GROWTH THROUGH CRITICISM**	**2.9**
ELABORATION QUESTIONS	**2.10**

GUIDING QUESTIONS

- What are the major elements/people in the environment that affect your behaviors and feelings?
- How strong are your primary drives compared to your friends?
- What are the major properties of human instincts?
- Give some examples of when you have acted on instincts.
- What is the internal model and how does it operate?
- What is the schedule of reinforcement?
- What does it mean when you receive punishment?
- Why do we perform "maladaptive" behaviors?
- What should you do when there is a conflict between your internal model and the environment?

INTRODUCTION

The forces that influence human behavior can be divided into two general categories: internal and external. Internal factors include instincts, feelings, memories, and intentions. External factors include physical surroundings, other people, and scarce resources. Our goal is to examine the important relationships among these forces so we can better understand and predict other peoples' behavior. We will begin by looking at the external factors that make up the environment.

Climate Change

THE ENVIRONMENT

At the most general level, the environment represents the immediate surroundings. For our purposes, it will be convenient to organize the environment into more specific sub-environments.

SUB-ENVIRONMENTS

Physical Environment. This category includes the tangible features of the environment such as: geography, climate, scarce resources, other life forms, etc.

Economic Environment. This category includes factors related to the distribution of scarce resources such as: specialization of labor, productivity, income distribution, consumption, etc.

Social Environment. This category includes the factors related to group interactions such as: social structure, social dynamics, social rules, social influence, etc.

Family Environment. This category includes the factors related to behaviors in your family of origin. For example, when acting as part of your family you are often expected to behave in customary ways that may differ dramatically from the way you act in your social environments.

Other sub-environments could be listed, depending on the level of specificity desired. Notice that although these environments are listed separately, they are normally closely interrelated. For example, a person who inherits considerable economic wealth will probably experience changes in other environments as well (e.g., physical, social, and political).

REQUIREMENTS FOR SURVIVAL

The most basic human behaviors are related to survival. To succeed at survival, each individual must perform a minimum of three activities which represent our most basic or primary needs.

NOURISHMENT

All life forms must perform behaviors to replenish their energy supply. This requirement typically produces specific plans for how to find, subdue, and digest protein.

Note there will be natural differences among people on these traits. For example, some people have a stronger hunger drive than others. These natural differences are assured due to "random gene combination" which means each person is a unique collection of human traits.

PROTECTION

The physical environment contains many dangers to survival. For humans, the major threat is other humans (war and violence) but other dangers exist as well, including: predators, natural hazards like insufficient water, volcanic eruptions, earthquakes, freezing temperatures, floods, etc. When a threat to survival is encountered, the individual can do one of three things:

Do Nothing. This is a bad choice because it tends to result in the individual being harmed or killed. Organisms that do nothing when their survival is threatened tend to get "selected out" quickly. Thus, this "non-response" option is rarely chosen in the face of a true threat.

Withdraw. One of the best ways to escape danger is to withdraw from it. For example, speed is a good protection for antelopes against predators. Similarly, soldiers are taught to retreat when faced with disadvantageous odds. Note that withdrawal from a legitimate threat normally minimizes the possibility that the individual will be harmed and is, therefore, a frequently used protection strategy. If organisms possess extremely sensitive evaluation processes, they are able to practice avoidance (i.e., to withdraw from a potential threat before it occurs). This makes avoidance the most adaptive protection strategy, since it involves the lowest risk of danger to the practitioner. Unfortunately, few life forms possess evaluation processes capable of avoiding all threats to survival.

Counterattack. The other adaptive response to a threat is for the organism to **attack** first or **counterattack** effectively. Unfortunately, because counterattack usually involves violence, there is a strong possibility that the individual will suffer considerable harm. As a result, counterattack is often considered a last resort, used only if withdrawal attempts fail.

Thus, withdrawal and counterattack represent the two basic reactions (behaviors) when an organism encounters a threat to survival. The level of a person's need for protection also varies among people. Some are focused on security and protection and some like to take risks and "live dangerously."

Counterattack

REPRODUCTION

The third primary drive revolves around DNA, the basic building block of life. Its unique property is that it can construct replicas of itself. Therefore, the very definition of life involves reproduction. To survive, your body constantly reproduces new cells that perform the same functions as the cells they replace. For a species to survive, individuals must create replacements through sexual reproduction. A species that cannot reproduce dies out. Therefore, any ongoing species must engage in behaviors designed for reproduction if it is to survive. Such behaviors include finding,

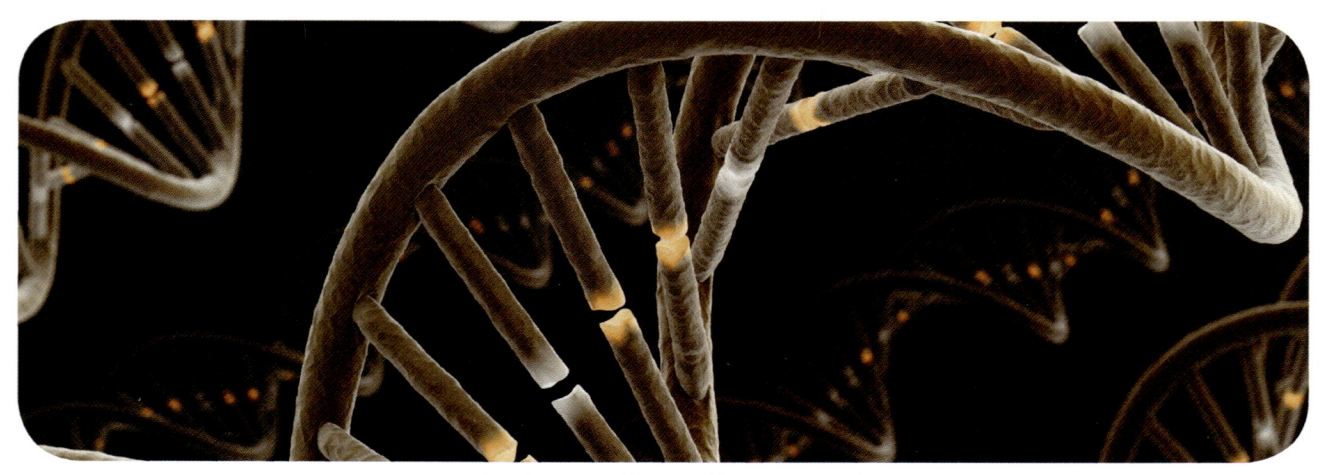

Instincts are Genetically Determined

attracting, and courting potential mates, sex, and parenting. Again, we should expect people to vary with regard to the level of their sexual drive. Some people have a strong sex drive and others have a weaker sex drive.

INSTINCTUAL EVALUATIONS

INTRODUCTION

We can predict from the preceding discussion that life forms will frequently perform behaviors associated with nourishment, protection, and reproduction. In order to accomplish these vital goals, each form of life possesses a repertoire of possible overt behaviors. Simple or "lower" forms of life normally have small behavioral repertoires (i.e., they can do only a few things). More complex or "higher" forms of life usually have larger behavioral repertoires and can thus **choose** from a larger number of available behaviors. These repertoires are collections of possible behaviors that the individual acquires from one of two sources: instincts and/or learning.

DEFINITION OF INSTINCTS

Your body consists of about a thousand-million-million cells. Each has 46 chromosomes (except sex cells, which have 23) that are made up of strands of genetic material called DNA. This DNA is arranged in specific patterns that form a genetic code. Importantly, this genetic code controls the cell's manufacture of protein - the fabric of your body. Thus, at the most fundamental level, your internal behaviors (digestion, immune responses, etc.) and your external behaviors (reproduction, withdrawal, counterattack, etc.) are controlled by your genetic programming.

By definition, instincts refer to genetically determined response tendencies. Instincts have evolved over time through the process of natural selection that favored instincts efficient at surviving. Indeed, from the genetic point of view, **human bodies** and their overt actions are complex **survival machines**. Because our ancestors encountered similar environments, they developed similar adaptive instincts. This means that the vast majority of human beings share basic survival related instincts and thus basic survival related behaviors. Indeed, many of the diagnostic traits used to separate different species involve how instincts are fulfilled (i.e., hunting, eating, aggression, protection, courting, mating, parenting, sleeping, etc.).

INSTINCTS ARE POWERFUL MOTIVATORS

Since some of our instincts are designed to serve the primary needs of survival (i.e., nourishment, protection, and reproduction), some mechanism is needed to assure that instincts are represented in the individual's selection of behavior. Accordingly, instinctual instructions are accompanied by physiological impulses (or energy) that exert strong pressure for their own satisfaction. Feelings of hunger, pain, or fatigue are examples of physiological motivations designed to fulfill survival oriented instincts. In general, an individual's primary motivation to comply with instincts is strong, especially at the cellular or somatic level. Indeed, instincts are impulses originating directly in the body and are characterized by **lack of freedom** and **compulsiveness**.

INSTINCTS ARE NONVERBAL

Another important characteristic of instincts is their automatic and unconscious operation. Neither careful thinking nor conscious control is required for instincts to perform their function. As an example, when your body is digesting food, your attention is normally focused somewhere else. The nonverbal nature of instincts makes it difficult to identify and/or express them in many situations.

INSTINCTS ARE FIXED FOR LIFE

Another feature that typifies instincts is their rigidity. The genetic code is fixed at conception and thus present before birth (i.e., they are "pre-wired"). In addition, most of these instructions cannot be changed after birth (i.e., they are "hard-wired") – although some changes occur due to maturation and mutation. However, major advances are being made in efforts to break the genetic code, and soon genetic engineering may discover techniques for altering instincts.

MODELS OF BEHAVIOR

THE INSTINCTUAL MODEL

We have seen that some of the first evaluations and overt behaviors of human beings were based on genetic instructions. These evaluations and choices did not depend on verbal thinking (i.e., cognitive) activities but on physiological stimulus response (S-R) associations. The instinctual model of behavior is based upon "primary perception" whereby individuals acquire data from the environment through their sensory apparatus. This information is internalized in neurochemical units to look, smell, sound, feel, and taste as close to the external object as possible. This "analog" model of the environment is fed into a sensory register and the impressions stay there for a short time (1/4 second) until they are automatically related to the appropriate overt behavior. Even in our early ancestors, this analog information display would trigger a genetically determined internal reaction to maximize the probability of an appropriate response. For example, the instinctual fear of snakes (which many modern humans have inherited) helps us jump away when we encounter them thereby lessening the risk of being bitten. To accomplish these behaviors, some physiological evaluative response or instinct (e.g., fear of snakes) would occur and overt behavior (jump away) would follow. This process is shown in Model 1.

THE COGNITIVE MODEL

In addition to our instinctual evaluations, we have developed the ability to think, plan, and reason – to construct a **cognitive** model of the external environment. This model is not scattered about the body in each cell like genetic instructions, but instead resides in the neocortex (memory) - the location of our learned evaluations. A model of the verbal/cognitive process is shown in Model 2.

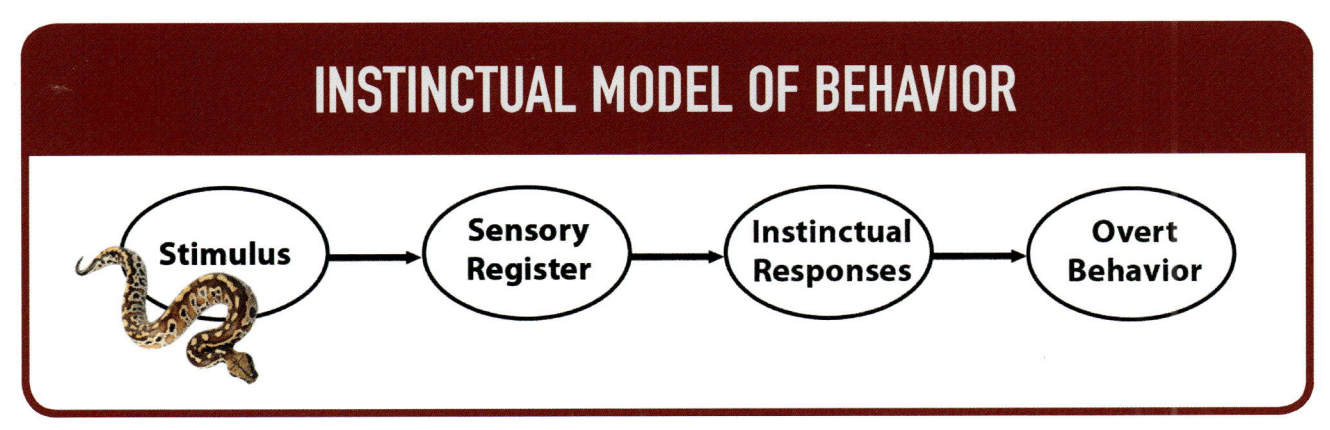

INSTINCTUAL MODEL OF BEHAVIOR

Stimulus → Sensory Register → Instinctual Responses → Overt Behavior

Model 1

THE COGNITIVE MODEL

Stimulus → Sensory Register → Cognitive Processing → Overt Behavior

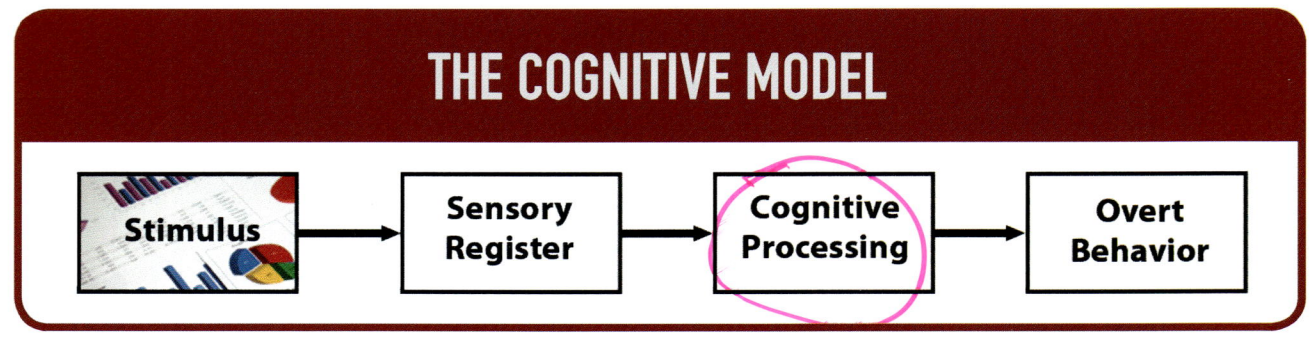

Model 2

THE INTERNAL MODEL

The ability to acquire, store, and remember verbal symbols enables the individual to construct an internal (symbolic) model of the external environment. This process has significant primary value because the verbal symbols can be used to **predict** future survival related events. In other words, the individual can learn important relationships in the environment (e.g., where to find food, water, protection, etc.), store the associations in memory as symbols (graphic or verbal), and then remember them on demand. As more and more associations in the environment come to be included in the internal model, the individual's ability to accurately predict the world increases. At the most general level, the internal model represents the way the individual sees the world. It is a portable model of the external environment that all of us carry around in our memory.

As a general example, we could compare the internal models of an optimist and a pessimist. An optimist usually sees a positive, hopeful, pleasant world. As a result of this model, such people usually behave in a positive, hopeful, pleasant manner. A pessimist, however, usually sees a negative, bleak, unpleasant world and also acts accordingly. This comparison demonstrates two major points:

1. Different people model the world quite differently. Indeed, because the overall environment is so complex, it is extremely unlikely that any two people will encounter identical experiences. As a result, we can expect people to have very different views of the way the world works, depending upon their personal encounters with it.

2. People almost always act in accordance with how their model of the world tells them they should. For example, we can expect people who have been lied to, cheated, or exploited to model the world pessimistically. Since people act according to their models, we can expect these people to be less likely to trust or help others.

SCHEDULE OF REINFORCEMENT

When an individual performs an overt or verbal behavior, it is often observed by other elements in the environment – especially other people. If these other people "like" the behavior, they will apply rewards in order to reinforce it (i.e., increase the probability that the behavior occurs again). **Positive reinforcement** occurs when rewards are applied (e.g., money, love, esteem, food, etc.). **Negative reinforcement** occurs when negatives (e.g., pain, discomfort, negative attitude, etc.) are removed. If the overt behavior is not well suited for the environment, it will be punished. **Punishment** is achieved by the application of disincentives (e.g., pain, discomfort, negative attitude, etc.), or the removal of rewards. Model 3 summarizes the relationships between the internal model, overt behavior, and the schedule of reinforcement.

Since people behave according to their internal model, and because behavior will be rewarded or punished by the environment, it is imperative that an individual's internal model reflects the true environment accurately. Clearly, an individual with an accurate (i.e., objective) picture of the world is in a better position

[handwritten annotation: "gives mental health issues, distort world"]

to identify and execute adaptive behaviors and thus receive rewards. Conversely, individuals who develop an inaccurate internal model will engage in behaviors that are "correct" for an environment that does not really exist. In this situation, the individual will suffer more punishments than those who have an accurate picture of the world. In the final analysis, everyone acts "the only way they know how;" those who most accurately model the environment will succeed, and those who construct an inaccurate model will fail.

If we view college education in this light, we can see that its purpose is to help the individual gain exposure to adaptive ideas. A true education is highly valued because it enables the owner to perform the "correct" behaviors in a variety of situations. As the internal model becomes more informed, it selects more adaptive overt behaviors, thereby maximizing rewards.

MALADAPTIVE BEHAVIORS

An individual may not be able to perform the most adaptive behavior in a given situation. There are three primary reasons for this.

INSTINCTUAL FAILURE
The individual may have received a negatively mutated or otherwise faulty genetic code. Maladaptations occur because the individual's behavioral repertoire is missing important behaviors or contains approximations not close enough to be rewarded.

PERCEPTUAL FAILURE
Failure of the sensory apparatus to properly identify the environment obviously can generate maladaptive behaviors. Here, an accurate associational process will trigger the proper behavior for the **perceived situation**, but the individual is actually encountering some other environment. Failure of the sensory apparatus can result from genetic variations (e.g., deafness, blindness), from the individual's failure to use this physical equipment carefully (e.g., poor listening skills), or from perceptual alteration (e.g., intoxication through binge drinking).

LEARNING FAILURE
Here the individual cannot adapt properly because the ability to learn from the schedule of reinforcement has been damaged or impaired. The damage may be physical (e.g., car accident) or mental (e.g., growing up in a deprived environment). In either case, the individual has trouble learning from mistakes and often repeats behaviors that have been punished.

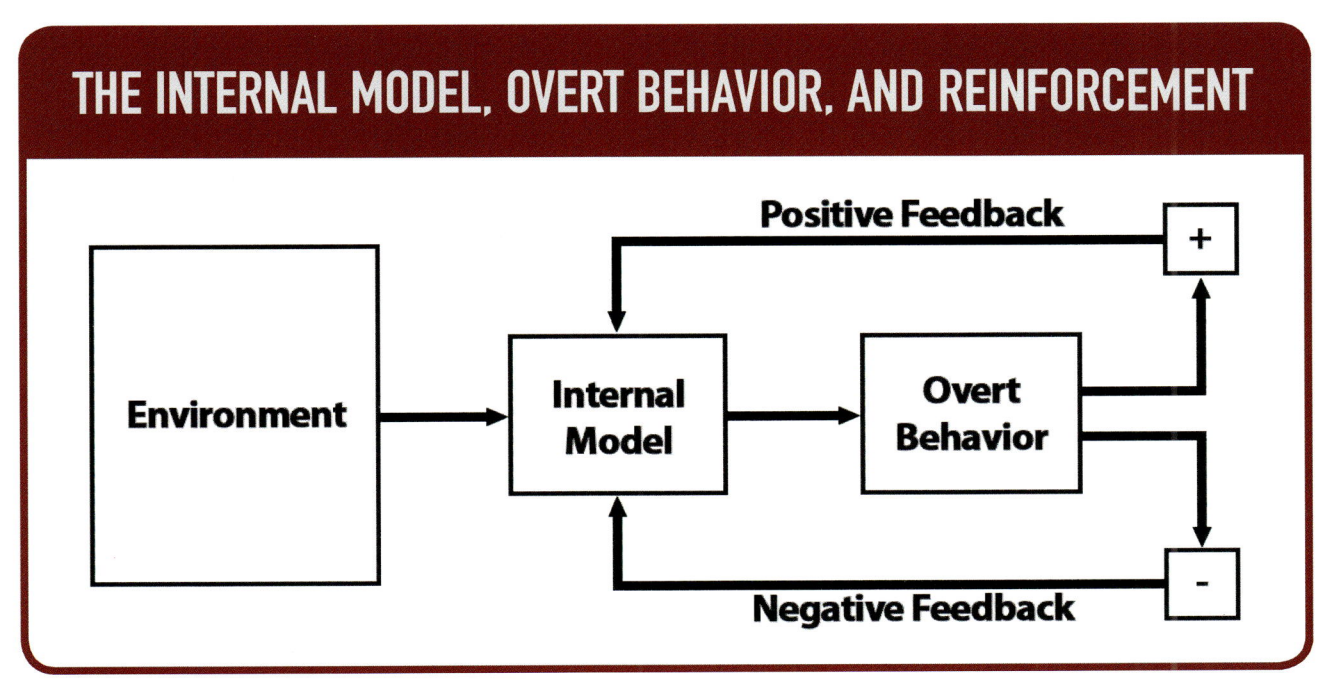

THE INTERNAL MODEL, OVERT BEHAVIOR, AND REINFORCEMENT

Environment → Internal Model → Overt Behavior → Positive Feedback (+) / Negative Feedback (−), with feedback loops returning to Internal Model

Model 3

THE EVOLUTION OF GIFT IDEAS

Figure 1

Another cause of learning failure is when the individual has strong intrinsic drives (e.g., sex or hunger drive) that are considered negative by the social/political environment but cannot be easily unlearned.

When any of the above failures occur, the individual is likely to perform an overt behavior that is maladaptive to some extent, and thus receive some form of punishment as a consequence.

CONFLICTS BETWEEN THE INTERNAL MODEL AND THE ENVIRONMENT

Since it is extremely unlikely that anyone has a perfectly accurate internal model, everyone will, to some extent, engage in maladaptive behaviors. Children who have not yet fully developed their evaluation processes make frequent mistakes and errors (e.g., physically, socially, economically, politically, etc.). In these cases, adults normally do not apply severe punishment, especially for first time (naive) errors. After all, the child must be given an appropriate period of time (16 to 18 years) to accumulate experience and construct an accurate model of the way the world works.

Ideally, each time the individual selects the correct behavior and is rewarded, s/he should remember that behavior for similar situations in the future (and indeed most people are quite good at learning from trials that are successful). In addition, however, the individual should remember behavioral selections that failed and avoid them in future similar situations. Many people have learning deficiencies in terms of "learning from their own mistakes." Yet, these failures when properly (objectively) analyzed give the actor just as much information about environment values as successes. Indeed, only by paying close attention to your entire schedule of reinforcement (i.e., both rewards and punishments) can you construct an accurate internal model. Unfortunately, human beings often have real difficulties here because self protection can cause us to defend our mistakes, which, in turn, **maximizes** the probability that we will repeat the errors in the future.

RESPONSES TO PUNISHMENT

In general, when an individual performs a behavior that is subsequently punished, s/he can do one of three things:

Learn and Change: Ideally, the individual will be able to identify which behavior was punished in which situation. This new information would then be combined with similar data in memory. The next time this situation is encountered, the individual will exclude from consideration the behavior(s) previously punished. Eventually, the person will find an adaptive behavior that will be rewarded and remembered.

This alternative simply means that people constantly revise their internal model as they encounter new environmental data.

Counterattack: Often, when people are punished because they have behaved maladaptively, they counterattack the environment (i.e., the person who delivered the punishment). Such counterattacks can take several forms including:

1. **Rejecting the discrepant information.** Some people, after receiving a punishment, refuse to believe they should have acted differently.

2. **Discounting the discrepant information.** For example, if we receive verbal punishment we might respond by saying something like:"That is only your opinion."

3. **Attempting to change the environment.** In this case we try to change other people's values to be more similar to our own (e.g., "I am not going to change my opinion, so you are going to have to change your opinion.")

Notice that when we counterattack punishments we do not learn from our mistakes. Since the internal model is not revised in this instance (i.e., no learning occurs), we can expect to make the same mistake again and again. In the long run this seriously reduces the amount of reinforcement received.

Withdraw. A very common response to punishment is to run away from it. Individuals normally develop this technique in childhood but may keep using it even when they become adults. Withdrawing from punishment is another method for refusing to admit that a mistake was made. We simply leave, and turn our attention elsewhere.

Unfortunately, if the individual encounters the environment in which s/he was punished again, s/he will again have to run away. Accordingly, if one is to succeed in an environment (e.g., marriage, sales, money, etc.), one must, sooner or later, develop some successful behaviors to display in the environment. These adaptive actions are unlikely to accrue to people who constantly run away from the environment when they do not like what is happening to them. When the inability to learn and change is added to the internal model it looks like Model 4.

Notice that rejection, withdrawal and counterattack are classic *threat* reactions. What is being threatened when individuals receive punishment? The answer lies

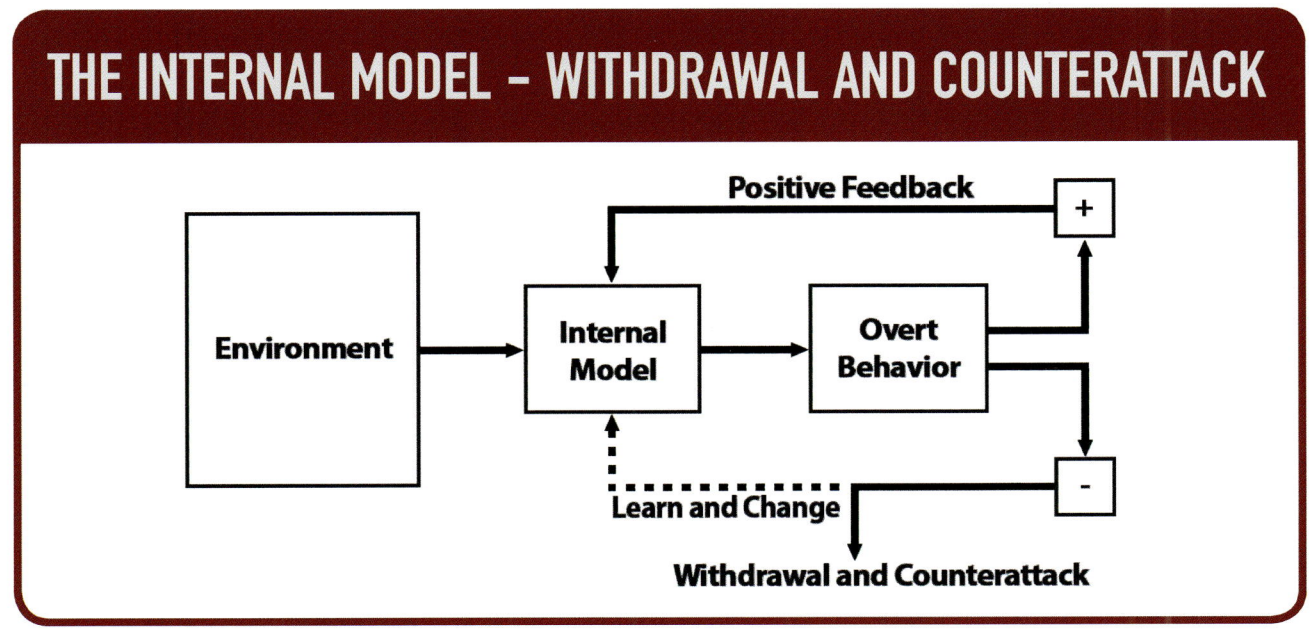

THE INTERNAL MODEL – WITHDRAWAL AND COUNTERATTACK

Model 4

in their self concept (which for most people is not very objective) and/or their perceived status within a group. In either case, acknowledging a mistake requires an "admission of wrong doing" that contradicts our self concept's desire for perfection and/or lessens our perceived group status. As a result, defensive reactions to environmental punishments are commonplace among human beings.

For the rest of your life you will be called on to decide whether you want to adapt to different environments or try to change them. In discussing this difficult and important question, past classes have identified the following situations where the environment should be changed through withdrawal or counterattack:

1. If you are asked to break a legal/social code. → counterattack
2. If you are asked to coerce or physically intimidate another person. → counterattack
3. If you are asked to restrict another person's freedom of choice. → counterattack
4. If you are asked to lie or misrepresent a material fact. counterattack
5. If you are asked to put yourself in physical danger. withdraw

Analyze and critique the list above. Can you add any items to the list?

EXPERIMENT 2.1
GROWTH THROUGH CRITICISM

Identify a situation where you have received constructive criticism but have rejected, withdrawn, or counterattacked it. Think about how you could accept some of the criticism and benefit from a change in your behavior. Make the change for two days and see: **1) how you feel, and 2) how the other person responds.**

ELABORATION QUESTIONS

- What happens when an individual has strong intrinsic drives that are considered "inappropriate" by society?

- How do most of your friends handle conflicts with the environment? Give some specific examples.

- How do you usually react when you receive punishment from another person? Give some specific examples.

- What is the best way to give a key account discrepant information?

- Give some examples of instinctual consumer behavior.

- Give some examples of cognitive consumer behavior.

CHAPTER 3
THE STRUCTURE OF MEMORY

DEFINITION OF KEY TERMS 3.1
    Workspace 3.1
    Coding 3.1
    Sensory Origin Input Form Examples 3.1
    Movement of Items Within the Memory System 3.3
    Loss of Information - Forgetting 3.4
    Definition 3.5
    Operation 3.5
    Definition 3.6
    Workspace 3.6
    Structure and Coding 3.6
    Transfer 3.6
    Forgetting 3.6
    Overt Behavior 3.6
LONG-TERM MEMORY 3.7
    Definition 3.7
    Workspace 3.7
    Structure and Coding 3.7
    Transfer 3.7
    Forgetting 3.8
    Overt Behavior 3.8
CONCLUSION 3.9
EXPERIMENT 3.1 MEMORY CODES 3.9
ELABORATION QUESTIONS 3.10

GUIDING QUESTIONS

- » What is the three-store memory model?
- » What is the sensory memory?
- » What is the short-term memory?
- » What is the long-term memory?
- » What is the amount of workspace in each memory?
- » How is information coded for placement in the memory system?
- » What are Level I, Level II, and Level III codes?
- » How is information moved into the memory system?
- » How is information retrieved from the memory system?
- » How does decay cause forgetting?
- » How does interference cause forgetting?
- » How does retrieval failure cause forgetting?
- » How much information can each memory hold?
- » How efficient is rehearsal at transferring information into long-term memory?
- » How does the long-term memory produce overt behaviors?

DEFINITION OF KEY TERMS

The cognitive part of the internal model (described in the previous chapters) is housed in the memory system. Therefore, understanding how your memory works is key to your adaptive mission. Fortunately, the natural intrigue of human memory has motivated people to study it since the beginning of science. Accordingly, there is now a wealth of objectively gathered data on how the memory system operates. While the memory system actually consists of an intricately related lump of gray matter in your cerebral cortex, it is easier to understand its operation by thinking of three types of memories: **Sensory Memory** *(sometimes called the sensory register),* **Short-Term Memory (STM)**, *and* **Long-Term Memory (LTM)**. *To organize our discussion, we will examine each of these memories on four dimensions:* **workspace, coding, moving information, and forgetting.**

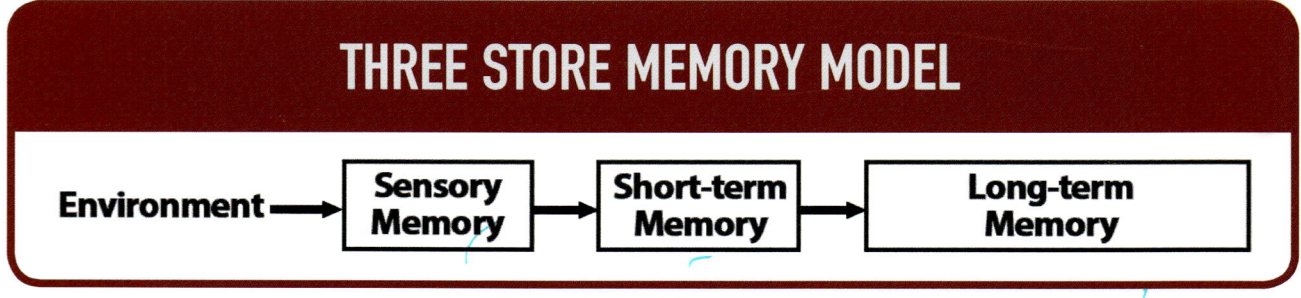

THREE STORE MEMORY MODEL

Environment → Sensory Memory → Short-term Memory → Long-term Memory

Model 1

WORKSPACE

This refers to the amount of information the memory system can process. As such, this dimension has two components. **Capacity** refers to the **number of items** that can be processed during a given interval of time. **Duration** refers to the **length of time** an item persists (i.e., is available) in the memory system.

CODING

Coding refers to how people structure, or represent, information for placement in the memory system (i.e., the input form of "to-be-remembered" items). A very useful theory of coding, called the "levels of processing theory," identifies three major types of input codes.

Level I Codes. Because incoming information is received from the sensory apparatus, it can take any of the five input forms as shown in Figure 1.

LEVEL I MEMORY CODES

SENSORY ORIGIN	INPUT FORM	EXAMPLES
1. Sight →	Visual →	Lines, angles, contrasts, colors
2. Hearing →	Acoustic (sounds) →	Bell ringing, ocean surf, gunshots
3. Smell →	Smells (odors) →	Garlic, rose petals, ammonia
4. Taste →	Tastes →	Sweet, sour, bitter, salt
5. Touch →	Touch units →	Textures, pressures, surfaces

Figure 1

These Level I codes are designed to look, sound, smell, taste, and touch as closely to the external stimuli as possible. As an example, your primary code for the color white is the color of the paper on which this page is printed. Because there is normally a close tie between the external stimuli and the Level I code, they are often referred to as "analog codes."

Level II Codes. After the initial process of recognition by matching incoming data to stored impressions, the individual may process (i.e., code) the information at a "deeper" level. Often, the second step in coding is to internally voice or articulate **words** that are associated with the **meaning** of the external stimuli. For example, can you remember the main color of the cover of this book? Chances are you performed this task using silently articulated words (i.e., "the cover is flesh") rather than using visual codes (i.e., closing your eyes and visualizing the color itself).

According to semantic theory, humans prefer to think using their "internal dialogue" (also called self-talk) because using language (verbal codes) makes it easy to associate **meaning** with the external object. This is accomplished by arranging the verbal codes into **an organized pattern** like a sentence. Thus, humans can conveniently internalize the outside world by using words and sentences to describe the meaningful relationships that exist. These words and sentences reside in the memory system as verbal codes.

Western Movies, White Hat Signifies "Good Guys"

For example, suppose someone drives up to you and asks how to get to a nearby lake. You might first visualize the lake's location by drawing on visual codes from your memory system. These codes are difficult to communicate, however, unless you have a visual aid like a pencil and paper. On the other hand, an easy way to direct the person is to transform your visual codes (Level I) to verbal codes (Level II), and then articulate them using words and sentences. In this case you might tell the person, "Drive east on this road to the second stoplight, turn right, then drive south for about six miles. Then, turn left just after you cross the bridge." In fact, you are probably so accustomed

LEVELS OF PROCESSING FOR THE COLOR WHITE

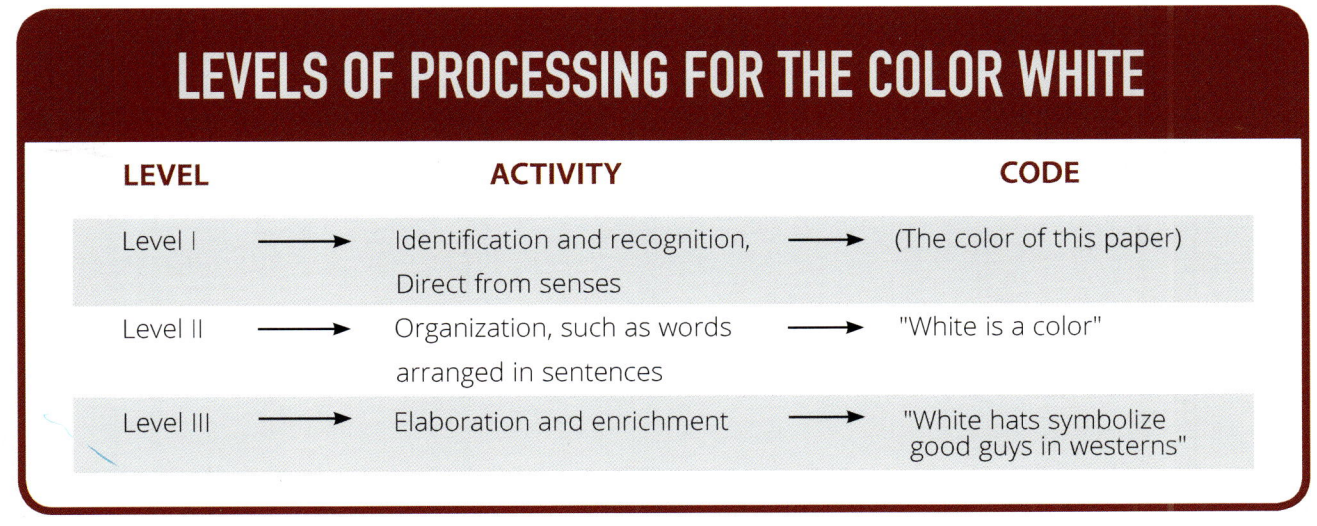

LEVEL	ACTIVITY	CODE
Level I	Identification and recognition, Direct from senses	(The color of this paper)
Level II	Organization, such as words arranged in sentences	"White is a color"
Level III	Elaboration and enrichment	"White hats symbolize good guys in westerns"

Figure 2

to constructing Level II codes that you are no longer aware of doing it.

Thus, the second level of processing (a Level II code) is to articulate the stimulus impressions as words in an organized or meaningful fashion. Another example of a Level II code would be describing this page color as "white" as in Figure 2.

Level III Codes. The third level of processing occurs when the individual "elaborates" or "enriches" the Level II codes. In this case, the individual adds something of personal meaning to the Level II codes. Examples here would include creativity and inferences (where we go beyond the information given to us). At this level, the individual combines the organized or self-articulated input codes (Level II) with material that has already been stored in memory. This produces a Level III code that includes features of the original stimulus as well as aspects of codes already stored in the internal model. An example of a Level III code would be remembering that "good guys in western movies wear white hats." The relationships among the three levels of processing are summarized next.

As another example of elaborated memory codes, suppose you had to learn the six major effects of climate change. Instead of mechanically repeating the effects you could connect them to material permanently stored in your memory. For example, you could tie the effects to the months of the year. Start by listing the first six months (Level I codes) and then think of the first thing that naturally comes to your mind (Level II codes). Next, make meaningful connections between your existing associations and the effects of climate change (Level III codes) as shown in Figure 3.

While it does take a little time to create these associations, the process is much more interesting than rote rehearsal, ultimately takes less time, allows you to remember the associations as long as you want, and gives you practice at creative thinking. This is why the elaboration study technique (described later) is so valuable to students.

MOVEMENT OF ITEMS WITHIN THE MEMORY SYSTEM

This dimension refers to how memory codes get moved around within the internal model. Such movement must take one of two directions:

Transfer. This term refers to how items are moved into the system from the sensory register to the short term memory (T1), and finally to the long term memory (T2). This is obviously an important issue since items cannot be remembered if they are not successfully transferred into the long term store.

Retrieval. This deals with how items are located and extracted from the LTM and returned to the STM. This is also a crucial memory function since retrieval

ELABORATING INFORMATION THROUGH CREATIVE ASSOCIATION

MONTHS	FIRST ASSOCIATION	CLIMATE CHANGE EFFECTS
January	→ Snow →	Increased Glacier Melt
February	→ Shortest Month →	Water Shortages
March	→ Comes in Like a Lion →	Animal Migration Changes
April	→ Showers →	Increased Flooding
May	→ Flowers →	Decreased Insect Pollination
June	→ Graduation →	Gradual Rise in Sea Level

Figure 3

failure makes the items inaccessible and, thus, of no value to the individual. Research indicates that people can search for information in several ways (e.g., in a serial or parallel fashion). In addition, retrieval appears to be facilitated if coding took place at a deep or meaningful level.

LOSS OF INFORMATION – FORGETTING

Information can be lost from the memory system on the way in (i.e., during transfer) or on the way back out (i.e., during retrieval). In other words, forgetting is caused by transfer failure and/or retrieval failure.

Transfer Failure. Two things can happen to prevent an item from being transferred into the memory system: it may be interfered with, or it may decay away.

1. **Interference.** A major reason that an item may not be transferred is because of interference. As we will see in a coming chapter, the "perceptual bottleneck" imposes capacity restrictions on the amount of information from the environment that can be processed. Only a small amount can be processed, and many environmental and internal stimuli compete for the available capacity. As a result, the large numbers of informational items interfere with each other for the restricted processing capacity of the STM. In other words, processing current data uses up the available space in the STM, thereby hindering transfer of previous and pending material.

2. **Decay.** In this case, the input code may disintegrate before transfer can be accomplished. According to this theory, the transient and vulnerable memory trace is quickly erased and lost unless it is refreshed in the active memory or processed at a meaningful level. There are many examples of items briefly stored in the STM that decay away before transfer. An example would be material you memorized to prepare for an exam but could not remember the following class period.

Perceptual Bottleneck

Retrieval Failure. The other major explanation of forgetting is called retrieval failure. According to this theory, the target item exists in the long-term store (i.e., has been successfully transferred) but cannot be located and returned to the STM on demand. A useful analogy is to think of the LTM as a large file drawer. If items are poorly indexed when they are originally filed (i.e., during transfer), they may be lost and, hence, inaccessible. There is a general consensus that retrieval failure is a major cause of "forgetting."

SENSORY MEMORY

DEFINITION

The sensory memory is the location where direct impressions from the external environment are input to the memory system via the five senses. As an analogy, you could think of the sensory register as a motion picture screen. The senses project raw impressions (Level I codes) onto this screen. Since new sensory information is constantly being fed into the sensory register, the duration of each image is limited to the length of the direct impression and its "afterimage" (about 1/4 second).

OPERATION

Research indicates that huge amounts of sensory data can be briefly held in the sensory memory and that coding is basically Level I (i.e., similar to the original stimuli). The individual then decides which items in the sensory memory deserve further processing. The selected items become candidates for transfer to the STM; however, large losses of information exist at this point due to the obvious opportunities for decay and interference. The major aspects of the sensory memory are shown in Model 2.

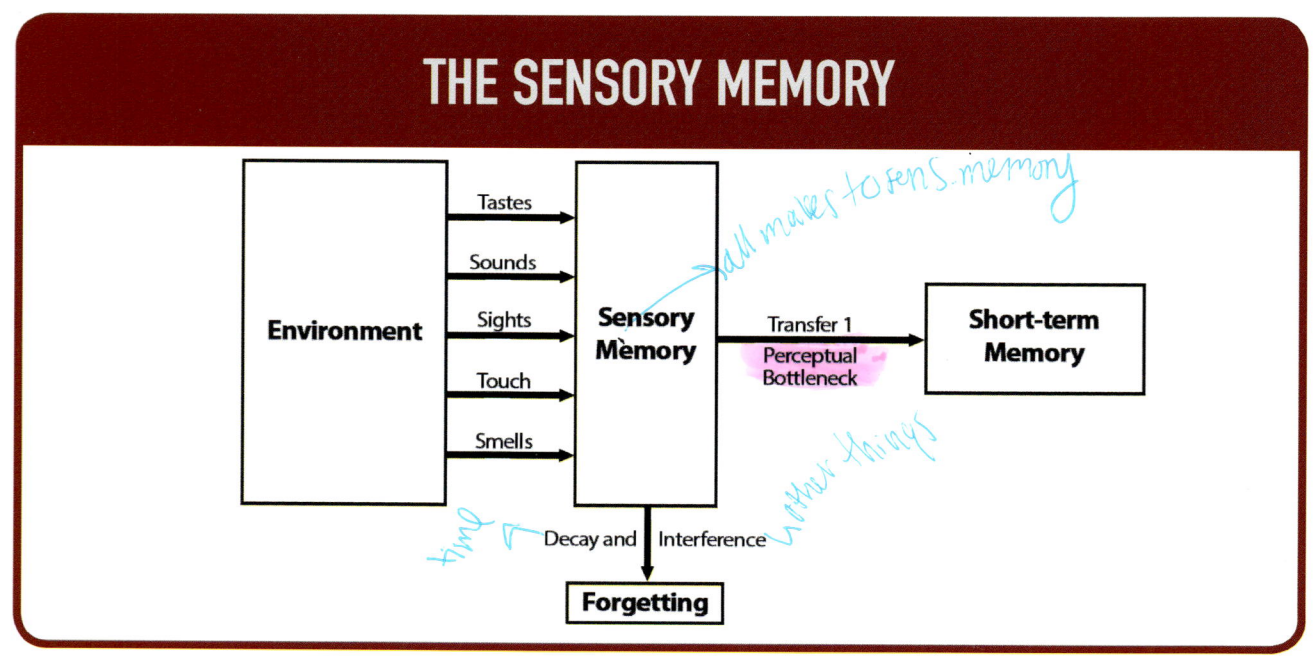

Retrieval Failure

THE SENSORY MEMORY

Environment → (Tastes, Sounds, Sights, Touch, Smells) → Sensory Memory → Transfer 1 / Perceptual Bottleneck → Short-term Memory

Sensory Memory → Decay and Interference → Forgetting

Model 2

3.5

SHORT-TERM MEMORY

DEFINITION

After preliminary processing, some of the information in the sensory memory can be transferred to the STM. Basically, your short term memory represents your current awareness, your current "train of thought," or your current consciousness. As such, your STM is the access point to your internal model (i.e., introspection). Our definition for the STM will be: **"the currently and temporarily activated memory cells."**

The STM is quite remarkable in terms of flexibility and control. It is extremely adaptable and can be set up quickly, take into account situational factors, make decisions, solve problems, and be creative. In addition, the STM is easily controlled by the individual's manipulation of the activation sequence. Indeed, it is our ability to use this most adaptive apparatus that gives human beings a material advantage over other life forms in our efforts to adapt to the environment.

WORKSPACE

The **capacity** of the STM is usually from five to nine "meaningful" chunks of information. Meaningful chunks of information can be words, sentences, song titles, nonsense syllables, brand names, or any other Level II or Level III code.

The **duration** of items in the STM is normally from 20 to 30 seconds, though items may be "refreshed" through rehearsal. Rehearsal refers to the rote (mechanical) repetition of an item, word, or image. Thus, by using the STM to repeat items, the individual can retain access to the desired information.

STRUCTURE AND CODING

The short term memory is often called a "buffer" because items are continually shifted in and out. A good way to envision the STM's structure is to imagine a seven-celled compartment with intake and output valves. Incoming information is the data transferred from the sensory register, and output is the data transferred to the LTM, or the information used to control overt behavior. The contents of the seven compartments can be instantaneously changed and/or arranged in any way desired.

In the Short Term Memory, Level II codes seem to be the easiest to manipulate and therefore, are the most commonly used. Level I and III codes can also be processed by the STM, but even strong visual data (like colors) are often transformed to verbal codes. It is also useful to think of the STM's workspace as expandable. With practice (e.g., thinking, reading, writing, etc.), the capacity and duration of the STM can be improved. This has the powerful effect of increasing the amount of information in the internal model, which often produces a more representative view of the world. Indeed, for many students, a major advantage of going to college is that they get ample opportunity to exercise their STM and thereby develop its efficiency.

TRANSFER

Items are transferred into the STM from the sensory register by the conscious control of the individual. As noted, each person selects candidates for transfer according to his/her current goals. Only a small fraction of the information in the sensory register can be transferred to the STM due to the processing capacity restrictions of the perceptual bottleneck.

FORGETTING

Given the small capacity of the STM, it is not surprising that most of the information loss at this stage occurs through **interference**. In addition, the relatively short duration of the STM means that decay can also cause information loss. However, although **decay** effects have been found in the STM, interference normally accounts for a larger share of forgetting at this stage.

OVERT BEHAVIOR

It is important to note that the contents of the STM often direct the individual's overt behavior. In other words, your STM tells your muscles how to act. These are called **controlled** (i.e., conscious) overt behaviors because they are performed under the awareness and planning of the individual. The major aspects of the human memory system are summarized in Model 3.

THE HUMAN MEMORY SYSTEM

Model 3

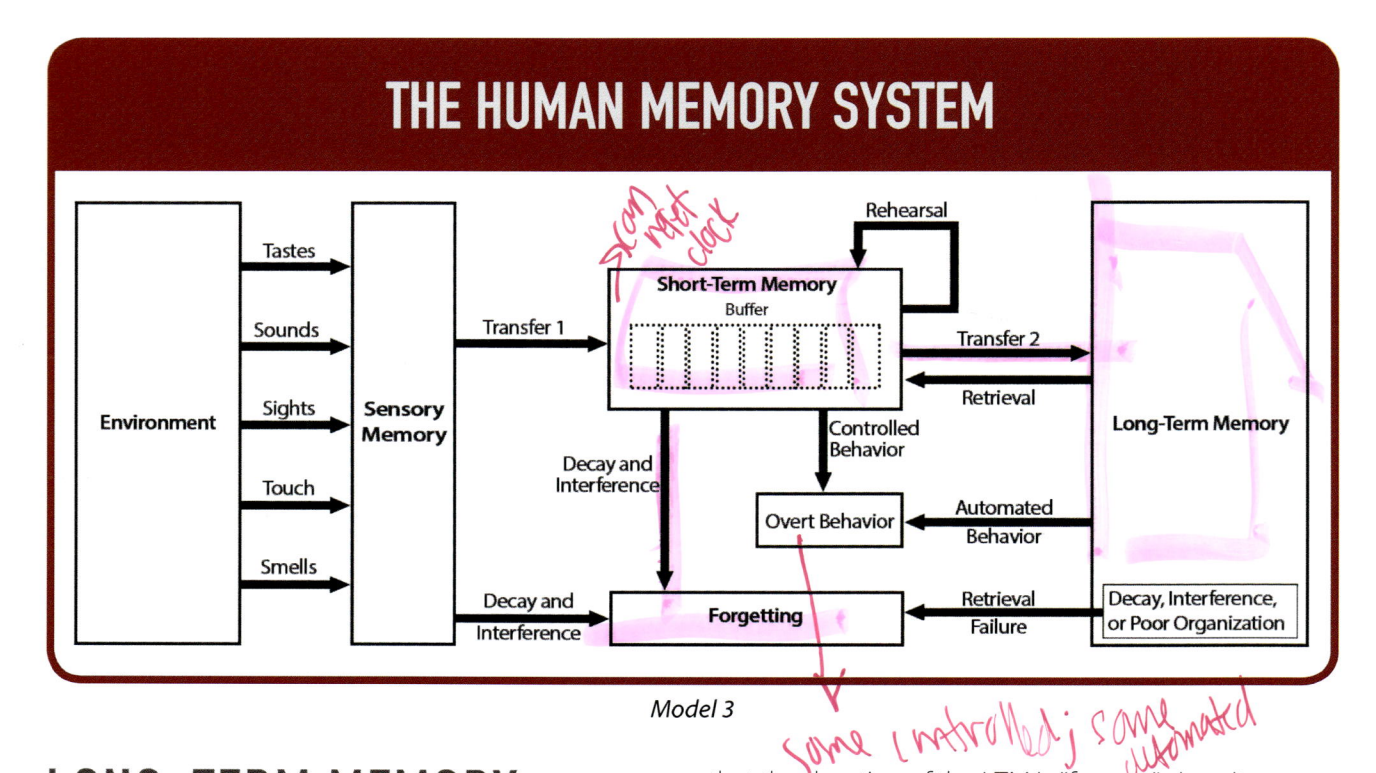

LONG-TERM MEMORY

DEFINITION

The LTM represents the permanent storage capacity of the memory system. Since the STM has a limited capacity, the vast majority of memory cells are inactive at any point in time. In this stage, the memory cells hold information for future access via activation by the STM. As an analogy, you could think of the memory system as a large warehouse composed of small containers that hold information. Think of the STM as a directed energy charge that can be focused on a particular cell to reveal its contents. Usually, this charge is strong enough to illuminate from five to nine cells for about 25 seconds. Thus, the cells that are currently lighted (activated) represent the STM. The majority of containers, however, are unlighted (inactive) at any point in time and represent the LTM.

WORKSPACE

Estimates are that the LTM can hold from 10 to 100 trillion binary associations (Sagan 1977). There is disagreement regarding the duration of items in the LTM. Some psychologists argue that items have varying duration in the long term store because they can be lost through decay and interference. Others maintain that the duration of the LTM is "forever" since items are not lost through forgetting (decay and interference), but rather are lost due to "retrieval failure" (i.e., the item is still there but cannot be located).

STRUCTURE AND CODING

A very important feature of the LTM is its structure. The easiest way to picture it is to think of a tree-like or pyramid-like structure as shown below.

As you can see, this is a carefully organized system for information storage and retrieval. In this system, semantic codes (i.e., symbols that represent **meanings**) are the easiest to manipulate (i.e., store and retrieve). This means the LTM prefers to handle Level II and Level III codes since they easily fit into the meaning structure. However, Level I codes of all kinds, including visual images (e.g., colors) or sound units (e.g., the sound of a siren), are also stored in the LTM.

TRANSFER

Items are transferred into the long term store by one of two methods: rehearsal or elaboration. Both, however, require the **active participation of the STM** in the form of attention given and/or adequate coding. The first method of transfer is through **rehearsal** of the to-be-remembered information. A good example

3.7

of this is when students "cram" for exams. In doing so, they normally just rehearse the material as much as they can and hope some of it "sinks in" (i.e., is transferred to LTM).

The rehearsal strategy is what most of us used as children to learn the alphabet, number system, spelling, etc. However, much of the information encountered later in life (like the material in this book) does not lend itself to rehearsal. To really remember this information, you will be much better off if you relate it to your past direct experiences by **elaboration** (i.e., creating Level III codes). This can be accomplished by thinking up dramatic examples of how you have personally experienced the concepts and then writing these examples in the margins of the text. When you study the concepts for an exam, you can associate the concepts in the text with your own meaningful experiences. Then, on the exam, if you can remember your past experiences you can use them as retrieval cues for the concepts.

While this is a much more efficient way to transfer the information, notice that it requires some creativity and elaboration. Moreover, because most people must start learning by using the method of rehearsal, they often continue to use this strategy in college even though more productive and efficient methods exist.

FORGETTING

This happens when a desired item cannot be located for retrieval by the STM. For example, if an item was poorly organized during transfer into the LTM, it may be difficult or impossible to find. This failure to find the right memory address means that the person has effectively "forgotten" the item on either a permanent or a temporary basis. An example of temporary retrieval failure is the familiar tip-of-the-tongue phenomenon, when a usually accessible memory location suddenly becomes hard to find.

OVERT BEHAVIOR

It is important to note that the contents of the LTM can direct the individual's overt behavior. In these cases, the LTM triggers action impulses that have become automated over time. These are called **automated** (i.e., subconscious) overt behaviors because they are performed without the awareness of the individual. The key elements of automated memory processes are discussed in the next chapter.

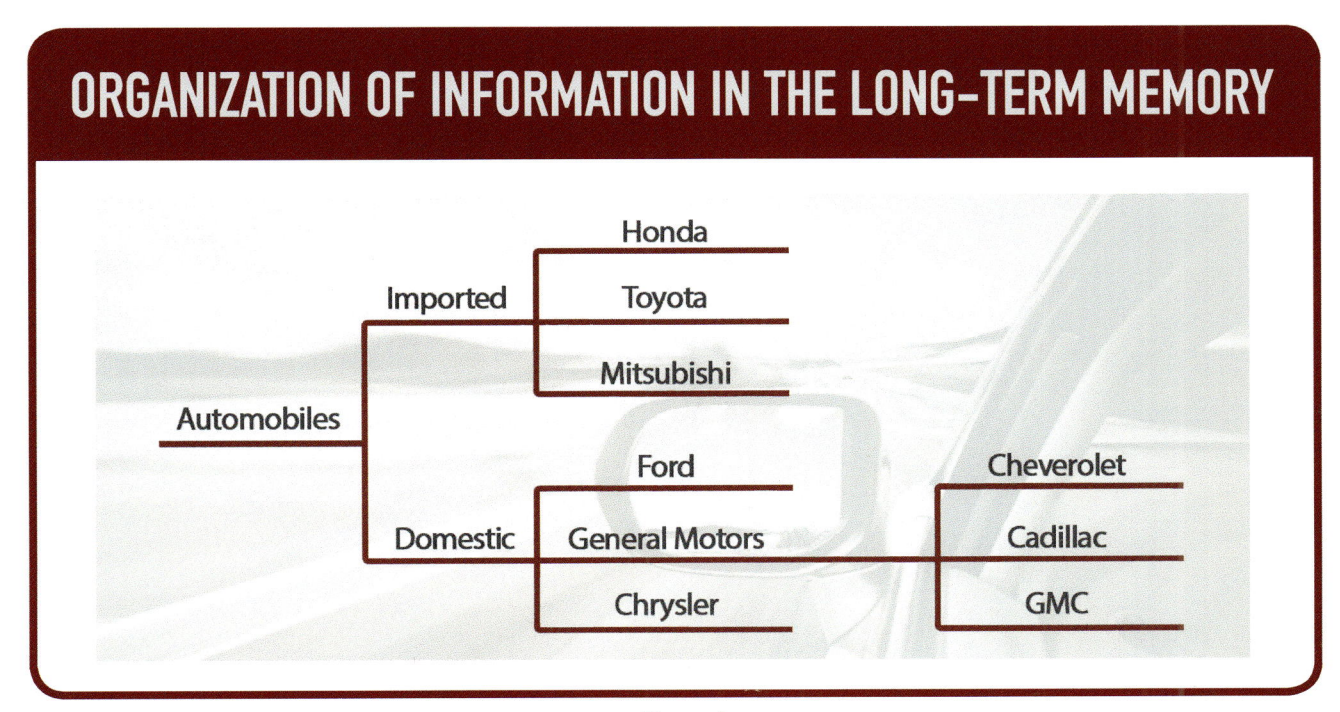

ORGANIZATION OF INFORMATION IN THE LONG-TERM MEMORY

Automobiles
- Imported
  - Honda
  - Toyota
  - Mitsubishi
- Domestic
  - Ford
  - General Motors
    - Cheverolet
    - Cadillac
    - GMC
  - Chrysler

Figure 4

CONCLUSION

In this chapter we have seen how the memory system operates as if there were three separate parts. The sensory memory receives large numbers of analog codes from the environment. Depending on the individual's current needs and goals, a small amount of this information will be selected for further processing and thus transferred to the STM.

The STM represents the currently activated memory cells under the direct conscious control of the individual. This memory provides the "work space" for solving problems, making decisions, and directing behavior. It is extremely flexible and can be quickly changed or set up to take into account whatever the individual believes to be important. This provides humans with a remarkable device to adapt to the environment.

The major disadvantage of the STM is its limited workspace. Because operation of the STM requires the individual's attention or awareness, and because this awareness is severely restricted by the perceptual bottleneck, the normal capacity of the STM is only from five to nine meaningful chunks. In addition, the relatively short duration of items in the STM (20-30 seconds) frequently requires the individual to rehearse items by repeating them. The overall result is that STM capacity is in great demand and short supply. This, in turn, forces the person to choose or somehow select the environmental stimuli that will be favored by active attention and awareness as discussed earlier.

The LTM is the permanent storage location for all learned associations. This information is organized in treelike structures, usually according to their meaning. Because of this, Level II and III codes are most easily remembered. Finally, it is important to note the intimate relationship between the STM and LTM since transfer into the LTM requires the limited attention of the STM, and retrieval out of LTM requires a controlled STM search.

EXPERIMENT 3.1
MEMORY CODES

1. Create Level-III memory codes for three different concepts in chapters 1-3 by relating them to experiences from your life.

2. Describe two ways to make level III connections with key accounts in your career - give specific examples of what you would do.

ELABORATION QUESTIONS

- Describe how you were trained to use your memory system as a child when you were learning the alphabet and number system. Was repetition and rehearsal involved? Did you ever change to a more elaborative study technique?

- Give an example of Level I, Level II and Level III codes.

- What is the major limitation of the short-term memory?

- What accounts for most of the forgetting in your internal model?

- What is the best way to get a key account to remember your messages?

- How efficiently have you used your memory system during college?

- Do you think you will need your memory more or less after college?

CHAPTER 4
MEMORY OPERATIONS

INTRODUCTION	**4.1**
CONTROLLED MEMORY PROCESSES	**4.1**
AUTOMATED MEMORY PROCESSES	**4.2**
Definition of Automated Processes	4.2
Automated Responses are Performed Without Awareness	4.3
Automated Responses are Difficult to Suppress	4.3
Automated Versus Semi-Automated Behaviors	4.4
Summary	4.4
FACTORS AFFECTING RECALL	**4.4**
Introduction	4.4
Level of Processing	4.5
Consistency	4.5
Frequency	4.6
Recency	4.6
Arousal and Survival Value	4.7
USING THE MEMORY TO STUDY	**4.7**
Cramming Can Hurt the Memory System	4.7
Cramming Relies on Superficial Codes	4.7
Cramming Can Perpetuate Itself	4.7
The Elaboration Study Technique	4.8
LEARNING	**4.9**
Learning Defined	4.9
Classical Conditioning	4.9
Operant Conditioning (Instrumental Learning)	4.9
Rules of Instrumental Learning	4.12
CONCLUSION	**4.13**
**EXPERIMENT 4.1	STUDY ELABORATIVELY**	**4.13**
ELABORATION QUESTIONS	**4.14**

GUIDING QUESTIONS

- » What are controlled memory operations?
- » What are automated memory operations?
- » Can memory perform more than one operation at the same time?
- » What are some of my automated behaviors?
- » What is a semi-automated behavior?
- » How does the level of processing affect consumer memory?
- » How does consistency affect consumer memory?
- » How does frequency affect consumer memory?
- » How does arousal affect consumer memory?
- » What are the disadvantages of the rehearsal study technique?
- » What are the advantages of the elaboration study technique?
- » What are the six steps in the elaboration study technique?
- » What study technique do you use?
- » What is classical conditioning?
- » What are the rules of classical conditioning?
- » What is instrumental learning?
- » What are the rules for instrumental learning?

INTRODUCTION

In the preceding chapter we noted how the memory system acts like it consists of three separate components: a sensory memory, a short term memory, and a long term memory. In this chapter we will examine topics that deal with the way the memory system operates and how humans learn. The first topic develops a distinction between "automated memory processes" and "controlled memory processes." The second topic explains how to get the memory system to most effectively recall a target stimulus. The third topic is the elaboration study technique. The fourth topic covers the two major models of learning.

CONTROLLED MEMORY OPERATIONS

Solving Puzzles | Listening

Taking Exams | Planning

Figure 1

CONTROLLED MEMORY PROCESSES

Controlled memory processes are those that are **consciously** directed by the individual's STM. As such, these processes represent the currently and temporarily activated memory cells. These memory operations require attention and therefore, are performed with full awareness. Examples of controlled memory processes include memory search, transfer, and retrieval, problem solving, decision-making, planning, speaking, and creativity. What you are doing now - reading words and sentences, is also a good example of a controlled process.

In general, these processes are designed to be flexible, adaptive, easily set up and altered, and applied to **novel** situations. Awareness, or introspection, to these controlled processes is normally accomplished by the **internal dialogue** (i.e., "self-talk") whereby the individual uses words and sentences to think, plan, and reason.

The tremendous flexibility of the STM is somewhat offset by its limited capacity (five to nine meaningful chunks), its limited duration (20-30 seconds), and its limited attention span. In addition, individuals can normally perform only **one** controlled process at a time, though there is some evidence that **two** controlled processes can be performed more slowly in a serial fashion. Finally, controlled processes tend to quickly reach maximum performance levels unless they become automated.

AUTOMATED MEMORY PROCESSES

DEFINITION OF AUTOMATED PROCESSES

An important feature of the memory system is its ability to carry out automatic processes. Automatic processes are defined as memory cells (or a sequence of cells) that are **almost always activated** in response to external or internal stimuli. In these cases, the activation sequence has become so familiar (i.e., over-learned) that direct supervision by the short-term memory (i.e., awareness) is no longer required. It should also be noted that the number of learning trials required before an activation sequence becomes automatic can vary greatly from a few to thousands.

As an example of an automated response, think about what happens to experienced drivers when they encounter a red stop light. The appropriate overt response (i.e., stopping the car by pressing the brake pedal) is easily learned and thus does not require continued use of scarce short-term memory capacity. As a result, the identification of the external stimulus (red light) and the retrieval from memory of the appropriate response (pressing the brake pedal) can occur **without awareness**. For example, it is not uncommon for people to arrive home from a routine drive, only to realize that they do not remember driving because they were "thinking of something else." Here, the identification of external stimuli (e.g., red lights, children, etc.) and the activation of the appropriate response sequence (e.g., stopping, slowing down, etc.) has been automated.

AUTOMATED MEMORY OPERATIONS

Smoking

Biting Fingernails

Study Habits

Driving Habits

Figure 2

AUTOMATED RESPONSES ARE PERFORMED WITHOUT AWARENESS

The most important aspect of automatic processes is that they are activated with **little or no awareness.** Research indicates that this lack of awareness occurs because (1) the activation can be extremely brief and thus easily lost from the short-term memory, or (2) the response may be so familiar or unimportant that conscious control of the activation sequence is not necessary. Indeed, the **speed and automation** of these processes normally keep them hidden from conscious view and control.

A major advantage of automatic processes is that since they do not require short-term memory awareness, they are not hindered by the capacity limitations of the short-term memory. Indeed, they have been shown to occur in parallel (i.e., at the same time) and independently from one another. There is obvious adaptive value to this arrangement since it allows the individual to use the short-term memory for important and/or novel stimuli while simultaneously automating numerous less important response sequences. This means, however, that human beings typically develop a host of automated behaviors for any response sequence that is deemed excessively familiar or relatively unimportant. As we will see in a later chapter, these automated responses can cause serious problems in our ability to adapt to important sub-environments (e.g., career or relationships).

AUTOMATED RESPONSES ARE DIFFICULT TO SUPPRESS

It is important to note that once established, **automatic processes are extremely difficult to suppress, alter, or eliminate.** This is to be expected since they are performed without awareness and therefore, are not subjected to rigorous conscious examination.

As an example, a teenager may start to smoke cigarettes for a variety of reasons. S/he may be seeking peer group approval, trying to project an "adult" image, rebelling against parental or societal authority, or trying to relax in a difficult social environment. Whatever the motivation, the response sequence of lighting up and smoking a cigarette is easily learned and then over-learned (habitualized). Once established, automated responses are exceedingly difficult to suppress or

Fully Automated Behavior - Brushing Teeth

eliminate. This is because the smoking behavior can be triggered without awareness the person may want to stop, but essentially "forgets" to do so. Identify five behaviors you have automated.

1. driving home from rec
2. prepping bfast
3. swimming
4. breathing
5. making snack @ night

AUTOMATED VERSUS SEMI-AUTOMATED BEHAVIORS

Behaviors triggered from the long-term memory can be fully automated or semi-automated. A ***fully automated behavior*** does not need any participation from the short-term memory. These behaviors are performed "mindlessly" and we usually do not remember them. Even complex behaviors can be fully automated including, exercise routines, driving a car (while thinking of something else), or preparing a meal the same way time after time.

A ***semi-automated behavior*** does require some use of short-term memory resources. In this case, the individual uses the short-term memory to assess the situation and decide which behaviors are appropriate. Then the individual activates an automated series of memory cells and performs the behavior without awareness. As an example, suppose you were at a party and saw someone you were interested in dating. Through experience you have probably automated several ways to attract attention from someone you are interested in. Once you decide which "script" to perform (based on the particulars of the situation) you can engage in a series of behaviors drawn from the long-term memory – short-term memory participation is no longer required.

SUMMARY

In summary, the human memory system has evolved to assist in adapting to the environment. In its current form, the human memory system can perform two types of operations: controlled and automatic. This "two process" system has two major advantages:

1. Normally the STM is used to solve the most pressing needs of the individual. In unusual or important situations, controlled processes can be used to react adaptively, though slowly. Unfortunately, these controlled memory processes are in short supply due to the restricted capacity of the STM.

2. In familiar or unimportant situations, responses can be automated, thereby freeing the limited short-term memory capacity to respond to more pressing problems.

FACTORS AFFECTING RECALL

INTRODUCTION

We have now examined the basic structure and operation of the human memory system. A thorough understanding of the memory system is important for two major reasons. First, the ability to adapt to any particular environment (e.g., a new job) is greatly facilitated by the efficient use of your memory. Many students believe that once they leave college, they will no longer need to use their memory efficiently. This mistake is normally made by students who equate "efficient use of memory" with a rehearsal strategy.

Of course, we know now that the term "efficient use of memory" almost never means rehearsal but instead, refers to a meaningful level of processing (organization or elaboration). If you begin training your memory system to organize and elaborate incoming information, you will not only get better grades right away, but you will also enjoy a tremendous advantage over your competitors in your first job.

The second reason you need to understand the memory system's operating features is also related to your career success. In any sales or advertising position, you will be required to construct presentations or advertisements that are memorable. If the consumer forgets your message, it cannot influence his/her behavior. Fortunately, the structural and operating characteristics of the memory system make it easier to

Cognitive Consistency

remember external information if it possesses certain features. Indeed, research indicates that each of the following factors can influence message retention.

LEVEL OF PROCESSING

As demonstrated in the preceding chapter, a deep level of processing produces a more organized and meaningful memory code. Not surprisingly, people can more easily remember meaningful information. Meaning facilitates semantic organization, and organization facilitates both transfer and retrieval. Thus, "to organize is to remember." As a result, to maximize the probability of a message being retained, you must make it **meaningful** and **organized** for your audience.

Of course, this means you must have some idea of the meaning structures (tree structures) that currently exist in the consumer's long-term memory. Indeed, a major function of marketing research is to examine the consumers' belief and value structure so that promotional information can be presented in the most organized and effective manner. Therefore, when you design a message to be remembered (or when **you** want to remember a message), take care to relate the message to material already stored in the long term memory.

CONSISTENCY

The "meaningfulness" of information usually depends on its relationship to material already included in the internal model. For example, an advanced calculus formula will have little meaning to you unless you have the background to understand its component parts. It should not surprise you that information **consistent** with already-established beliefs and values is more easily organized and integrated into the long-term memory.

In contrast, discrepant information is relatively difficult to understand and integrate since relevant knowledge structures may be missing or poorly developed. In addition, it is hard to accurately comprehend discrepant information since the individual is often (though not always) engaged in counterattack or withdrawal. Not surprisingly, this limits transfer opportunities to the long-term memory and minimizes subsequent retrieval. Finally, most people demonstrate a significant lack of motivation to recall discrepant data since it creates cognitive dissonance.

One of the real challenges of marketing communications (both personal and commercial) is to frame the persuasive message as consistently as possible with

Point-of-Purchase Display

the consumer's existing beliefs and values. However, if the goal is to **change** the consumer's internal model (e.g., to induce brand switching), discrepant information **must** be provided, even though there is a small likelihood of its acceptance. Indeed, if you become adept at getting people to accept and remember discrepant information, you can be very successful in the marketing communications field.

FREQUENCY

Items that are frequently encountered are easier to remember for several reasons. First, there is greater opportunity for transfer into the long-term memory since the short-term memory encounters the item on a frequent basis. In essence, each short-term memory encounter is a rehearsal opportunity which, over time, maximizes transfer. In addition, constant repetition may facilitate the "automatic" transfer of the item to long-term memory **without awareness**. Indeed, several theories that will be discussed later (like the low involvement learning theory) rely on this process to explain some overt behaviors.

Repetition may also facilitate familiarity, which provides a deeper level of processing and/or better organization of the incoming material. Frequency seems to be especially important for getting people to remember material that is incidental or superficial since such information is difficult to organize or elaborate. As a result, advertising for many products relies heavily on repetition to get the message remembered.

RECENCY

Because items in the short-term memory can last for up to 30 seconds, one way to improve recall is to make the information recent. Obviously, recency reflects the operation of the short-term memory. To use the recency effect to their advantage, many marketers create point-of-purchase displays or other in-store promotions that consumers can encounter just before a purchase decision is made.

AROUSAL AND SURVIVAL VALUE

Studies have shown that recall is enhanced if the individual is "aroused" while learning. This effect likely comes from the increased attention and short-term memory processing that occurs during heightened states of arousal. In addition, material that is related to physical survival or important secondary goals, will tend to be better remembered due to its obvious saliency. Again, increased attention and/or better organization of such important data likely explains this effect.

The arousal effect may explain, in part, why sexually oriented advertisements are so commonly employed. If the arousal level becomes too great, however, the awakened primary drive chemistry may interfere with transfer or distract the STM's attention. Therefore, it is recommended that the learner's arousal level be kept within reasonable boundaries.

In summary, if you want to maximize your recall of certain material, or if you want others to remember your message, follow these guidelines:

1. Attach the incoming items to information already stored in long-term memory.
2. Organize the material.
3. Understand the material.
4. Make the material frequent.
5. Make the material recent.
6. Arouse the learner.
7. Attach the material to survival or important secondary goals.
8. Make the material consistent

USING THE MEMORY TO STUDY

A familiar memory operation for most college students is the use of a studying strategy called "cramming." In using this technique, the student tries to force as much information as possible through the short-term memory by mechanically rehearsing the information. This rote repetition is often timed to commence a night or two before the exam, and may require the student to stay up all night. Notice, however, that this study method is inefficient for several major reasons.

CRAMMING CAN HURT THE MEMORY SYSTEM

First, it takes a long time to accomplish transfer using rehearsal, and the human attention span was not designed for long, boring tasks. Instead, it likes to process information in short, intensive bursts. In addition, the capacity and duration of the short-term memory are small. Therefore, forcing yourself to laboriously rehearse material often causes boredom and fatigue, and may even impair your short-term memory (as manifested for instance, by headaches or drowsiness). In this condition, the short-term memory has a difficult time searching the long-term memory during retrieval. In fact, studies have clearly demonstrated that studying in short intensive bursts is much more effective for recall than massed practices like cramming.

CRAMMING RELIES ON SUPERFICIAL CODES

Secondly, the information that is transferred via rehearsal is normally processed at a very superficial level (e.g., memorizing a formula as a set of symbols as opposed to remembering the meaning of the symbols). Unfortunately, the organizational structures and relationship of the material cannot be easily identified through rehearsal. This practice, therefore, tends to obscure the most meaningful aspects of the material in return for a short run ability to repeat certain parts of it - a poor trade indeed.

CRAMMING CAN PERPETUATE ITSELF

Because rehearsed information is quickly lost after the exam, and because the meaning and organization of the study material has not been acquired, rehearsal for one exam makes studying for the next exam doubly difficult. The foundation material that would be required for future understanding was never transferred to the LTM at a deep level. Therefore, the only viable study technique for future exams will again be inefficient rehearsal.

Cramming for Exams

THE ELABORATION STUDY TECHNIQUE

The elaboration study technique is designed to form Level III memory codes the first time you process new information. If this is accomplished it is much easier for the internal model to retrieve the information at a later date. To accomplish elaboration follow these steps:

1. **Organize study episodes into 30 minute segments.** Studying past your attention span (usually about 30 minutes) is inefficient and cannot produce Level III codes. This is because Level III codes require careful attention to incoming information. Therefore, elaboration can be achieved only when the learner is alert and focused on the information to be learned. ***Note:*** Lack of time management skills prevents the use of the elaboration technique and leads to cramming.

2. **Study the organizational structure of the information before learning it.** To achieve this, study the table of contents or other outline if available. Think about how each chapter relates to the overall structure of the class. Think about the structure of the chapter to be read. The idea is to set up "retrieval cues" or organized memory addresses for the to-be-consumed information. For example, in this book, the ***guiding questions*** at the beginning of each chapter are designed to help you understand the structure of the material before you read it.

3. **Think about how the new information relates to your existing memories.** Think about situations from your own life that exemplify the concept. Spend some time thinking up good examples – this is the key to the elaboration technique. The example(s) you pick should allow you to remember the essentials of the concept being learned. ***Note:*** Do not proceed if you do not understand a concept. This is because

future information often builds on previous concepts. Therefore, go back until you understand the information and can think of a good example for it.

4. **Write the best (i.e., most vivid) example from your life in the margins of the text.** The notation should be detailed enough to allow you to remember the concept when you think of the example. You should write down one example for each major concept being learned.

5. **Try to be creative.** Think of interesting questions or innovative applications for the new information and also write these notations in the margins.

6. **When you review the material before the exam go over both the concepts and the examples you entered.** Then if you cannot remember a concept on the exam you should be able to "reconstruct" the correct answer using your examples as guides.

LEARNING

LEARNING DEFINED

The formal definition of learning is ***a change in behavior not due to instincts, maturation, or temporary states.*** Individuals can acquire associations (i.e., learn) in two basic ways, classical conditioning and operant conditioning (or instrumental learning).

CLASSICAL CONDITIONING

Here, an "unconditioned stimulus" (UCS), like food powder automatically elicits an overt behavior, called an "unconditioned response" (UCR), like salivating. If a neutral or "conditioned stimulus" (CS), like a bell, is repeatedly paired with the food powder (UCS), the individual will learn to salivate (conditioned response (CR)) upon hearing the bell. This learning paradigm is shown below.

As another example, suppose a child cries (UCR) when put to bed (UCS). If the child hears the word "bed time" (CS) before going to bed on repeated occasions, s/he will soon begin to cry (CR) upon hearing the word "bed time." Research has shown that the factors influential in determining classical conditioning are the frequency with which the UCS and CS are paired (as the number of pairings increases, the more the CR resembles the UCR) and the temporal relation between UCS and CS. (For maximum learning, the CS should **precede** the UCS by a short time interval like 0.5 seconds.)

It is important to note that classical conditioning occurs only when an unconditioned response exists (e.g., reactions to pain or fear, or involuntary responses like salivation). As a result, this type of learning usually accounts for a smaller number of beliefs and values than operant conditioning.

CLASSICAL CONDITIONING

1. UCS (food powder) ⟶ automatically elicits ⟶ UCR (salivating)

If:

2. UCS (food powder) ⟶ is preceded by a ⟶ CS (bell),

Then, over repeated associations:

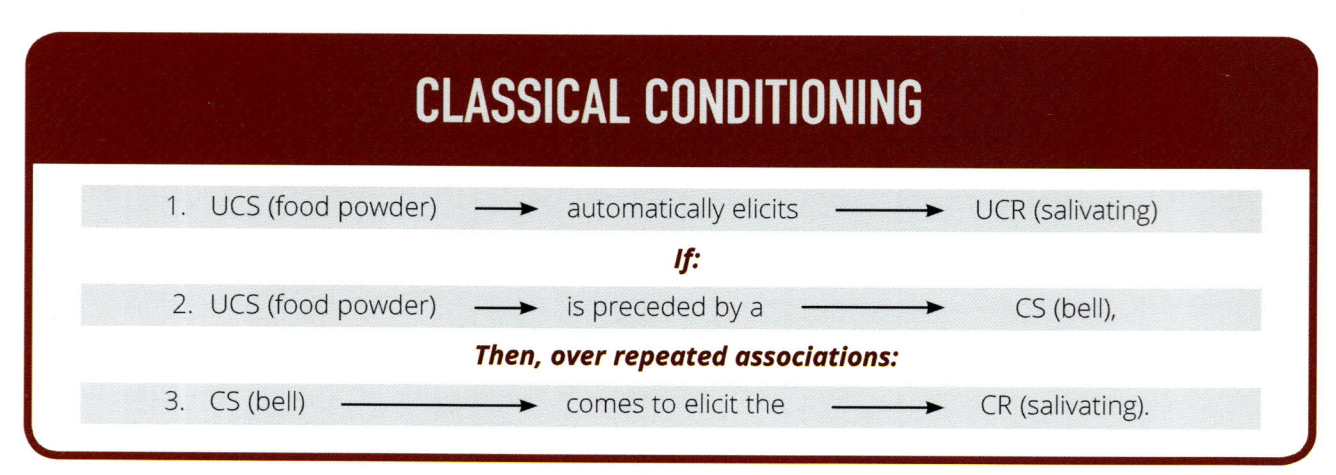

3. CS (bell) ⟶ comes to elicit the ⟶ CR (salivating).

Figure 3

Conditioned Response

OPERANT CONDITIONING (INSTRUMENTAL LEARNING)

Operant conditioning (also called instrumental learning) begins when the individual performs any overt behavior. These can be purposeful or random actions. After an individual performs the behavior, the environment reacts in one of three ways:

1. The environment **rewards** the individual for performing the behavior.
2. The environment **punishes** the individual for performing the behavior.
3. The environment **does nothing**.

The basic rules of instrumental learning are that rewards increase the probability of the behavior being repeated, and that punishments decrease the probability of the behavior being repeated. Thus, learning occurs as individuals:

1. Add to their behavioral repertoire actions that have been rewarded.
2. Eliminate from their behavioral repertoire actions that have been punished.

The itinerary of rewards and punishments is called the **schedule of reinforcement**, and it is the major mechanism by which operant conditioning is accomplished. Rewards will be any environmental response that facilitates need satisfaction. The degree of the reward is determined by the extent to which it fosters goal attainment (instrumentality) and the current priority level of that goal.

Notice that many of these rewards and punishments are determined by the **reaction of other people to your behavior**. Since we already know that the basis for our behavior is **expected-benefits**, you can expect to be rewarded when you behave in a fashion "instrumental" to "significant others," and punished

REINFORCEMENT VERSUS PUNISHMENT

	Reinforcement *"increase behavior"*	**Punishment** *"decrease behavior"*
Positive *"add"*	 Give Love	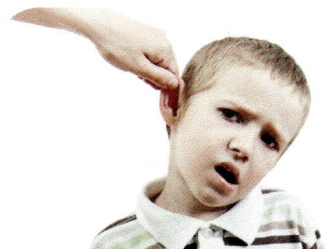 Give Time Out
Negative *"remove"*	 Remove Pain	 Remove Freedom

Table 1

when your behavior conflicts with their goal attainment. This means that a large part of your schedule of reinforcement depends upon your ability to identify and perform behaviors that are instrumental to other people.

For example, suppose a sports oriented father wants (i.e., values) his son to be "athletic." Since this is a goal for the father, he will reward any behaviors that he associates with being athletic and may punish any behaviors that he associates with being "non-masculine." Any child placed in this environment will quickly learn that athletic behaviors are rewarded and "non-masculine" behaviors are punished. In this situation the child will usually (though not always) quickly acquire a host of athletic behaviors due to their obvious instrumentality. Notice that here, the child has learned a value (i.e., athletic behaviors are good).

While this example demonstrates how values are stamped into the internal model, it does not mean that children will have the exact same values as their parents. This is because the individual also learns values from other information sources like web sites, peer groups, television programs, movies, books, etc. In many cases these values will conflict with parental values, and thus cause behavior conflicts. Also, if a parent applies excessive punishments in the schedule of reinforcement the learner may reject the teacher's values and "rebel"(i.e., learn to dislike the behaviors the parent is trying to stamp in – often called the "boomerang effect").

Thus, regardless of who applies the schedule of reinforcement, we learn to positively value anything that brings us perceived rewards and to negatively value anything that brings us perceived punishments.

INSTILLING VALUES

Figure 4

Indeed, if you stop and think about your own beliefs and values, you will find a large number of them reflect the schedule of reinforcement you encountered as a child.

In addition, since no two individuals receive identical schedules of reinforcement, no two people will have identical beliefs and values. The greater the difference in schedules of reinforcement, the greater the difference in beliefs, values, and behavior. This means that disagreements about the value of things usually reflect that different schedules of reinforcement were encountered and learned. This also accounts for the remarkable differences in values found in different cultures of the world.

RULES OF INSTRUMENTAL LEARNING

Because operant conditioning is so important, it received a great deal of attention from learning psychologists in the mid 1900s (see for example Hull 1943, or Skinner 1957). Some of the more important findings are summarized as follows:

1. The target behavior will be learned faster if the individual is reinforced **every time** the behavior is performed (i.e., in a continuous schedule of reinforcement) than if the individual is rewarded intermittently.

2. Learning occurs faster if the **reward immediately** follows the target behavior. As the time between the performance of the target behavior and the administration of the reward increases, more (non-target) behaviors are likely to be performed. As a result, the learning organism cannot easily identify which behavior has been rewarded.

3. **Extinction** refers to the "unlearning" of a previously acquired association (e.g., trying to stop smoking). Studies show that when rewards are terminated for performance of the target object (or punishment applied), behaviors acquired from a continuous schedule of reinforcement are extinguished faster than behaviors acquired via an intermittent schedule.

4. The acquisition of complicated behaviors is facilitated by **modeling,** where the learning organism is shown someone else performing the target behavior **and being rewarded.** For example, advertisements do not just show people buying the target product, but also receiving rewards instrumental to goal attainment (i.e., happiness, prestige, group esteem, etc.).

5. The acquisition of complicated behaviors is facilitated by **shaping,** where simpler but similar behaviors are learned which successively approximate the target behavior.

6. The acquisition of complicated behaviors is facilitated by **chaining,** where the complex target behavior is broken down into simpler components and then "chained" together.

In summary, if you want to modify or influence another person's behavior, you should apply a schedule of reinforcement that best suits your goal. Of course, this will require a knowledge of what the learning organism values. In general, you can expect people to value anything that is instrumental to need satisfaction.

CONCLUSION

We have now concluded our preliminary examination of the thinking apparatus of the internal model. Basically, the internal model represents an individual's "view of the world" that is stored in the memory system. To understand how this internal model works, we must understand its most fundamental components - beliefs and values.

EXPERIMENT 4.1
STUDY ELABORATIVELY

Use the elaboration study technique to prepare this chapter.

1. Describe how you achieved each of the six steps in the strategy,

2. Prepare two Level III questions,

3. Be sure to form personal connections to the material by relating it to your current life - give two examples,

4. Describe how well you were able to achieve the elaboration study technique.

ELABORATION QUESTIONS

- How do college students compare to non-students in terms of their controlled memory operations. Give some specific examples.

- Identify some of the major automated behaviors of your key accounts.

- Identify some of your own major automated behaviors.

- What are some automated behaviors of consumers?

- Explain how you could use the levels of processing theory to get key customers to remember your sales points.

- Explain how you could use consistency to get key customers to remember your sales points.

- Explain how you could use arousal to get key customers to remember your sales points.

- Compare your study strategy to the elaboration technique.

CHAPTER 5
BELIEFS AND VALUES

INTRODUCTION 5.1
BELIEFS 5.1
    Definition 5.1
    Belief Format 5.1
    Dimensions of Beliefs 5.3
    Belief Formation 5.4
    Belief Function 5.4
BELIEF TYPES 5.5
    Descriptive Beliefs 5.5
    Informational Beliefs 5.6
    Inferred Beliefs 5.6
BELIEF VERIFIABILITY 5.7
    Tangible Versus Intangible Attributes 5.7
    Factual Versus Non-factual Associations 5.7
    Hardening of Non-verifiable Beliefs 5.8
BELIEF CHANGE 5.9
VALUES 5.9
    Introduction 5.9
    Characteristics of Values 5.10
    Types of Values 5.10
VALUE RIGIDITY 5.10
THE HUMAN VALUE SYSTEM 5.10
    Human Values 5.11
    Cultural Values 5.11
    Peer Group Values 5.11
    Family Values 5.11
    Personal Values 5.11
    Value System 5.11
EXPERIMENT 5.1 | THE RIGIDITY OF BELIEFS AND VALUES 5.12
CONCLUSION 5.12
ELABORATION QUESTIONS 5.13

GUIDING QUESTIONS

- What is the definition of beliefs?
- How are beliefs formatted in memory?
- What is belief strength and why is it important?
- How are beliefs formed?
- What function do beliefs play?
- What are the different types of beliefs?
- What types of beliefs are people most confident of?
- Why are inferred beliefs usually wrong?
- What is belief verifiability?
- What are tangible attributes?
- What are factual associations?
- Why is verifiability so important in marketing?
- Why do non-verifiable beliefs harden over time?
- Why is belief change so important?
- What are values, and how are they defined?
- How are values similar to beliefs, and how are they different?
- What is the difference between instinctual values and learned values?
- Why our values so rigid?
- What major values have been identified in consumer situations?

INTRODUCTION

We have seen that the cognitive component of the internal model contains symbolic units that we somehow use to think and reason. In this chapter we will examine the most fundamental components in the internal model - beliefs and values. In addition, in Chapter 13 we will see how these verbal symbol units are arranged in a meaningful pattern to form thoughts and feelings.

BELIEFS

DEFINITION

The human memory system provides internal storage for symbolic representations of external objects or events. In addition, this system is highly associative and connects related representations by a "memory trace." Thus, the memory system performs two major functions:

1. **It stores items** (e.g., descriptions, meanings, events, etc.), and
2. **It connects them** (i.e., associates them).

The simplest form of these functions would be a connection between two items. For example, the memory system might associate "fire" with "hot" or "college education" with "a successful career." These associations between two items are labeled "beliefs," and they represent the most fundamental building blocks in your model of the world. These examples demonstrate that beliefs contain three basic components:

1. An **object** or event,
2. An **attribute** of the object or event,
3. **A degree of association between them** (i.e., a subjective probability of association).

This leads to the formal definition of a belief as "the subjective probability of association between an object (or event) and an attribute." These relationships are shown in Figure 1.

BELIEF FORMAT

Each belief component (i.e., the object and the attribute) is stored in its own **memory cell** and connected by an neural-chemical **memory trace.** This memory trace represents the probability of association between the contents of the two memory cells. As an example, consider a consumer's memory representation for beliefs about cars. The consumer in this example associates BMW's with prestige, durability, and high price as shown in the diagram in Figure 2.

BELIEF COMPONENTS

OBJECT	PROBABILITY OF ASSOCIATION (P)	ATTRIBUTE
Fire	→ (is associated with) →	Hot
	$0.0 < p < 1.0$	

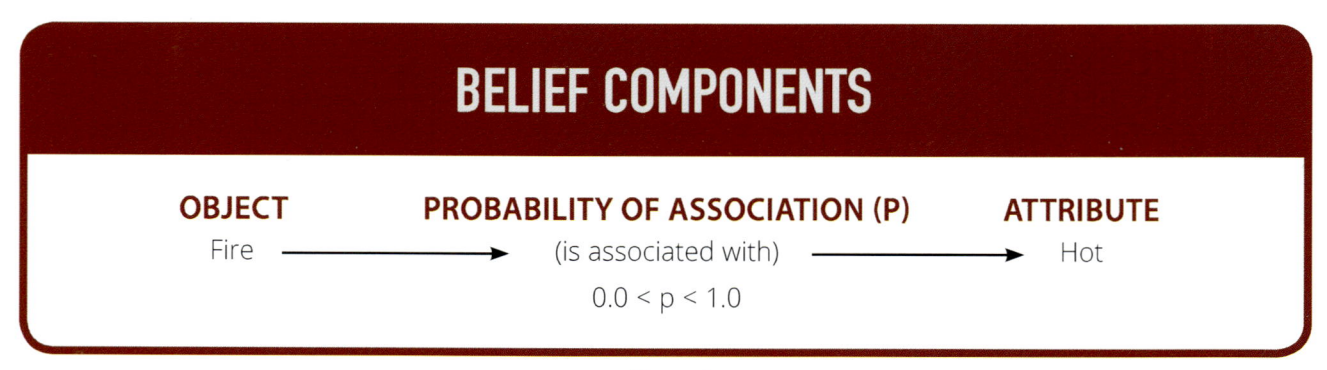

Figure 1

5.1

BELIEFS AS FORMATTED IN MEMORY

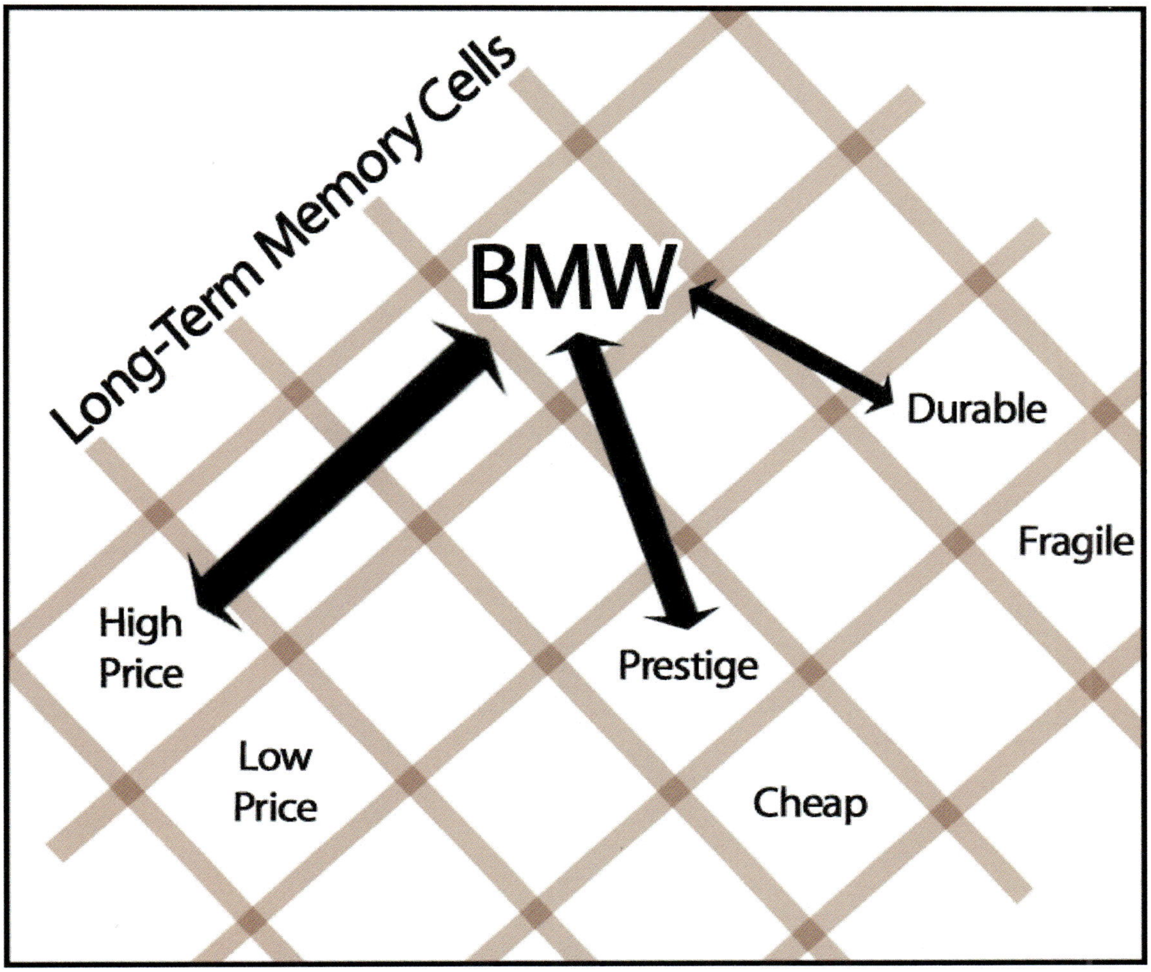

Figure 2

Notice that the memory traces in the diagram above have differences in the strength of the associations (as represented by the thickness of the arrows). In mathematical terms, the memory trace can be represented as a probability estimate. Thus, the probability of association between any object and any attribute (i.e., p) can range numerically from 0.0 to 1.0. When p = 0, the individual does not "believe" that any association exists between the object and the attribute. In the diagram above for example, there is no association between BMW and "low price." Conversely, when p = 1.0, the individual is "certain" that the object and attribute are associated. In the diagram above for example, there is a very strong association between BMW and "high price."

To identify some of your own beliefs, circle the appropriate probability on the scales in Table 1.

PERSONAL BELIEF SCALES

OBJECT	PROBABILITY OF ASSOCIATION	ATTRIBUTE
Cigarette smoking	0.0 .1 .2 .3 .4 .5 .6 (.7) .8 .9 1.0	Lung cancer
God	0.0 .1 .2 .3 .4 .5 .6 .7 .8 .9 (1.0)	Creator of life
Your personality	0.0 .1 .2 .3 .4 .5 .6 .7 (.8) .9 1.0	Very social
Capitalism	0.0 .1 .2 .3 .4 .5 .6 .7 (.8) .9 1.0	Good
Cramming	(0.0) .1 .2 .3 .4 .5 .6 .7 .8 .9 1.0	High exam grade
BMW	0.0 .1 .2 .3 .4 .5 .6 .7 .8 .9 (1.0)	High price
College	0.0 .1 .2 .3 .4 .5 .6 .7 (.8) .9 1.0	Social education
College degree	0.0 .1 .2 .3 .4 .5 (.6) .7 .8 .9 1.0	Intelligence
50 different people	0.0 (.1) .2 .3 .4 .5 .6 .7 .8 .9 1.0	Identical responses on these scales

Table 1

DIMENSIONS OF BELIEFS

By completing these scales, you have identified three dimensions of your beliefs: strength, centrality, and subjectivity.

Belief Strength. Notice that your subjective probability of association (p) varies depending on how likely you think it is that the objects and attributes are connected. When p is small (i.e., p < .3), beliefs are referred to as **lower order** since they represent a low probability of association. When p is large (i.e., p > .7), beliefs are referred to as **higher order** since the probability of association is strong.

Belief Centrality. Some objects and attributes are more important to you than others. Greater importance normally occurs when objects and/or attributes are closely tied to your values, goals, ego, or self concept. Beliefs related to such objects and/or attributes are said to be "central" and therefore, enjoy more attention from you in terms of time spent thinking, information acquired, personal interactions, etc. Central beliefs tend to resist change because they are tied to, and form the foundation of, so many other beliefs.

Belief Subjectivity. It is important to note that your responses to these belief scales represent **only** your view and depend largely on the information to which you have been exposed (especially when you were young). There is no reason to expect other people to have the same belief strengths and centrality, unless they have encountered the same information as you. Indeed, it is generally true that the extent of similarity between any two people's beliefs depends upon the similarity of the information they have encountered in life.

Belief subjectivity is a very important dimension of the internal model because it means that people can be expected to hold different beliefs. When people with different beliefs interact on matters related to those beliefs, conflict will inevitably occur. For example, people with different religious beliefs (which tend to be central and strongly held) often engage in long arguments trying to "enlighten" one another in an attempt to change the other person's beliefs to be more like there own. This outcome is rarely achieved, however, and both people will normally leave the argument more convinced than ever of their original beliefs. This is because they have just recalled and expressed their original beliefs (i.e., activated them) a process which usually has the effect of making the beliefs more accessible from memory.

BELIEF FORMATION

Beliefs are "formed" or "acquired" when an individual **accepts** information from the environment that relates an object to an attribute. For example, if you believe that BMW's have smooth rides, then at some point you have **accepted** information that connects them. This acceptance could be based upon direct experience (e.g., a test ride) or on a general belief that BMW's are superior cars. In any event, belief formation occurs whenever a person identifies evidence that connects two items and stores this association in the internal model.

BELIEF FUNCTION

Why do people form beliefs? The answer lies in their **predictive ability.** If you know what attributes are associated with an object, you can predict future events regarding that object. For example, if you experience huge traffic jams while trying to drive through Chicago at 4:30 p.m., you will form a belief that associates traffic jams in Chicago with 4:30 p.m. If you have this experience several times, the belief will gain strength. In other words, your internal model will accurately reflect the real world's traffic patterns for Chicago at 4:30 p.m. Notice that once formed, this belief can allow you to **predict** traffic jams at 4:30 p.m. in Chicago. This prediction, in turn, gives you greater **control** over your interactions with your environment if you can **avoid** traffic jams by not driving in Chicago at 4:30 p.m.

Thus, the major function performed by beliefs is that they allow us to better predict, and thereby control, our relationship with the environment. Because control has significant survival and reinforcement value, modeling the world internally by forming beliefs is **adaptive** and thus "selected for." This means we can expect all normally equipped people to be able to form beliefs and actually to do so through information acceptance. The resultant prediction and control are extremely functional, adaptive, and instrumental to goal attainment. However, these benefits accrue **only** if the beliefs **accurately model** the real world.

Avoiding Traffic Jams

BELIEF TYPES

The information that forms beliefs can come to the internal model from three sources that produce three identifiable types of beliefs.

DESCRIPTIVE BELIEFS

Descriptive beliefs are formed through **direct sensory experience** with the object and its attributes. An example would be actually getting stuck in Chicago traffic at 4:30 pm on a weekday. In addition, because "descriptive" beliefs are processed directly by the senses, they are normally **strong and confidently held**. Because of their strength, descriptive beliefs play a prominent role in the internal model's evaluation of the environment. After all "seeing is believing."

In marketing, descriptive beliefs are formed when consumers have direct experience with the product or brand. One of the best ways to form confidently held beliefs in consumers is to offer a **product trial**. When consumers are able to directly experience the attributes that are associated with a brand (e.g., taste test) they typically form strong beliefs. This is especially true for **"experiential attributes,"** which by definition can be evaluated by trial. Even expensive products can offer trial as part of their marketing strategy. As an example, major automobile manufacturers sometimes offer a 24 hour trial of new cars – the consumer can keep the car for an entire day to judge how it performs. This can be expected to form strongly held descriptive beliefs about the car which can lead to purchase if the attributes associated with the car are favorably evaluated.

INFORMATIONAL BELIEFS

These are beliefs that are formed when you accept ("believe") what another person tells you or what you read. An example would be a friend telling you to avoid Chicago at 4:30 p.m. because the traffic is bad. Lacking personal confirmation, the strength of these beliefs varies widely, depending on the perceived credibility of the information source. This is a critical point for marketing because promotions seek to associate our brand with positive attributes.

Direct Sensory Experience Test Driving a Car

Before purchase, this is primarily done by web sites, advertising and sales people (after purchase the consumer will have his/her own descriptive beliefs). However, because these sources have a **vested interest** in promoting the brand, their credibility is in question. Indeed, consumers normally **discount** the information they receive from vested-interest sources and form lower order beliefs. For example, the informational beliefs formed when a consumer reads an advertisement for a product are frequently weak due to the low perceived credibility of the source.

Because of these dynamics, perceived credibility is critically important to develop if you work in marketing. Because we actively promote our brand we must expect people to discount what we say. Accordingly, we need to be able to support or document any claims we make.

We will examine the issue of source credibility in more detail in a later chapter.

INFERRED BELIEFS

Sometimes, your internal model will "go beyond the information given to it" and create beliefs of its own. For example, you may notice that all of the major cities experience heavy traffic problems at rush hour. Looking at a map of Chicago, you also may notice that downtown Chicago can only be approached from the west, north, and south since it is next to a lake. From these observations you may **infer** that Chicago traffic at rush hour would be quite bad since there is no eastbound traffic from downtown. In this case, your internal model has formed its own new belief that "Chicago traffic is probably very bad at rush hour" even though you have not experienced it.

THE SUBJECTIVITY OF INFERRED BELIEFS

Figure 3

It turns out that inferred beliefs play a central role in the internal model due to their large number. People continually find themselves in situations where they must infer the causation of effects they observe. For example, suppose the person you have been dating for a month calls you at the last minute and cancels a date you were looking forward to; saying there is no time to explain right now, then hangs up.

In situations like this (many of which are less dramatic and often unnoticed), most people will immediately try to figure out (i.e., infer) what is happening and why. Lacking direct knowledge of the actual events, **we must go beyond the information given to us**. Perhaps the person was intoxicated; perhaps s/he was in trouble. Maybe s/he is losing interest in the relationship and had second thoughts about going through with the date. Whatever the true circumstances, the inference we make will have a big effect on our overt behavior. If you inferred your date was intoxicated, you might get angry and therefore, perform negative overt behaviors like ripping up the person's picture or refusing further calls. Conversely, if you inferred your date was in trouble, you might get worried and therefore, perform positive overt behaviors like calling the police or some friends to try and be of help. If you inferred your date had changed his/her mind, you might feel insecure, become depressed and perform a negative overt behavior like pouting, over-drinking, or over-eating.

Studies on inferred beliefs demonstrate that people generally are **not** very good at making accurate inferences. A major reason for this is that people often project their own motives or feelings onto others (e.g., "I am usually angry when I raise my voice so the person talking in a loud voice must be angry"). In other cases, people just guess at the motives of others and these guesses are often wrong (e.g., If a friend does not say "hi" to you on campus you might infer that he is mad at you, when he was thinking about something else and did not notice you). These inaccuracies in making inferences are not surprising in a complex world that is difficult to understand, but they do cause many maladaptive behaviors that are subsequently punished.

The processes by which consumers make inferences about products has been studied in marketing research. For example, a common consumer inference is that there is a correlation between price and quality. If you want to buy the "best" but are not familiar with the product category you may infer the highest priced product has the best quality. Notice that in this case, the purchase of a product rests solely on an inferred belief.

BELIEF VERIFIABILITY

In marketing, it is important to distinguish between beliefs that are verifiable and those that are not. Verifiable beliefs are said to exist when the attribute is tangible and the association is based on provable facts.

TANGIBLE VERSUS INTANGIBLE ATTRIBUTES

Tangible attributes are those that can be **directly assessed through the senses** by ordinary people (especially the sense of touch). Advertising claims like "this car has steel-belted radial tires," or "this car has a V-8 engine," are examples of tangible attributes. Intangible attributes are not physical and cannot be directly assessed through the senses. Examples of intangible attributes would include: "pride of ownership" and "beautiful styling."

FACTUAL VERSUS NON-FACTUAL ASSOCIATIONS

Factual associations exist when the attribute-object link can be supported or documented by facts. Facts are specific information that can be verified using a standard (agreed upon) scale **not** subject to individual interpretation. For example, it is a fact that water boils at 100 degrees centigrade (at standard temperature and pressure). Similarly, a verifiable scale is used to determine the MPG ratings for automobiles. Sometimes verifying facts requires special training or equipment. As an example, carbon dating of organic material requires special equipment and training but is a verifiable process. Non-factual associations exist when the attribute-object link cannot be supported or documented by facts. Instead, non-factual (also called impressionistic) information is subject to individual interpretations. Examples would include: "beautiful styling" or "truly excellent gas mileage."

In marketing, verifiable beliefs exist when the consumer associates a product with tangible attributes and the association between the brand and attribute can be factually documented. As an example, suppose a new car is advertised as getting 33 miles per gallon of gas. This is a verifiable advertising claim because how far a car can go on a gallon of gas is tangible (readily observed through the senses) and factual (can be verified on a standard scale). The reason this is important is that if verifiable claims about a brand are false – the consumer can sue the company for false or misleading advertising. Similarly, salespeople who make verifiable claims about a brand that are false can be sued in court for misrepresentation of a material fact. Because of this marketers must be very careful not to give consumers false verifiable beliefs about their brand.

No such problem exists for non-verifiable claims where the consumer associates a product with intangible attributes and the association between the brand and attribute cannot be factually documented. As an example, think about the advertising claim that a new car is the "most beautiful" car available. This is a non-verifiable claim because beauty is an intangible attribute and the claim is non-factual because there is no standard scale to measure beauty. Because of these dynamics, many marketers prefer to advertise non-verifiable claims about their brands. Exaggerating non-verifiable claims is known as ***puffery*** and is permitted within reason.

HARDENING OF NON-VERIFIABLE BELIEFS

It is apparent from the above discussion that humans should be able to reach a consensus on verifiable beliefs because of their testable nature. However, it is also apparent that humans will not reach a consensus on non-verifiable beliefs (e.g., beauty, religion, politics, etc.). This means we should be reasonably tolerant of differences on many of these subjective issues. However, as we will see in the next chapter, when "cognitive consistency" controls the information sample, even non-verifiable beliefs become hardened

Verifiable Scales: Temperature and Gas Mileage

over time. This often causes adults to become intolerant and to defend non-verifiable beliefs with skepticism, disdain, and even violence.

BELIEF CHANGE

Changing beliefs is an important topic in marketing. In the modern marketplace things change quickly and technology and innovation can cause major changes in product preferences. Most belief change comes from within through experience and growth. For example, you may think your computer game is the best but then play a new game that is much better. This experience would form new descriptive beliefs that differ significantly with old beliefs. You should be able to identify many beliefs you once held that have changed over time and with experience (e.g., Santa Claus).

When influence agents (e.g., advertisements and salespeople) try to change consumers' beliefs the process is very different. As we will learn in the next two chapters, consumers process incoming information using cognitive consistency as implemented by four selective defense mechanisms (selective exposure, selective attention, selective comprehension, and selective retention). This means it can be very difficult, and in many cases impossible, to get other people to accept discrepant information and change their beliefs.

VALUES

INTRODUCTION

The second basic components of the internal model are values. Like beliefs these are associations stored in memory but instead of linking an object to its attributes, values link the attributes to good (+) or bad (-). These valenced states (+, -) include properties like ***favorable/unfavorable, like/dislike, good/bad,*** or ***right/wrong.*** The reason values are so important is that they determine which objects in the environment we **approach** or **avoid**. Therefore, values give **direction** to our behavior by guiding it toward positively evaluated alternatives. People interact positively with things they value (+ valence) and interact negatively with things they disvalue (- valence). The only way we can

Belief Change - Santa Claus

successfully understand and predict other people's behavior is by knowing their values.

CHARACTERISTICS OF VALUES

Value Strength and Centrality. Because values are similar to beliefs they share the important characteristics of strength and centrality. Some values are strong (held with more confidence) and some are weak. Some values are central (e.g., religious values) and some are not central. Normally, these two traits are related such that the more central the value, the stronger it becomes.

Value Subjectivity. Values are subjective because they are largely determined by the cultural and social environments which vary dramatically around the world. Because of this, we can expect that no two individuals will possess identical values. When people interact with respect to objects that they value differently, conflict occurs (this topic will be discussed in later chapters). To identify some of your values, circle the appropriate number on the scales in Table 2.

TYPES OF VALUES

Instinctual Values. We have already discussed the strong primary values of nourishment, protection, and reproduction and how people are instinctively motivated to satisfy these drives. In addition, Maslow's model (covered later in the book) identifies secondary motives associated with social reinforcement (belongingness and love) and personal reinforcement (self-esteem and self-actualization). It is clear that humans value any object that helps them achieve any of these primary or secondary needs.

Learned Values. Humans have many values that they learn from the environment (culture) around them. Indeed, the specific ways in which the general motives are achieved is usually determined by values the individual has learned over time. Like beliefs, values are created whenever the individual accepts information from the environment that relates an object to "good or bad," or "right or wrong." Values are primarily learned in two ways: classical conditioning and instrumental learning.

PERSONAL VALUE SCALES

VALUE	EXTREMELY BAD									EXTREMELY GOOD
Financial success	-9	-7	-5	-3	-1	0	+1	+3	+5	+7	+9
Peer group approval	-9	-7	-5	-3	-1	0	+1	+3	+5	+7	+9
Premarital sex	-9	-7	-5	-3	-1	0	+1	+3	+5	+7	+9
Extramarital sex	-9	-7	-5	-3	-1	0	+1	+3	+5	+7	+9
Cheating on an exam	-9	-7	-5	-3	-1	0	+1	+3	+5	+7	+9
Telling a lie	-9	-7	-5	-3	-1	0	+1	+3	+5	+7	+9
Withholding the truth	-9	-7	-5	-3	-1	0	+1	+3	+5	+7	+9
Drug use	-9	-7	-5	-3	-1	0	+1	+3	+5	+7	+9
Getting intoxicated	-9	-7	-5	-3	-1	0	+1	+3	+5	+7	+9

Table 2

VALUE RIGIDITY

The discussion in Chapter 4 explained how people learn new values, especially as children. As values (and beliefs) are acquired, the child assembles them into an organized view of the world. Research indicates that normally, by the age of eight to ten, the individual has a consolidated value structure that is organized by (1) his/her immediate environment, and (2) the rules of cognitive consistency.

Once assembled, the value structure becomes the judge of all new information. Indeed, we will see in future chapters how the selective defense mechanisms work to screen out, and thus minimize the acceptance of value-discrepant information. This has the effect of making the value structure highly resistant to change attempts. An internal model that was once open-minded and eager to learn, now becomes protective and defensive. It regards discrepant information as a threat to the solidity of the value structure (as well as reflecting poorly on past behaviors). **In essence, information that just happened to be encountered and accepted early in life now controls the process by which new data is accepted or rejected.** It is this rigidity of values that makes influence attempts so difficult to accomplish.

Thus, values encountered and accepted at an **early age** will be **overly represented** in the individual's **value structure**. As a result, the beliefs and values encountered and accepted as a child frequently control the individual's behavior after they become an "adult." In addition, since children are naive, they attribute high credibility to adults and hence, often learn whatever values the adults in their environment display. In this situation, maladaptive beliefs and values accepted and expressed by adults can become permanently ingrained in the child's belief and value structure. These values will subsequently be defended, resist change, and can cause the individual large amounts of environmental punishment.

THE HUMAN VALUE SYSTEM

Any individual's value system is composed of values at different levels. These can be arranged on a continuum ranging from very broad to very specific.

HUMAN VALUES

Human values, or what Maslow called species values, are those inherited by virtually all human beings. In Maslow's model these values include five preconditions (striving, freedom, curiosity, need to know, and self expression), the deficiency needs (survival, safety, security, affiliation, love and esteem), and growth needs.

CULTURAL VALUES

Cultural values are those shared by most members of society. For example, cultural values that are associated with the United States include materialism, youthfulness, achievement, success, individualism, freedom, activity, and progress. It is important to recognize that the cultural environment often determines which behaviors are rewarded and which are punished. We know that all humans seek belongingness and affiliation, but the appropriate way to introduce yourself depends on local customs and values. Similarly, what is regarded as proper in business dealings, courtship behaviors, and group settings will vary depending on the cultural environment. Your ability to identify the values of the environments you encounter, and to select exchange behaviors that will be rewarded in these environments, is crucial if you will be traveling in your career.

PEER GROUP VALUES

Peer group values are those of the groups to which you belong. Indeed, the reason you normally choose to join a group is because you share values with other members of the group. Much of consumer behavior takes place in groups (e.g., family decision-making and group decision-making) so these values are of special interest to marketers vending social products (e.g., music, video games, sports equipment, etc.).

FAMILY VALUES

Family values represent those that were taught to you in your family of origin. These normally play an important role in establishing your early values, although you do not necessarily accept all family values that you are exposed to.

Family and Personal Values, Education

PERSONAL VALUES

These are values that you have acquired during your personal journey through life. These values may be idiosyncratic (yours alone) and they help distinguish you from your key accounts. Indeed, **personal identity** requires that some values of the individual differ from those of the social groups to which s/he belongs.

VALUE SYSTEM

We can see that any individual's value system -- what humans consider to be right and wrong, good or bad -- is complex. One reason for this is that sometimes **cultural** values will conflict with **peer** group values or **peer** group values will conflict with **family** values, etc. Also, what a person values depends, in part, on which sub-environment s/he is in. This suggests that when you are with your peers you may engage in behaviors that would be considered wrong by the values of your family. In these cases, the individual must decide which value(s) to favor. Often, this decision is difficult because the individual must choose between the two values in the internal model or must fluctuate back and forth depending on the current environment.

CONCLUSION

We have now examined the most fundamental building blocks in the internal model – beliefs and values. These elements are mostly acquired as we grow and evolve and are designed to be the software of the internal model - to be flexible depending on the contingencies in the current environment. However, over time beliefs and values can harden to the point where they resist change attempts – not a good scenario for marketers. Indeed, to fully understand the dynamics of beliefs and values we must know how **cognitive consistency** works (next chapter).

EXPERIMENT 5.1
THE RIGIDITY OF BELIEFS AND VALUES

1. Identify three of your key accounts:
    a. one of whom has a verifiable belief you think is wrong,
    b. one of whom has a non-verifiable belief you think is wrong,
    c. one of whom has a value you think is wrong,

2. Try to change the belief/value. If you are unsuccessful, ask them what it would take to make them change the belief/value.

3. Report results in class.

4. What is the key to having a successful relationship with a person who has different beliefs and values?

ELABORATION QUESTIONS

- Why do different cultures have such different beliefs?

- What are some of your strongest beliefs?

- What happens to children who are exposed to radical beliefs (e.g., neo-Nazis), but are too young to have their defense mechanisms in place?

- How much source credibility do you have with people who know you well?

- Can you give some examples of product-related inferred beliefs that caused you to buy a product but turned out to be false? How did you react?

- Is anything ever really objective?

- Do you have any non-verifiable beliefs that you hold with high confidence? - give some consumer examples.

- How tolerant are you of beliefs that are discrepant?

- While it is important to understand that other people will have different beliefs and values and it is important to tolerate these differences, is there a point at which we should choose not to tolerate another person's beliefs and values?

- When does a person or country have the right to impose its values on someone else?

- What is the best way for someone working in international marketing to reconcile the differences in cultural beliefs and values that exist?

- Give some examples of instinctual values and learned values that influence consumer behavior.

- What are some of the ways that you reward and punish your key accounts?

- If you had the task of changing another person's values, how would you go about it?

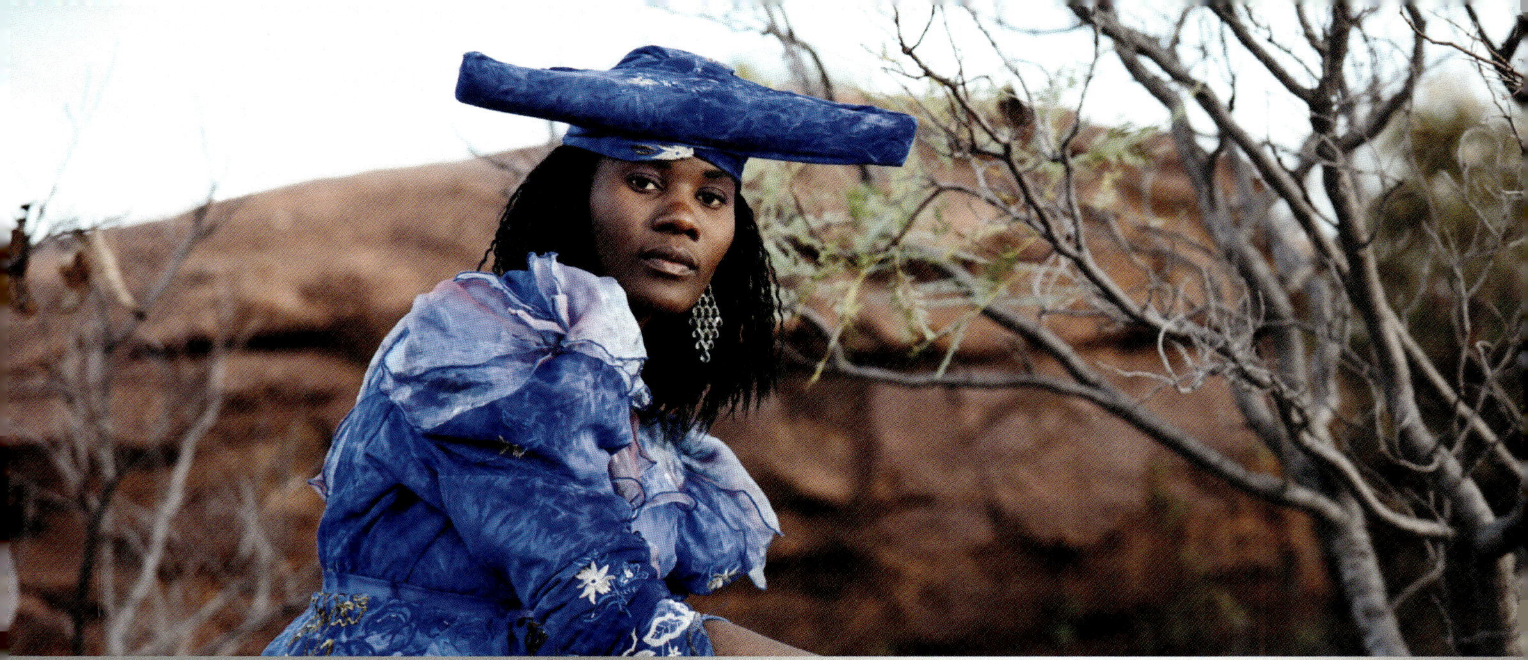
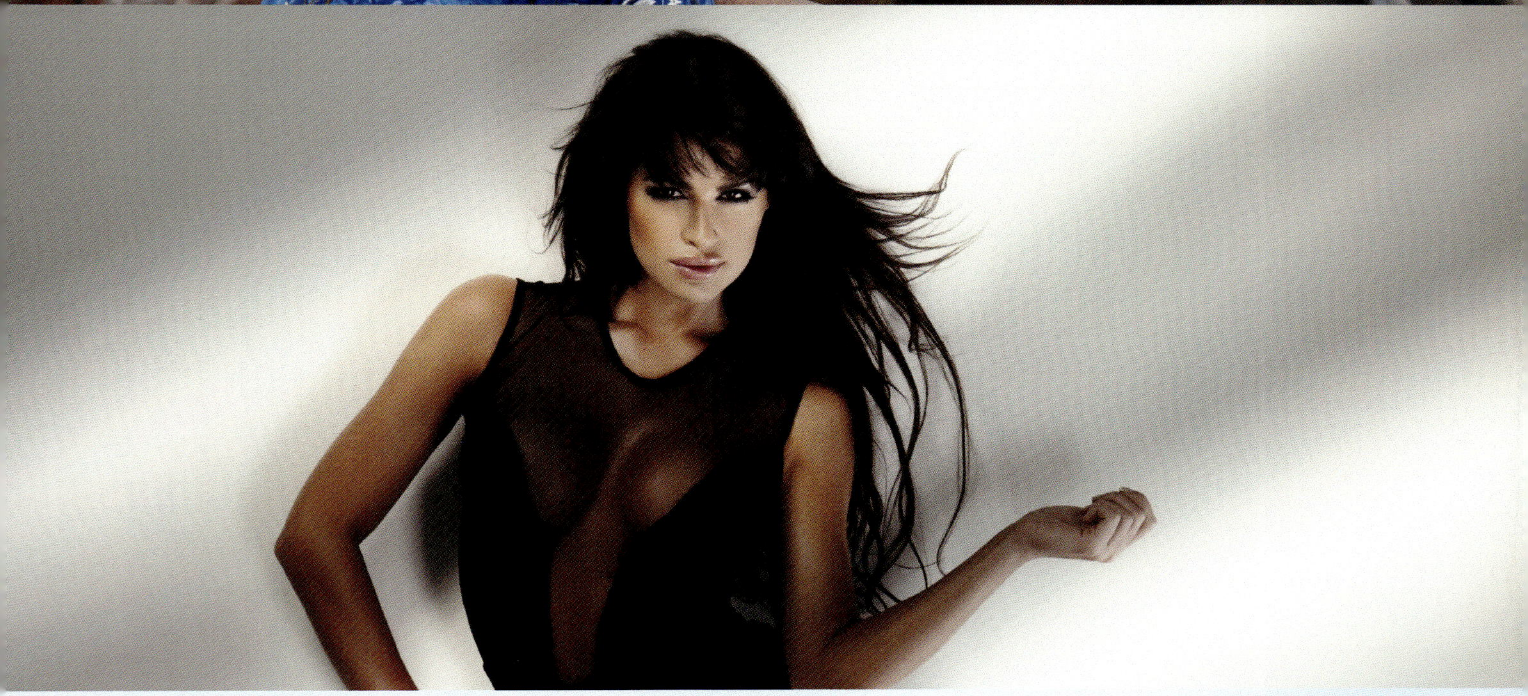
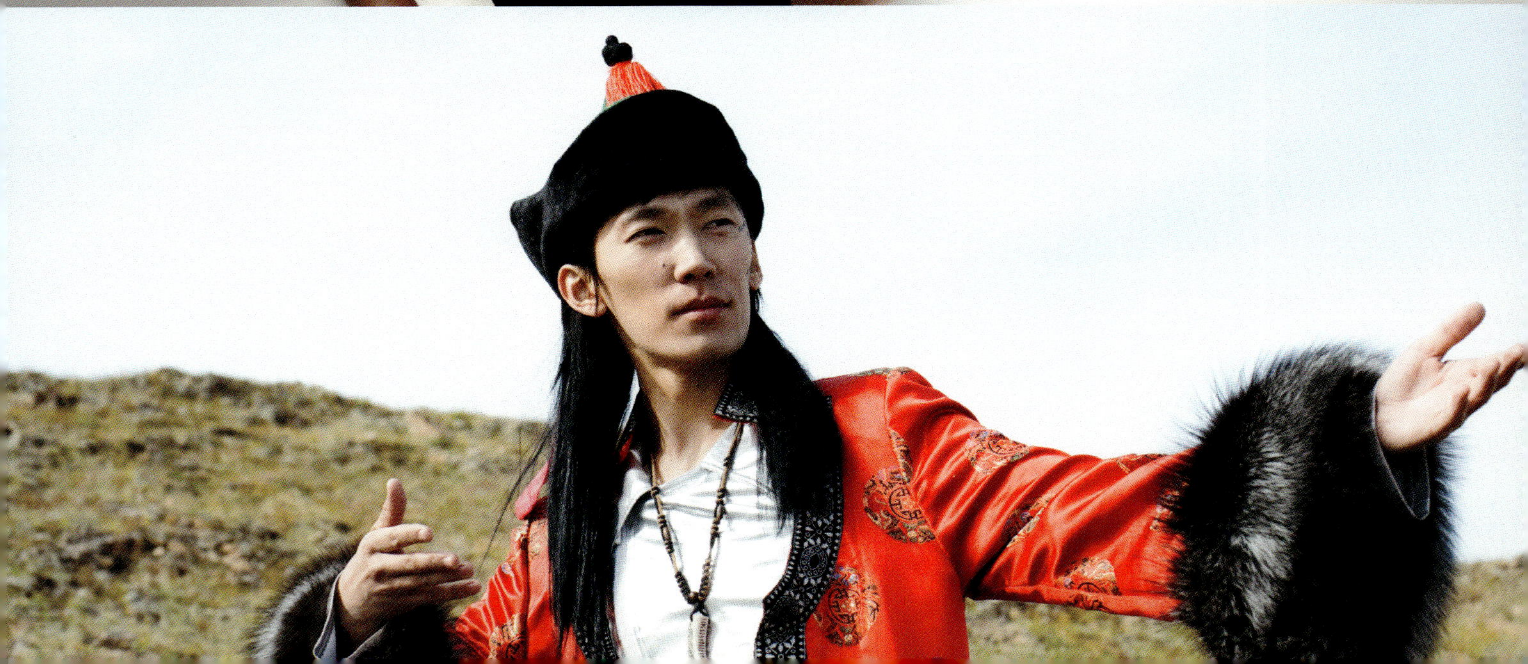

CHAPTER 6
COGNITIVE CONSISTENCY

INTRODUCTION
THE PROBLEM - A PERCEPTUAL BOTTLENECK
THE SOLUTION - INFORMATION SAMPLING
TRUTH SEEKING
COGNITIVE CONSISTENCY
    Definition of Cognitive Consistency
    Motivation for Cognitive Consistency
CONCLUSION
EXPERIMENT 6.1 | ACCEPTING INCONSISTENT INFORMATION
ELABORATION QUESTIONS

GUIDING QUESTIONS

- » Why is our ability to correctly perceive the environment limited?

- » How have the informational complexities of the environment changed in the last 100 years?

- » What is the major cause of our inability to process large amounts of environmental information?

- » What type of plan do most people use to select a sample of information from the complex environment?

- » When are people most likely to seek the truth?

- » When are people most likely to avoid the truth?

- » What is cognitive consistency?

- » What motivates people to be cognitively consistent?

- » How well do you handle uncertainty?

- » How often do you admit to mistakes you have made?

- » Why is it so hard to change people's minds?

INTRODUCTION

The internal model is designed to facilitate success and survival by enabling us to construct an accurate model of the environment. A major question in understanding the operation of the internal model is: "How do people decide which information to accept and store in their model of the world?" The answer ultimately defines our overt and verbal behaviors.

THE PROBLEM – A PERCEPTUAL BOTTLENECK

If you could see what life was like long ago, when our perceptual apparatus was developing, you would find a relatively simple world. Life forms were quite rudimentary, and they basically performed primary functions like reproducing, protecting, and food gathering. There were no web sites, newspapers, bars, television, or other verbally complex stimuli to concern human beings. In such a world, most survival related events occurred in the **immediate vicinity** of the individual. As a result, natural selection favored sensory apparatus designed to identify the **immediate environment.** In addition, because this environment was fairly simple, life forms could survive by processing relatively **small amounts** of information.

Thus, to survive, our ancestors developed perceptual skills that emphasized **short, intensive bursts of close-by, survival-related, data collection**. For example, they might walk for a while, stop, look around for food or predators, and then move on if all was safe. In this regard we were (and still are) like many other forms of life - designed to process the environment in small intensive chunks of information. This is a major reason why humans have short attention spans.

There is no doubt that this equipment served our ancestors well, but we no longer live in their environment. However, even though we live in a much more informationally complex society, we still have the old equipment - a short attention span and limited short term memory capacity. This situation has occurred because physiological evolution (i.e., changes in our physical equipment) requires millions of years, while humans have developed an informationally complex world in a much shorter period of time (about 6,000 years and especially the last 50 years).

This means that sensory equipment originally designed to process small amounts of close by, survival related data is now being used in social, political, economic, and other sub-environments. Thus, humans have constructed a world so complex that few (if any) of us are physically equipped to process sufficient information to understand how this world actually works. Indeed, trying to be successful (i.e., adaptive) in these various sub-environments has placed a heavy burden on our sensory and evaluation systems.

It is important to note that the major obstacle in modeling the complex environment is **not** found in the long term memory system. In fact, it is estimated that the average human memory is capable of holding 10 to 100 **trillion** associations (Sagan 1977, p. 43). In comparison, the average American has a listening vocabulary of 25,000 words and a speaking vocabulary of 5,000 words. Clearly, most people never even come remotely close to utilizing the full potential of their long term memory system. The reason for this enormous shortfall is not a lack of storage capacity, but is due instead, to the limited capacity of the short term memory.

Notice that one of the inherent perceptual limitations (i.e., restriction of range) has been overcome through sensory extensions like microscopes, telescopes, amplifiers, etc. Nevertheless, humans are still unable to expand the amount of information they can **attend to and comprehend.** So even with these extensions, people still encounter the problem of the perceptual bottleneck.

Thus, a major problem in the human information processing system is that we must construct a model of the environment **based on extremely limited data.** If we could use our long term memory system to anywhere near its capacity, we could probably construct a very accurate model of the world. Unfortunately, our limited short term memory forces us to construct a world view that is based upon scanty and incomplete data. The result is that everyone's model of the world contains large gaps and considerable missing information. Because these gaps cause maladaptive behaviors in everyone, it turns out that to err is indeed human.

THE SOLUTION – INFORMATION SAMPLING

Even though our short term memory capacity is quite limited, we must still attempt to model the world accurately. If we could just get more information into our huge long term memory, we could do a much better job - but we cannot. Therefore, we are forced to construct the best model we can, given the fact that we can process only a small amount of environmental data.

Notice that this situation is, in fact, a sampling problem. That is, the individual must somehow decide which items of information will be selected, processed, and stored in memory, knowing that only a very small amount of the available data can be processed through the working memory. In this regard, we can define an individual's **information sample** as the informational items selected from the much larger environment, stored as beliefs and values, and used to model (i.e., understand and predict) that environment.

Thus, as people attempt to model the environment, they are exposed to a certain sample of environmental data. This information is stored in memory as an internal model of the way the world works. Since people react to their perception of the world, it is imperative that their internal model portray the world accurately. If the model is correct, the individual will engage in adaptive behaviors and will be rewarded by the true environment. If the model is inaccurate or incomplete, however, the individual will perform behaviors designed for a world that does not really exist, thereby increasing the probability of maladaptive actions.

Given this scenario, it is obviously crucial to the individual's interests that the information sample accurately reflect the larger environment. The individual must somehow select informational items that generate a representative sample of the elements contained in

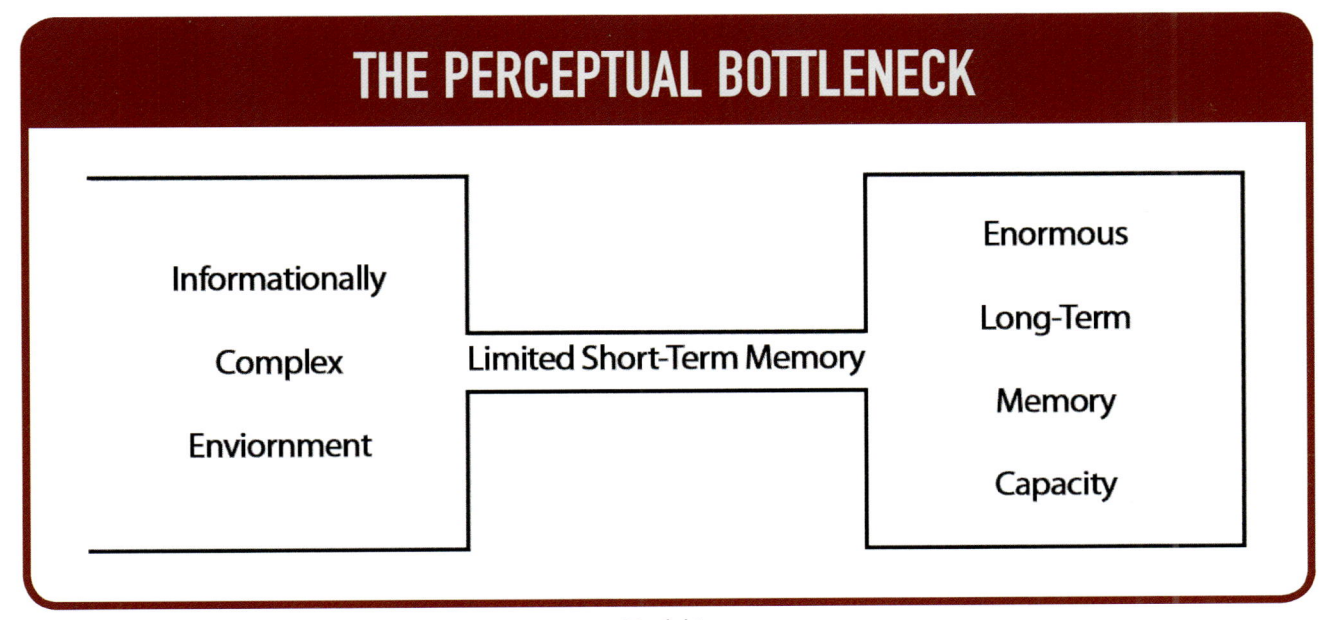

THE PERCEPTUAL BOTTLENECK

Informationally Complex Enviornment → Limited Short-Term Memory → Enormous Long-Term Memory Capacity

Model 1

the actual environment. It is well known that the best way to obtain a **representative sample** from any larger domain is to use a sampling rule called a "simple random sample." Here, all elements from the larger domain are identified and placed on a list. From this list, the sampler selects units at random and with replacement. Use of this procedure means that each and every item from the larger domain has a known and **equal** probability of being selected.

To use a simple random sample in selecting information for the internal model, the individual would be required to randomly sample information from all sources, media, countries, etc. Clearly, this is impossible for most of us. No such list exists, and even if it did, few people would be interested in the majority of its items (which would not directly affect them). For example, what would be the expected benefits from reading a blog that is related to issues you do not care about? Obviously, most of us are not at all motivated to use the rule of simple random sampling in the construction of our internal model. Thus, an important question is: "how does each individual decide which information from the environment is sampled and accepted?" It turns out that the sampling plan used by most people is heavily influenced by one of two important missions: (1) truth seeking, and (2) cognitive consistency.

TRUTH SEEKING

A major goal for humans is to construct an accurate model of the world (so we can be rewarded for our behaviors). To achieve this goal we must seek the truth wherever it leads us. Many times this is our overt goal, as for example, a college student whose main job is to discover the truth about the world by studying various subjects.

The truth seeking mission of humans is especially powerful early in life after the cognitive equipment becomes operational. Children ask many questions about relationships and associations in the world, and build their internal model based on the answers they receive (note that if the child gets inaccurate answers to these questions the internal model can be permanently damaged). However, humans also seek the truth when there are significant consequences for a bad choice (i.e., we will pay a high price for inaccuracies in the internal model). Also, people who are "meta-motivated" (growth oriented) have a strong truth seeking mission, as truth is one of the meta-motives. When people are in "truth seeking" mode, they tend to be open-minded and guided by factual evidence and objective arguments.

However, once the individual has assembled a reasonably organized view of the world, the truth seeking mission often declines. This is because the internal model has a pre-existing point of view (stored in memory) that may **conflict** with incoming environmental information. At this point, (usually around age 10) the individual starts to mix two very different missions: (1) seeking the truth about the world, and (2) defending the internal model's existing views. This second, defensive, mission is achieved by tendencies toward cognitive consistency.

COGNITIVE CONSISTENCY
DEFINITION OF COGNITIVE CONSISTENCY

Cognitive consistency can be defined as the **tendency** for people to sample, accept, and retain informational items (i.e., beliefs and values) that are consistent or "in harmony" with one another. Actually, the suggestion that people like to maintain harmonious beliefs and values is one of the oldest hypotheses in social psychology, dating back to Heider (1944) and others from the "Gestalt" school. Specific theories of cognitive consistency include **Balance Theory** (which holds that people strive for balance or consistency in their beliefs and values), **Congruity Theory** (which suggests that beliefs and values tend toward equal polarization); and **Cognitive Dissonance Theory** (which concludes that inconsistency between beliefs and values is psychologically uncomfortable and therefore avoided). Thus, some of the earliest investigations into the structure of the internal model found a pronounced tendency for individuals to **purposefully** seek, sample, and retain informational items that are consistent with each other.

Truth Seeking Students

MOTIVATION FOR COGNITIVE CONSISTENCY

If people are motivated toward cognitive consistency as proposed in these consistency theories, there must be obvious reasons why. Actually, cognitive consistency is prominent for two major reasons:

1. **Human Beings Usually Dislike Uncertainty.** Because beliefs represent object attribute associations, they help the individual **understand** the environment by identifying which attributes go with which objects. This understanding, in turn, allows the individual to **predict** which objects possess certain desirable or undesirable attributes. Since these predictions can be used to interact with objects possessing positively valued traits and to avoid objects possessing negatively valued traits, the individual gains a certain degree of control over his/her relationship with the environment. This control is itself highly desirable because it has obvious survival (success) value. Thus, individuals rightfully expect tremendous benefits from the understanding, prediction, and **control** afforded by the creation of beliefs and values. Accordingly, we can expect all individuals to display powerful tendencies to sample information and represent it in their internal models as beliefs and values.

Unfortunately, this natural sequence of events is confounded whenever the individual encounters information that does not agree with already established beliefs and values (i.e., discrepant information). Confusion results from a **loss of predictive ability** that occurs whenever discrepant information is encountered. For example, suppose that over the last several years an individual tried drinking coffee on several occasions, and, as a result of this experience, formed the beliefs and values shown in Figure 1.

HYPOTHETICAL BELIEFS AND VALUES

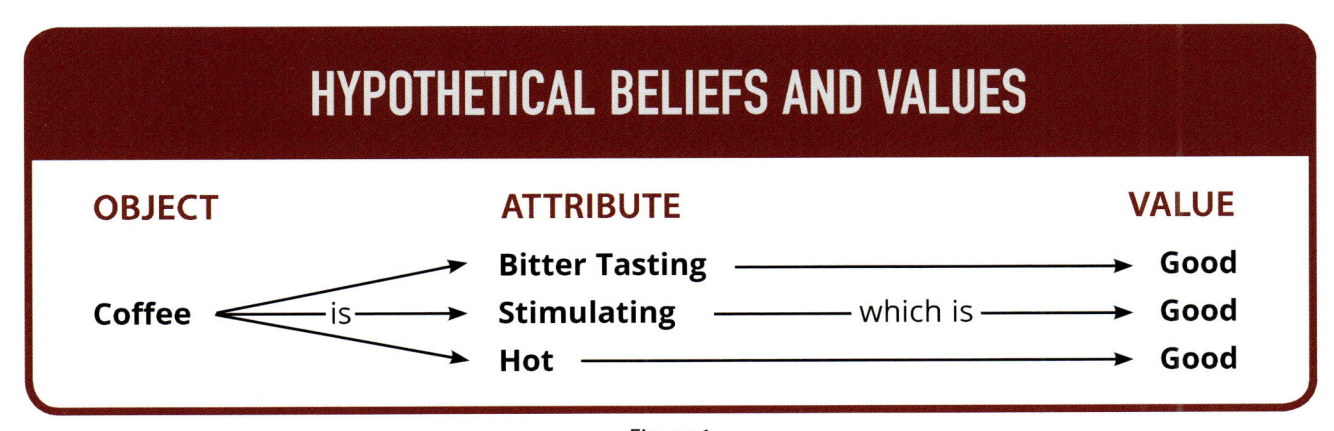

OBJECT	ATTRIBUTE		VALUE
	Bitter Tasting		Good
Coffee —is→	Stimulating	—which is→	Good
	Hot		Good

Figure 1

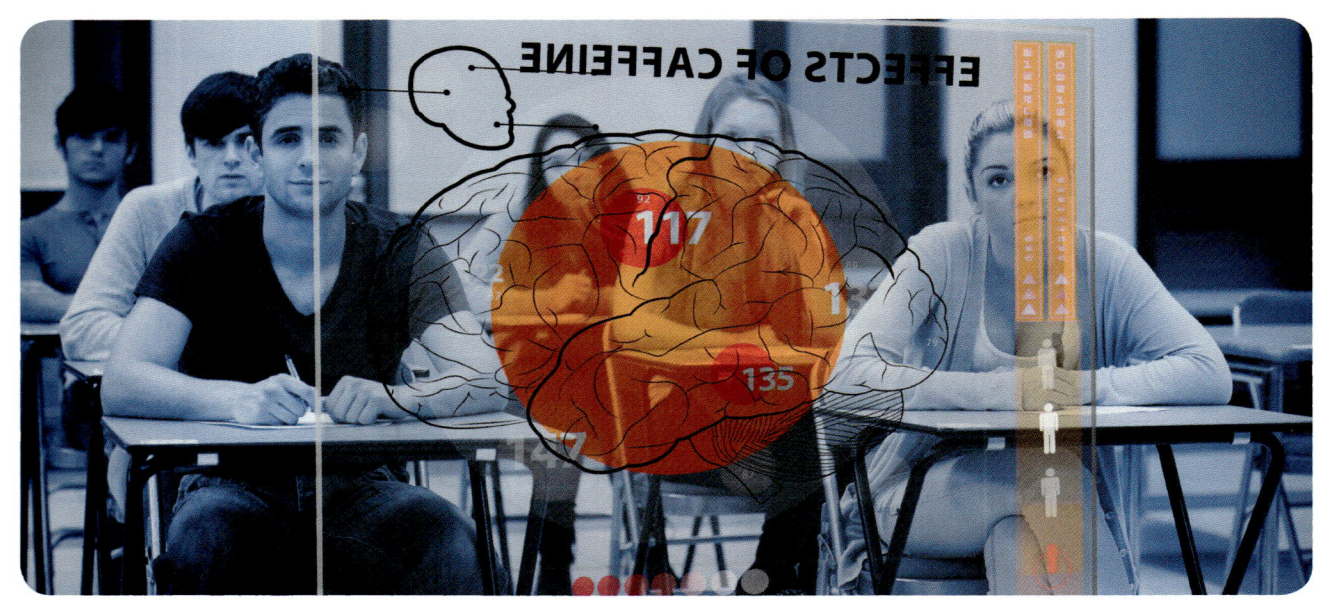

Learning the Effects of Coffee on the Body

Based upon this sample of information, the individual could be expected to drink coffee in situations where s/he wants a bitter, stimulating, hot beverage. Notice that it is the **beliefs** and **values** that allow the individual to **predict the benefits** of this object. Notice also, that all of these attributes are positively valued (i.e., "good") and therefore, highly **consistent** in the internal model of coffee as a "good" drink. This high degree of consistency makes it **easy** for the individual to **predict** positive benefits from coffee and thus to **drink it** with little or no expectation of negative effects. However, suppose this individual suddenly encounters the discrepant information that high levels of coffee consumption have been linked to sleeplessness and stomach ulcers. The individual's new belief and value structure is shown in Figure 2.

Now the individual has beliefs regarding coffee that are in conflict (i.e., they are discrepant) since the object is associated with both positively **and** negatively valued attributes. This person will be **uncertain** whether s/he should drink coffee since s/he expects both positive and negative consequences from its use. In these cases, the ease and confidence of prediction associated with consistently evaluated attributes is lost.

Human beings have a powerful desire to model the environment and control their interactions with it. We accomplish this goal by using our beliefs and values to predict good or bad consequences from interacting with certain objects, people, etc. A highly consistent cognitive structure creates strongly held predictions

HYPOTHETICAL BELIEFS AND VALUES AFTER DISCREPANT INFORMATION

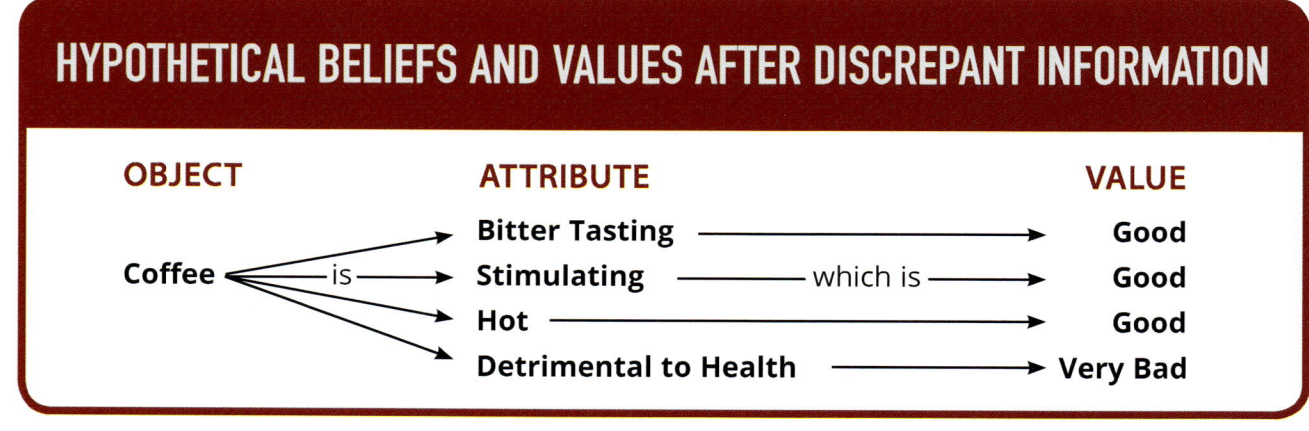

OBJECT	ATTRIBUTE		VALUE
Coffee is	Bitter Tasting		Good
	Stimulating	which is	Good
	Hot		Good
	Detrimental to Health		Very Bad

Figure 2

and personal confidence. In these cases we act with conviction and determination (though we may not be correct).

This sequence of events is threatened, however, when the individual encounters discrepant information. In this case, the confidence and certainty of prediction that go with consistent information is replaced by ***uncertainty and indecision.*** Since most people find this state of uncertainty psychologically uncomfortable, they avoid it whenever possible. The easiest way to resolve uncertainty is to seek out supportive information while avoiding discrepant information. When people act in this way, scientists say that they are displaying their tendencies toward cognitive consistency.

2. **Human Beings Usually Dislike Being Wrong.** When an individual has confident beliefs and values, they show up in his/her verbal and overt behaviors. For example, in the coffee example above, the person likes coffee for its perceived benefits. Most likely, this person performs several positive behaviors regarding coffee. S/he might recommend it to his/her friends or buy some as a housewarming gift for a new neighbor. But when this person reads the information linking coffee consumption to stomach ulcers, s/he has a problem. S/he has recommended a dangerous product to friends, served it to friends, etc. No doubt, this would make any of us feel bad about ourselves ***provided that we accept the conclusion that coffee does, in fact, cause stomach ulcers.*** One way to resist this conclusion -- one way not to accept that we were wrong -- is to avoid, counterargue, or reject the information that links coffee to stomach ulcers. And that is exactly what people often do when told they are wrong. If you do not believe it, tell someone s/he is wrong (especially in front of other people) and see how s/he accepts the discrepant information.

Conversely, when people encounter consistent information, it makes their view of the world seem correct and accurate. This is normally perceived as a personal accomplishment and serves as an immediate positive reinforcer (reward). Not surprisingly, people tend to gravitate toward consistent information as a convenient method of self gratification.

When people avoid discrepant information (because it hurts to be wrong) and seek out consistent information (because it feels good to be right), scientists say they are displaying their tendencies toward cognitive consistency.

CONCLUSION

In this chapter, the concept of the personal information sample has been developed. Due to the perceptual bottleneck, our internal models' are based upon an extremely small amount of environmental data. The individual's sample of information is critical because missing and/or erroneous information causes "blind spots" in the internal model. These informational gaps often result in maladaptive behaviors and environmental punishments. To make our information samples more objective (representative), we could make better use of random sampling. Unfortunately, few of us are motivated or able to do this.

Often, though not always, people use the sampling plan of cognitive consistency. Here, the individual's information sample is purposely biased to favor consistent information (because it generates confidence and immediate rewards) and to avoid or counterattack discrepant information (because it causes uncertainty and the immediate punishment of being wrong). This is the information sampling rule that ***often*** determines which informational items will be selected for inclusion in the internal model of adults. Notice that use of such a rule will generate an information sample that has an extremely small chance of being representative because major and ***legitimate parts of the world are deliberately not included.*** Accordingly, the chances are remote that any individual will have an internal model that accurately reflects the real world. Therefore, we can expect most people to construct internal models that contain major gaps and missing data, resulting in maladaptive behaviors and environmental punishment. In this light, it is easy to see that environmental punishments are usually evidence that your internal model (i.e., information sample) is inaccurate and needs revision.

The human tendency toward cognitive consistency also causes a major problem for influence agents such as salespeople and advertisers, since their communications often have the goal of **_changing_** a specific target behavior (for instance, the purchase of a particular brand of soft drink). Essentially, changing a person's behavior can be accomplished only by providing new and/or discrepant information (consistent information would, of course, lead to continued purchases of the current brand). Therefore, a common goal of marketing communications is to provide discrepant information in the most effective fashion. Unfortunately, the selective defense mechanisms discussed in the next chapter make it exceedingly difficult to circumvent the consumer's tendency to process consistent information. In fact, if you can develop the talent to circumvent these tendencies you can expect to make considerable amounts of money as a copywriter or salesperson.

EXPERIMENT 6.1
ACCEPTING INCONSISTENT INFORMATION

Describe an occasion where you have recently refused to accept cognitively inconsistent information from a key account - even though you would benefit from it.

1. What was your true motivation for resisting?

2. Make a serious effort to be more open-minded and process the discrepancy to the best of your ability.

3. How did you feel afterwards?

4. How did your key account respond to your efforts?

ELABORATION QUESTIONS

- » Based on your experiences, what are some of the most common ways that people avoid discrepant information?

- » How do you handle uncertainty?

- » How do you handle admitting mistakes?

- » Do your friends consider you to be stubborn once you make up your mind?

- » When are you most likely to seek the truth – even if it means changing your opinion?

- » What is the best way to interact with key accounts who hold different opinions of your own?

CHAPTER 7
SELECTIVE DEFENSE MECHANISMS

INTRODUCTION	7.1
SELECTIVE EXPOSURE	7.1
SELECTIVE ATTENTION	7.2
SELECTIVE COMPREHENSION	7.3
Comprehending New Information	7.3
Comprehending Related Information	7.3
SELECTIVE RETENTION	7.5
SELECTIVE DEFENSE MECHANISMS AS A THREAT REACTION	7.6
PEOPLE DO PROCESS DISCREPANT INFORMATION	7.6
CONCLUSION	7.6
**EXPERIMENT 7.1	PROCESSING DISCREPANT INFORMATION**	7.7
ELABORATION QUESTIONS	7.8

GUIDING QUESTIONS

- » What is selective exposure?
- » What is selective attention?
- » What is selective comprehension?
- » What is selective retention?
- » How do these selective defense mechanisms influence attempts to persuade people?
- » What is being protected by selective defense?
- » When do people process discrepant information?
- » How does selective defense affect personal and professional growth?

INTRODUCTION

We have seen in the previous chapter that environments contain enormous amounts of information while human sensory capacity is very small. This arrangement means that every day, we select a small sample of environmental information according to some explicit or implicit sampling plan. The purpose of this information sample is to construct an internal model (housed in memory) that reflects the true environment as accurately as possible. Because people react to their model of the world (rather than the world itself), it is clear that when their model is accurate, they will perform adaptive behaviors, and receive reinforcement. Conversely, when their internal model is inaccurate, they will often perform maladaptive behaviors, and receive punishment. As a result, it is important for the individual's information sample to be representative of the environment at large.

Unfortunately, the selection plan best suited to generating a representative sample (i.e., simple random sample) is rarely used. Instead, people routinely follow a subjective sampling plan that is heavily influenced by tendencies toward cognitive consistency. Thus we often misrepresent the true environment.

Perhaps the biggest problem in correcting human tendencies toward cognitive consistency is the **unconscious nature** of their operation. Most of the time that these defense mechanisms are "turned on," the individual is **not aware** that s/he is selectively screening information. This is because these mechanisms are easily learned, then over learned, and finally automated as an information processing "script."

As an example, are you aware that when you visit your favorite web sites, you are engaged in selective exposure? What makes these sites favorites is that they coincide with some of your values. Therefore, you are selecting web sites that tend to be consistent with already established beliefs and values. When people act in this fashion, scientists say they are displaying tendencies toward cognitive consistency. In studying these tendencies, scientists have isolated four specific selective defense mechanisms: selective exposure, selective attention, selective comprehension, and selective retention.

SELECTIVE EXPOSURE

Selective exposure, the first information screen, refers to the problem created by a complex environment and the perceptual bottleneck: We can expose ourselves to only a small portion of the total information in the environment.

For example, college students usually have a wide variety of class offerings to choose from when constructing their class schedule. They have to select specific classes to enroll in (i.e., to expose themselves to). We have already seen that if students wanted to get a **representative sample** of courses from the university, they would employ a simple random sample when choosing classes. This rarely happens in practice, however, because most students have certain subjects they do not like at all. Accordingly, they tend to select a disproportionately large number of electives they like and a disproportionately small number of classes they dislike.

This example is directly analogous to people's everyday encounters with information sources. As individuals, we tend to expose ourselves to information sources that we like and avoid those we do not like. Moreover, a major basis for liking or not liking a certain information source is whether or not it can be expected to provide information that is **consistent** with already established beliefs and values (since this makes us feel confident and correct).

In summary, the first way that cognitive consistency affects the individual's information sample is called selective exposure. This phenomenon motivates people to expose themselves mostly to information sources that they expect to contain data that is consistent with already established beliefs and values. Of course, they also run into some discrepant information, especially that which is heavily represented in the environment.

SELECTIVE ATTENTION

Mere exposure to information certainly does not guarantee that data will ultimately be included in the internal model. In addition to information exposure, the individual must focus his/her sensory apparatus on the information (i.e., attend to the information). Selective attention is an important part of the perceptual bottleneck because studies have shown that people are usually capable of attending to only one information source at a time. In addition, it has been noted that the human attention span is usually quite short. These factors mean that large amounts of environmental data constantly compete for the individual's **limited attention.**

Usually, people attend to stimuli that "demand attention" or "deserve attention." Factors found to increase the demand for an individual's attention to stimuli include size, motion, intensity, color, novelty, and contrast. Here the stimulus "demands attention" by its physical properties and characteristics. Thus, for example, advertisers often manipulate the movement, novelty, color, intensity, etc. of their commercials in order to maximize audience attention.

In addition to these physical traits, a stimulus may "deserve attention" if it is pertinent to the individual's current needs or goals. Such pertinence results from the information's ***"instrumentality"*** (i.e., the extent to which the information is perceived to lead to goal attainment). Another reason a stimulus may "deserve attention" is because it reaffirms (i.e., is consistent with) the individual's internal model. Here, in return for the attention given, the individual feels comfortable because his/her view of the world has been supported and affirmed.

In general, we can see that a person's ***motivation*** to pay attention to a particular information source is determined by a cost-benefit analysis. There are

Provocative Photography Demands Attention

important opportunity costs related to time spent and effort required (i.e., we could be paying attention to something we enjoy). There can also be monetary costs like paying to see a movie or buying new music. Expected benefits include belief or value consistency, amusement, or goal attainment. If multiple information sources are competing for an individual's limited attention, s/he will establish a preference by conducting a cost-benefit analysis.

In summary, information that is interesting, consistent, amusing, shocking, useful, or otherwise pertinent to the individual's goals will be favored to receive attention. Conversely, withdrawing attention is one of the easiest (and therefore, most common) techniques for avoiding discrepant information. Almost all of us can remember occasions when, in the face of discrepant information, we simply chose not to listen.

Comprehension Can Be Difficult

The phenomenon of selective attention means that attempts at persuasion frequently fail because people with opposing views tend to "tune out" the message. In this light, it is not surprising that more non-smokers than smokers attend to anti-smoking commercials. One of the keys to marketing is finding ways to get your message heard by consumers who prefer other brands.

SELECTIVE COMPREHENSION

As discussed above, environmental information must be sampled and attended to before it can be included in the individual's internal model. In terms of comprehension, it is useful to think of two major types of environmental information: (1) new information, and (2) information that is related to previously stored beliefs and values.

COMPREHENDING NEW INFORMATION

New information is comprehended when it is encoded (or formatted) as a belief and stored in the memory system. That is, the individual must accurately comprehend (encode) the information as a belief or value. Unfortunately, accurate comprehension of new information is a demanding task that presents ample opportunity for errors to occur. Specifically, individuals may encounter the following problems:

1. Associating an object with attributes it does not possess.
2. Failing to associate the object with attributes it does possess.
3. Incorrectly specifying the strength of the association between the object and attribute.

Misrepresentations often occur when the individual uses cognitive consistency to comprehend the new information to be as consistent as possible with already established beliefs. Numerous other errors will occur because of such factors as information overload, minimal or wandering attention, complex or difficult-to-interpret events, etc. Whatever the source, it is clear that when information is miscomprehended, the accuracy of the internal model is impaired.

COMPREHENDING RELATED INFORMATION

In addition to encoding new information, people must constantly comprehend data that are related to information already stored in the memory system. This type of processing is normally accomplished by what behavioral scientists call the "cognitive response process." Here, people compare the incoming information to their existing beliefs and values by generating cognitive responses through their internal dialogue (self talk). These cognitive responses relate the incoming information to items already stored in memory. For example, suppose a coffee drinker reads a newspaper story linking caffeine consumption to stomach ulcers in rats. While reading the report, the individual will be comparing what s/he reads with beliefs and values already stored in memory. This comparison process generates a series of "primary thoughts," as shown in Model 1.

As shown above, comprehending information related to existing beliefs and values usually involves accepting or rejecting the message. Acceptance occurs if the individual is willing to encode the message as a belief or value. For this to happen, the message must somehow fit in coherently with the existing internal model. To freely accept discrepant information would create conflicting beliefs in the internal model, violating our powerful desires for an easily ordered and organized world.

Obviously, the primary thoughts shown in Model 1 have a lot to do with whether the message claims are accepted or rejected. Notice that if the incoming message is consistent with already established beliefs, the individual will be likely to generate support arguments and/or engage in source bolstering. Both of these cognitive responses enhance message acceptance while simultaneously reaffirming the accuracy of the current internal model. Essentially, the internal model agrees with, and therefore, accepts, the external information, adding it to memory for future reference.

When the incoming information disagrees with previously stored beliefs and values, the individual encounters difficulties. Specifically, we have seen that the acceptance of discrepant information causes two serious problems for the internal model: 1) uncertainty, and 2) the acknowledgement of wrongdoing. To avoid these unpleasant states the individual can refuse to accept the discrepant information by ***rejecting*** it or ***miscomprehending*** it.

Rejection. An easy way for a coffee drinker to avoid dissonance is to reject the information that connects

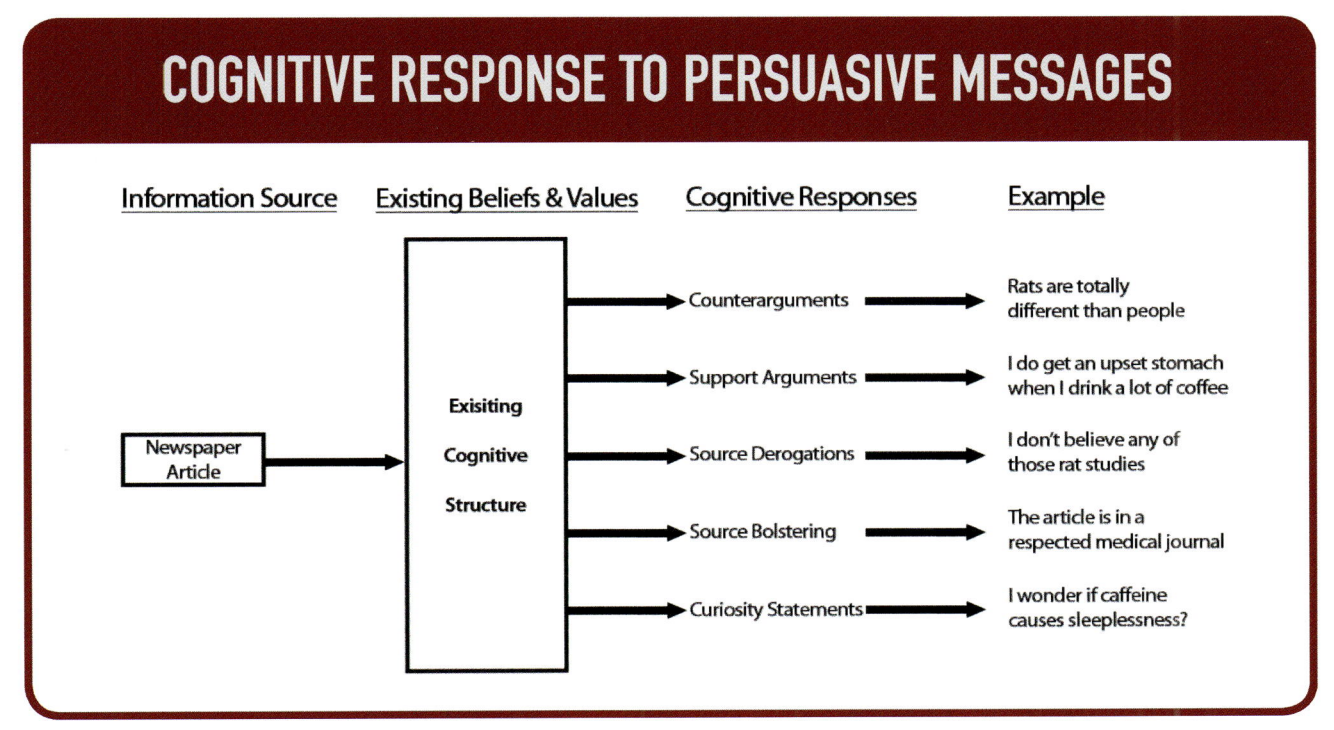

COGNITIVE RESPONSE TO PERSUASIVE MESSAGES

Information Source	Existing Beliefs & Values	Cognitive Responses	Example
Newspaper Article	Existing Cognitive Structure	Counterarguments	Rats are totally different than people
		Support Arguments	I do get an upset stomach when I drink a lot of coffee
		Source Derogations	I don't believe any of those rat studies
		Source Bolstering	The article is in a respected medical journal
		Curiosity Statements	I wonder if caffeine causes sleeplessness?

Model 1

caffeine to stomach ulcers by generating counter arguments and/or source derogations. Rejection is accomplished if the individual assigns a probability of zero (or near zero) to the object (coffee)-attribute (may cause stomach ulcers) link. In some situations this rejection will occur without any articulated justification but when called upon, people can easily verbalize their counterarguments and source derogations.

1. **Counterarguments.** Here, the individual summons from memory (or external sources) information that contradicts the inconsistent data. This action has the effect of reaffirming the existing beliefs and values in the internal model by arguing in their defense. Various types of counterarguments are possible, but all rely on the tactic of defending presently held beliefs against discrepant, but possibly legitimate environmental information.

2. **Source Derogation.** An easy way to reject discrepant information is to derogate the credibility of its source. Normally, this is accomplished by attacking the honesty (trustworthiness) or accuracy (expertise) of the discrepant information source. In the caffeine example, the source derogation that "rat studies cannot be believed" questions the accuracy of the research. This invalidates the [coffee-stomach ulcer] link in the coffee drinker's internal model. In addition, the individual may discount or reject the discrepant information by questioning its truthfulness. Consumers often discount the credibility of advertisements and personal salespeople since these sponsors have obvious vested interests in selling the product.

Miscomprehension. Another way to selectively screen out discrepant information is to encode the message in an altered or subjective form. Here, some aspect of the discrepant object-attribute association is changed to make it more consistent with already held beliefs. This can be accomplished by changing the attribute (e.g., "caffeine may cause stomach ulcers" encoded as "coffee may cause an upset stomach") or the magnitude of the association (e.g., "coffee may cause stomach ulcers, but only if consumed in large quantities over extended periods of time").

To summarize, it can be said that comprehending external information is a very fragile process. We can all think of times when other people took something we said in the "wrong way" - that is, they encoded a message that was very different from the one we tried to send. This happens to almost everyone on a regular basis because we all use our existing beliefs and values to judge the validity of incoming data. In so doing, we end up encoding a disproportionately large amount of consistent information and a disproportionately small amount of discrepant information. In such cases, the individual miscomprehends the true environment by excluding legitimate parts of it from his/her internal model. When this happens, behavioral scientists say we are exhibiting tendencies toward selective comprehension.

SELECTIVE RETENTION

Even if the individual encounters, attends to, and accurately comprehends external information, it must be retrieved on demand to be useful in planning and action. Unfortunately, no one has 100% recall of encoded information. More importantly, the information lost from the internal model through forgetting is **not** random. Instead, there is a pronounced tendency to remember consistent information and forget discrepant information. Indeed, one of the easiest methods to avoid inconsistent information is quite simply to "forget it."

As we learned earlier, retrieval of information from memory is heavily dependent upon how well that information is ***organized and integrated*** into the existing belief and value structure. Not surprisingly, consistent information is much easier to organize and integrate and therefore, is easier to retrieve. In contrast, inconsistent information not only "will not fit" into the internal model but also suffers from the individual's general lack of motivation to attempt retrieval of discrepant information. Thus, the phenomenon of selective retention refers to the

THE COGNITIVELY CONSISTENT INTERNAL MODEL

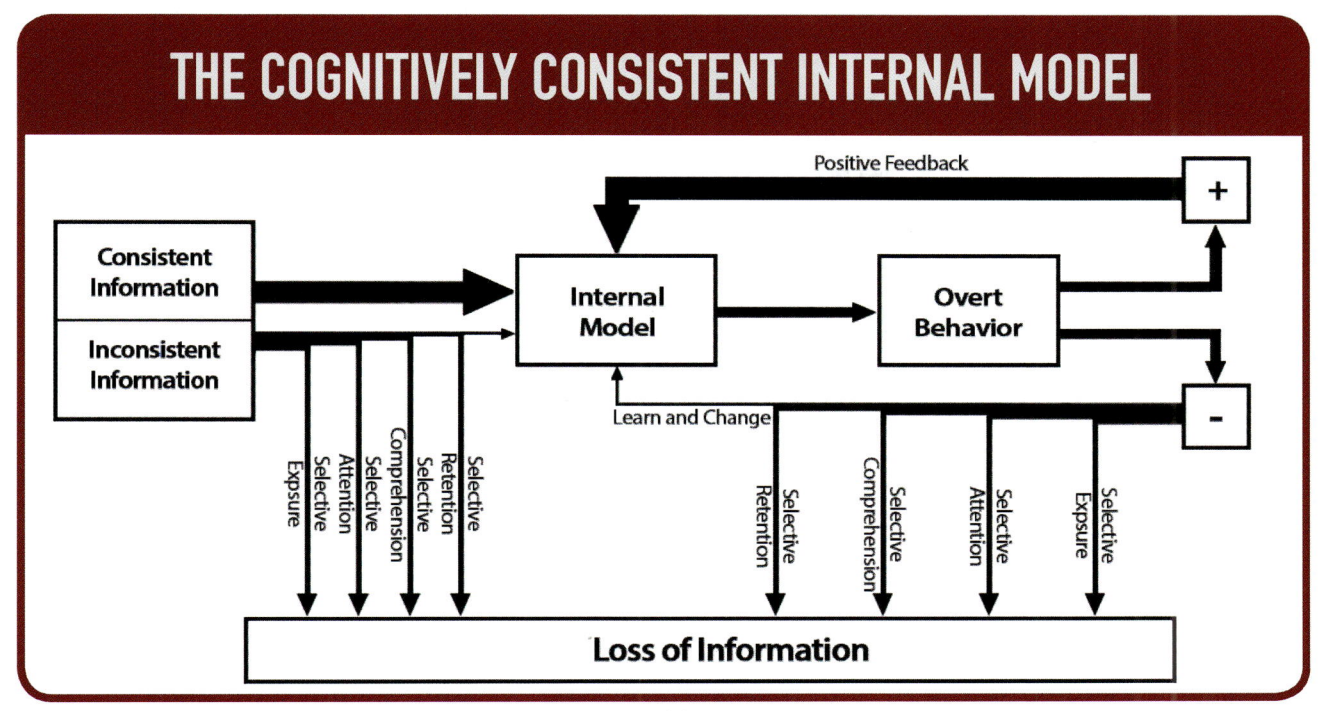

Model 2

tendency for individuals to remember information that is consistent with already established beliefs and values.

Together, the four selective defense mechanisms produce a cognitively consistent internal model as shown in Model 2.

SELECTIVE DEFENSE MECHANISMS AS A THREAT REACTION

As we have seen, individuals are generally motivated to process consistent information. In this light, discrepant information can be viewed as a clear and present **threat** to cognitive consistency and psychological tranquility. Since perceived threats to survival are almost always followed by withdrawal or counterattack, we might expect the defense mechanisms to parallel these reactions. Indeed, selective exposure, selective attention, and selective retention are all ways that people withdraw from discrepant information by using the process of perceptual avoidance. Similarly, people employ techniques for selective comprehension (i.e., rejection, counterarguing, and source derogation), which involve counterattack of discrepant environmental data.

PEOPLE DO PROCESS DISCREPANT INFORMATION

It is also important to note that movement toward consistent information is ***ONLY A TENDENCY***. Everyone can think of occasions when they have been exposed to, attended to, comprehended, and retained discrepant information. For example, a discrepant belief may be so heavily represented in the environment that the individual cannot avoid frequent exposure to it. Similarly, discrepant information may be accepted because it comes from a highly credible source or from direct experience. However, the amount of discrepant information included in the internal model is normally significantly smaller than the amount of consistent information included.

CONCLUSION

In this chapter we have seen that the individual's attempts to model the world accurately are severely

AN EXAMPLE OF THE SELECTIVE DEFENSE MECHANISMS

SELECTIVE EXPOSURE | SELECTIVE ATTENTION | SELECTIVE COMPREHENSION | SELECTIVE RETENTION

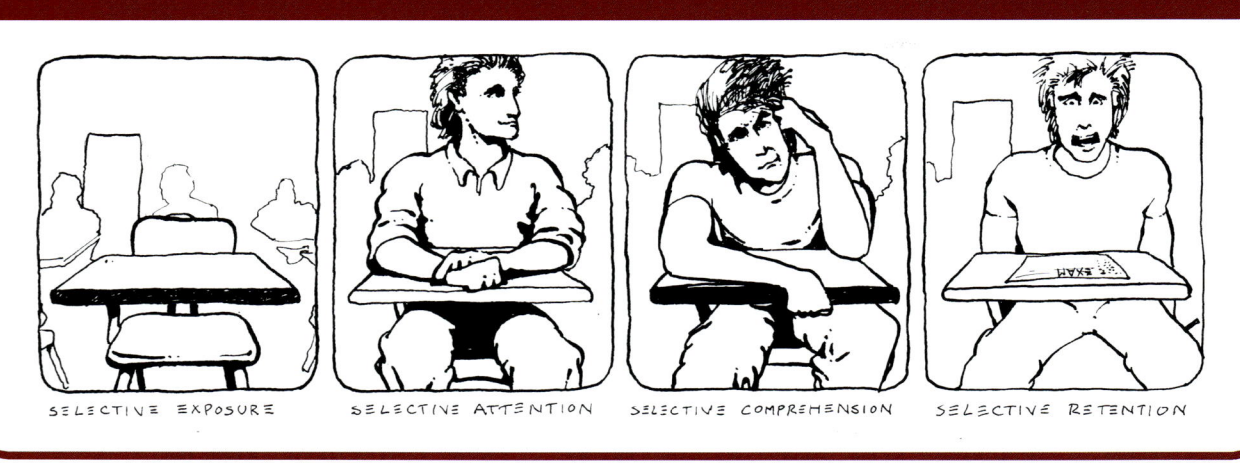

Figure 1

limited by the perceptual bottleneck and tendencies toward cognitive consistency. First, limitations occur when human sensory apparatus which is designed to model small amounts of near by, survival related, information is used to model an informationally complex world (including many sub-environments important to the individual). This bottleneck forces everyone to sample information from the environment in the hopes of constructing a reasonably representative internal model.

An accurate model could be built if the individual followed a simple random sampling rule. Unfortunately, such a rule is not feasible, and tendencies toward cognitive consistency motivate us - intentionally and unintentionally - to favor consistent information. These tendencies toward cognitive consistency are operationalized through selective exposure, selective attention, selective comprehension, and selective retention. Together, these defense mechanisms form an impressive sequential filter that makes it difficult for people to process information objectively and adaptively.

EXPERIMENT 7.1
PROCESSING DISCREPANT INFORMATION

1. Describe a controversial issue that you have strong feelings about. Describe at least one occasion when you have engaged in:
   a. Selective exposure
   b. Selective attention
   c. Selective comprehension
   d. Selective retention

2. What effect do the selective defense mechanisms have on your ability to have a successful relationship with people who hold different opinions?

3. Minimize the selective defense mechanisms for two days and report what happens.

ELABORATION QUESTIONS

- What are some of the types of information you often avoid? Why?

- What happens in selective information processing when the information is boring or delivered in a boring way?

- How do the selective defense mechanisms influence the outcome of arguments?

- How do you react when you cannot understand information in a class?

- How much information can you recall from the classes you took last semester?

- How would you try to minimize the tendencies for consumers to screen out your message?

CHAPTER 8
CONSUMER INVOLVEMENT

INTRODUCTION	**8.1**
CONCEPTUALIZATION OF INVOLVEMENT	**8.1**
Definition	8.1
Allocation of Attention	8.2
Types of Involvement	8.2
DETERMINANTS OF INVOLVEMENT	**8.3**
Intensity of Thought	8.3
Quality or Depth of Thought	8.3
Persistence of Thought	8.4
LIFE CYCLES OF INVOLVEMENT	**8.5**
The Involvement Life Cycle	8.5
The Role of Arousal	8.6
The Law of Diminishing Returns	8.6
Summary	8.7
EFFECTS OF INVOLVEMENT ON LATITUDES OF ACCEPTANCE AND REJECTION	**8.8**
CONSUMER INVOLVEMENT	**8.8**
Determinants of Involvement	8.8
Longevity of Involvement	8.9
The Focus of Involvement	8.9
**EXPERIMENT 8.1	LIFE CYCLE OF INVOLVEMENT**	**8.10**
Consequences of Involvement	8.10
CONCLUSION	**8.10**
ELABORATION QUESTIONS	**8.11**

GUIDING QUESTIONS

- What is the definition of involvement?
- What are the determinants of involvement?
- How do motivation, opportunity, and ability influence involvement?
- What is the difference between current involvement and accumulated involvement?
- What determines the intensity of thought?
- How is effort related to involvement?
- What is your effort span?
- How is arousal related to involvement?
- What are the three levels of thought?
- How is persistence related to involvement?
- How do frequency and duration of thought affect persistence?
- What are the normal stages of involvement?
- How long does involvement last?
- What is the chemical bath?
- What is the law of diminishing returns?
- What are latitudes of acceptance and rejection and how are they related to involvement?
- What are some of the different patterns that emerge in consumer involvement?
- What are the consequences of consumer involvement?

INTRODUCTION

In earlier chapters, it was noted that the perceptual bottleneck forces the internal model to select a small sample of information from the environment. Basically, this means the short-term memory can pay attention to only one thing at a time (when trying to attend to more than one stimuli, we must shift our attention back and forth). Because attention is in short supply and great demand, the allocation of it becomes an important decision with significant consequences.

It is also important to note, that the quality of the attention given can vary greatly from full concentration to barely listening. The quality of attention is a function of two major determinants: the depth of processing given to the object, and whether the interest in the object is intrinsic or requires effort. It also turns out that our level of involvement with any particular object is dynamic (i.e., it fluctuates over time). Indeed, we will see that there is a regular pattern of involvement that usually unfolds over time – the "life cycle of involvement."

Another important aspect of this construct is that when people are involved with a product or service they process information about it much more actively. Indeed, understanding the difference between an involved consumer and a passive consumer is critical to effective marketing strategy. Accordingly, the purpose of this chapter is to examine the topic of consumer involvement. We will develop a model that explains the basic determinants of involvement, look at each of these components, and then see what happens to involvement over time.

CONCEPTUALIZATION OF INVOLVEMENT

DEFINITION

Involvement can be defined as the extent to which an individual's **attentional resources (i.e., short-term memory) are committed to an object.** Thus, involvement is determined by the proportion of total processing resources that are allocated to a particular object. This definition has several important implications. First, **attention** is the substance of involvement – the more we are involved with an object, the more attention we give it. This means it is the thought contents of the short-term memory that determine one's current involvement with any

Involved Consumer

8.1

Consumer Imagining Using the Shampoo

object. Second, involvement can be directed toward any tangible stimulus (e.g., a new automobile) or intangible stimulus (e.g., imagining the product in use). Third, the allocation of involvement (i.e., granting attention) implies a **conscious choice** since the short-term memory is under the individual's control.

ALLOCATION OF ATTENTION

Because most environments are informationally complex (i.e., contain many objects of potential interest), the internal model must decide how to allocate its limited attention. In general, the allocation of attention is determined by three factors: motivation, opportunity, and ability.

Motivation to Attend. An individual's motivation to attend to a particular stimulus is determined by that object's **instrumentality** (i.e., the extent to which it facilitates goal attainment). As we will see in the next chapter, motivation is related to gratification of five preconditions, the deficiency needs, neurotic needs, and the growth needs.

Opportunity to Attend. An individual's opportunity to attend to a particular stimulus is determined by the environment. Opportunity to attend is high when there is little or no interference in our communication with the environment (i.e., messages from the environment that are clear and easy to understand). Opportunity to attend is low whenever significant interference or static exists that interfere with communication. An example would be trying to understand a person who is speaking a language that you are not familiar with. You may be motivated to listen and understand but you have little opportunity to do so.

Ability to Attend. An individual's ability to attend to a particular stimulus is determined by whether the person is physically and mentally sound. For example, you cannot attend to a stimulus with maximum ability if you are physically impaired by fatigue, illness, intoxication, etc.

TYPES OF INVOLVEMENT

Because the short-term memory is time-restricted, one can think of involvement at two levels:

Current involvement. Current involvement is defined as the current contents of the short-term memory. Basically, this means you are involved with whatever you are thinking about. Your stream of consciousness reflects your current involvement and is the same thing as the allocation of attention.

Accumulated Involvement. Accumulated involvement is defined as the **pattern of attention** that has been granted to an object **over time.** The residue from each of these involvement episodes is stored in long-term memory. Over time, the representation of the object in the memory system (i.e., what it means) is determined by the quantity and quality of attention granted to it.

DETERMINANTS OF INVOLVEMENT

Involvement is determined by three characteristics of attention: (1) relative intensity, (2) relative quality (depth), and (3) relative persistence.

INTENSITY OF THOUGHT

This refers to the power of concentration allocated to the stimulus. Intensity is a function of effort and arousal.

Effort. Effort refers to giving attention based on mental discipline or "force of will." In these instances, the individual feels "obligated" to pay attention, but does not necessarily enjoy doing so. The obligation is usually based on **extrinsic motivation,** that is, the person will benefit or gain in some way by giving attention to the target stimulus.

Effort is an input variable under **conscious control** of the individual. It refers to the individual directing the short-term memory to concentrate on a stimulus. For example, a student studying for an exam by forcing his/her short-term memory to rehearse course material.

The relative nature of effort can be accounted for by considering the percentage of short-term memory capacity devoted to the stimulus. A student who studies with the TV on is less involved than a student studying with the TV off, since presumably some amount of short-term memory is devoted to the TV, thereby reducing the percentage of the short-term memory occupied by study-related stimuli.

Each individual has an **effort span.** This is the length of time a person can concentrate on an object through force of will alone. Notice that the length of the effort span is closely related to what most people consider a person's **will power** or **work ethic.** Also notice that college students who get an acceptable grade point average using their effort span are very attractive to businesses with less glamorous positions to offer. This is because the students have shown that they can stay focused on a task even if they do not enjoy it. This is a big plus in many entry level positions where new employees are expected to "pay their dues" (i.e., perform the non-intrinsic tasks).

Arousal. Arousal refers to involvement that is based on a natural or **intrinsic interest** in the target stimulus – the "natural engagingness" of the object. Like effort, arousal can produce a highly concentrated state in the short-term memory. The major difference is that arousal naturally demands short-term memory capacity, so will power (effort) is not necessary. Often, when an individual is highly aroused s/he enters a state called "flow." In this condition, time passes very quickly, and one has a sense of enjoyment and/or pleasure. For example, in marketing, sexually suggestive advertisements might arouse some viewers, thereby attracting their attention, without requiring undue effort (which is unlikely to be given in a voluntary exposure situation).

Arousal often has physical manifestations that can be readily observed by others. For example, heavy breathing, perspiration, dilated pupils, blushing, excited tone of voice, etc. In summary, intensity of thought is determined by arousal and effort and influences involvement as shown in Table 1.

QUALITY OR DEPTH OF THOUGHT

In an important memory article, Craik and Lockhart (1972) identified three "levels of processing" that reflect three different types of attention. The quality of the attention given is based on the degree of

SUMMARY OF AROUSAL AND EFFORT

	Effort Low	Effort High
Arousal Low	Low Involvement	Moderate Involvement
Arousal High	Higher Involvement	Highest Involvement

Table 1

cognitive elaboration that is achieved. We have already examined the "levels of processing" theory which identified three levels of thought as follows:

Level I Thought. This includes superficial thoughts like simple feature recognition, counting the words in a message, memorizing without understanding, etc.

Level II Thought. At this level, the individual is able to place some type of meaningful organization onto the incoming information. This includes putting stimuli into meaningful categories, understanding the underlying relationships of the material, formulating relevant questions, etc.

Level III Thought. This requires the individual to elaborate and enrich the incoming information, usually by creating personal connections. In marketing and advertising, personal connections occur when consumers relate a product (or advertisement) to meaningful parts of their own lives (e.g., imagining how a product will solve one of their problems).When level III thought is achieved there are profound consequences for the individual including longer lasting memory of the information and the ability to use this information to solve problems and be creative.

Depth and Involvement. As consumers become more involved with a product they reach a point where the quality of their product-related thought improves. For example, they become more aware of the attributes that differentiate brand performance, and more aware of their own tastes and preferences. And, as consumers think more deeply about a product, they further increase their level of involvement with it. This increased quality of thought might be demonstrated in a variety of ways like becoming an opinion leader, being better able to compare alternatives, being better able to remember brand-related information, etc.

Thus, one way to identify the level of involvement is to examine the quality or depth of thought. Deep thinking indicates that considerable cognitive investment has been allocated to the stimulus and that a state of high involvement exists.

PERSISTENCE OF THOUGHT

This reflects the total accumulation of short term memory thought-time allocated to the stimulus. This total accumulation can be conveniently partitioned into (1) frequency of thought, and (2) duration of thought.

Frequency of Thought. This represents the number of thought episodes allocated to the stimulus. To be most meaningful this measure should have a time frame to reflect its relative nature. For example, the number of different thought episodes per day, week, month, or year. This is especially important in marketing applications of the involvement concept because frequency may increase dramatically just before and after product purchase.

Duration of Thought. This represents the elapse time per thought episode. It can be measured with self-reports, eye cameras, amount of time spent on a page, or experimentally controlled.

When involvement is in the growth stage, thought episodes regarding the object are both frequent and long-lasting. However, when the object becomes familiar through adaptation the number and length of thought episodes usually decreases.

In summary, persistence of thought is determined by frequency and duration and influences the level of involvement as shown in Table 2.

LIFE CYCLES OF INVOLVEMENT

According to this conceptualization, it is important to distinguish between current involvement and accumulated involvement. Accumulated involvement is the pattern of attention that has been allocated to the stimulus object over time. Therefore, different *patterns of attention* should result in different types of influence on the individual's decision-making.

THE INVOLVEMENT LIFE CYCLE

Involvement often has a "life-cycle" with respect to its four major components: effort, arousal, depth, and persistence. Specifically, each of these components can go through several basic stages as shown in Model 1.

Growth Stage. Growth can be based on any or all of the components of involvement. When arousal is a major player, growth usually shows a rapid rise. By the end of this stage, the rate of growth slows dramatically or stops altogether and involvement levels off. Note that overall involvement is still quite high but no longer growing. This often marks the maximum level of involvement with an object, product, person, etc.

Maturation Stage. As we become highly involved during the growth and maturation stages, we spend more and more time thinking about, and interacting with, the object, product, or person. However, an inescapable consequence of involvement is ***familiarity.*** As the once unknown and exciting becomes known and familiar there is a normal tendency for involvement to level off. At this point involvement usually fluctuates with declines and corresponding rises. However, over long periods of time we can become ***adapted*** to a stimulus that was once new and interesting. At this point arousal lessens and overall involvement starts a corresponding decline.

Decline Stage. At this stage, involvement begins to drop rapidly. For example, a new car that was once our most prized possession (and washed every week) now has become familiar and has acquired a series of dents, scratches, and dirt. We still use the car but we do not give it much attention. At some point, involvement can drop steeply, for example we may suddenly decide our old car needs to be replaced. When involvement starts a rapid decline the relationship is in danger of terminating unless regrowth occurs.

SUMMARY OF FREQUENCY AND DURATION

	Frequency Low	Frequency High
Duration Low	Low Involvement	Moderate Involvement
Duration High	Moderate Involvement	High Involvement

Table 2

THE LIFE CYCLE OF INVOLVEMENT

LIFE CYCLE OF INVOLVEMENT

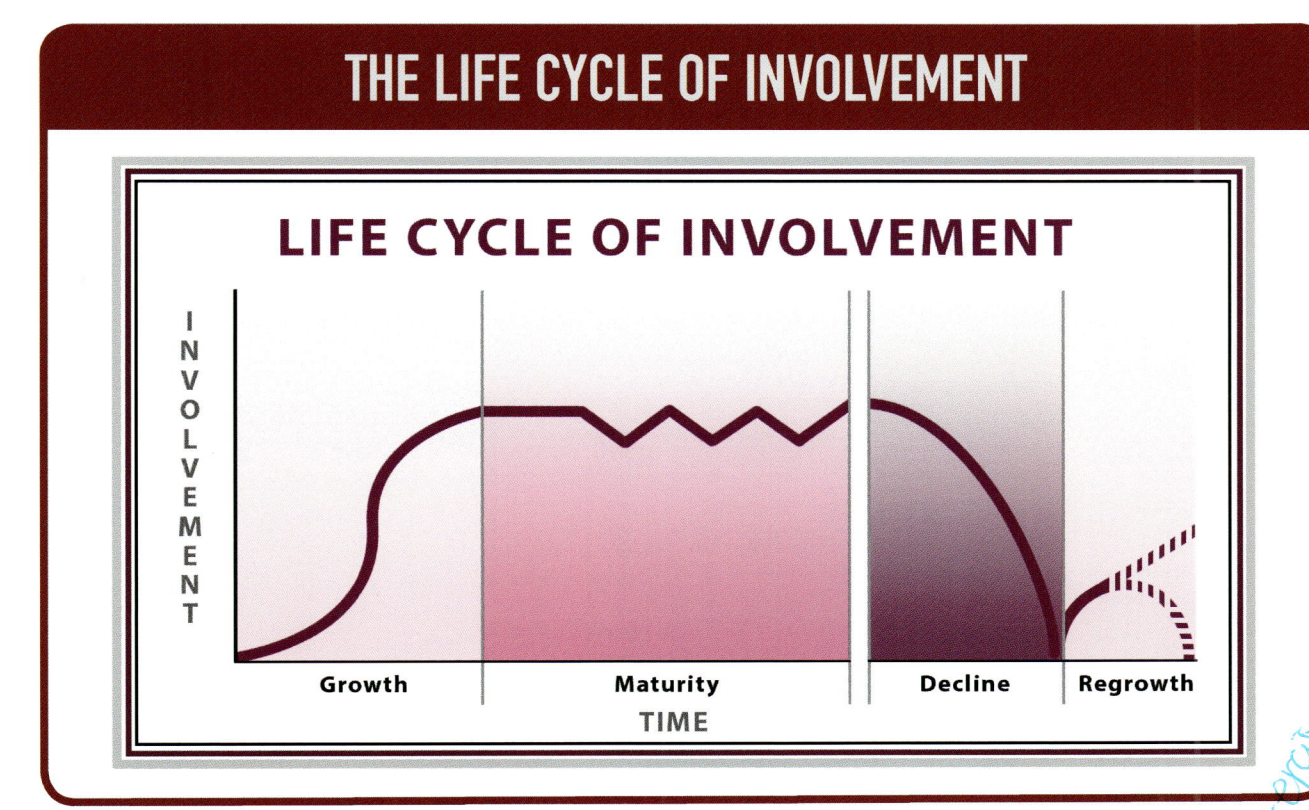

Involvement vs *Time*: Growth, Maturity, Decline, Regrowth

Model 1

Regrowth Stage. Sometimes when involvement declines, people have second thoughts about losing the relationship. This can be due to long term intrinsic interest or the fear of losing a loved one or loved object. At this point one or both parties to the exchange may attempt an intervention to stop the decline and return to previous times when involvement was higher. For example, a couple in a declining relationship may seek counseling in an effort to re-engender growth. Notice however, that due to familiarity, the regrowth stage often relies on **effort rather than arousal.** Because it is very difficult to produce increasing involvement without arousal, the regrowth stage often does not last. For example, instead of buying a new car we may spend money fixing up our old car so that some parts of it are "new again." This can work for a while but ultimately most consumers move on and buy a new car.

THE ROLE OF AROUSAL

Arousal is an especially important component of involvement. It can create an intense **chemical bath**, which is a body chemistry that includes high levels of **adrenalin** and natural **body opiates**. These chemicals produce extreme positive reinforcement and vivid memories (due to heightened adrenalin) both of which are often involved in feelings of "love." However, over time familiarity builds and people normally become adapted to objects that were once highly arousing. Over extended periods of time the law of diminishing returns takes effect.

THE LAW OF DIMINISHING RETURNS

The law of diminishing returns states that as people obtain an increasing amount of a commodity, they will reach a point where additional units of that commodity generate less utility (or value) than the preceding unit. In other words, people tend to become bored with things they possess in large quantities. For example, each additional dollar is valued less by a millionaire than by a poor person. If a person eats three candy bars in a row, the first is likely to taste better than the last. Indeed, it is the law of diminishing returns that gives marginal utility curves their familiar shape as shown by Model 2.

8.6

Notice the discontinuity (gap) in the utility curve. It is drawn to show that it may take a long time for additional units to begin losing value. This gap is used to explain why relationships with some objects or people have high value and involvement over extended periods of time. With the discontinuity included, the principle of diminishing returns gains "law" status , (i.e., it is expected to apply to all situations sooner or later).

The law of diminishing returns is the basis for many well-known sayings like "familiarity breeds contempt," "all things in moderation," "variety is the spice of life," or "you can get too much of a good thing." Virtually everyone can think of objects, products, or people that were once liked but have lost their value over time due to familiarity. The law of diminishing returns also plays a major role in human dissatisfaction because the **perceived value** of an object **declines** with more object-related interactions. Therefore, over time, many people experience less value than they expected when dealing with objects, products, or people.

SUMMARY

The law of diminishing returns indicates that humans will be prone to cycles of involvement. When we discover a new source of pleasure (e.g., object, product, person, job) we will tend to value it highly and devote considerable time and attention (involvement) to it. The irrevocable result of this involvement is familiarity. Once the source of reinforcement begins to become familiar, the marginal utility will, at some point, begin to decline (it may take a long time to reach this point, however). Once this value decline starts, we can predict a decrease in involvement. At this point, individuals will look to new objects or events to maximize their satisfaction. These unusual dynamics between involvement and the law of diminishing returns cause considerable human dissatisfaction.

Indeed, over time, most consumers show a **need for novelty** in the products they buy (and the promotions they attend to). Part of this is due to natural changes in our interests as we age and mature. For example, when people have children, they usually become highly involved in a whole new set of products and services. In addition to natural growth, adaptation, and diminishing returns can cause consumers to lose involvement with almost any product over time. This tendency highlights the importance of personal growth and creativity in **continuing** exchanges to prevent or minimize boredom.

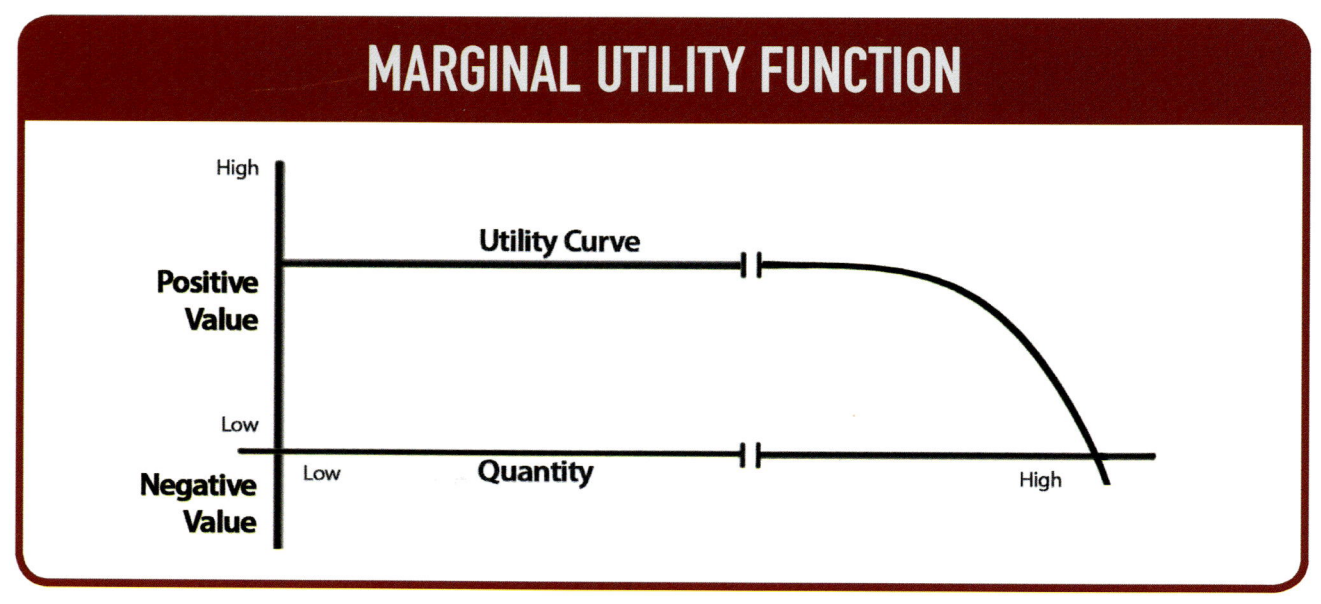

MARGINAL UTILITY FUNCTION

Model 2

EFFECTS OF INVOLVEMENT ON LATITUDES OF ACCEPTANCE AND REJECTION

As consumers become more involved, their decision-making skills evolve and improve. Latitudes of acceptance are defined as your range of acceptable positions and latitudes of rejection are defined as your range of unacceptable positions. Latitudes of non-committal are defined as the range of positions where you are undecided. In marketing, this would relate to whether a consumer perceives the range of a product's attributes as acceptable or unacceptable. For example, assume you had to buy a bottle of wine for a dinner party this week-end. If you know little about wines your latitudes of acceptance will be wide – you would be willing to buy almost any wine. Your latitudes of rejection will be narrow because you have little knowledge as to why you should not buy a certain wine. Often in this case, the consumer will sub-contract the decision-making to the store clerk and ask for a recommendation from a more knowledgeable source.

Now, assume that over time you become involved with wines and start to study, buy, and sample them. As you learn more about the product (through your involvement) you become a more demanding judge. This is because you now have a large amount of experience and knowledge (accumulated involvement) and therefore, know what attributes to consider and how to judge them. Thus, consumers normally become more discriminating (harder to please) as they become more involved with a product causing their latitudes of acceptance to shrink and their latitudes of rejection to expand as illustrated by Model 3.

CONSUMER INVOLVEMENT

Based on the discussion above we can identify different characteristics of consumer involvement that are important to marketing strategy. The factors to be considered are the determinants of involvement (intensity, depth, and persistence), how long involvement lasts, the target of involvement, and the consequences of the involvement.

DETERMINANTS OF INVOLVEMENT

One reason consumer involvement is a complex topic is that different types of involvement can exist depending on the level of the determinants. **Arousal** is a particularly important component of involvement and when it is high, growth is present and pleasure is high. **Effort** is required in many exchange relationships but when arousal is low and the effort required is high, involvement is less sustainable over time. **Depth** of processing is also a very important element of

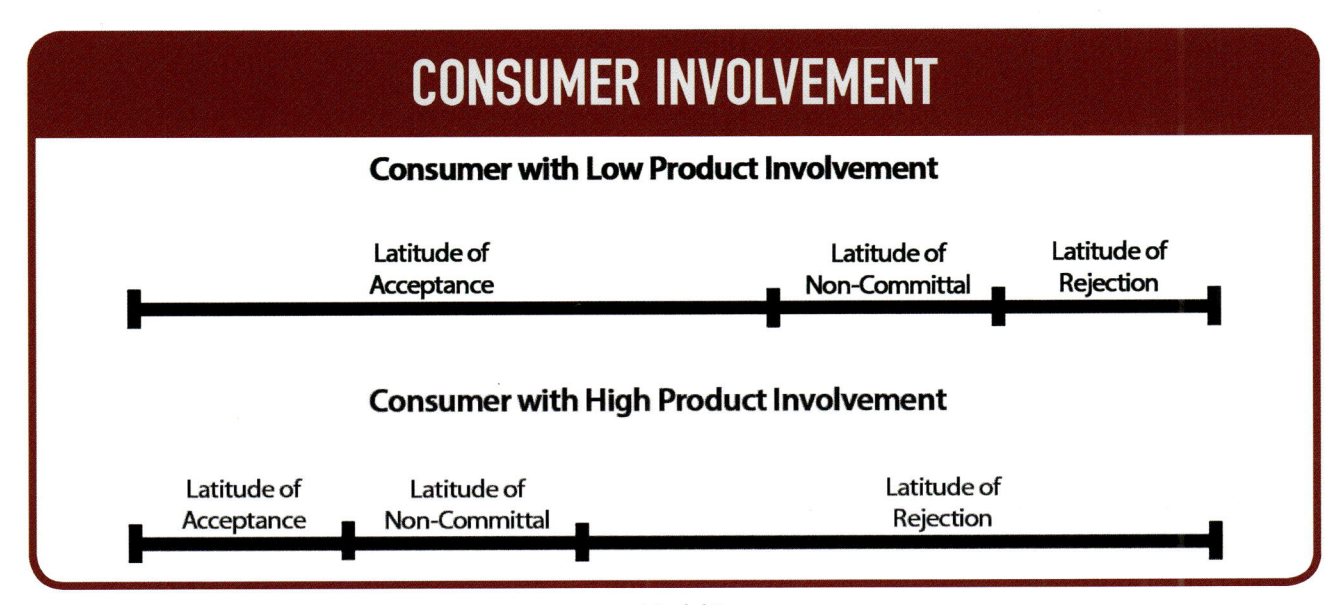

CONSUMER INVOLVEMENT

Consumer with Low Product Involvement

| Latitude of Acceptance | Latitude of Non-Committal | Latitude of Rejection |

Consumer with High Product Involvement

| Latitude of Acceptance | Latitude of Non-Committal | Latitude of Rejection |

Model 3

LONGEVITY OF INVOLVEMENT IN EXCHANGE RELATIONSHIPS

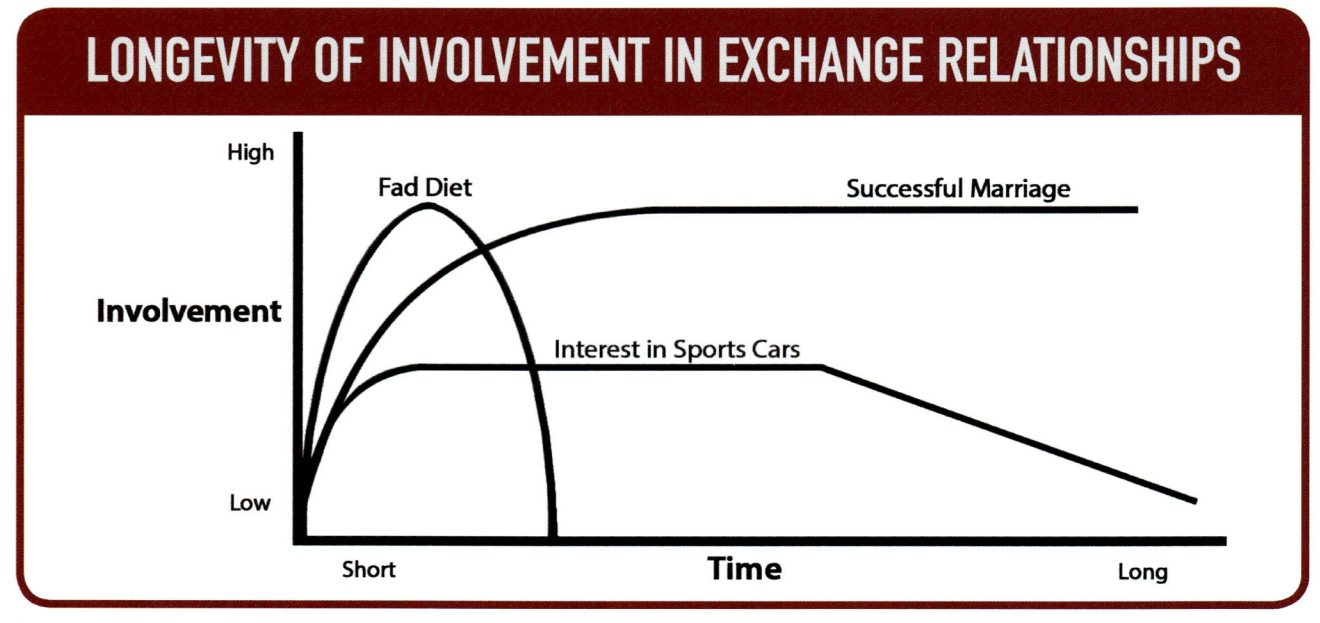

Model 4

involvement. Indeed, Level III processing produces elaboration and creativity which have the potential to prevent the loss of involvement over time. This is because creativity introduces new and unusual elements to the relationship thereby enhancing arousal and decreasing familiarity and boredom. In any event, different combinations of arousal, effort and depth can produce very different patterns of consumer involvement.

LONGEVITY OF INVOLVEMENT

Although involvement shows a general life-cycle pattern, each specific case has its own dynamics. One way to examine involvement in exchange relationships is to consider how long the involvement remains high (i.e., how long the relationship remains vital and meaningful). For example, at the short end of the longevity continuum is a **fad** type of involvement where rapid growth occurs but then a correspondingly steep decline occurs. For example, the total involvement episode for a fad diet may last only days, weeks, or months but the involvement and arousal can be intense during this time.

In the middle of the longevity continuum, would be a consumer's relationship with a product that lasted for a period of time but then declined. For example, involvement with sports cars may give way to involvement with mini vans as an individual traverses the cycle of life. At the other end of the longevity continuum are the most enduring relationships like our family and friends and products we are loyal to for life. Although it is true that such relationships usually have ups and downs in the level of involvement, the law of diminishing returns can be postponed with intrinsic bonds, creativity, and Level III processing.

THE FOCUS OF INVOLVEMENT

In marketing, there is a special interest in the target of involvement because consumers are quite dynamic in their allocation of attention. Indeed, consumers can be involved with a brand (e.g., Coca-cola), a company (e.g., Harley-Davidson), a product category (e.g., opinion leader), an industry (e.g., movie buff), advertisements (that are humorous or creative), or even the process of product acquisition (e.g., bargain hunters) or product disposition (e.g., re-cyclers). Note that some product categories benefit from intrinsic arousal (e.g., sports, gold, vacations, pets, etc.) and can achieve higher levels of consumer involvement and longevity. However, other products have a naturally short involvement period though it can be very intense (e.g., prom dress).

CONSEQUENCES OF INVOLVEMENT

One reason involvement is such a dynamic construct is that it has both positive and negative ramifications. On the positive side, involvement allows us to: fulfill our curiosity and knowledge needs, get to know and judge objects accurately, decrease our latitudes of acceptance (so we are less likely to be taken advantage of), and lead to elaboration and creativity which facilitate growth and success. On the negative side, involvement necessarily produces familiarity which can result in boredom, declining utility, adaptation and even contempt for a once-valued object. We can also expect consumers to be dynamic over time and have a series of involvement cycles with a wide variety of products and services throughout their lifetime.

CONCLUSION

Consumer involvement is an important and interesting construct that has been heavily studied in consumer research and has a significant impact on marketing strategy and success. Your ability to give high involvement to your professional key accounts, to the products and services you represent, and to your personal key accounts will be an important determinant of your success. In addition, your ability to attract high involvement from your professional and personal key accounts will also have a big impact on your success in marketing. Accordingly, a level III understanding of consumer involvement is a valuable asset for any marketer.

EXPERIMENT 8.1
LIFE CYCLE OF INVOLVEMENT

1. Construct a graph (in months) for the average life cycle of involvement for the following (discuss with friends to reach a consensus):

   a. Undergraduate student's involvement with college over four years

   b. The "average" romantic relationship in college

   c. An entry-level marketing position in sales or retailing

   d. A consumer's relationship with a new car

2. What factors prolong the life-cycle of involvement?

3. What factors shorten the life-cycle of involvement?

ELABORATION QUESTIONS

- Does the law of diminishing returns apply to personal relationships in the same way it applies to products and services?

- What are some specific ways to prevent the loss of involvement in key account relationships over time?

- How many personal key accounts can you have high involvement with at one time?

- What does it mean to "be in love with love?"

- Can you have a successful long-term relationship without level III thought? Give some examples.

- What does the involvement life cycle look like for "on-again, off-again" relationships?

- Are you susceptible to fad involvement cycles with products and services? If so, which product categories?

- How long is your effort span?

- What happens when you exceed your effort span?

- What is the best way to make products and services arouse consumers?

- What are the signs that a relationship is entering the decline in involvement stage?

- What types of relationships can withstand a decrease in involvement but still work?

- What products and services have you been involved with the longest?

- Is it easier or harder to maintain high levels of involvement with key accounts who evolve and change as they mature?

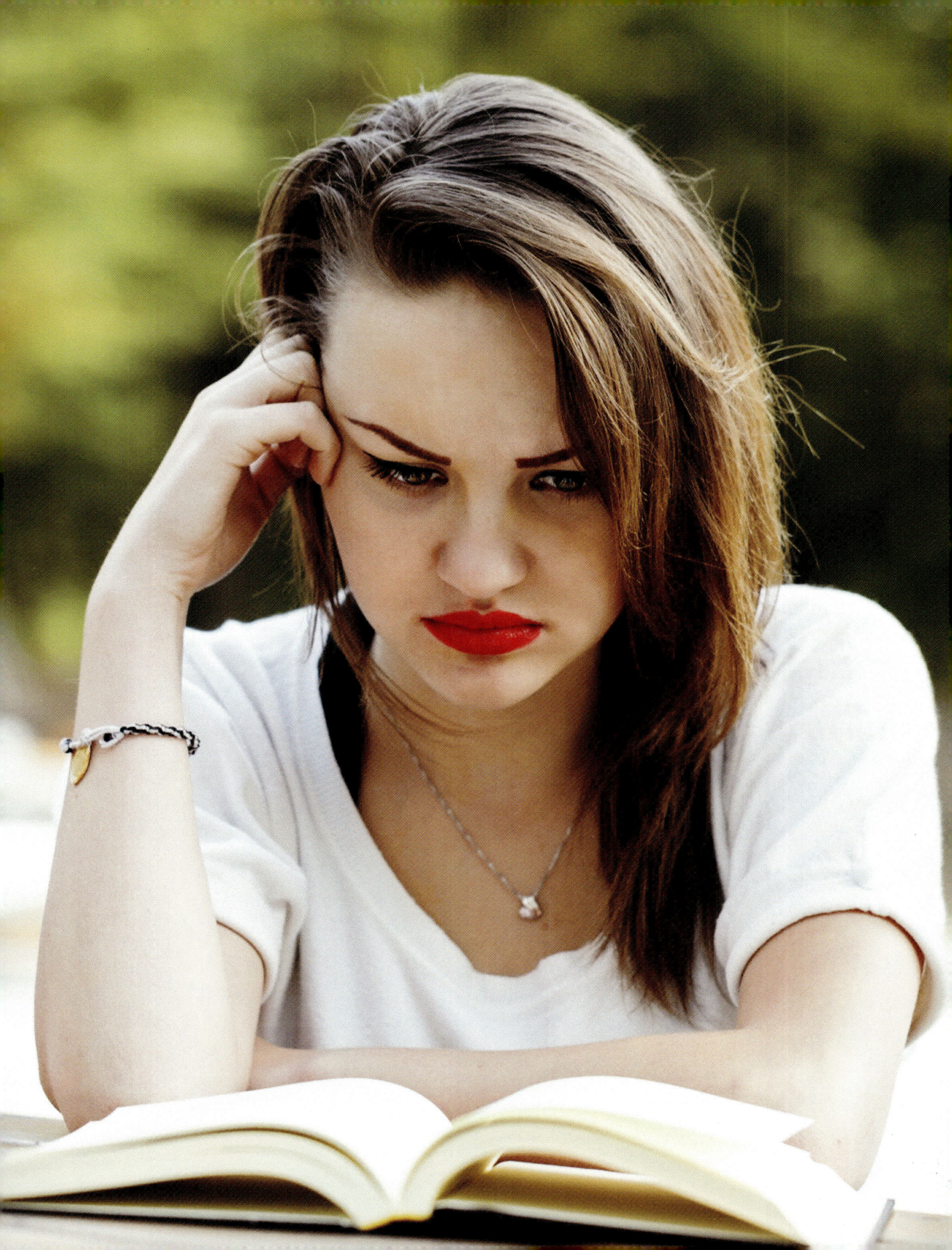

CHAPTER 9
MOTIVATION I: THE PRECONDITIONS TO NEED SATISFACTION

EXCHANGE THEORY	**9.1**
Background	9.1
Humanistic Psychology	9.2
Origin of the Hierarchy of Needs and Motives	9.2
BACKGROUND DEFINITIONS	**9.3**
Needs Versus Desires	9.3
Prepotency	9.3
Multiple Motives	9.3
The Striving Cycle	9.3
Ascending the Hierarchy	9.4
Deficiency Needs versus Growth Needs	9.4
Stages of Development	9.4
THE PRECONDITIONS FOR NEED SATISFACTION	**9.5**
Humans are Striving Organisms	9.5
Humans Must Have Freedom of Choice	9.6
Humans Are Curious	9.7
Humans Have a Need to Know and Understand	9.7
Humans are Self-Expressive	9.7
THE PRECONDITIONS – INNATE, INTRINSIC, AND UNIVERSAL	**9.8**
**EXPERIMENT 9.1	PRECONDITIONS ANALYSIS**	**9.9**
ELABORATION QUESTIONS	**9.10**

GUIDING QUESTIONS

- In general, why do people make certain exchanges and avoid others?
- Do people always have to make a profit in their exchanges?
- What do people value?
- Who was Abraham Maslow?
- What is humanistic psychology?
- What is the difference between a need and a desire?
- What is multiple motivation?
- How are needs arranged?
- What are the preconditions to need satisfaction?
- How does the striving nature of humans affect consumer behaviors?
- How does the need for freedom affect consumer behaviors?
- How does curiosity affect consumer behaviors?
- How does the need to know and understand affect consumer behaviors?
- How does self-expression affect consumer behaviors?
- What is the difference between coping behavior and expressive behavior?

EXCHANGE THEORY

The previous chapters described the basic equipment and operation of the internal model which we use to identify the environment and select behaviors that we believe are likely to be rewarded. This section identifies what types of rewards we seek. **Motivation** *refers to* **why** *people select specific behaviors. In the most general terms, motivation can be described by exchange theory. According to this theory, the motivation for exchange is always* **profit** *(but not necessarily monetary profit). Specifically, each party must be better off after the exchange than before (if we were worse off we would not engage in the exchange for very long). That is, the perceived value of what we gain must exceed the perceived value of what we give. If the exchange involves only a single transaction, then the equation below must hold. If the exchange involves a series of transactions over time, then it is the totality of exchanges that must meet the equation (i.e., we may not gain from every transaction but we do gain over the long term).*

> **PERCEIVED VALUE GAIN > PERCEIVED VALUE GIVE**

However, this equation is not complete because all exchanges involve transaction costs that must be included. These are the physical, financial, and mental costs of making the transaction. These can include: shipping costs, waiting for delivery, effort to go to a store, etc. Thus, the final equation is: the perceived value of what we gain must exceed the perceived value of what we give by more than our transaction costs.

> **PERCEIVED GAIN > PERCEIVED GIVE + TRANSACTION COSTS**

A good example of the power of exchange theory is that we rarely see people exchanging items that both parties value equally (e.g., trading quarters). Ultimately, the "profit" that people seek in their exchanges is **need satisfaction** which can include any of the following shown in Figure 1:

PROFITS FROM NEED SATISFACTION

1. Gratifying the "preconditions"
2. Gratifying deficiency needs
3. Reducing drive states (tension)
4. Gratifying neurotic needs
5. Gratifying growth needs
6. Gratifying subconscious needs

Figure 1

ABRAHAM H. MASLOW

BACKGROUND

The most widely cited model of human motivation was developed by Abraham Maslow and forms the basis of our approach to consumer motives. Abe Maslow began his career in psychology at the University of Wisconsin where he received three degrees (a B.A. in 1930, a M.A. in 1931, and a Ph.D. in 1934). There, he worked with Harry Harlow during the famous experiments that were designed to investigate what happened to adult behavior when monkeys were raised with limited love and affection. The results showed that the degree of affection and nurturing a baby receives has a lot to do with how s/he acts as an adult. Maslow's early research investigated the motivation of adult primates (Maslow 1936a, 1936b), but he soon noticed major similarities between animal and human motivation and turned his attention to humans.

In 1954, Maslow published **Motivation and Personality**, which contained his basic theory of the hierarchy of needs and motives. In 1970, he revised the book and added a preface that responded to some criticisms and outlined the new additions. He continued to speak and write about human motivation but was primarily interested in meta-motivation in his last 15 years (Maslow died of a heart attack in the summer of 1970 but a collection of his speeches was published in 1971).

HUMANISTIC PSYCHOLOGY

Maslow studied psychology in the 1930s and 1940s when abnormal psychology was the rage. Freud had discovered that psychological disorders produced physical illnesses, so there was a great desire to understand diseases based on mental disorders (e.g., psychiatry). The research on mild psychological sicknesses (neuroses) suggested that almost everyone had these problems, so the study of psychology became a bit morose and sullen -- often focusing on the abnormal. Maslow ultimately became dissatisfied with a study of the human mind that emphasized **negative** deviations from the norm.

In reaction, by the 1960's Maslow was focusing on what he called "humanistic" psychology or a study of the human mind that emphasized **positive** deviations from the norm. Specifically, the theory of meta-motivation was developed by interviewing subjects who had unusually **good** psychological health. Also, he emphasized a "holistic" approach that integrated concepts from many theories including the Taoistic movement. Finally, the humanistic label emphasized that his model was based on observations of humans and not rats or monkeys (this was because humans were the only species that could achieve meta-motivation).

Note that Maslow never denied the negative side of human psychology:

> "and yet there are also other regressive, fearful, self-diminishing tendencies as well ..." (1970, p. xiii).

Abraham Maslow

He believed that there should be a balanced approach to the study of psychology -- since so many focused on the abnormal aspects, he focused on the best part of being human.

ORIGIN OF THE HIERARCHY OF NEEDS AND MOTIVES

Maslow (1970, p. xi) developed his original theory of motivation by asking the following questions (note the heavy clinical orientation as he searched for a cure to the behavioral problems of adults):

1. Which early deprivations produce neuroses?
2. Which psychological medicines cure neuroses?
3. Which psychological medicines prevent neuroses?
4. In which order are the psychological medicines demanded?
5. Which are most powerful?
6. Which are most basic?

Humanistic Psychology is Based on People, Not Animals

Maslow concluded that satisfying needs should be considered a human right. For example, the sexual revolution of the 1960's was seen, by some, as a rebellion against repression of the human sex drive. The idea that all humans should have the right to pursue the basic needs has obvious moral and ethical implications that Maslow did not shy away from (he wanted to create a better society and said so often).

BACKGROUND DEFINITIONS

NEEDS VERSUS DESIRES

Needs are **universal** human necessities. They are necessary because if they are not satisfied, the individual will become **physically sick.** Because of this humans are strongly motivated to satisfy their needs (to avoid illness). These motives give rise to "desires" which are means to the universal ends (e.g., an individual **desires** a fancy car because he **needs** social approval). Desires are culturally determined but the underlying needs are the same for all humans.

PREPOTENCY

Certain needs can be arranged in a hierarchy of strength. The strength (or position) of any two needs can be determined by depriving a person of both (e.g., safety and social needs) and noting which one is satisfied first. The results are predictable and represent the theoretical basis for the hierarchy concept.

MULTIPLE MOTIVES

Each individual has **multiple motives** active at any point in time. Accordingly, it is a mistake to focus on a single need in the hierarchy (e.g., social needs) because many are active at the same time. As Maslow (1970, p. 54) notes: "if prepotent need A is satisfied only 10%, then need B may not be visible at all. However, as this need A becomes satisfied 25 percent, need B may emerge 5 percent, as need A becomes satisfied 75 percent, need B may emerge 50 percent, and so on." As a result, consumer motivation is very dynamic and complex and often difficult to understand unless we know the total set of active needs.

THE STRIVING CYCLE

To satisfy our needs, people go through a "striving cycle." The person will usually have to work to satisfy a need (e.g., buy and fix food for dinner). After this effort is expended and a need (hunger) is satisfied there is usually a period of rest and relaxation.

However, due to multiple motivation this window of rest and relaxation is often much shorter than most realize. Almost immediately, the next most important unmet need will motivate the person to start another striving cycle.

ASCENDING THE HIERARCHY

To move up the hierarchy, lower needs must be "reasonably" fulfilled. Because individuals have different levels of demand for each need (e.g., some people need more social approval than others), what is a "reasonable" level of gratification can only be defined on an individual basis. As noted above, multiple needs may be active at the same time but progression up the hierarchy can only be achieved by **reasonably satisfying** each lower need. Specifically, an individual is unlikely to be **focused** on esteem needs if s/he is not gratified in the physiological, safety, and love needs. However, this does not mean that people who are insecure will be uninterested in self-esteem (e.g., it may be 5% active).

DEFICIENCY NEEDS VERSUS GROWTH NEEDS

Deficiency needs are universal human necessities that cause **physical illness** if they go ungratified. **Growth needs** (meta-motives) are less necessary for survival, but they are crucial to the full development of human potential. If these needs are not gratified, they produce a **spiritual illness** in the individual.

STAGES OF DEVELOPMENT

People go through stages of development starting with infancy where there is complete (100%) dependency on other people for need gratification. As people age they learn to satisfy their own needs (to one extent or another). Ultimately, in Maslow's model, the goal is to achieve **functional autonomy**, whereby an adult is able to satisfy his/her own basic needs.

Window of Rest and Relaxation

Spiritual Illness

THE PRECONDITIONS FOR NEED SATISFACTION

One of the biggest omissions in summaries of Maslow's model is the absence of the "preconditions for need satisfaction." These preconditions represent five characteristics of human nature that facilitate need gratification. Individuals will have difficulty gratifying their needs and ascending the hierarchy if the preconditions are restricted by internal factors (e.g., gene mutation, sickness, etc.) or, more commonly, external factors (e.g., social and political constraints).

For example, Maslow sees the cognitive abilities of humans as a set of adjustive tools that enable need gratification. Thus, to facilitate need satisfaction, humans must be free to inquire (e.g., humans have a need for curiosity). Any threat to the preconditions is considered a danger and reacted to as if the needs themselves were threatened.

> *"There are certain conditions [that are] immediate prerequisites for the basic need satisfactions. Danger to these is reacted to as if it were a direct danger to the basic needs themselves. Thwarting in these freedoms will be reacted to with a threat or emergency response. These conditions are defended because without them the basic satisfactions are quite impossible, or at least, severely endangered."* **(Maslow 1970).**

Despite their importance, the five preconditions have seldom been recognized in summaries of Maslow's model.

HUMANS ARE STRIVING ORGANISMS

This first precondition is central to Maslow's model because humans are viewed as being in a nearly constant quest: "Man is a wanting animal and rarely reaches a state of complete satisfaction except for a short time. As one desire is fulfilled another pops up to take its place . . . It is a characteristic of the human being that throughout his whole life he is always wanting something" (Maslow 1970, p. 24). The idea that satisfaction is **short-lived** and that striving is the greater human impulse has major implications for consumer satisfaction theories. Satisfaction from routine products and services may amount to a small portion of overall human satisfaction.

In fact, striving is so valued that people seem to naturally cheer for "underdogs" and reserve deep scorn for those considered "lazy." Another implication of the striving orientation in humans is the importance of employment. Indeed, unemployment figures are one of the leading indicators of an economy's health. When unemployment is high, the striving impulse is often redirected to anti-social activities including crime, rebellion, and violence.

HUMANS MUST HAVE FREEDOM OF CHOICE

The second precondition reflects the vital importance of personal freedom. True motivation can be observed only when people are free. Indeed, threats to freedom often produce the "reactance effect" whereby people undertake actions to reestablish their freedom of choice (Clee and Wicklund 1980). In particular, freedom of choice and expression must be present before internal motives will be displayed in overt behavior.

This is an important precondition because freedom of choice is a requirement to maximize need gratification. Choices made without full freedom will be less expressive (intrinsic) and thus, typically provide less satisfaction. For example, prisoners cannot achieve the same level of satisfaction with the food they are given as they can when they are free to choose their favorite foods. Similarly, consumers cannot achieve maximum levels of personal satisfaction if their product and service choices are constrained (e.g., by budget limitations, parental control, social norms, peer pressure, group decision making, advertising, etc.). This suggests the necessity to examine both personal satisfaction and social satisfaction (i.e., the pleasure one receives by gratifying the needs of others).

In summary, **freedom** is a necessary component if consumers are going to maximize their satisfaction. This is true not only with respect to basic need gratification, but perhaps even more importantly, to enable consumers to make progressive choices relating to higher-level needs. This is important because according to Maslow (1971) gratifying the higher needs produces more pleasure than gratifying the lower ones.

Consumer Freedom of Choice

HUMANS ARE CURIOUS

The third precondition focuses on human curiosity. This is an important drive because it causes people to explore different ways to satisfy their needs. Indeed, there seems to be a direct relationship between curiosity and surprise (both positive and negative). This is important in marketing because surprise is the basis for the disconfirmation model of consumer satisfaction (negative surprise leads to dissatisfaction and positive surprise leads to satisfaction).

Curiosity also seems to be directly related to the human need for variety, novelty, and divergent thought. There is an obvious relationship between curiosity and risk-taking behavior. The more curious the individual, the more risks they are willing to take. Curiosity and risk-taking also show patterns over time as both tend to decline with age. For example, adults with low curiosity, may prefer to repurchase the same product over and over even when the law of diminishing returns has eroded the satisfaction received. Conversely, consumers with high levels of curiosity and variety drive may achieve significant satisfaction by switching brands and/or categories (i.e., consumer promiscuity) rather than buying the same brand repeatedly. Also note that differences in perceived levels of "acceptable risk" between parents (low) and children (high) often contribute to the "generation gap."

HUMANS HAVE A NEED TO KNOW AND UNDERSTAND

The fourth precondition focuses on the human need to know and understand. This drive can direct curiosity to a specific task or goal until closure, understanding, and control are achieved. The implication to marketing is that consumers seek information regarding products both **before** and **after** the purchase decision. In fact, some consumers pay such great importance to information seeking that **information satisfaction** is an important determinant of overall satisfaction.

Only by knowing and understanding ourselves and our environment can we reach full potential in terms of need gratification. Indeed, colleges and universities are devoted entirely to knowing and understanding, and they are among the best places on earth.

HUMANS ARE SELF-EXPRESSIVE

The fifth precondition focuses on the human need to be self-expressive. In Maslow's model, "self-expressive" behaviors are those performed for intrinsic motives (i.e., **internal** rewards) rather than extrinsic motives (i.e., **external** rewards). Thus, self-expressive behaviors are performed to express our true thoughts, and feelings. As an example of this difference, an artist who paints a portrait of a client for a fee is engaged in extrinsically motivated behavior while an artist who paints a portrait of his/her ideal of beauty is engaged in intrinsically motivated behavior. The implication to marketing is that, in many cases, consumers buy products to express their own identity and this can be the most important purchase criterion for personal products. Self-expression is also important because the inability to express one's true self causes low self-esteem which is at the root of many modern problems (including consumer problems like addictions).

Characteristics of Expressive Behavior. Expressive behavior cannot be determined by external constraints. It simply expresses some state of the individual (e.g., the hopeless expression of a desperate person, or the glee of a person in love). In addition, coping (extrinsic) behavior is responsive to external reward/punishment but expressive behavior is not (at least so long as it remains expressive). Expressive behavior can be related to "purposeful spontaneity," and can also be a catharsis or "release behavior" (e.g., primal screaming).

Maslow notes that the psychology of his day focused almost exclusively on coping behaviors but had "notoriously little to say ... about beauty, art, fun, play, wonder, awe, joy, love, happiness, and other 'useless' reactions and end-experiences. It is therefore of little or no service to the artist, ... the humanist, ... or to other end- or enjoyment-oriented individuals." (1970, p. 131). This is perhaps surprising given that Maslow concluded that expressive behaviors can yield some of life's greatest pleasures.

Most psychology literature deals with coping behaviors and the same is true of consumer research. Many researchers have emphasized the importance of

SUMMARY OF COPING AND EXPRESSIVE BEHAVIORS

Coping Behavior	Expressive Behavior
Purposeful and motivated	Often unmotivated
More determined by environment and culture	Determined by the state of the organism
Learned	Unlearned, released, or disinhibited
More easily controlled	More uncontrollable and sometimes uncontrollable
Designed to change something in the environment	Not designed to change anything- if it does, it is often an unintended outcome.
Means to an end	End in itself
Usually conscious	Often unconscious
Externally determined	Internally determined
Effortful	Effortless

Table 1

(extrinsic)   (intrinsic)

coping behaviors in consumption. However, in so doing they overlook an important group of consumption behaviors -- those which are expressive in nature and truly reflect an extension of the self.

The distinction of expressive vs. coping behavior is important in that it represents different underlying mechanisms for seemingly identical consumption behaviors. One example would be commitment. Consumers who stay in a relationship may be driven by very different underlying motivations. The commitment may be coping in nature in that the consumer stays because of the instrumental worth of the relationship to them (e.g., greater financial benefits, avoidance of loneliness, etc.). Alternatively, the commitment may be expressive in nature because the consumer has achieved a sense of identity with the relationship. The choice is made, not purely on instrumental worth, but based on the achieved sense of identity (i.e. the relationship is expressive). However, the consequences of consumption behaviors (coping vs. expressive) are expected to differ.

THE PRECONDITIONS — INNATE, INTRINSIC, AND UNIVERSAL

Maslow did not develop the preconditions in the same detail as the deficiency needs. However, they are intrinsic and innate universal drives or dispositions that all (normal) human beings are born with. These intrinsic dispositions must not be deprived, in order for an individual to fully satisfy the deficiency needs, and progress up the hierarchy. Thus, striving, freedom, curiosity, need to know, and self-expression are necessary yet insufficient conditions for gratifying needs and maximizing satisfaction. When the preconditions are restricted individuals will not be able to satisfy their needs. This, in turn, leads to numerous problems as summarized in Table 2.

PRECONDITIONS FOR NEED SATISFACTION

Precondition	Effects of Deprivation or Absence
Humans are striving organisms.	Lack of meaning to life, lethargy, inactivity
Humans must be free.	Anger, violence, self-destruction
Humans are curious and are born with the intrinsic capacity for variety, novelty, and divergent thought.	Boredom, unquestioning acceptance, acceptance of status quo, routine behavior, declining utility due to diminishing returns
Humans are born with the intrinsic capacity to know and understand.	Lack of metal evolution, limited ability to satisfy higher needs, routine and automated behavior
Humans have a need to express their true feelings.	Anger, frustration, rebellion

Table 2

EXPERIMENT 9.1
PRECONDITIONS ANALYSIS

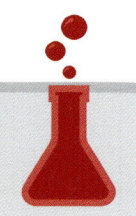

Select a key account who is having problems:

1. Ask them to what extent they believe they have achieved each of the five preconditions.

2. See if they can draw any connections between deprivation of the preconditions and their current problems.

3. Can you see any relationship between how self-expressive your key account is (high or low) and his/her health, satisfaction in life, and general level of motivation?

ELABORATION QUESTIONS

- Do different management styles facilitate or restrict the five preconditions? Ultimately, what is the relationship between management and the preconditions?

- What happens when self-expressive behaviors are punished by the environment?

- What are the most self-expressive products and services you have purchased? How much satisfaction do these products/services bring you compared to the other things you buy?

- What is the relationship between self-expression and tolerance?

CHAPTER 10

MOTIVATION II: DEFICIENCY NEEDS AND NEUROTIC NEEDS

HIERARCHY OF DEFICIENCY NEEDS	**10.1**
DEFICIENCY NEEDS	**10.2**
The Physiological Needs	10.2
Sensory Pleasure and Hedonistic Tendencies	10.2
Homeostatic Needs and Drive Reduction	10.4
The Safety Needs	10.6
The Belongingness Needs	10.6
The Love Needs	10.6
The Esteem Needs	10.7
Limitations to the Deficiency Needs Hierarchy	10.8
NEUROTIC NEEDS	**10.8**
Definition of Neurotic Needs	10.8
Characteristics of Neurotic Needs	10.8
Origins of Neurotic Needs	10.8
Probability of Developing Neurotic Needs	10.9
Neurotic Needs and Marketing	10.9
CONCLUSION	**10.10**
**EXPERIMENT 10.1	NEUROTIC NEEDS**	**10.10**
ELABORATION QUESTIONS	**10.11**

GUIDING QUESTIONS

- » What is the hierarchy of needs and motives model?
- » What are the hedonistic needs?
- » What are the homeostatic needs?
- » What is drive reduction?
- » What are the physical safety needs?
- » What are the psychological security needs?
- » What are the belongingness needs?
- » What are the love needs?
- » What are the social esteem needs?
- » What are the self esteem needs?
- » What are the limitations to the hierarchy of needs and motives model?
- » What are neurotic needs?
- » How do people acquire neurotic needs?
- » What happens when people develop neurotic needs?
- » Who has neurotic needs?
- » How do neurotic needs affect marketing and consumer behavior?

HIERARCHY OF DEFICIENCY NEEDS

The hierarchy of deficiency needs is the most widely referenced part of Maslow's model of motivation and is normally presented as a pyramid with five or six stages. The pyramid shape indicates that the most basic needs are satisfied first (prepotency) and that a smaller percentage of people satisfy each category of needs as we move toward the top. Our pyramid model will differ in some important ways. First, the important influences of the preconditions to need satisfaction are noted by showing them as the foundation of the pyramid model. Second, our model will have nine stages or categories of needs.

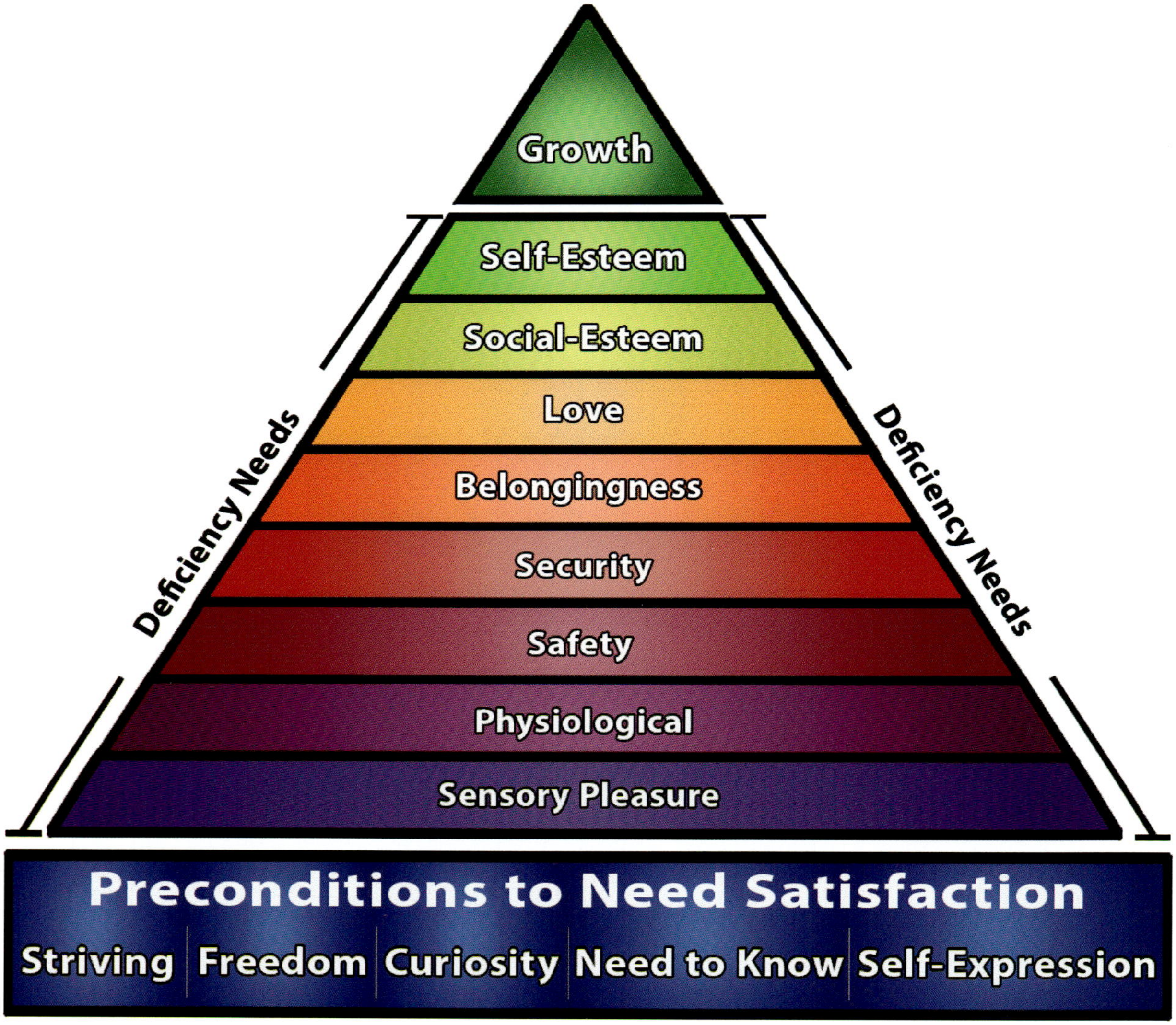

Growth
Self-Esteem
Social-Esteem
Love
Belongingness
Security
Safety
Physiological
Sensory Pleasure
Deficiency Needs
Deficiency Needs
Preconditions to Need Satisfaction
Striving
Freedom
Curiosity
Need to Know
Self-Expression

Model 1

The hierarchy of deficiency needs is the most widely referenced part of Maslow's model of motivation and is normally presented as a pyramid with five or six stages. The pyramid shape indicates that the most basic needs are satisfied first (prepotency) and that a smaller percentage of people satisfy each category of needs as we move toward the top. Our pyramid model will differ in some important ways. First, the important influences of the preconditions to need satisfaction are noted by showing them as the foundation of the pyramid model. Second, our model will have nine stages or categories of needs.

DEFICIENCY NEEDS

THE PHYSIOLOGICAL NEEDS

The physiological needs include hunger, sex, sleep, activity, exercise, and sensory pleasures (tastes, smells, tickling). If all needs are unsatisfied, the physiological needs will dominate the organism. Once these needs are satisfied, "at once other (and higher) needs emerge" (Maslow 1970, p.38). It is important to note that Maslow divided the physiological needs into two categories: **sensory pleasure** and **homeostatic.**

SENSORY PLEASURE AND HEDONISTIC TENDENCIES

Theories of humans as pleasure seekers go back as far as Epicurus (circa 320 B.C.E.). No theory of motivation can reliably predict human behavior without this critical component. Desires for short-term pleasure, immediate gratification, expensive products and services, conspicuous consumption, etc. are clearly related to this human universal. It is important to draw attention to these hedonistic tendencies as they can often provide a direct explanation for consumer behaviors.

Philosophers commonly distinguish between **psychological hedonism** and **ethical hedonism**. Psychological hedonism is the view that behavior is motivated by the desire for pleasure and the avoidance of pain. Ethical hedonism is the view that our fundamental moral obligation is to maximize pleasure or happiness. Ethical hedonism is most associated with the ancient Greek philosopher Epicurus (342-270 BCE) who taught that life's goal should be to minimize pain and maximize pleasure.

> *"We recognize pleasure as the first good innate in us, and from pleasure we begin every act of choice and avoidance, and to pleasure we return again, using the feeling as the standard by which we judge every good."*
> **[Letter to Menoeceus]**

Epicurus gives advice on how to decrease life's pains, and explains the nature of pleasure. As to decreasing life's pain, Epicurus explains how we can reduce the psychological anguish that results from fearing the gods and fearing death. Concerning the nature of pleasure, Epicurus explains that at least some pleasures are rooted in nature and, as a rule, every pain is bad and should be avoided, and every pleasure is good and should be preferred. However, sometimes simply minimizing life's pains is not sufficient to attain happiness, and we need to go a step further and actively increase pleasure. He argues that we should not pursue every possible pleasure, such as when they produce more pain (e.g., over eating). He also argues that the fewer desires we have, the easier it will be to experience happiness. It is also important to decide which type of pleasure is most preferred – intense but short or mild but long. He concluded the latter is better and that ultimately the best source of pleasure was **friendship**.

During the middle ages, Christian philosophers largely denounced hedonism, which they believed was inconsistent with the Christian emphasis on avoiding sin, doing God's will, and developing the Christian virtues of faith, hope and charity. Renaissance philosophers such as Erasmus revived hedonism and argued that its emphasis on pleasure was in fact compatible with God's wish for humans to be happy. In his famous work Utopia (1516), British philosopher Thomas More explains that "the chief part of a person's happiness consists of pleasure." More defends hedonism on religious grounds and argues that, not only did God design us to be happy, but that He uses our desire for happiness to motivate us to behave morally. He also argues that we should pursue pleasures that are more naturally grounded, so that we do not become preoccupied with artificial luxuries.

There is little doubt today that people are strongly motivated to seek pleasure and avoid pain – though sometimes we endure pain to gain long run pleasure. Indeed, one of the first signs of depression is the loss of interest in pleasure. Because of this we can make some generalizations about human motivation. First, people will often put off doing things that are not pleasing in order to pursue fun. Second, we can predict that pleasure (like money) has a time value (i.e., pleasure today is worth more than pleasure tomorrow). This means that **procrastination** is a major component of many peoples' behavioral

HEDONISM

Figure 1

repertoire. Third, people will be motivated to attend to stimuli that promise the attainment of pleasure (a common advertising technique). Fourth, the drive for hedonism is so strong in some people that they cannot control their consumption of pleasurable products and services. This can lead to addictions and self-destructive behavior.

> *"A man hath no better thing under the sun, than to eat, and to drink, and to be merry."*
> **Hebrew Bible** *Ecclesiastes 8:15*

> *"It is only by enlarging the scope of one's tastes and one's fantasies, by sacrificing everything to pleasure, that the unfortunate individual called man, thrown despite himself into this sad world, can succeed in gathering a few roses among life's thorns."* **Marquis de Sade** *(1740–1814)*

Ethical/political Implications. Do consumers have the right to pursue sensory pleasures in a free-market democratic society? Currently, the answer depends on the **type** of pleasure. Some types of consumer activity have a long history of prohibition and taboo including: sexual pleasure (e.g., prostitution, and homosexuality), gambling, alcohol (minors), drugs, etc. Even though important historical figures like Lincoln and Jefferson concluded that prohibition of consumption was inconsistent with democratic values, there are many products and services that are prohibited in today's marketplace.

This raises the issue of illegal markets and their promotion and distribution systems, which actively stimulate the use of prohibited products (e.g., free trials). This also means there is no regulation of these banned products and services, which also causes much harm to consumers. Maslow believed that humans have universal rights to gratify their deficiency needs.

Shopping Excessively

This raises many questions about national policies regarding prohibition from drug policy to motorcycle helmet laws.

HOMEOSTATIC NEEDS AND DRIVE REDUCTION

Homeostasis. The second type of physiological needs are homeostatic in nature. The human body has a chemistry equilibrium position known as homeostasis. When an individual is in homeostasis, there is a condition of inner harmony or a lack of tension in the system. This is the preferred or most healthy position because the entire organism (including the critical immune system) operates most efficiently at homeostasis (by definition). The physiological needs of *hunger, sex, sleep, activity, and rest,* are considered homeostatic needs because they are regulated by the body's "automatic effort to maintain a constant, normal state in the blood stream" (Maslow 1970, p. 36).

Drive States. Drive states occur when the body's equilibrium position is altered because an internal resource is needed (e.g., food), or because aversive stimuli from the environment are present (e.g., threats). Most people are familiar with the internal tension (i.e., negative drive states) associated with hunger, tiredness, fear, etc.

Action Impulses. When drive states occur, they produce action impulses or physical energy intended to lead directly to an appropriate approach/avoidance overt behavior. For example, when the body gets hungry, it produces a series of chemistry changes that, in turn, produce strong action impulses to find and consume food. Thus, action impulses connect drive states to specific overt behaviors.

Drive Objects. Drive objects are any items in the environment that **naturally** and **fully** satisfy the internal tension caused by the drive state. For example, when a person is hungry (drive state), the natural drive object is food. Attainment of the drive object alleviates the drive state tension and returns the body to homeostasis. Thus, in a drive reduction model, drive states motivate people to approach drive objects as shown in Figure 2.

Substitute Drive Objects. These are objects that, though not necessarily related to the original drive object, can at least **partially** reduce the drive state energy. For example, a very hungry person on a diet may feel considerable drive state pressure to eat. The dieter may deny the normal drive object, however, and find a partial release by smoking a cigarette instead. In this case, the cigarette is a substitute drive object for food as shown in Figure 3.

Successful Motivational Sequence. The model below shows what happens when action impulses are naturally and fully satisfied.

DRIVE STATES AND DRIVE OBJECTS

INSTINCT	DRIVE STATE	DRIVE OBJECT
Revitalization →	Hunger →	Food
Reproduction →	Sexual Desire →	Sex
Protection →	Fear →	Security

Figure 2

Maslow notes that not all physiological needs have been proven to be homeostatic (i.e., all needs do not have rising and falling appetites depending on levels of blood chemicals). In addition, he notes that **sensory pleasures** are not homeostatic, and that ultimately they, "may become the goals of motivated behavior" (Maslow 1970, p. 36). One of the biggest problems with the way Maslow's model has been summarized is the exclusion of sensory pleasure as a major motivating force in humans. Accordingly, the best way to illustrate the physiological needs is to divide them into two categories – homeostatic needs and sensory pleasure needs.

SUBSTITUTE DRIVE OBJECTS

Figure 3

DRIVE REDUCTION MODEL

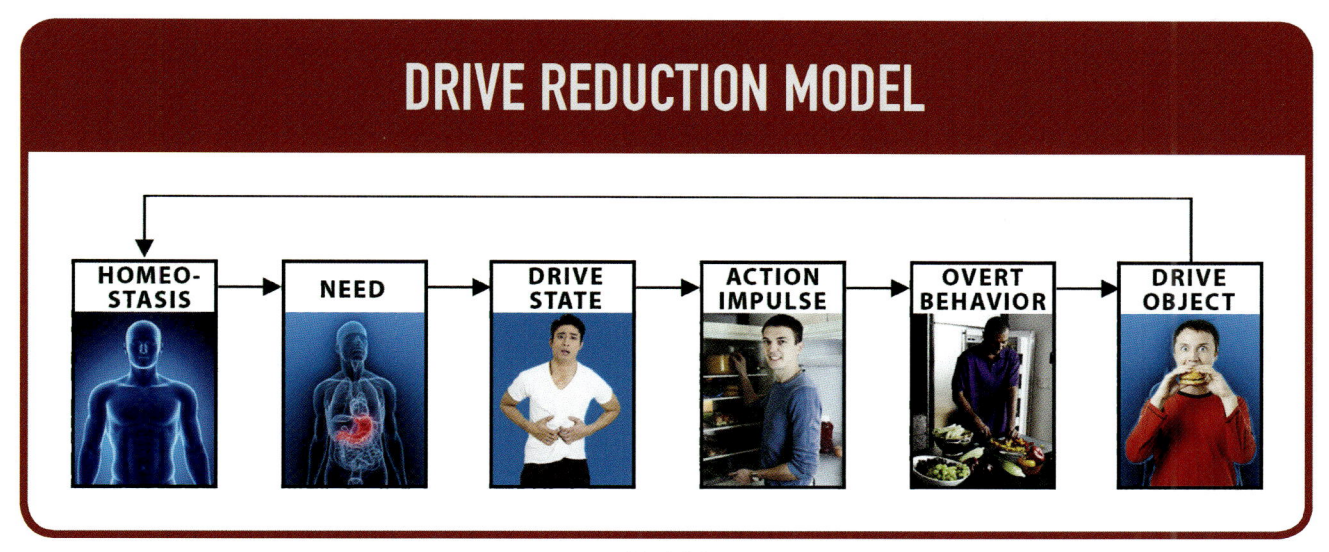

Model 1

THE SAFETY NEEDS

Personal safety includes the need for: **security, stability, dependency, protection, freedom from fear, anxiety, and chaos, structure, order, law, limits,** etc. This set of needs leads to preference for familiar rather than unfamiliar things, for the known rather than the unknown. Individuals who have pathologies related to safety can become, at the extreme, compulsive-obsessive such that they try to arrange their world so that nothing unexpected can occur. Implicit in Maslow's list are two different types of safety needs:

1. Physical Safety. The need for: **security, stability, protection, order, law,** etc. Threats to physical safety usually evoke a physical "Flight/Fight" response (e.g., withdraw or counterattack). In addition, Maslow (1968) notes that many major decisions in life represent a choice between safety and growth. Often, safety is preferred, due to the power of the deficiency needs. This suggests that safety will play a major role in the general motivation of human beings.

2. Psychological Security. The need for: **freedom from fear and chaos, psychological stability, structure, and order.** Threats to psychological security usually evoke a psychological "Flight/Fight" response (e.g., cognitive consistency, selective perception, denial, etc.). Psychological security plays a big role in marketing where inducing change in beliefs or attitudes is a common goal. However, changing these cognitive/affective structures in adults can be very difficult due to tendencies toward security and the resulting distaste for discrepancy (i.e., tendencies toward cognitive consistency).

THE BELONGINGNESS NEEDS

These needs are based on the desire for social contact with other humans. These include the need for **contact, friendship, and intimacy; and the need to avoid loneliness and alienation.** Often, affiliation needs are deficiency based – that is humans are powerfully motivated to **avoid** loneliness and will affiliate with a bewildering array of people and groups to do so. As an example of how these tendencies might affect marketing, it is interesting to speculate how many consumers who shop but do not buy are looking for human companionship (e.g., shopping with friends) instead of products.

THE LOVE NEEDS

Humans need love and affection all through their life, but especially in the first three years. The love needs are very important because failing to satisfy them can have serious consequences. Indeed, most theories of psycho-pathology have stressed thwarting of the love needs as basic in the picture of maladjustment and abnormal behavior. It is also important to note that the love needs involve both **receiving and giving love.** Different types of "love" can be identified, for example,: romantic love, family love, "being-love," the love of a good friend, or even loving one's job.

A major component in all types of love seems to be **intimacy.** Intimate relationships are based on uncensored, open communication, where true self-identity is revealed. This is a vulnerable state that requires maximum trust and respect. Intimate relationships may be easily lost, hard to recover, and probably infrequent in number over one's life. There are significant implications here for relationship marketing models where commercial – but psychologically intimate -- exchanges could be a source of real customer loyalty. The love needs will be discussed in detail in a later chapter.

THE ESTEEM NEEDS

Esteem from Others. These needs include: *reputation and prestige, status, fame, glory, dominance, recognition, attention, importance, and appreciation.* Especially important in this group are **dominance** needs. Dominance has received some attention in marketing (e.g., power in the channel of distribution) but plays a small role in the consumer behavior literature. This seems to contrast with real-life exchanges where dominance is a frequent goal of both exchange partners (and often plays a critical role in the success and duration of relationships).

Self-Esteem. These needs include: *strength, dignity, achievement, adequacy, mastery, competence, confidence, independence, and freedom.* It is interesting to note that when social esteem is placed before self-esteem, we can predict that many people will give up self-esteem in order to achieve esteem from others.

Ultimately, self-esteem is critically important. Maslow (1970) notes that every falling away from species values is registered in the subconscious and causes self-loathing. In a real sense, self-esteem becomes the "guardian" of the growth motives (see below) because achieving self-esteem (while gratifying the other deficiency needs) is a necessary condition for moving to a focus on growth.

In Maslow's model, self-esteem goes up whenever we perform an intrinsic behavior but self-esteem goes down when we perform extrinsic behaviors. Social-esteem goes up when we perform behaviors (intrinsic or extrinsic) that please other people and social-esteem goes down when we perform behaviors (intrinsic or extrinsic) that displease other people. The relationships between social-esteem and self-esteem are shown in Table 1.

SOCIAL ESTEEM AND SELF ESTEEM

	Intrinsic Behaviors	Extrinsic Behaviors
Approved by Others	Self Esteem **High** Social Esteem **High**	Self Esteem **Low** Social Esteem **High**
Disapproved by Others	Self Esteem **High** Social Esteem **Low**	Self Esteem **Low** Social Esteem **Low**

Table 1

LIMITATIONS TO THE DEFICIENCY NEEDS HIERARCHY

The needs hierarchy is an attempt to interpret complex human behavior through a simplified model. This requires limitations and qualifications:

Integrated Whole. Maslow identifies the need to see the individual as an integrated whole. There are many motivations as well as many other influences on behavior -- all must be considered as an integrated unit. Maslow rejected atomistic views that focused on one thing (e.g., subconscious) while assuming all else is held constant.

Possibility of Attainment. Maslow suggests that people primarily wish for things that are obtainable. As one's income rises, the wishes for cars become wishes for yachts. This suggests that wishes are the (normally obtainable) desires that lead to motivation. The relationship between wishing and motivation is strong, according to Maslow. Also, an important question to consider is what happens when wishes are suppressed (e.g., hopelessness or depression) by harsh realities (e.g., refugee camps, ghettos) or long-term inability to achieve them (e.g., illness or unemployment).

Psychological Health. Any study of motivation must also include the motivation of psychologically healthy people -- those that are meta-motivated).

Instinctoids. Maslow believed that humans do inherit behavioral tendencies (e.g., aggressiveness) in the genetic code that can be subconscious. However, he felt that for modern humans these instincts were very weak. Because of this, they can be easily overwhelmed by training or acculturation. In fact, it was because instincts are "very plastic, superficial, easily changed, easily stamped out," that it was so easy to produce "all sorts of subtle pathologies" (Maslow 1970, p. xviii). However, Maslow probably underestimated the strength of instincts which have remained strong in many modern humans.

NEUROTIC NEEDS

DEFINITION OF NEUROTIC NEEDS

Maslow discovered that when deficiency needs (D-needs) go unsatisfied – especially in the first three years of life – people develop unnatural need states. Maslow called these "neurotic" needs.

CHARACTERISTICS OF NEUROTIC NEEDS

Increased Need Activity. People who have been deprived of D-needs early in life develop ***unnaturally high*** need states. For example, if love is deprived, the basic need state enlarges and the individual will need ***significantly more*** love in an attempt to satisfy the neurotic need. Note that this is the opposite of growth toward ***functional autonomy*** because adults with neurotic needs require large amounts of perceived love (which only other people can give).

Persistence of the Need Past the Normal Period of Time. Essentially this means that adults will act "childish," and continue to seek large amounts of the deprived need from others -- often all through life. Even when the basic need is adequately gratified, people with neurotic needs will continue to seek additional reinforcement.

Less Satisfaction from Need Gratification. Gratification of the neurotic needs does not carry the positive reinforcement value that comes with the satisfaction of a normal need. Usually, only tension reduction occurs (though this still can be of benefit to the person). This makes it extremely difficult to satisfy neurotic needs and thus progress up the hierarchy to meta-motivation.

ORIGINS OF NEUROTIC NEEDS

Neurotic needs are caused primarily by need deprivation. However, Maslow (1970) found neurotic needs can be based on any of the following:

Deprivation. When basic needs are under-satisfied the result is need deprivation which can create neurotic needs. Indeed, need deprivation, ***especially***

in the first three years, was undoubtedly the major cause of adult neuroses and psychoses in Maslow's time.

Affluence. When basic needs are over-satisfied, the person may become "spoiled" and take need satisfaction for granted. Maslow referred to this as ***psychological affluence*** – e.g., children being over-loved, adored, and worshiped. This causes a variety of neuroses in adults including the mocking of basic need satisfiers, the devaluing of basic needs, resistance to growth, and a reduction in striving effort. Similar to deprivation, affluence can create adult neurotic needs for excessive attention, love, etc.

Satisfaction. When needs are satisfied, Maslow found that there was 1) a reduction in the drive state, and 2) an accompanying positive emotion (satisfaction) – sometimes, and 3) a brief period of rest or relaxation. In most cases, when needs are satisfied, there is minimal chance for neurotic needs to emerge. However, satisfaction of basic needs can create negative dynamics. According to Maslow, these include disdain for the old satisfiers, loss of appetite, boredom, etc. Thus, while need satisfaction minimizes the probability of neurotic needs, it does not totally prevent them.

PROBABILITY OF DEVELOPING NEUROTIC NEEDS

Whether neurotic needs develop depends on whether the basic D-needs are under-satisfied, satisfied, or over-satisfied. If we consider the preconditions (5), and the basic D-needs (8) there are 13 universal impulses (or "near universals") that form the foundation of human motivation and personality. Therefore, we can consider the individual's demand for each of these 13 end goals. For example, person A may have an unusually high need for love but a low need for curiosity. Person B may have strong hunger needs (poor family) but low belongingness needs (large family).

For each of the 13 demand functions, there is a corresponding level of perceived supply -- the amount of food, belongingness, freedom, etc. that the person receives. Suppose person A receives the right amount of love and therefore is well adjusted (neurotic love needs do not emerge). Suppose person B cannot find much food as a child (e.g., large but poor family) and therefore, develops a neurotic need for food (which causes overeating as an adult). Suppose person C gets too much love (e.g., only child) and develops a neurotic need (for extra love as an adult) based on over-satisfaction.

Each of the 13 end goals can be under-satisfied, satisfied, or over-satisfied. If the need is under-satisfied or over-satisfied, neurotic needs emerge and remain. It appears unlikely that a person can evolve to adulthood and receive the perfect level of need satisfaction (i.e., not too much, not to little) for all 13 universals. Thus, virtually all adults have neurotic needs. As Maslow (1970, p. xxv-xxvi) observed "one becomes saddened by the ease with which human potentiality can be destroyed or repressed, so that a fully-human person can seem like a miracle, so improbable a happening as to be awe inspiring"

NEUROTIC NEEDS AND MARKETING

Understanding Consumers' Neurotic Needs. Because the majority of human beings have some neurotic needs, we can expect many consumer behaviors to be influenced or driven by them. Consequently, understanding consumer neurotic needs should become an important area of consumer research, since it is directly related to topics such as: shoplifting, consumer addictions, impulsive buyer behavior, over-consumption, profane consumption, sacred consumption, prohibition of consumption, etc.

Impulsive Behavior. It seems likely that many impulsive behaviors are driven by neurotic needs. With the likelihood of need deprivation and the resulting inability to achieve full satisfaction, consumers can be easily encouraged to over-purchase and over-consume -- even when they consciously know that the behavior will not bring them positive utility in the long run. For example, feelings of guilt after eating an extra meal often outweigh the pleasure that was obtained by eating when not hungry.

Down-Leveling. Note that once neurotic needs emerge, they may cause a tendency to down-level. For example, when people find it impossible to satisfy neurotic needs, they may shift their attention and try to reduce tension or seek pleasure from the satisfaction of lower needs. Thus, if a person is rejected in love s/he may switch to eating as a way to release frustration or seek short-term sensory pleasure. This is problematic because it stops progression up the hierarchy.

Also, there are occasional up-leveling tendencies after neurotic needs occur. Sometimes when people find their lower needs at risk or unsatisfied, they may seek security from the satisfaction of higher needs. For example, repressed people may focus their attention on freedom, justice, and order rather than security and safety.

Leadership Behaviors. It's common to see managers who are not open to subordinates' suggestions or are uncaring toward those they manage. Though leadership research has identified the character traits of charismatic leaders, it is very difficult, if not impossible, for managers to change themselves into the desired type. Understanding managers' neurotic needs, which often have a heavy but sometime unconscious influence on their leadership style, can help managers change their behaviors and become more humanistic leaders (i.e., provide their people with more valuable rewards).

CONCLUSION

In this chapter we have examined the all important deficiency needs in detail. They are important because they represent the first needs encountered on the path up the pyramid. Also, the vast majority of humans must satisfy these needs on a recurring basis making them a natural target for much advertising and promotion. If you carefully observe advertising claims you will note that most are directly related to the deficiency needs of consumers. Unfortunately, there are serious consequences if the D-needs are under-satisfied or over-satisfied. In either case neurotic needs develop and produce unnaturally large drive states. It is very important to understand neurotic need states because virtually everyone you work with will have some. It is easy to over-react in such instances and, thereby, demonstrate your own neurotic needs. If you can develop a successful strategy for coping with the neurotic needs of key accounts you will achieve more pleasure and less pain at work and in life.

EXPERIMENT 10.1
NEUROTIC NEEDS

Identify two key accounts who have a neurotic need. For each person:

1. Describe the neurotic need.

2. Explain how the neurotic need was developed – deprivation or affluence.

3. Describe how the neurotic need affects this person's exchange relationships.

4. Is the neurotic need related to any self-destructive behavior?

5. In your opinion, what would be the most effective way to reduce the neurotic need?

ELABORATION QUESTIONS

- What restrictions should be placed on people's hedonistic tendencies?

- Can the self-esteem of your key accounts influence you own self-esteem?

- What factors cause people to seek higher needs before the lower needs are satisfied?

- What are some of the signs that a job recruit has neurotic needs?

- Identify some advertising campaigns that exploit neurotic needs.

- How are neurotic needs cured or reduced?

- Which of the preconditions or deficiency needs has brought you the most satisfaction? The most dissatisfaction?

- What percentage of the time are you at homeostasis?

- Give some examples of products and services that are substitute drive objects.

- Are you more interested in social esteem or self-esteem at this time in your life?

- Are neurotic needs based on deprivation worse than neurotic needs based on affluence?

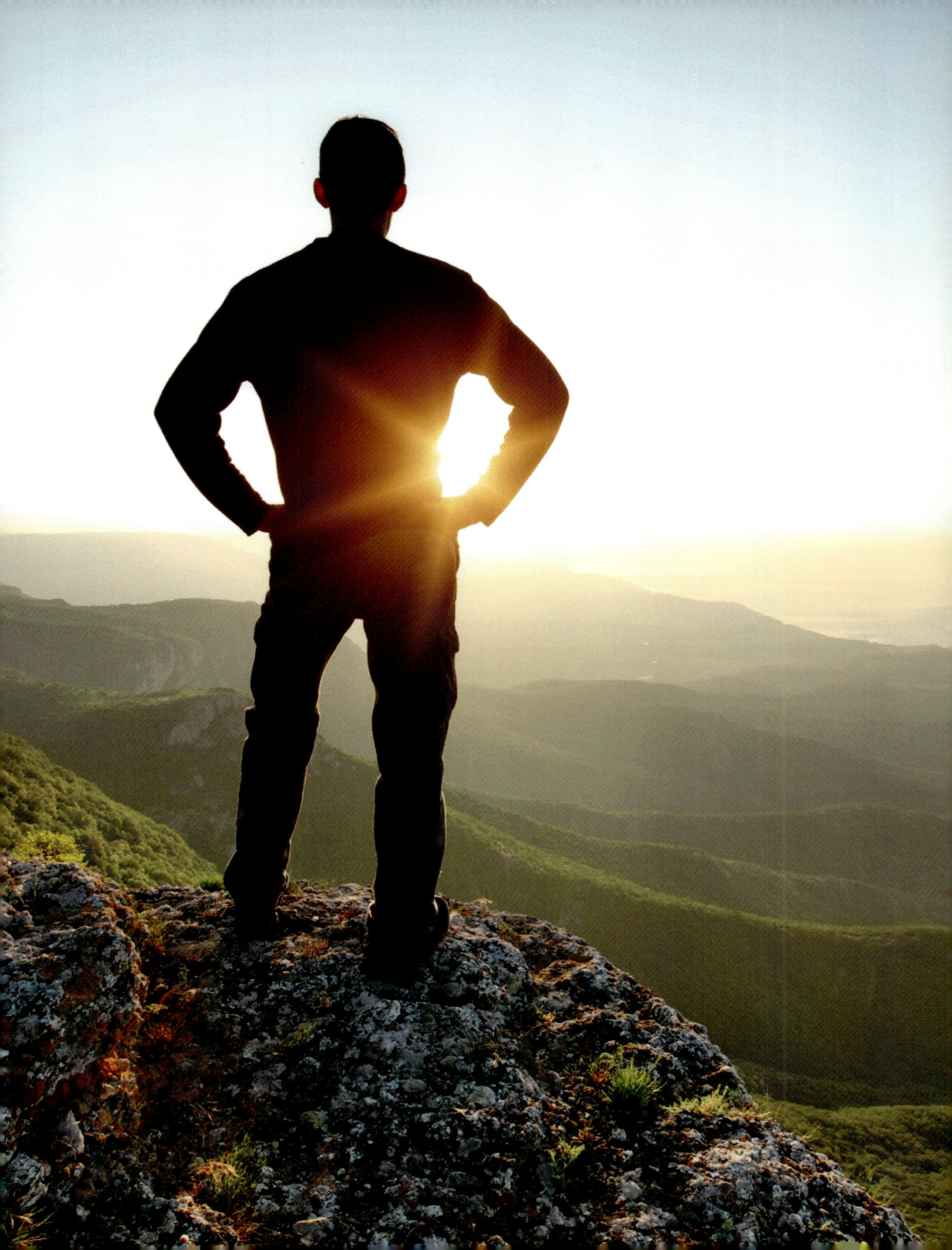

CHAPTER 11
MOTIVATION III: GROWTH NEEDS

GROWTH NEEDS AND META-MOTIVATION	**11.1**
Meta-needs and Meta-motives	11.1
Growth Needs (Higher) vs. Deficiency Needs (Lower)	11.1
Meta-Pathologies	11.3
Summary of Meta-Motives	11.3
Conceptual Definitions of Meta-Motives	11.3
Requirements for Meta-Motivation	11.5
Growth Failure	11.7
Meta-Motivation and Creativity	11.7
THE EXTENDED HIERARCHY OF NEEDS AND MOTIVES	**11.7**
LIFE'S JOURNEY	**11.7**
Preconditions for Need Satisfaction	11.8
Deficiency Needs	11.8
Neurotic Needs	11.8
Growth Needs	11.8
**EXPERIMENT 11.1	ADDING VALUE TO A KEY ACCOUNT**	**11.9**
ELABORATION QUESTIONS	**11.10**

GUIDING QUESTIONS

- What are the growth needs?
- How do growth needs differ from deficiency needs?
- Who is most likely to focus on growth?
- How many people focus on growth?
- What are the consequences of achieving growth?
- What happens to people who never focus on growth?
- What are the meta-motives and how are they defined?
- What are the requirements to achieve a focus on growth?
- Why is career choice so important in achieving growth?
- What are peak experiences?
- What causes "human diminution?"
- What is the relationship between growth and creativity?
- What are the important components in the full hierarchy of needs and motives model?
- According to Maslow, what is the purpose of human life?

GROWTH NEEDS AND META-MOTIVATION

META-NEEDS AND META-MOTIVES

*If the deficiency needs are suitably fulfilled, people become motivated by other, higher motives called meta-motives (also called "Being-cognition" or "B-values"). Meta-motives are universal values (to which all people aspire) that are thought to be "a-cultural" and are instinctual in nature, falling along the same biological continuum as the basic needs. While basic motives are based on **deficiency** needs, meta-motives are caused by **growth** needs. The process of satisfying meta-needs is known as self-actualization. After many years of study, Maslow concluded that all humans are born with growth needs. However, these needs remain largely dormant until the deficiency needs are reasonably fulfilled. Specifically, before the meta-needs become active a person must ". . . have a feeling of belongingness and rootedness, [have] satisfied their love needs, have friends and feel loved and love worthy, have status and place in life and respect from other people, and have a reasonable feeling of worth and self-respect." (Maslow 1971, p. 289)*

Obviously, it is difficult for most people to achieve this status because most never reasonably satisfy the preconditions, deficiency needs, and neurotic needs. Indeed, Maslow found that only a very small percentage of people reach self-actualization (about 1%). Perhaps that is why this part of Maslow's theory has been largely ignored. However, it is critical to remember that self-actualization is an evolving, never-ending process by which humans continue to strive. This aspirational or striving quality has significant implications for how marketing views the exchange-of-value process.

GROWTH NEEDS (HIGHER) VS. DEFICIENCY NEEDS (LOWER)

Equal Potency. According to Maslow, the meta-needs are "equally" potent and cannot be arranged in a hierarchy like the D-needs.

Deprivation of Deficiency Needs and Emergence of Growth Needs. Higher needs may occasionally emerge after either a voluntary or forced period of deficiency need deprivation.

Increasing Strength. Unlike the deficiency needs that grow weaker (temporarily) when satisfied, Maslow discovered that growth needs tend to get stronger the more they are fed. This hypothesis possesses significant implications for key marketing constructs such as: satisfaction, desire, expectations, delight, regret, frustration, loyalty, etc., as we will discuss later.

Higher Needs Evolved Later. Higher needs are later evolutionary developments. The higher the need, the fewer life forms share it with us. Self-actualization is the only need that other animals do not display (i.e., it is uniquely human).

Growth Needs - Travel

Higher Needs Occur As Humans Age. Higher needs are later ontogenetic developments - they occur as people age and develop. This is a key consideration and must be taken into account when analyzing consumer growth. Younger consumers can be expected to focus on their deficiency needs – only after they are reasonably fulfilled will they focus on growth.

Higher Needs Are less Common and less Urgent. The higher the need the less imperative it is for survival, the longer gratification can be postponed, and the easier it is for the need to disappear completely. Nonetheless, all normal individuals are born with an innate orientation to strive for meta-motivation, ranging from minor episodic occurrences (most common) to fairly continuous self actualized behavior (rare). Indeed, Maslow noted that almost all humans have peak experiences when meta-motives are achieved (i.e., latent meta-needs do occasionally surface). In this respect we can define the **Meta-Motivation Quotient** (MMQ), as the proportion of total motivation accounted for by the meta-motives.

It is interesting to speculate what this quotient would look like when plotted over time. One could hypothesize that the MMQ shows a declining gradient as enculturation occurs and D-needs are satisfied. However, as people age the MMQ should start to grow – if D-needs are satisfied. How far and how fast it grows depends on the environment and the individual's character. Thus, the MMQ may be expected to range from minor aspirational occurrences to fairly continuous self-actualized behavior (though this is rare about 1% of the population in Maslow's time). This distinction is important for marketing researchers and managers because it is the higher needs that provide the greatest satisfaction.

Unfortunately, because growth needs are less pressing it has been easy for marketers to provide products and advertising messages that focus on lower, more urgent, more instantly gratifying needs. However, this comes at the expense of less urgent, but ultimately more satisfying meta-needs (Maslow 1970). This can cause individuals and societies to down-level by focusing excessively on lower needs (e.g., materialism).

Higher Needs are More Healthy. Living at higher need levels is healthier and more efficient. Indeed, betraying these intrinsic values produces intrinsic guilt of the "real" biological self.

Higher Needs Produce More Satisfaction. Gratifying higher needs produces greater satisfaction, happiness, and a fuller life. People who have gratified lower and higher needs prefer higher needs. However, the satisfaction literature is focused mainly on the lower needs. This may explain some of the mixed results regarding the satisfaction construct. To the extent that marketing can help consumers become more aware of, aspire to, and ultimately, satisfy their growth needs, it can provide consumers with a more intense, longer lasting, and ultimately, healthier kind of satisfaction (i.e., "meta – satisfaction").

Higher Needs Have More Preconditions. The deficiency needs are "prepotent" to the meta-needs (i.e., all lower needs must be reasonably satisfied). However, this is not an absolute maxim, but rather only a "statistical" statement of varying degree, depending on the individual, the society/culture, the economic infrastructure, etc. In general, higher needs require better environmental conditions to make them possible. While deficiency need satisfaction requires the five preconditions, growth need satisfaction requires these preconditions plus the reasonable gratification of deficiency and neurotic needs.

Higher Needs Are Pro-social. Pursuit of higher needs have positive civic and social consequences. In fact, Brooker (1976) discovered a correlation between socially conscious behavior and self-actualization and noted that individuals who exhibited higher self-actualization scores were also more likely to purchase "ecology-related products [which] implies concern for the long-term survival of a healthy environment." With the recent events surrounding corporate dishonesty and corruption, it would seem that the pro-social component of meta-motivation could add significant value.

Higher Needs Reveal Self-Identity. Pursuit and gratification of higher needs lead to greater individualism and self-identity. Self-expression is especially critical at this stage as meta-motivation causes the self to enlarge to include new and growth-based elements.

META-PATHOLOGIES

When a meta-need goes unsatisfied too long it produces a spiritual deficiency in the person, which in turn, produces a meta-pathology (i.e., a sickness of the spirit or soul). Examples of meta-pathologies in marketing include bate and switch tactics, hard-selling, corporate collusion scenarios, predatory pricing schemes,"public relations" spin-doctoring, etc.

SUMMARY OF META-MOTIVES

A summary of the meta-motives (Maslow 1968, 1970) are listed in Table 1 along with their associated meta-pathologies which occur if the meta-motives are not fulfilled. Note that the meta-motives are **not** arranged in a hierarchy of potency like the deficiency needs.

CONCEPTUAL DEFINITIONS OF META-MOTIVES

Truth. Truth refers to sincerity and honesty in an individual's actions and words. It involves a desire to seek and accept the truth about oneself, others, and the world and accuracy in description or portrayal. The truth reflects the body of real things, events, and facts as can be scientifically verified and/or corroborated by a majority of scholars (e.g., fundamental reality).

Justice. Justice refers to the feeling or the quality of fairness (e.g., being just and impartial). Self-oriented justice refers to a person's desire to be fair and impartial to other people and society. People seeking justice try to treat others with fairness even at the cost of their own personal interests.

Beauty/Art. Beauty is the quality of being pleasing to the senses or appealing to the mind or spirit. Art is a typical source of beauty; however, other objects or events may also possess the value of beauty if they are of aesthetic value. People who have the meta-motive of beauty are not only capable of noticing and appreciating beauty, but also like to take time and effort to create things and environments that are beautiful.

Goodness. Goodness refers to the act of putting other people's needs ahead of your own. It is the desire to give value to others -- unconditionally. Examples include: a willingness to help others grow, receiving value from others with gratitude, being tolerant, and possessing pro-social values.

Playfulness. Playfulness refers to a fondness for having fun and playing games with others. An individual who values joviality and attempts to maintain a sense of humor and lightheartedness exhibits playfulness as does someone who strives to maintain a healthy balance between work and recreation/leisure related activities. Playfulness includes an ability to

Dare to be Different

SUMMARY OF META-MOTIVES

Meta-Motive	Description	Associated Meta-Pathology
Truth	Honesty, reality, simplicity, richness, beauty, pure, clean and unaltered, completeness	Dishonesty, distrust, cynicism, suspicion
Justice	Fairness, orderliness, lawfulness, "oughtness"	Insecurity, anger, cynicism, lawlessness, selfishness
Beauty	Rightness, form, aliveness, simplicity, richness, wholeness, perfection, completion, uniqueness, honesty	Vulgarity, specific unhappiness, tension, fatigue
Goodness	Rightness, desirability, "oughtness", justice, benevolence, honesty	Selfishness, hatred, repulsion
Playfulness	Fun, joy, amusement, gaiety, humor, exuberance, effortlessness	Grimness, depression, loss of ability to enjoy
Uniqueness	Idiosyncrasy, individuality, non-comparability, novelty	Feeling interchangeable, anonymous, not really needed
Perfection	Necessity, just-right-ness, just-so-ness, inevitability, suitability, justice, completeness, "oughtness"	Discouragement, hopelessness, nothing to work for
Unity	Wholeness, integration, tendency to one-ness, connectedness, simplicity	Loss of connectedness, either/or thinking, arbitrariness
Order	Organization, structure, order	Loss of safety and predictability, tension, vigilance
Comprehensiveness	Richness, complexity, intricacy	Depression, uneasiness, loss of interest in world
Aliveness	Process, non-deadness, spontaneity, self-regulation, full-functioning	Deadness, robotizing, boredom, loss of zest for life
Self-sufficiency	Autonomy, independence, not-needing-other-than-self-in-order-to-be-itself, self-determining, environment-transcending, separateness, living by its own laws	Dependence on others
Meaningfulness	True value, understanding, rightful order	Despair, senselessness of life
Simplicity	Honesty, nakedness, essentiality, abstract, essential, skeletal structure	Confusion, disconnectedness, disintegration
Effortlessness	Ease, lack of strain, striving or difficulty, grace, perfection, beautiful functioning	Fatigue, strain, gracelessness
Completion	Finishing, bringing to an end, closure	Hopelessness, no use trying, incompleteness

Table 1

Effortlessness and Self-Sufficiency

comprehend that hedonism, pleasure seeking, and self-expressive behavior are important to one's overall psychological health, creativity, and productivity.

Uniqueness. Uniqueness is the quality of being different and uncommon. A unique person is divergent from the majority by possessing unusual talents or personality traits. Uniqueness is an important part of our self-identity and individuality. People possessing uniqueness seek to achieve differentiation from other people.

Perfection. Perfection is the feeling or the quality of being perfect (e.g., free from fault or defect). Self-oriented perfection involves striving to attain impeccability in one's endeavors as well as striving to avoid failures. Lack of perfection may lead to discouragement and hopelessness.

Unity. Unity refers to belonging to something greater than oneself and a feeling of being connected to important parts of the world. This involves understanding the natural order of things and your place therein. Unity can be achieved by accessing the meta-motives with others or creating a Level III bond with anyone or anything.

Order. Order reflects the laws and principles that organize and rule the world. People seeking order are able and willing to detect the underlying regularity beneath the surface. They seek to learn the organizing principles that connect the elements of the world together. By seeking order, people gain a better understanding of the world and therefore, the feeling of control. Lack of order results in wariness due to a loss of safety and predictability.

Comprehensiveness. Comprehensiveness refers to a totality of reinforcement. Individuals exhibiting this trait satisfy all needs – including the growth needs. People who exhibit comprehensiveness can solve a variety of problems and have a richness of reinforcement.

Aliveness. Aliveness refers to being full of energy and vigor and would be typified by an individual who displays a zest for, and interest in, life. It is the quality of being active or animated, highly engaged, full of activity, with a sense of excitement.

Self-Sufficiency. Self-sufficiency refers to an ability to maintain oneself without the help of other people. It also involves the ability to satisfy one's own needs. Essentially, self-sufficiency involves the pursuit and achievement of ***functional autonomy.***

Meaningfulness. Meaningfulness refers to an ability to relate past experiences to future problems. This includes the ability to organize and elaborate (Level III value) to produce deep understanding. This trait also reflects an ability to resolve conflicts and inconsistencies as well as knowing and achieving one's purpose in life.

Simplicity. Simplicity is the quality of being concise and essential. This meta-motive is seen in Eastern philosophy, especially Taoism. It means simplifying life by getting rid of unnecessary possessions and memories. People with the meta-motive of simplicity will not be disturbed or perplexed even in complex situations. Instead, they seek the simple yet essential elements and ignore noises and less valuable information.

Effortlessness. Effortlessness refers to the performance of activities with grace and ease. It is by-product of self-expressive behavior, whereby the striving process (although a highly effortful undertaking) is perceived as fun and effortless (e.g., a labor of love). An individual displays effortlessness when s/he performs behaviors with the appearance of little effort.

Completion. Completion refers to the feeling or the quality of being complete, including all necessary parts, elements, steps, etc. This includes the desire to attain closure and the resolve to finish a task that has been started.

REQUIREMENTS FOR META-MOTIVATION

To achieve meta-motivation people must sufficiently satisfy their preconditions, deficiency, and neurotic needs. However, satisfying the lower needs do not guarantee people will move on to meta-motivation. Indeed, for most people, the meta-motives remain largely dormant even after the lower needs are satisfied. Maslow referred to this as the "weak link" in his theory. Thus, fulfilling the deficiency needs is a **necessary** but **insufficient** condition for meta-motivation to occur.

The other factor that determines whether a person will advance to meta-motivation is the individual's ***character.*** Character is determined by how the deficiency needs are satisfied and by the strength of one's "inner voice." The following is a list of character traits that are needed to reach meta-motivation.

1. **Beloved Occupation.** All meta-motivated people are devoted to some calling or beloved work. Less evolved persons use work as a means to satisfy basic needs while self-actualizers use work to express powerful intrinsic values. Inner requiredness ("I want to") coincides with external requiredness ("I must"). It is interesting to consider the idea of finding one's "beloved occupation" in relation to the typical college placement service and the level of effort expended by students during the interview process.

2. **Elaborative Learner.** The person must absorb completely what is to be learned. In devotion to this goal the individual gives up his/her defenses and redirects the energy to learning everything available about his/her chosen path.

3. **Growth Choices.** The person must make growth choices rather than regressive choices. Regressive choices are usually based on fear and movement toward what is safe and known. Growth choices involve personal challenge and moving toward the unknown.

4. **Honesty.** The person must be honest rather than dishonest. We must accept the responsibility for being truthful and any uncertainty it causes.

5. **Courage.** The person must be courageous. We must express our meta-motives honestly, even if doing so is embarrassing or unpopular.

6. **Self-Improvement.** The person must be dedicated to improving the self. This entails using one's intelligence to realize the possibilities that are available. For this, the person must be devoted to doing something that (1) s/he really wants to do, (2) at which s/he really wants to be successful, and (3) at which s/he can succeed. The person must want to be the best s/he can be at this endeavor.

7. **Elimination of Defense Mechanisms.** The person must identify existing defense mechanisms (selective defenses and defense structures) and act to give them up. The unpleasantness associated with defense mechanisms must be eliminated before meta-motivation can occur.

8. **True Self Emerges.** The person must listen to the true self, and must let this self emerge. This requires the individual to act the way s/he really feels and not to be guided by social rules. We should look deep inside ourselves and allow the true self (i.e., the **biological intrinsic self**) to emerge. Resistance to total enculturation is another example of this trait.

9. **Peak Experiences.** The person must strive for peak experiences. Peak experience is "a generalization for the best moments of the human being, for the happiest moments of life, for experiences of ecstasy, rapture, bliss, of the greatest joy" (Maslow 1971, p.101). These are moments of ecstasy, which usually include an element of surprise and/or attainment. Such experiences provide pure joy and irreversibly alter the character of the individual in a positive way. Maslow believed that most people have a few peak experiences in life, but for the majority this is as close as they will ever come to self-actualization. In Maslow's model the purpose of life is to strive for growth and peak experiences play a major role by validating that growth has taken place.

True Self

GROWTH FAILURE

For humans to reach meta-motivation, they have to encounter "good preconditions." For example, they must have need-satisfying parents (and friends), be raised in a healthy culture, not get to much or too little of the D-needs, etc. As Maslow (1970, p. xxv-xxvi) observed:

> "These physical, chemical, biological, interpersonal, and cultural conditions matter for the individual finally to the extent that they do or do not supply him with the basic human necessities and "Rights" which permit him to become strong enough, and person enough, to take over his own fate. As one studies these preconditions, one becomes saddened by the ease with which human potentiality can be destroyed or repressed, so that a fully-human person can seem like a miracle, so improbable a happening as to be awe inspiring."

Maslow (1967) applied a medical/clinical model to aid in the understanding of what impedes a human being's achievement of personal growth. He introduced two concepts: **full-humanness**, and **human diminution.** Being "fully human" allows one to satisfy the lower needs and ultimately achieve the growth needs. Human diminution occurs when the lower needs are not met, neurotic needs develop, and a focus on growth is never realized. This may lead to spiritual disorders such as loss of meaning, doubts about the goals of life, grief and anger over a lost love, seeing life in a negative way, loss of courage or hope, despair over the future, low self-esteem, etc. Human diminution also makes it more difficult for people to detect their inner signals and/or answer them. Maslow discovered that in some cases, human diminution can be reversed by satisfying the unmet needs but in other cases, it is not reversible.

META-MOTIVATION AND CREATIVITY

Maslow (1970, p. 55) suggests a strong relationship between creativity and meta-motivation noting:

> "My feeling is that the concept of creativeness and the concept of a healthy, self-actualizing, fully-human person seem to be coming closer and closer together, and may perhaps turn out to be the same thing."

This is true because creativity is usually defined as **divergent** ideas that are **relevant.** However, simply being divergent or different is not the same as being creative (which requires relevance). It is more accurate to view both divergence and relevance as necessary for a person to lead a healthy, self-actualizing, and fully-human life. This is because relevant divergence stimulates positive growth which is basically the same thing as self-actualization.

It is important to note that Maslow differentiates two types of creativity. **Primary creativeness** comes out of the unconscious and is the source of new discovery. Maslow called this "real novelty"and it is equivalent to **divergence**. **Secondary creativeness** is based on logic, common sense, and reasoning and is equivalent to **relevance** component of creativity.

Maslow also mentions the importance of effectively **managing creative people** (a common task in marketing). He suggests permitting employees to be more individualistic in organizations. Employees should be given a certain level of freedom and the chance to express their own thoughts.

Finally, Maslow attributed lack of creativity (in part) to the fear of change. Some people simply repress everything unconscious or uncontrollable in order to be sure that the dangerous portions of the subconscious do not get out. One solution he offered is to force people to confront novelty and to improvise.

THE EXTENDED HIERARCHY OF NEEDS AND MOTIVES

We have now examined Maslow's model of human motivation in detail. The model is far more complex and profound than the simple five or six stage pyramid that is often used to represent it. Specifically, we expanded the list of needs to include the preconditions, the deficiency needs, the neurotic needs, and the growth needs. A summary of Maslow's complete model (i.e., the extended hierarchy) is presented in Figure 1.

LIFE'S JOURNEY

When born, we are 100% dependent on others for the satisfaction of our deficiency needs. Even as we age, we need things that only other humans can give. The first three years are critical in the formation of the individual's character. A major part of the personality is determined by how many neurotic needs are developed during youth.

If the preconditions or D-needs are under-satisfied or over-satisfied, neurotic needs emerge and tend to remain. It appears unlikely that a person can evolve to adulthood and have the perfect level of need satisfaction (not too little, not to much) for all the preconditions, deficiency needs, and growth needs. Therefore, virtually all adults have neurotic needs and the resulting pathologies. Given this scenario it is not

EXTENDED HIERARCHY OF NEEDS AND MOTIVES

PRECONDITIONS FOR NEED SATISFACTION

1. Humans are striving organisms
2. Humans must be free
3. Humans are curious
4. Humans have a need to know and understand
5. Humans have a strong need for expression

DEFICIENCY NEEDS

6. Humans seek reinforcement and have hedonistic tendencies
7. Humans seek satisfaction of homeostatic needs (food, sleep, water, sex, etc.)
8. Humans seek physical safety
9. Humans seek psychological security (cognitive consistency)
10. Humans seek belongingness
11. Humans seek love
12. Humans seek respect from others
13. Humans seek self-esteem

NEUROTIC NEEDS

14. Neurotic needs related to the preconditions
15. Neurotic deficiency needs

GROWTH NEEDS

16. Truth
17. Justice
18. Beauty,
19. Goodness
20. Playfulness
21. Uniqueness
22. Perfection
23. Unity
24. Order
25. Comprehensiveness
26. Aliveness
27. Self-Sufficiency
28. Meaningfulness
29. Simplicity
30. Completion
31. Effortlessness

Figure 1

surprising that Maslow found only 1% of humans were able to focus on growth.

This is perhaps why the meta-needs have been neglected in the marketing literature. However, as people in a society are increasingly able to trust that their lower level needs will be met, they should naturally begin to explore their higher needs. This suggests that in the future we can expect an increasing number of consumers to reach a focus on growth and a significant proportion of such activities will come from using products and services (i.e., meta-consumption").

Maslow concluded that the purpose of life is to strive for growth so we can reach the ultimate goal of functional autonomy, whereby an individual can satisfy his/her own needs. This is possible because after years of satisfying the deficiency needs (i.e., getting the needed things from other people), a person builds immunity to deprivation and can exist for extended periods of time without receiving love, if that person feels worthy of love. This frees the individual to pursue growth and unfettered creativity in an attempt to meta-motivate. For an individual to be successful at this endeavor: (1) the preconditions, deficiency needs, and neurotic needs must be reasonably satisfied, and (2) the individual must have developed a self-worthy (as opposed to self-important) character while satisfying the lower needs.

EXPERIMENT 11.1
ADDING VALUE TO A KEY ACCOUNT

1. Select a key account who is having problems and ask them for help completing a motivation assignment.

2. Go through the extended Maslow Model on pages 11.13 - 11.14 with them to identify which preconditions, D-needs, neurotic needs, or growth needs are not being satisfied.

3. Select a lower need that is unsatisfied and try to come up with an idea for how you could help them satisfy this need.

4. Select a growth need that is unsatisfied and try to come up with an idea for how you could help them satisfy this need.

5. Implement your ideas and summarize if you added value to your relationship with this key account.

6. Did your key account's problems get better?

ELABORATION QUESTIONS

- Estimate your MMQ and compare it to your friends and family.

- Do you agree or disagree with Maslow's conclusion about the purpose of human life? Why?

- What percentage of people your age focus on growth as opposed to the D-needs?

- Describe some of your peak experiences.

- Which of the meta-motives are most important to you at this time in your life?

- How many of the "requirements for meta-motivation" do you currently possess?

- When are you most creative?

- Where are your key accounts in the hierarchy? Can you use the model to identify their main needs and therefore, how to add meaningful value to your relationships with them?

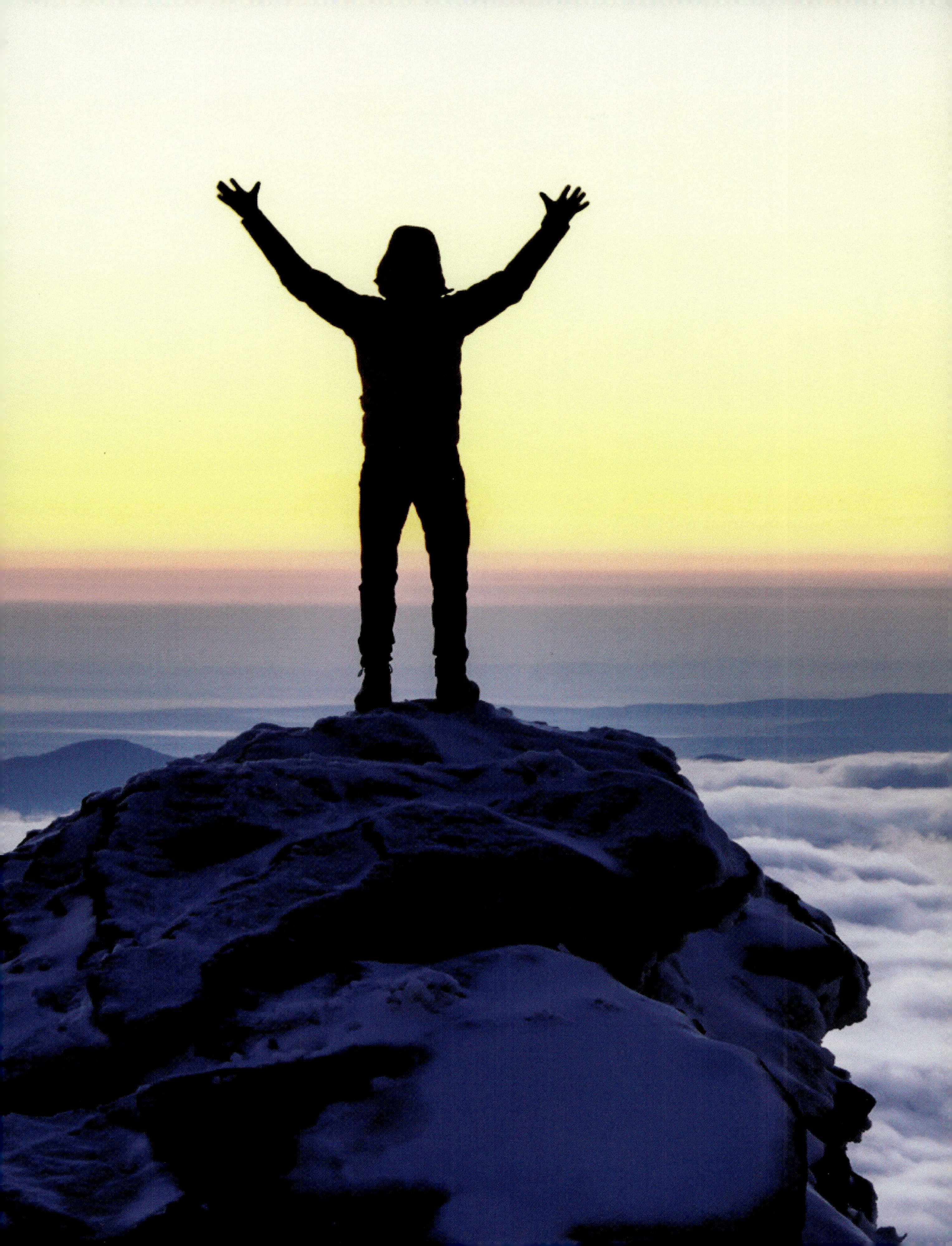

CHAPTER 12
MOTIVATION IV: SUBCONSCIOUS MOTIVATION

INTRODUCTION — 12.1
THE CONSCIOUS, SUBCONSCIOUS, AND UNCONSCIOUS MIND — 12.1
   The Conscious Mind — 12.1
   The Subconscious Mind — 12.1
   The Unconscious Mind — 12.1
   Communicating with the Subconscious and Unconscious Mind — 12.2
SUBCONSCIOUS MOTIVATION — 12.3
   Frustration — 12.3
   Repressing Frustrated Energy — 12.3
   The Frustration Pool — 12.4
   The Guilt Pool — 12.4
   The Fear Pool — 12.4
   Releasing Frustrated Energy — 12.5
   Automation of Coping Techniques — 12.6
   Cycles of Frustration — 12.7
   Consequences of Frustration — 12.7
   Implications of Frustration — 12.8
CONCLUSION — 12.8
EXPERIMENT 12.1 | REDUCING FRUSTRATION — 12.9
ELABORATION QUESTIONS — 12.10

GUIDING QUESTIONS

- » What is the conscious mind?
- » What is the subconscious mind?
- » What is the unconscious mind?
- » How do the subconscious and unconscious minds manifest themselves?
- » What is subconscious motivation?
- » What is frustrated energy?
- » Where does frustration come from?
- » Where does frustrated energy go?

- » What is the frustration pool?
- » What is the guilt pool?
- » What is the fear pool?
- » What are control structures?
- » What are defense structures?
- » What happens when defense structures become automated?
- » What are cycles of frustration?
- » How does frustrated energy influence consumer behavior?

INTRODUCTION

In the early 1900s, Sigmund Freud discovered that when drive state energy cannot be discharged in a "normal" fashion it becomes "repressed to the subconscious." In other words, if a person cannot achieve the drive object to gratify his/her needs and return to homeostasis, the body continues to produce drive state energy for extended periods of time. Freud found that this repressed frustration can seek release in behaviors not related to the original drive state, and thus, he identified the subconscious as a major cause of human behavior (especially "abnormal" or anti-social behavior).

Sigmund Freud

THE CONSCIOUS, SUBCONSCIOUS, AND UNCONSCIOUS MIND

One of the major challenges in understanding subconscious motivation is the lack of standardized definitions in this area. For our purposes we will distinguish among three levels of consciousness: the **conscious mind**, the **subconscious mind**, and the **unconscious mind**.

THE CONSCIOUS MIND

This is equivalent to the **short term memory** (STM) which we defined as the currently (but temporarily) activated memory cells. By definition we always have full awareness of the STM so the contents of the conscious mind represent our stream of consciousness (i.e., what we are currently thinking about). Indeed, the STM is a powerful tool for problem solving and need satisfaction. The key element of the conscious mind is that it has **awareness** of the information held in memory. So we can say that you are aware of all your actions that are currently in your STM and any information that you can easily retrieve from memory with no help or coaching. These "addressable" memory locations hold information that the individual has full awareness of, and access to.

THE SUBCONSCIOUS MIND

For our purposes, the subconscious mind represents the memory cells that hold information in "semi-addressable" memory locations. In these cases, the individual can still get to the information but it is difficult to do so. There are many reasons we may not be able to quickly address the memory cells. For example, they may hold information we are ashamed of and that we purposely try to repress. Or, they may hold old information that was not elaborated at encoding and has decayed over time. Often, this information is only available if we receive a "retrieval cue" that triggers our memories through spreading activation. For example, psychoanalysis includes a series of probe questions by the therapist to try and activate important information in memory. Three categories of information turn out to be strong candidates for repression by forgetting, these are: **guilt, fear,** and **frustration.**

THE UNCONSCIOUS MIND

We will define the unconscious mind as the information that is held in the long term memory (LTM) but that is no longer addressable – even with help. Some of the unconscious is emotional information that we have inherited but cannot deal with in a conscious or cognitive manner. As an example, Carl Jung believed that all humans share a "collective unconscious" which holds primal fears like the fear of snakes. In addition, information stored in specific memory locations can decay away or become inaccessible over time. As an example, over your life you have probably done some things you are ashamed of. Many of these, however, are minor things that do not warrant much conscious thought and others are bigger things that you purposely want to forget. Over time we lose the ability to address this information (i.e., we can no longer remember the details of these events) but it can still affect us because it remains in the LTM as a vague feeling.

To demonstrate the different levels of consciousness, think of someone you know that has low self-esteem. If this person were to search his/her conscious mind they would probably discover some issues related to guilt, fear, and frustration. If they dealt constructively with these issues their self-esteem would increase. At the next level, the person could get therapy where an analyst tries to delve into the subconscious and cue the recall of important information. If these issues were dealt with effectively, self-esteem would increase again. However, the person probably also has some vague feelings of guilt, fear, or frustration that are no longer accessible. This material is very difficult to deal with and often keeps self-esteem from reaching maximum levels. These definitions are summarized in Figure 1.

COMMUNICATING WITH THE SUBCONSCIOUS AND UNCONSCIOUS MIND

After studying these issues, Freud concluded that information below the conscious level sometimes could appear in everyday activities. These include slips-of-the-tongue, dreams, jokes and sarcasm, doodles, response to trauma, creativity, and when people are under the influence of some drugs and alcohol. To communicate with the subconscious mind Freud and his colleagues developed a series of techniques. The most famous of these was psychoanalysis (which is still actively practiced by many therapists) but also included projective tests, dream analysis, hypnosis, etc. Importantly, the information and feelings held in the subconscious and unconscious can be the source of powerful motivation. This means if we want to fully understand consumer behavior, we must understand the basic elements of subconscious motivation.

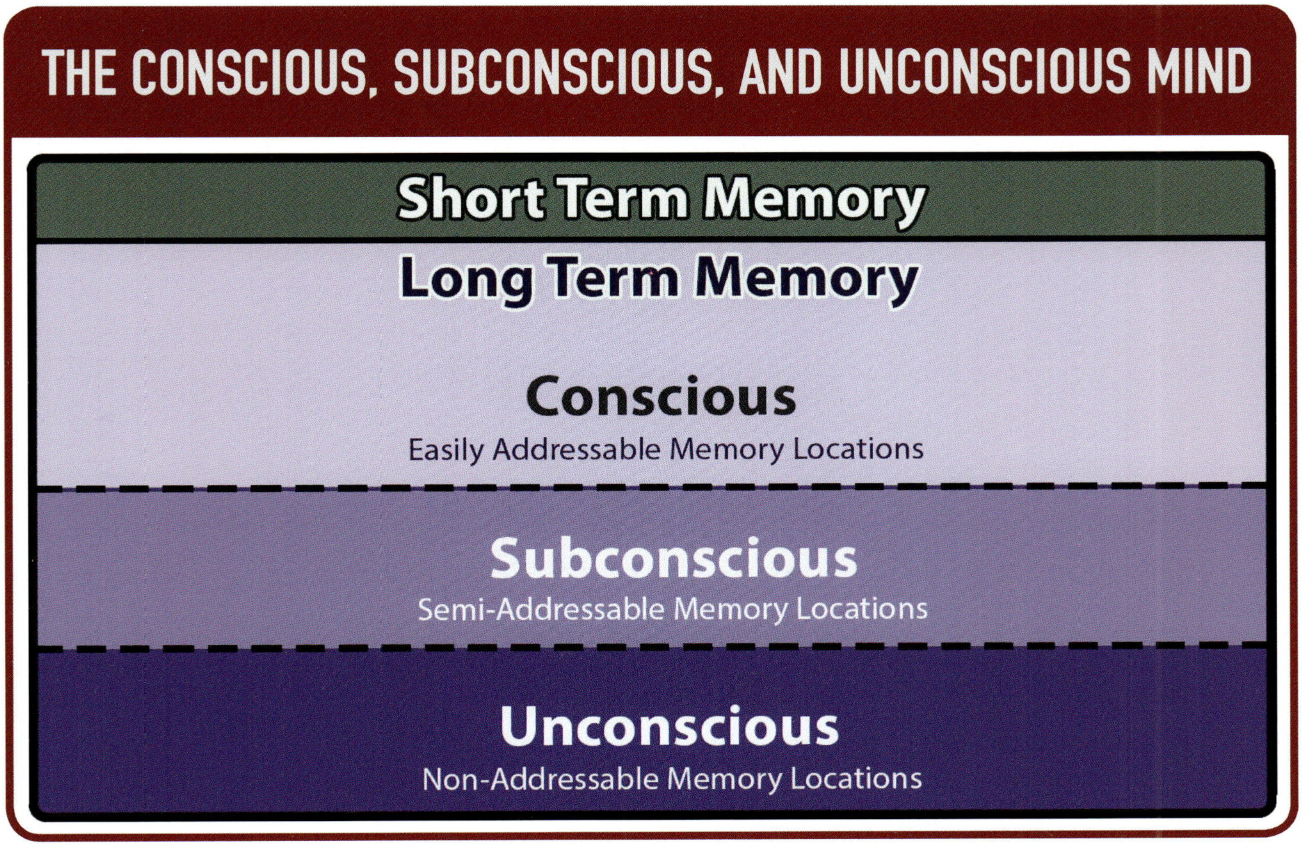

THE CONSCIOUS, SUBCONSCIOUS, AND UNCONSCIOUS MIND

Short Term Memory
Long Term Memory

Conscious
Easily Addressable Memory Locations

Subconscious
Semi-Addressable Memory Locations

Unconscious
Non-Addressable Memory Locations

Figure 1

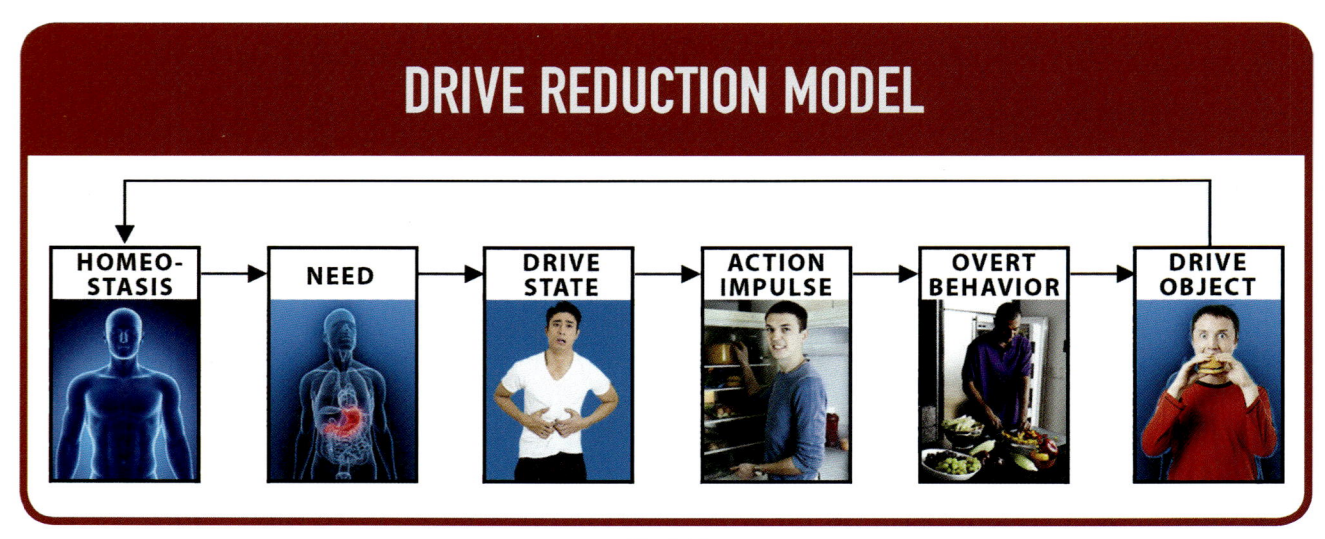

DRIVE REDUCTION MODEL

HOMEO-STASIS → NEED → DRIVE STATE → ACTION IMPULSE → OVERT BEHAVIOR → DRIVE OBJECT

Model 1

SUBCONSCIOUS MOTIVATION

FRUSTRATION

In an earlier chapter we examined satisfied feelings in the **Drive Reduction Model.**

In many instances, the individual will not be able to naturally release **all** of the drive state action impulses by achieving the drive object. This unfortunate circumstance can occur in any of the following situations:

1. The drive object is not available.
2. The drive object is available, but is self-denied (e.g., refusal to eat due to a diet).
3. The drive object does not completely satisfy the drive state (e.g., a small meal).
4. A substitute drive object fails to discharge all of the action impulses.
5. Competing drive states exist that cannot be mutually fulfilled (e.g., a very hungry person on a very strict diet).

In these situations, the individual has a problem -- **conflict** exists between what the body chemistry is urging the individual to do and what s/he can do (or chooses to do). When this happens, action impulses that are not discharged through overt behavior are described as "frustrated energy."

This frustrated condition exists because the body's chemistry cannot return to homeostasis until the action energy is released by an appropriate overt behavior and drive object. In these cases, the individual undergoes the "frustrated feelings" sequence shown by Model 2.

When frustration occurs we have two basic choices: (1) we can **repress** the frustrated energy to long term memory and deal with it later, or (2) we can **resolve** the frustration through venting or coping behaviors.

REPRESSING FRUSTRATED ENERGY

In many situations, people choose to repress frustrated energy rather than acknowledge it. This may happen for many reasons: we may be ashamed of our action impulses; we may not be able to express physiological (instinctual) action impulses verbally; we may be pressed for time; we may be in a setting where our attention is needed for other activities; we may not understand the source of the frustration; it may be socially inappropriate to deal openly with the frustration; etc.

In such cases, we can minimize our awareness of the internal tension by not paying immediate attention to it. This is accomplished by focusing the short-term memory on something else, which causes the drive state impulses to be channeled (repressed) to the unconscious (long-term memory). This strategy is equivalent to saying, "I can't do anything about this

FRUSTRATED FEELINGS SEQUENCE

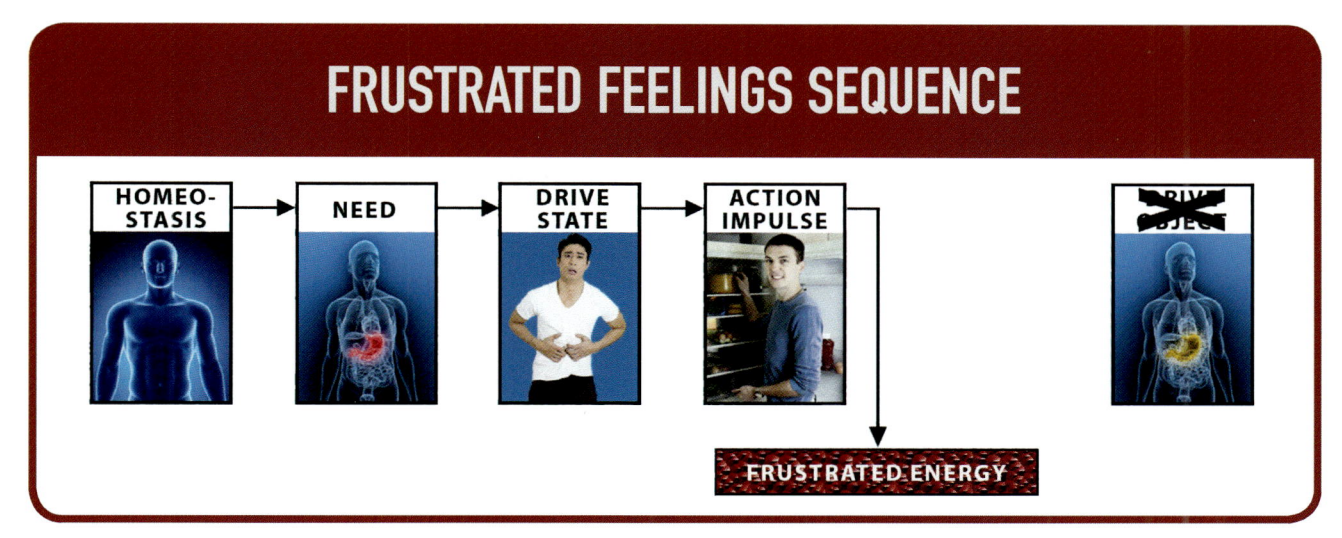

Model 2

frustration now, so I'll think about it later, or maybe forget it altogether." This temporarily eliminates the individual's awareness of the drive state urges, **but in no way eliminates the action impulses themselves.**

As a classic Freudian example, a young man who feels strong drive state pressure to engage in sex may be unable to find a willing partner. To help repress the strong urges, the man may drink alcohol to depress his central nervous system. The alcohol helps "numb" the short-term memory to the natural drive states, but **does not satisfy** the action impulses. As the man continues to drink, he might become obnoxious and start a fight. Subconsciously, the man has powerful sexual urges accumulating in the long-term memory. These urges may see a chance for expression in overt behavior by starting a physical brawl (i.e., substitute drive object) with another man. In this case, a major antisocial overt behavior (i.e., fighting) is really caused by the repression of sexual instincts, though few people would be able to understand the true motivation.

THE FRUSTRATION POOL

In this example, it is important to note that repression merely delays the ultimate venting of unreleased action impulses, but it does not eliminate the need to vent them. In this regard, the concept of the **frustration pool** becomes relevant. As frustrated action impulses from various drive states are repressed, they are added to the existing pool of frustrated energy accumulating subconsciously in the long-term memory.

This accumulating frustration also causes changes in body chemistry that may go unnoticed in the short run, if the individual is accustomed to high levels of tension. At some point, however, this pool of frustrated energy reaches its maximum threshold or "boiling point." When this happens, the individual is forced to discharge the frustration by using whatever coping techniques are available. The concept of repression and the frustration pool are shown in Model 3.

THE GUILT POOL

Frustration, occurs when our drive states cannot be satisfied with an appropriate drive object, and this accounts for much of subconscious motivation. However, we can think of a corresponding **guilt pool.** This part of long term memory holds our awareness of the shameful things we have done -- especially to other people. In Maslow's model, every shameful or selfish act is registered in the memory system -- we cannot easily eliminate our awareness of these events because they were important. It is this guilt pool that lowers self-esteem for many humans. In other words, it is difficult for us to feel self-esteem when we are aware of our lies, cheating, stealing, selfishness, etc. Indeed, the guilt pool is often the source of low self-esteem which prevents growth and creativity. It seems likely that the guilt pool can only be reduced by admission of wrong doing and some type of meaningful atonement.

FRUSTRATION AND REPRESSION

Short Term Memory

Repressed Frustration

Long Term Memory

Frustration Threshold

Model 3

THE FEAR POOL

Another section of long term memory holds our fears. Some of these are well known to us, while others are part of Jung's "collective unconscious." These are archetypes or patterns that evolved over time and are, therefore, shared by most humans. Included here would be fear of snakes, reptiles, bugs, the dark, etc. Also in the **fear pool,** are any fears that have been learned or "stamped in" through the schedule of reinforcement.

Together, the pools of frustration, guilt, and fear combine to influence many human behaviors. This is because as the pools reach their thresholds, some of the negative energy must be discharged. This often involves substitute drive objects so these motives can show up anywhere and everywhere. As Maslow (1971, p. 151) observed:

> *"Those portions of ourselves that we reject and repress (out of fear or shame) do not go out of existence. They do not die, but rather go underground. Whatever effects these underground portions of our human nature may thereafter have upon our communications tend either to be unnoticed by ourselves or else to be felt as if they were not a part of us, e.g., "I don't know what made me say such a thing,"... We must talk about the instinctoid elements of human nature, those intrinsic aspects of human nature which culture cannot kill but only repress and which continue to affect our expression - even though in a sneaky way."*

RELEASING FRUSTRATED ENERGY

Because frustration is a negative internal state, people are required to develop techniques for expressing or eliminating the unreleased action impulses. Such venting behaviors or coping techniques are especially necessary when a large amount of repressed drive state energy accumulates in the frustration pool. Sometimes people can cope with frustration in an adaptive, prosocial, creative way. For example, a man might concentrate on sports activities in order to vent sex drive action impulses that cannot be fulfilled. In this

Self-Enhancing Behavior - Exercise

case, the coping technique is prosocial and physically beneficial. We will call adaptive coping techniques **control structures.**

Often, however, people cope with frustration in maladaptive, anti-social, and self-destructive ways. We will call these coping techniques **defense structures**, because they make people defensive and/or antisocial. Some of the more common maladaptive coping techniques are:

1. Depression and Moodiness
2. Aggressive counterattacks (verbal or physical)
3. Transference (taking out your frustration on someone less powerful)
4. Rationalization (making up reasons to justify acting foolishly)
5. Sarcastic humor and social negativism
6. Isolation (social withdrawal)
7. Psychosomatic illnesses (e.g., some ulcers, heart disease)
8. Excessive indulgence (e.g., drugs, food, spending money)

AUTOMATION OF COPING TECHNIQUES

According to Freud, coping techniques eventually become **independent** of the original drive state, once they are over-learned through use and practice. In this regard, defense structures become automated responses that are independent of their original action impulses. Like any automated behavior, defense structures can become an ingrained aspect of the individual's personality.

For example, sarcasm is a common response to frustration when other actions (i.e., solving the problem) are not possible. However, this substitute drive object may become an acquired habit to the extent that the individual is sarcastic even when not frustrated. Once defense structures become habitual, they are highly resistant to extinction - just like any other automated behavior. As a result, socially unacceptable actions can become routine items in the individual's behavioral repertoire (e.g., negative humor, being late for appointments, emotional outbursts, etc.).

CYCLES OF FRUSTRATION

The fully developed model of frustration is summarized by Model 4.

Notice the "frustration loop" in this model. Maladaptive coping and venting techniques that are employed to deal with frustrated energy have a direct impact on the individual's **schedule of reinforcement.** Specifically, since defense structures are by definition, antisocial, they ultimately have a negative effect on the schedule of external reinforcement. The resulting punishments, in turn, create more conflict, more frustration, and the use of more maladaptive coping techniques. This cycle of events can gain a momentum of its own, causing continuing frustration for the individual. In this way, defense structures can cause continuous cycles of external and internal punishment, and upon careful inspection, appear inconsistent with the greater adaptive mission of the individual.

CONSEQUENCES OF FRUSTRATION

The long-run effect of frustration depends on the way it is handled. If control structures are employed, the individual can use reasoning and creative problem solving to avoid, eliminate, or minimize the negative consequences of frustration. For example, productive substitute drive objects (like physical exercise) can release some action impulses while keeping the body fit. If control structures are used effectively, the body can return to near homeostasis chemistry with minimum frustration in the pool. No long-term negative consequences result.

Unfortunately, in real life, people often use a host of defense structures to vent frustration. These maladaptive responses have serious long-term negative consequences for both the internal and external schedule of reinforcement.

Internally, if the body's chemistry is not returned to homeostasis, serious medical problems can result. Indeed, prolonged exposure to high levels of altered body chemistry has been implicated in many types of illness. A major reason for this is that the body's immune system operates less effectively when homeostasis is not achieved. Externally, frustration causes many antisocial venting behaviors, such as sarcastic humor, slips-of-the-

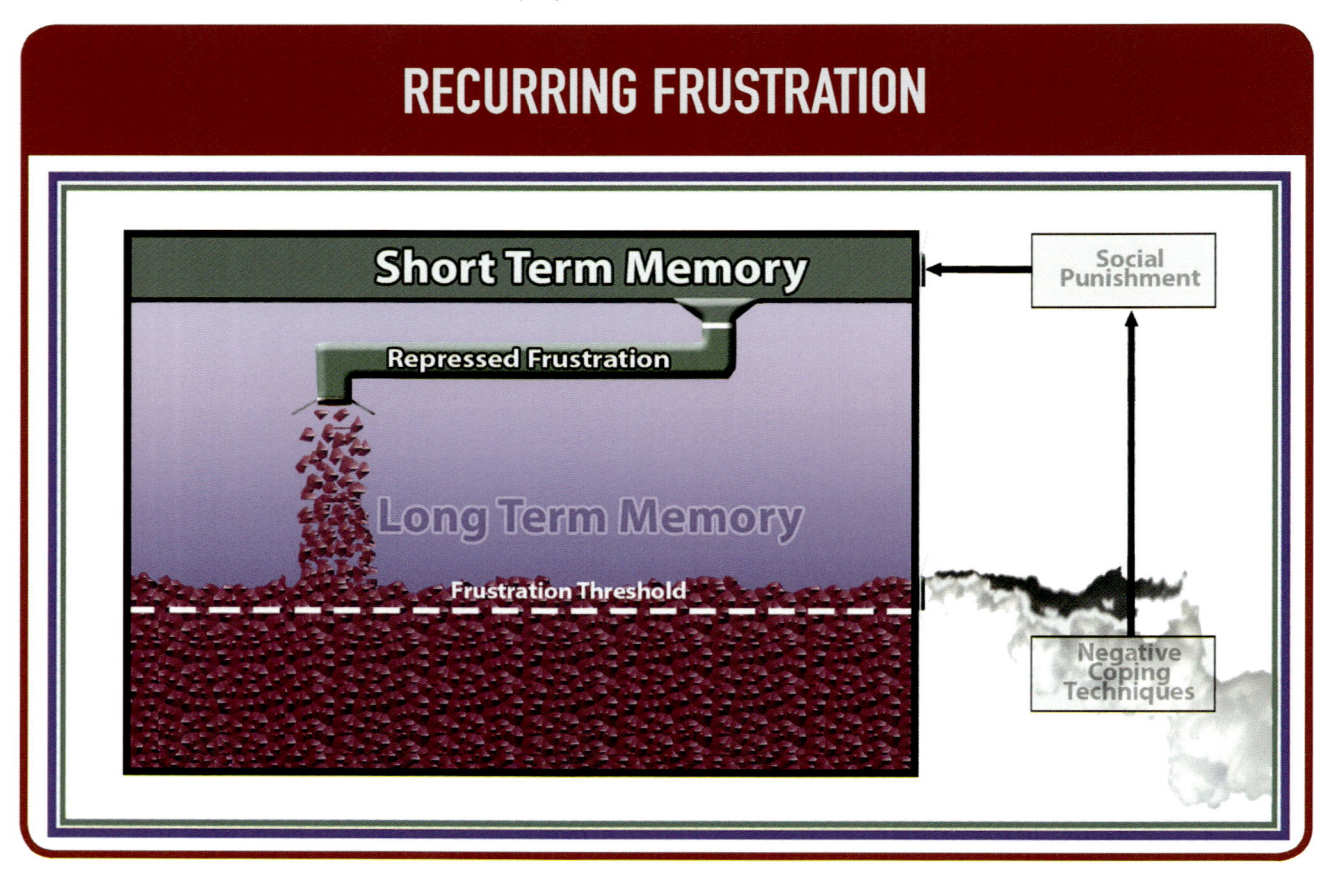

Model 4

tongue, short temper, depression, moodiness, excessive indulgence (e.g., food, sex, drugs, etc.). Ultimately, many of these actions are punished by the social environment, adding to the individual's level of frustration.

IMPLICATIONS OF FRUSTRATION

Not surprisingly, Freud's discoveries regarding subconscious motivation eventually influenced marketing research and theory. Specifically, in the 1950's authors such as Vance Packard (The Hidden Persuaders) and marketing researchers like Ernest Ditcher (Institute of Motivational Research Inc.) related many ordinary consumer purchases to subconscious motives under the heading, **Motivation Theory.** These analyses were based on subjective techniques like depth-interviewing which purported to delve into the consumer's subconscious to reveal hidden purchase motives. Conclusions reached by Ditcher included that men buy red sports cars as surrogate mistresses and women prefer to bake cakes from scratch because they are symbolically giving birth to a baby. However, this approach quickly fell out of favor due to its high subjectivity and low predictive ability.

Today, we have a better understanding of subconscious motivation, and this leads to serious implications. First, it is easy to predict from the model developed here that people in the modern world will be frustrated over many things. Manufacturers and advertisers try to turn this knowledge into profits by producing and selling products that promise to eliminate or reduce frustration. Some of these attempts are direct descriptions of how the product will serve as a substitute drive object (e.g., recommending the consumer buy and chew a diet gum instead of eating chocolate), or will reduce symptoms of frustration (e.g., headache remedies).

The model of frustration also suggests great potential to influence people by using their subconscious pent-up instinctual motivation. For example, a whiskey manufacturer may advertise its product making blatant use of sexual associations. This might form an image (possibly subconscious) that consumption of the product is associated with sexual gratification. Accordingly, if consumers are experiencing repressed sexual energy at the same time they are buying whiskey, the subconscious may see an opportunity to release some tension by purchasing the whiskey associated with sexual gratification. Here, the mere association (and therefore expectation) of sexual wish fulfillment might be strong enough to trigger purchase. Whether the product actually fulfills its subconscious promise in the long run does not really matter.

In addition, product purchase is a **control structure.** Indeed, few behaviors could be more socially acceptable in a materialistic society than satisfying frustrated urges by purchasing commercial products. It could also be argued, however, that sexually oriented advertisements have greatly increased individual frustrations by constantly provoking instinctual urges.

CONCLUSION

Tension and frustration are the undoing of many people, in both personal and professional environments. These forces typically have a prolonged negative impact on internal and external reinforcement. Maladaptive coping techniques (many of which are automated and unrecognized) only add to the frustration pool by creating continuing cycles of stress. Given the large amount of frustration the average person encounters, it is no wonder that "self-help" books on how to reduce or cope with modern stress abound.

Note that a very significant amount of modern human behavior is motivated, at least in part, by attempts to vent displaced frustrated energy. If you do not understand the prevalence of defense structures in exchange relationships, it is easy to take these actions personally and produce frustrated energy of your own.

While continuing stress is the destiny of many people, it is not inevitable. Human beings are equipped with a flexible and creative internal model that can be used to change maladaptive coping techniques into control structures. However, exercising this option requires that we edit our beliefs and values and discard those that have proven ineffective. This is a very difficult undertaking due to tendencies toward cognitive consistency.

EXPERIMENT 12.1
REDUCING FRUSTRATION

Interview one of your key accounts who is experiencing a lot of frustration.

1. Identify and list what the major sources of frustration are.

2. Describe the major techniques your key account uses to cope with frustration and categorize them as control or defense structures.

3. Help your key account replace one or two major defense structures with new control structures - how successful were they?

ELABORATION QUESTIONS

- Can the use of defense structures ever be a good thing?

- Give two examples of advertisements that appeal to subconscious motives.

- How can we change defense structures into control structures for ourselves? For our friends and family?

- What are creative ways to prevent repressing drive state energy?

- How does repressed energy affect the business world?

- When are you most likely to use defense structures?

- What are your major frustrations on campus? In your first job?

- How does your threshold for frustration compare with your key accounts? What factors reduce your ability to handle frustration (i.e., lower the threshold)?

CHAPTER 13
FEELINGS I: EXPECTED VALUE

INTRODUCTION	**13.1**
FEELINGS	**13.1**
Definitions	13.1
Expected-Value	13.1
Affect	13.1
Attitudes and Stereotypes	13.1
EXPECTED-VALUE	**13.1**
Definition	13.1
Formation of Expected-Value	13.2
Expected-Value is Flexible	13.2
Expected-Value Triggers Emotions	13.3
Expected-Value is Verbal/Rational	13.3
Calculating Expected-Value Exercise	13.3
THE ROLE OF BELIEF STRENGTH	**13.3**
The Importance of Belief Strength	13.3
Factors Affecting Belief Strength	13.4
SOURCE CREDIBILITY	**13.4**
Expertise	13.4
Trustworthiness	13.5
Source Credibility is a Perceived Phenomenon	13.6
Loss of Credibility	13.6
CONSISTENCY	**13.7**
QUANTITY OF INFORMATION	**13.7**
CONCLUSION	**13.8**
CALCULATING EXPECTED-VALUE	**13.8**
**EXPERIMENT 13.1	CREATING EXPECTED-VALUE IN A JOB INTERVIEW**	**13.9**
ELABORATION QUESTIONS	**13.10**

GUIDING QUESTIONS

- What are feelings?
- How do feelings determine overt behavior?
- What are the major types of feelings and how are they different?
- What is expected-value?
- What is affect?
- What are attitudes?
- What are stereotypes?
- Can feelings be rational?
- What are the three steps in the calculation of expected-value?
- Is expected-value flexible?
- How is expected-value related to emotions?
- What is the role of belief strength in persuasion?
- What factors determine belief strength?
- How is source credibility determined?
- Why is credibility so important in marketing?
- How do people lose credibility?
- How is consistency of information related to belief strength?
- How is quantity of information related to belief strength?

INTRODUCTION

*In earlier chapters we examined the internal model, its component parts, and its basic operations. Now we will examine more complex internal states called feelings. In an earlier chapter, we learned that values are different from beliefs because they have a directional charge (i.e., valence) that allows people to evaluate whether they should approach or avoid objects in the environment. These basic values (learned or inherited) are transformed into more elaborate feeling states which ultimately direct behavior. Therefore, if we are to understand why consumers make certain choices we must understand human **feelings** or **evaluations**.*

FEELINGS

DEFINITIONS

A major problem in discussing feelings and evaluations is the lack of commonly accepted terminology. Scientists often use the same labels to refer to different kinds of feelings. Therefore, it is important to define the terms we will use in our discussion. The terms "evaluation" and "feeling" will be used interchangeably. Both will represent **an internal state that has a positive or negative direction.** Thus, feelings are any internal valenced state that helps the individual decide whether s/he should approach (+), avoid (-), and/or counterattack (-) any particular environmental object.

For our purposes, three different types of feelings will be defined and discussed. The names we will use to distinguish these evaluations are: expected-value, affect, and attitudes.

EXPECTED-VALUE

These are defined as **rationally** determined feelings and are discussed in detail in this chapter. Essentially, expected-value comes from combining **beliefs** (the expectancy component) and **values** (the value component) in the short-term memory to evaluate an external object. These feelings are based primarily on learned values and vary greatly from one culture to the next. As an example of expected-value, think about evaluating different cars. Because the costs are substantial and sub-optimal choices have long lasting consequences most consumers will read and study different options and try to make the most logical choice.

AFFECT

This category of feelings includes **emotions, moods,** and **affective tones.** These feelings are based on instinctual evaluations (i.e., inherited values) that all humans share. In many cases, these feelings are similar to our ancestors and have not changed much in many years. Unlike expected-value, affective responses like emotions are not at all logical and often cause problems in the modern world. As an example, if you get stuck in traffic on the way to an important job interview you will probably have a strong, negative, emotional reaction that includes increased adrenalin levels, rising blood pressure, and a faster heart rate.

ATTITUDES AND STEREOTYPES

These feelings are learned over time and are composed of expected-value and/or affect. As we repeatedly encounter an object or person, it becomes tiring to have to re-evaluate them over and over. To save this extra effort, people learn their evaluations and then store them in the long-term memory for future use. In this way, known objects are pre-judged and therefore, much easier to evaluate. Indeed, we will define attitudes as **automated feelings** because they are often used without awareness.

EXPECTED-VALUE

DEFINITION

Human beings have the ability to produce verbally based feelings. This type of feelings is called **expected-value**, and consists of the spontaneous calculation of costs and benefits. These evaluations are created in the STM using beliefs and values. It is important to note that since the STM implies awareness, people are, by definition, conscious of their calculations of expected-value for objects or people in the environment. Expected-value is a mentally or **cognitively based feeling.**

FORMATION OF EXPECTED-VALUE

The expected-value (EV) of an object or person is developed in three steps: (1) information acceptance, (2) implicit evaluation, and (3) information integration.

Step 1: Information Acceptance (Belief Formation). Beliefs relate attributes to an object. As an example of this step in EV formation, suppose you were interested in buying a new car. You decide to investigate BMWs first so you visit the local dealership where you talk to a salesman and test drive a sport sedan. During your visit, you would obtain object-related data that associates important product attributes to the BMW. For example, after driving the car you might believe that it has a smooth ride:

$$BMW \xrightarrow[P=.8]{Has\ a} Smooth\ Ride$$

Step 2: Implicit Evaluation. Associated with each attribute belief (b_i) is an implicit evaluation (e_i). This means that individuals routinely arrange attributes into value categories like good-bad, right-wrong, and pleasant-unpleasant. In essence, people demonstrate their personal values by identifying which attributes they like and which they do not like. This step is called "implicit" because for most people, it has become "second nature." In other words, you so routinely evaluate attributes as good or bad, that you no longer are aware of doing it. So, even though people are aware of their current EV feelings, they often are not aware of the evaluation stage. Fortunately, people can easily gain awareness to the implicit evaluation process if their attention is directed to it. A common way this is done in marketing is by asking consumers to fill out value scales. For example, you might evaluate a smooth ride as moderately valuable.

$$BMW \xrightarrow[P=.8]{Has\ a} Smooth\ Ride \xrightarrow{Which\ is} Good\ (+4)$$

Over time and through conditioning (i.e., learning), the evaluative responses originally associated with the attributes become associated with the object. For the BMW example it would go like this:

$$BMW \xrightarrow[P=.8]{Has\ a} Smooth\ Ride \xrightarrow{Which\ is} Good\ (+4)$$
$$Becomes$$
$$BMW \xrightarrow{is} Good\ (+3.2)$$

Step 3: Information Integration. The final step in the calculation of expected-value is the summation of evaluative responses ($b_i e_i$) for all salient (important) attributes. At this step, the positive features of an object are considered along with the negative features to form an overall (all things considered) evaluation. Because good features can "compensate" for bad features, this is often called a "compensatory model." In other words, the EV from all salient attributes are added together, and the overall result summarizes the current expected-value from the object. An example of this integration process is shown by Figure 1.

Thus, in the example above, the person has an overall negative feeling (EV = -3.4) toward BMWs after spontaneously evaluating them. We could therefore predict that this individual would be unlikely to purchase a BMW.

EXPECTED-VALUE IS FLEXIBLE

Expected-value can change at a moment's notice. This is because spontaneous calculations of expected-value are verbal feelings, composed of potentially flexible beliefs and values. Therefore, EV changes whenever the salient beliefs and values change. In the BMW example, if the person suddenly inherits a large amount of money, the negative expected-value from the "high price" and "poor MPG" beliefs may become unimportant and therefore, not entered into the calculation of expected-value. In this case, the valence of the EV would be instantly reversed the person would now have a favorable feeling toward BMW's.

This means that EV is by far the most flexible way of evaluating the environment. Notice, however, that spontaneous calculations of EV require the capacity

CALCULATION OF EXPECTED-VALUE FOR A BMW

	ATTRIBUTE	BELIEF		VALUE		EXPECTED VALUE
1.	Smooth Ride	.8	*	+4.0	=	+3.2
2.	Beautiful Styling	.8	*	+2.0	=	+1.6
3.	High Prestige	.3	*	+9.0	=	+2.7
4.	High Price	1.0	*	-6.0	=	- 6.0
5.	Poor MPG	.7	*	-7.0	=	- 4.9
Total Expected-Value ($\Sigma b_i e_i$)					=	**-3.4**

Figure 1

of the STM for work space. This means that the actual amount of spontaneously calculated EV is limited by the restricted capacity of the STM.

EXPECTED-VALUE TRIGGERS EMOTIONS

Since EV is produced in the STM, the individual is, by definition, aware of the resultant feeling. If the feeling that is verbally calculated is negative, it touches off the corresponding negative emotion. For example, if someone verbally threatened your life, you would probably produce an immediate emotional response. Similarly, if someone threatens your self-importance or self-worth, you normally experience negative chemistry. This is why people engaged in arguments often turn "red in the face," experience a pounding heart, and end up shouting.

EXPECTED-VALUE IS VERBAL/RATIONAL

Because calculations of expected-value are based on beliefs that predict the future, we can say that EV is forward thinking. In fact, whenever an individual feels a decision is very important (e.g., what job to take, whom to marry, what new car to buy), s/he will normally use the STM to calculate EV. Because of this, decisions based on EV can be as informed and objective as the internal model's sample of information. When we take the time to carefully research our choices, there is a much greater probability of making a rational (i.e., adaptive) choice.

CALCULATING EXPECTED-VALUE EXERCISE

At the end of the chapter there is an exercise to see if you can compute expected-value correctly.

THE ROLE OF BELIEF STRENGTH

THE IMPORTANCE OF BELIEF STRENGTH

Belief strength plays a major role in determining the magnitude of expected-value. The first reason has to do with certainty. When b_i is strong (higher order), it means that the individual is certain of the belief. Conversely, when b_i is lower order, it means the individual is uncertain of the association. Thus, as the individual calculates expected-benefits, higher order beliefs will be more strongly represented since the individual is certain of their expectation.

In contrast, lower order beliefs are not particularly helpful in calculating expected-benefits because the individual is uncertain which attributes to expect from the object. Since it is expected-benefits that direct behavior, higher order beliefs direct more overt behaviors than lower order beliefs. As a result, information acceptance as reflected in belief strength is an extremely important concept in understanding and predicting human behavior.

Expertise - Doctors

FACTORS AFFECTING BELIEF STRENGTH

The level of belief strength depends on the extent to which the internal model accepts an external message as accurate. Research has identified three major factors that directly influence the level of message acceptance: source credibility, consistency, and quantity of information.

SOURCE CREDIBILITY

For an information source to be perceived as credible, it must possess two characteristics: **expertise** and **trustworthiness**. Before defining these traits, it is important to note that the overall credibility attributed to the source will be low if **either** expertise or trustworthiness is perceived to be lacking. Therefore, attempts to maximize message acceptance must offer information from a source that is perceived to be both expert (i.e., informed) and trustworthy (i.e., honest). If either component is missing, message acceptance will be dramatically reduced.

EXPERTISE

Expertise refers to the ability of the source to make accurate assertions about object-attribute associations. For example, a movie star speaking about makeup techniques would probably possess sufficient expertise to make valid statements. A movie star speaking about military operations or defense spending, however, may not possess sufficient experience to qualify as an informed source. The most direct technique to establish expertise is to present objective evidence that verifies the source is "informed." Such credentials can vary depending on the situation and subject of persuasion but often include educational accomplishments or relevant direct experience.

Persuasiveness (i.e., message acceptance) also is strong when the source is perceived to be high in status or prestige or if the source is self-confident. It seems likely that these effects are caused by the audience attributing more expertise to high status or confident sources.

TRUSTWORTHINESS

Trustworthiness refers to the willingness of the source to convey an accurate version of the true environment. When this willingness is compromised by vested interests (e.g., profit motive), credibility is reduced. Thus, trustworthiness is usually determined by the audience's perception of the source's intent. If the source will profit, advance, or otherwise benefit from the message's acceptance (which is often the case), the audience can easily reject the information by attributing it to a "self-serving" source. As a result, it is important for influence attempts to be constructed in a manner that maximizes perceived trustworthiness.

One way to accomplish this is to present a two-sided argument to the audience. For example, it has been demonstrated that if advertisers disclaim superiority on relatively unimportant product features, their claims of superiority on major product features are perceived to be more truthful. Thus, some amount of objectivity in terms of presenting alternative views can be used to increase source credibility.

Persuasive attempts also have been shown to be improved if the audience perceives the source to be "likable" or "similar" to the audience in any way. Presumably, these effects occur because people are more likely to "trust" people if they like them or resemble them.

Of course, the most trustworthy information source is the individual's own direct experience. Influence attempts that must rely solely on external information sources (i.e., based on only informational beliefs) cannot compare to the credibility of the individual's own encounters with the world (i.e., descriptive beliefs). This means that some of the most successful persuasive messages will be those based upon direct experience with the advocated item or issue. If such "trial" is unavailable, the influence agent might try to associate his/her position with former direct experiences of the audience. Such "surrogate trial" may be sufficient for higher order message acceptance in some cases.

Trust

SOURCE CREDIBILITY IS A PERCEIVED PHENOMENON

It is also important to note that credibility is a *perceived* phenomenon. It does not really matter how accurate the information really is, what is important is how much credibility the information is perceived to possess. Suppose, for example, that an insurance salesman poses as a "federal Social Security agent" in order to persuade an elderly couple to purchase an insurance policy. In this situation, the elderly couple may perceive the salesman to be a highly credible source and therefore, accept his recommendation that they purchase the policy.

LOSS OF CREDIBILITY

Many people engage in behaviors (overt and verbal) that lower their own credibility. Some of the most common ways are described below.

People often exaggerate the truth to make events seem more dramatic than they really were. This often holds the attention of the audience better (for a short time) but it also has the effect of eroding your source credibility. We have already seen that "puffery" or exaggeration of non-verifiable attributes is expected in marketing and interpersonal interactions. Many people exercise some "artistic license" in their verbal behaviors by embellishing here and there. While some of this exaggeration is expected and harmless, it can easily be rewarded and get stamped-in through operant conditioning. At some point, puffery becomes counter productive so it is important to know where to draw the line.

People often make predictions of their own behavior that they do not fulfill. Similarly, people often claim to possess characteristics and traits that do not show up in their overt behavior. This is not really surprising since, as we have seen, the correspondence between verbal and overt behavior is usually not very high. Nevertheless, people who are always going to stop smoking or begin a diet, but never actually do so, gradually destroy their credibility.

People often try to speak with confidence regarding issues they really know little about. Uninformed people masquerading as experts are numerous, and we can all think of experiences where we trusted someone's advice, only to discover later that the source lacked credibility. Yet, it is hard for some people to resist the temptation to gain social esteem by pretending knowledge or skills they do not actually possess. Over time, as the truth is exposed, the person loses credibility.

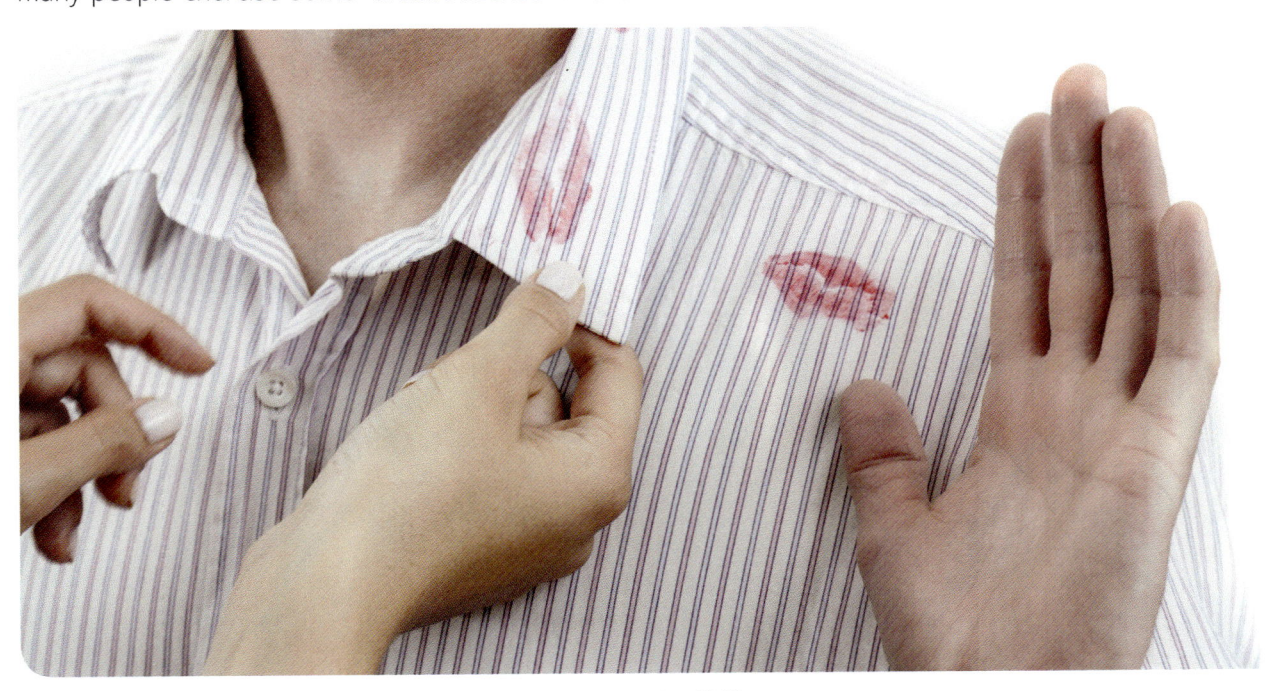

Losing Credibility

People do not want to hurt other peoples' feelings. People often withhold or tone down their real thoughts if they think they will hurt someone's feelings. This seems like a nice idea and is probably appropriate in some cases. However, **excessive non-disclosure** of true feelings will ultimately be inconsistent with the individual's over all behaviors (both verbal and overt). When others observe this inconsistency, it causes them to question the individual's trustworthiness and reduces his/her credibility.

People often brag about deceiving or lying to others. You have probably heard people describe with great pride how they "fooled" their boss by calling in with a fake sore throat on the first warm, sunny day of spring. People also brag about excuses they have used to avoid a deserved environmental punishment – for example, "I told my girlfriend I was studying late when I was really out drinking with the boys, and she believed me."

To one extent or another, most of us are probably guilty of some or all of the above traits. If you can avoid them and become known as a credible source, your ability to influence people with words will be greatly enhanced. Conversely, if you lose your credibility, it is very difficult to get it back. Clearly, risking your credibility is not in your own long-run interest – especially in professional environments.

CONSISTENCY

As you know from the discussion of cognitive consistency, people are highly motivated to accept information that is consistent with previously established beliefs and values. Influence agents often exploit this tendency in order to gain message acceptance. If a persuasive message begins by agreeing with the audience's views (on anything), the audience will be more likely to accept a later discrepant message. For example, suppose the dean of students wants to convince students of the need to raise the legal drinking age. Often, influence attempts begin with consistent information such as: "We all agree that social activities are very important to the overall mission of the university. We also realize that students need opportunities to rest and relax from the daily grind of classes and studying."

Such initial agreement not only **rewards the audience** by making them feel good (accurate) about their views, but also establishes the speaker as a **credible source** since the introductory information is consistent with the audience's experiences. This dual effect can be a powerful lever when trying to maximize message acceptance. After the audience's confidence has been gained, discrepant information can be presented in a more effective way. For example, the dean of students could then go on to say, "However, we also recognize the need for students to mature at school, so they can socialize and solve their problems, without relying on alcohol as a crutch."

As it turns out, almost everyone is receptive to consistent information. Flattery, for example, is really no more than an exercise in cognitive consistency. In fact, you might be surprised at how receptive most people are to flattery, even when it is false! However, false flattery quickly loses its positive reinforcement power because the receiver, sooner or later, realizes that it cannot be believed (i.e., message acceptance declines as the flatterer loses credibility). You might experiment with this technique to find the boundaries of where initial agreement stops generating positive effects and begins to be perceived as false. You will find that almost everyone is receptive to small and sincere agreements with their position.

QUANTITY OF INFORMATION

A third factor that affects message acceptance is the amount of data the individual has about the object attribute link. As information regarding the association increases, the internal model becomes more informed. Once the individual has accumulated sufficient data, s/he will hold the belief(s) with greater confidence, which has the effect of increasing belief strength.

As an example, suppose between classes you overheard someone say, "The President has resigned." Since this is an unlikely event, and you do not know the credibility of the source, you would probably accept the message at lower order levels. You would also probably generate curiosity statements like, "I wonder if the President really resigned." Now, suppose you overhear several other people saying the same thing. As the quantity of information regarding the event increases, your acceptance of the association normally will increase.

CONCLUSION

Belief strength is an important component in the individual's calculation of expected-benefits. Beliefs will normally be accepted at higher order levels when the information is delivered by a source perceived to have high credibility, when the information is consistent with already established beliefs, and when sufficient information is available.

Notice that due to the tendencies toward cognitive consistency information sampled and accepted ***early in life*** is overly represented in the internal model and thus in the individual's behavior. This is a major reason why the beliefs and values formed during childhood tend to be so important throughout life (i.e., they are used as a basis to sample and accept or reject subsequent information).

Notice also that early information is necessarily encountered when the child is young and "impressionable" (i.e., before the selective defense mechanisms are fully operative). As a result, even when the child matures into an adult, his/her internal model and behavioral repertoire are often heavily biased toward information encountered early, regardless of whether these beliefs and values are representative of the broader environment. "As the seed is sown, so grows the tree."

CALCULATING EXPECTED-VALUE

Olivia has been dating Andre, Ryan, and Archit, all of whom have proposed to her. Who should she marry?

OLIVIA'S VALUE STRUCTURE   OLIVIA'S BELIEF STRUCTURE

	ATTRIBUTES	VALUE	ANDRE	RYAN	ARCHIT
1.	Intelligence is highly valued	(+9)	.9	.6	.7
2.	A sense of humor is valued	(+7)	.6	.5	.7
3.	A college degree is valued	(+7)	1.0	.7	.8
4.	Appearance is somewhat valued	(+4)	.4	1.0	.7
5.	Drinking alcohol is negatively valued	(-8)	.5	.6	.4
6.	Smoking is negatively valued	(-6)	0.0	1.0	0.0

BELIEF STRENGTH PER SUITOR

Figure 2

ANSWER TO THE CALCULATION OF EXPECTED-VALUE EXERCISE

Andre = 16.9 units of expected-value
[(+9 *.9) + (+7*.6) + (+7*1.0) + (+4*.4) + (-8*.5) + (-6*0.0)]

Ryan = 7.0 units of expected-value
[(+9 *.6) + (+7*.5) + (+7*.7) + (+4*1.0) + (-8*.6) + (-6*1.0)]

Archit = 16.4 units of expected-value
[(+9 *.7) + (+7*.7) + (+7*.8) + (+4*.7) + (-8*.4) + (-6*0.0)]

Olivia should marry Andre since her expected-value is the highest for him.

Figure 3

EXPERIMENT 13.1
CREATING EXPECTED-VALUE IN A JOB INTERVIEW

1. Identify a specific job that you would like (but is hard to get).

2. Identify the major attributes that are needed to get this job (at least five)

3. Produce a creative resume and/or a set of interviewing props designed to enhance your credibility and document your claims regarding these attributes.

4. Practice using these materials in a mock interview or a real interview if you have one before this assignment is due.

5. Present the materials you made in class and summarize how the interview went. Turn in a copy of the resume and/or props.

ELABORATION QUESTIONS

- Give two examples of when you have made a major consumer decision using expect-value. Identify the salient evaluative criteria that you used.

- If a consumer is using expected-value to buy your product, what is the best way to maximize your persuasiveness?

- Analyze the perceived credible of several sources including sales people, advertising, and college students.

- Give some specific ways you could raise your perceived trustworthiness and expertise with a key account?

- Observe your peers and describe the major ways you see them lose their credibility. What is their underlying motive?

- Construct a sales message that has a high degree of consistency for a key account of interest to you (e.g., recruiter).

- If you lose credibility with a key account what is the best way to regain some of it?

- How is the calculation of expected-value related to cognitive consistency?

- **"Radical honesty"** means you tell your key accounts the truth, the **whole** truth, and nothing but the truth. How realistic is this idea?

CHAPTER 14
FEELINGS II: EMOTIONS

INTRODUCTION	14.1
EMOTIONS	14.1
Definition	14.1
SOURCE OF EMOTIONS	14.1
CHARACTERISTICS OF EMOTIONS	14.2
Emotions are usually strong	14.2
Emotions are Temporary	14.2
Emotional Reactions are Fixed for Life	14.3
Emotions Are Nonverbal	14.3
Emotions are Hard to Measure	14.3
Emotions are Directly Related to Health	14.4
Emotions and Stress	14.4
Emotions are Triggered by Expected-Value	14.7
LESS INTENSE AFFECT	14.8
Mood States	14.8
Affective Tones	14.8
CONCLUSION	14.9
**EXPERIMENT 14.1	EMOTIONAL PERSUASION**	14.9
ELABORATION QUESTIONS	14.10

GUIDING QUESTIONS

- » What are emotions?
- » What are the properties of emotions?
- » What is the source of emotions?
- » When did emotions developed?
- » Why are emotions so strong?
- » How long to emotions last?
- » Are emotions fixed for life?
- » Are emotions verbal or nonverbal?
- » How are emotions measured?
- » What is the relationship between emotions and health?
- » How are emotions related to stress?
- » What is modern stress syndrome?
- » What happens when people worry?
- » What is the relationship between the short term memory and emotions?
- » What are mood states?
- » What are affective tones?
- » What role do emotions play in consumer behavior?

INTRODUCTION

*The last chapter introduced three types of feelings and examined the calculation of expected-value in detail. In this chapter we will examine the second category of feelings, affect. The term **affect** is used because this type of feeling refers to how external and internal stimuli affect the chemistry of your body. The first type of affect is emotion which reflects the most intense internal reactions. Next are mood states which are less intense than emotions but often longer lasting. Finally we will examine affective tones which are small and fleeting fragments of affect.*

EMOTIONS

DEFINITION

Emotions refer to how the chemistry of your body reacts (positively or negatively) to external and internal stimuli. Unlike other types of feelings, emotions are tangible. They are instinctually determined evaluations composed of hormonal, neurochemical, physiological substances. Examples include levels of adrenaline, endorphins, testosterone, estrogen, white blood count, perspiration, and tears. Emotions have two major dimensions:

Valence. Emotions are positive/favorable (+ valence) or negative/unfavorable (- valence). The goals of emotions depend on whether they are positive or negative.

Positive emotions have as their goal to reward the selection of correct (adaptive) behaviors by producing positive internal body chemistry. The "thrill of victory," or a positive surprise are two examples of positive emotions.

Negative emotions have as their goal to return the individual to homeostasis by removing negative stimuli from the immediate environment. This goal is achieved by a series of withdrawal (flight) and/or counter attack (fight) behaviors.

Arousal. Emotions range from strong/intense to moderate. Weak affective responses are given a different label – affective tones. Examples of emotions include **distressed, angry, scared, hostile, bored, guilty, nervous, alert, excited, proud, determined,** etc.

The Thrill of Victory

SOURCE OF EMOTIONS

Originally, emotions were designed for primary survival value, so many are related to the primary needs: (a) **protection** (white blood count, immune responses, adrenaline, or perspiration all of which facilitate withdrawal or counterattack), (b) **food processing** (saliva, stomach acids, digestive enzymes), and (c) **reproduction** (testosterone and estrogen).

According to natural selection, people with "good" emotions had body chemistry that directed them to adaptive overt behaviors. As a result, they lived longer and produced more offspring who inherited similar emotions. In this way our emotional responses evolved over many years. Over this long period, humans developed a rich set of internal feeling states that made people avoid (i.e., withdrawal, counterattack), or approach stimuli they encountered. Indeed, from a behavioral point of view, life is a series of approach/avoidance decisions.

The emotions that evolved in humans represent a rich mosaic of internal feelings. However, given the dangerous world that existed during the great majority of human evolution, many emotions are related to defense. Especially important here are the emotions that produce "flight or fight" responses. For example, whenever humans perceive stress or threat in the environment, they produce emotional responses designed to prepare the body for a physical encounter (i.e., run away or fight back). To facilitate this physical action, the emotional syndrome includes increased heart rate, blood pressure, and respiration (to oxygenate the muscles); increased perspiration (to cool the body); increased adrenalin (to enhance muscle actions), etc.

However, if the threat is not physical (e.g., job interview) this emotional response to threat can easily deteriorate performance. Specifically, hands and voice tremble (due to increased adrenalin), perspiration collects on the brow, the heart pumps audibly, etc. Internally, the body wants to run away or physically attack the source of perceived threat. If these action impulses are blocked from overt behavior, the emotions continue to build and the person appears "nervous."

CHARACTERISTICS OF EMOTIONS

EMOTIONS ARE USUALLY STRONG

For emotions the level of arousal ranges from moderate to high. For example, the early stages of love typically produce powerful feelings based on a **chemical bath.** This bath is a complex syndrome of strong emotions including adrenalin and endorphins.

It is important to note that when negative emotions are engaged at full arousal, they force body organs (1) to work at peak performance levels, and/or (2) to secrete noxious chemicals in high levels (e.g., stomach acids). The body makes an implicit judgment that overworking key organs (e.g., the heart) is a good idea even though doing so takes minutes off the end of your life. In the old world, this used to be a good trade because physical threats to survival could end life immediately. However, the emotional response system could not envision a world where most threats would be non-physical and therefore, not life threatening (i.e., the modern world). It has taken humans only 10,000 years to develop cities and complex social rules -- a drop in the bucket by evolutionary timetables. As a result, many modern humans vastly overwork their defensive emotions (e.g., staying in a job they hate for the money) and unwittingly take large amounts of time off the end of their life.

EMOTIONS ARE TEMPORARY

The high to moderate intensity of emotions is designed to be temporary. As soon as the external stimuli is no longer in the visual field (or short-term memory), the body's chemistry returns to homeostasis.

Stress Associated with an Interview

EMOTIONAL REACTIONS ARE FIXED FOR LIFE

It is important to note that emotional responses, as defined here, are fixed for life and cannot be changed. When you encounter certain stimuli (e.g., a threat), you are pre-programmed to have a specific emotional response. These internal emotions (i.e., instinctual evaluations) are designed to facilitate the performance of adaptive overt behaviors (e.g., withdrawal or counterattack). These overt behaviors have as their goal the elimination of the stimuli that aroused the individual's emotions. Once the triggering stimuli are eliminated from the field of perception, the body's chemistry returns to its normal state (homeostasis).

Because emotions are fixed, however, problems occur when the individual is prevented from performing the overt behavior that instinctually corresponds to the emotional state. These "emotional failures" prevent the return to homeostasis, and instead, they prolong the production of negative chemistry designed to motivate the individual to somehow change the environment. As an example, when the internal model perceives a threat in the environment, it will direct the emotional equipment of the body to prepare for a threat reaction. As long as the perception of threat persists, the body will continue to produce abnormally high levels of adrenaline.

Conversely, if emotions are successfully expressed in the individual's overt behavior (e.g., procurement of food, protection, and reproduction), there is usually a strong positive feeling. Examples here include the satisfaction from eating or sleeping, sexual climax, or the "thrill of victory." These positive feelings (i.e., positive chemistry) are the internal reward for following your emotions. Continued fear, anxiety, hunger, and anger are internal punishments for failing to satisfy your emotions.

EMOTIONS ARE NONVERBAL

Another important feature of emotions is their nonverbal nature. We have seen that people often use the internal model to calculate expected-value (a verbal process) in order to act "rationally." Emotional

Emotional Expressions

reactions like fear and anger, however, often produce "irrational" behavior because they are neurochemical and thus cannot be arranged in logical sequences as easily as words and sentences.

This means it can be very difficult to express your emotions verbally in conversations with friends and loved ones. Indeed, understanding others' emotions is an area where human relationships often show communication breakdowns. An obvious reason is that emotions are difficult to describe in words and sentences. In addition, since emotions are designed for the immediate environment, they can often produce **dramatic** behaviors (e.g., angry outbursts) that have detrimental effects in the long run (e.g., loss of a job, or friend). It is important to remember that our emotions are not forward thinking.

EMOTIONS ARE HARD TO MEASURE

Associated with the tangible emotions are general psychological states like fear, sadness, disgust, anger, joy, etc. These general descriptive labels are normally used by people to describe an individual's emotions because measures of the precise neurochemical responses are not available. As a result, when a person is engaged in an instinctive threat reaction that involves heightened adrenaline, perspiration, and aggressive actions, we say s/he is "angry."

However, the label "angry" also applies to other situations, making it difficult to isolate this general emotion for precise scientific scrutiny. Today, science is showing an increased interest in measuring emotional reactions. For example, lie detector tests measure specific emotional responses (Galvanic skin response, pulse, blood pressure, respiration) that accompany verbal statements.

EMOTIONS ARE DIRECTLY RELATED TO HEALTH

Because emotions are physical, they have an important impact on the physical wellbeing of the individual. The body was designed to prefer the condition of homeostasis. However, it is emotionally equipped to produce dynamic chemistry changes in life threatening situations. When the emotional response is dramatic in nature, it requires major organs (like the heart) to work at peak performance levels. Thus, if an individual continually runs into survival threats, his/her emotional response would overwork important parts of the body. Not surprisingly, this can cause the body to become sick or fail prematurely.

Unfortunately as noted earlier, the perception of a physical threat to survival is not the only environmental stimulus that provokes emotions. For maximum effectiveness at surviving, natural selection favored a rather automated connection between the perception of threat and the production of appropriate emotions. So as it turns out, whenever an individual perceives a threat in the environment and this includes verbal threats s/he produces automatic changes in chemistry. Not surprisingly, this means that people can become physically ill due to threatening verbal or social situations. Moreover, this emotional effect applies not only to threats to physical survival, but also to threats to social or personal success.

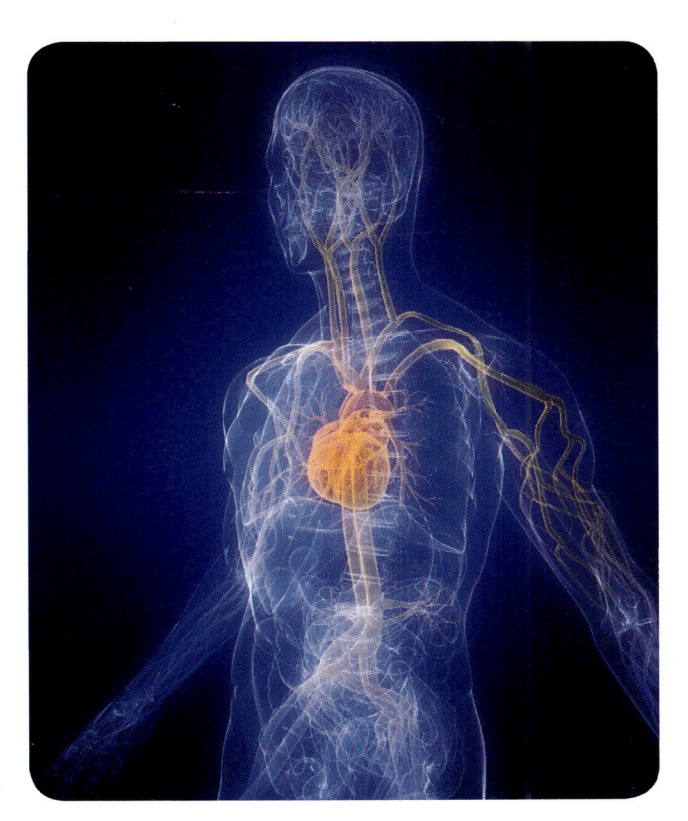

Emotions and Health

As an example, prolonged exposure to stressful environments that evoke fear and anger produces unnaturally high blood pressure, heart rate, and adrenaline. Thus, if you continually place yourself in a stressful environment, you could easily wind up with a premature heart ailment or circulatory problem. The intimate relationship between emotions and health means that we can gain valuable information about our physical well being by paying close attention to our emotional responses. Indeed, "biofeedback" techniques are direct attempts to identify current emotional states and then use this information to benefit the individual.

EMOTIONS AND STRESS

It is not surprising that human beings encounter considerable stress in the modern world. Basically, our emotional system was designed for a predator-filled world that no longer exists. Emotions that were selected for only 10,000 years ago (e.g., aggressiveness) can get you in big trouble in a "civilized" world. Unfortunately, the process of natural selection could not foresee impending civilization, and fixed the perception of threat to dynamic emotional responses. Now, in a world where words can be threatening, many people unwittingly overwork their emotional system. The major source of verbal threat is discrepant information, especially when

1. The degree of discrepancy is high, and/or
2. The threatened value is central or strong (e.g., self concept, religious beliefs, etc.).

Once the emotions are activated by the perception of threat, they produce powerful "fight or flight," action tendencies. The emotions are trying to motivate the individual to act in a way that will remove the threat. However, if the individual cannot or does not withdraw or counterattack, the powerful action tendencies are not released through overt behavior. This, in turn, prevents the body's return to homeostasis, and activates the further production of fight/flight chemicals (stress hormones).

As an example, in a program of research on human stress, Redford Williams (Anger Kills, 1994) has developed the following chemical (emotional) profile of flight/fight responses:

1. Hypothalamic nerve cells send signals to the adrenal glands sitting on top of the kidneys to pump large amounts of both adrenalin and cortisol into the bloodstream. This causes the heart to pump harder and faster raising the blood pressure.

2. The activated hypothalamus "emergency center" stimulates sympathetic nerves to constrict the arteries carrying blood to the skin, kidneys, and intestines while adrenalin causes the arteries to muscles to open wide. This is because if one is being attacked by a sabre-toothed tiger there is no need to waste precious body fluids on digestion or urine formation. In addition, if the skin is slashed its better to keep blood away from the skin on the body's surface. Instead, the blood is needed in the muscle groups that allow fight or flight responses.

3. The cortisol prolongs and amplifies the effects of the adrenalin on the heart and arteries.

4. The fired-up hypothalamus shuts down the parasympathetic nervous system so the effects of adrenalin cannot be quickly calmed down.

5. The adrenalin and cortisol also cause the immune system to go into a holding pattern. If you are slashed and bleeding you do not need your immune system to start making antibodies to your own tissues.

6. The body, if not engaged in physical response, continues to send messages to the brain about the extreme physiological effects - pounding heart, sweaty palms, rapid breathing - which reinforces the perception that real danger is close at hand.

7. As blood pressure rises the smooth inner linings of the coronary arteries (endothelial cells) can be eroded by rapidly swirling currents of blood (similar to a raging river eroding its banks).

8. Platelets (subcellular clotting agents) hurry to the damaged spot in the artery. If the artery were slashed by a tiger the platelets would stick to the spot, seal the hole, and stop the bleeding. If the artery lining is only scratched by the swirling blood the platelets clump there instead.

9. The adrenalin stimulates fat cells to empty their contents into the bloodstream -- to provide energy for the effort needed to counter a physical emergency. If physical activity does not occur, the liver converts the fat into cholesterol. This cholesterol is absorbed into the clump of platelets on the scratched artery and some of it makes its way into the artery wall. The cholesterol filled platelets do not clear out but remain there. Over years they mature into arteriosclerotic plaque that blocks the

flow of blood into the coronary artery. As the artery restricts over time platelet clots can completely block blood to the heart muscle causing a portion of it to die.

10. The effects noted above are more pronounced for people with high levels of irritability and aggression (i.e., "hostility syndrome").

In addition, recent research at Stanford University shows that prolonged exposure to stress hormones has the negative effects shown in Figure 1.

Notice that if the individual's beliefs and values are not representative of the environment, s/he is very likely to encounter significant discrepant information and internalize it as stress. In this way, people who have firmly held, but incorrect, beliefs and values pay

CONSEQUENCES OF CHRONIC STRESS

1. **Cardiovascular** - high blood pressure, arterial plaque.

2. **Suppressed Immune System** - resistance to all types of disease is decreased (e.g., the bacteria that cause stomach ulcers spreads more easily in stressed people).

3. **Obesity** - Stress hormones influence the number, type, and distribution of fat cells, and increases bad cholesterol.

4. **Aging** - as people age the ends of their chromosomes (telomeres) start to unravel which decreases the copy quality of the replacement cells. Exposure to stress hormones causes the telomeres to unravel more quickly causing accelerated aging.

5. **Cognitive Disfunction** - Stress causes an accelerated loss of brain cells thereby degrading cognitive function. In addition, stress degrades memory function (transfer, search, and retrieval).

6. **Depression** - Exposure to stress hormones makes people less able to feel pleasure and more able to feel pain.

7. **Sleep Deprivation** - Stress interferes with sleep thereby magnifying all of the above effects.

Figure 1

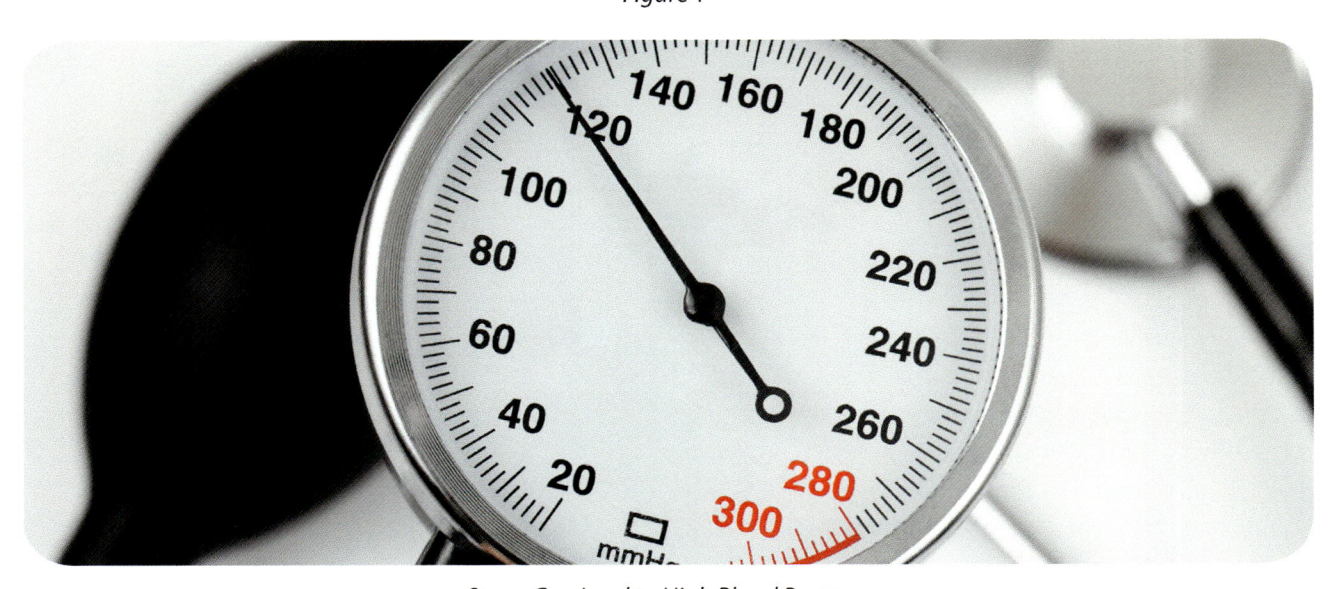

Stress Can Lead to High Blood Pressure

COPING WITH EMOTIONAL STRESS THEN . . . . AND NOW

Figure 2

a serious price for their maladaptive internal models. This is a big part of **Modern Stress Syndrome** and while there are countless Self-Help books and tapes available to improve the way people handle stress, it is very difficult to eliminate the cause.

EMOTIONS ARE TRIGGERED BY EXPECTED-VALUE

In the last chapter it was noted that because expected-value is produced in the STM, the individual is, by definition, aware of the resultant feeling. If the feeling that is verbally calculated is negative, it touches off the corresponding negative emotion. If someone verbally threatened your life, for example, you would probably produce an immediate emotional response. Similarly, if someone threatens your self-importance or self-worth, you normally experience negative chemistry.

This is why people engaged in arguments often turn red in the face, experience a pounding heart, and often end up shouting.

Earlier, we discussed how the external environment rewards or punishes overt behavior. It was noted that the accuracy of the internal model is directly reflected in the amount of positive reinforcement it receives. Now we see that there is also an internal schedule of reinforcement the emotions that are produced by spontaneous verbal evaluations.

As an example, if your beliefs and values regarding job interviews are inaccurate, you will have a hard time finding a job (external punishment). This situation can cause you to "feel bad" internally since the perception of stress and/or threat (negative EV) turns on the body's negative chemistry. In effect, people with inaccurate internal models pay a continual physical price when the world disagrees with their beliefs and values. In this light, people who believe they can hold any belief they wish (e.g., prejudice) often live shorter lives for their misjudgments. The relationship between emotions and expected-value is diagrammed in Model 1.

LESS INTENSE AFFECT

It has been noted that emotions are typically strong feelings. However, there are affective responses that are less intense: moods and affective tones.

MOOD STATES

Moods are internal states that are usually less intense than emotions but often last longer. Moods are influenced by the immediate environment and the contents of the STM. If the internal model is in a negative mood, it tends to place interpretations on the environment that correspond to the mood state. For example, recall the previous example for inferred beliefs. Your date calls at the last minute and cancels the date. If you were in a good mood you would be more likely to draw a positive inference from the event (your date is in trouble and may need help). If you were in a bad mood you would be more likely to place a negative inference on the event (your date is blowing you off). Moods can last from minutes to hours, days, and even longer, so they can have an important impact on behavior.

AFFECTIVE TONES

Affective tones are the weakest and most transient forms of affective response. These internal states are usually brief (seconds or minutes) and of low intensity (e.g., amusement at a joke in an advertisement). Although the impact of any single affective tone is minor, they can accumulate over time (with repetition), and without conscious awareness. This will be discussed later under the topic of low involvement learning.

As an example, of how affective tones can be important, think of your friend who has the best sense of humor. Every time this person makes you laugh, they evoke a positive affective tone. While each laugh may be incidental, over time they accumulate into significant reinforcement. The result is that you may like this person better, invite him/her to more social events, be more likely to lend him/her money, etc. Similarly, if products (or ads for them) can induce positive affective tones repeatedly in consumers, the effects can add up over time to a significant brand advantage.

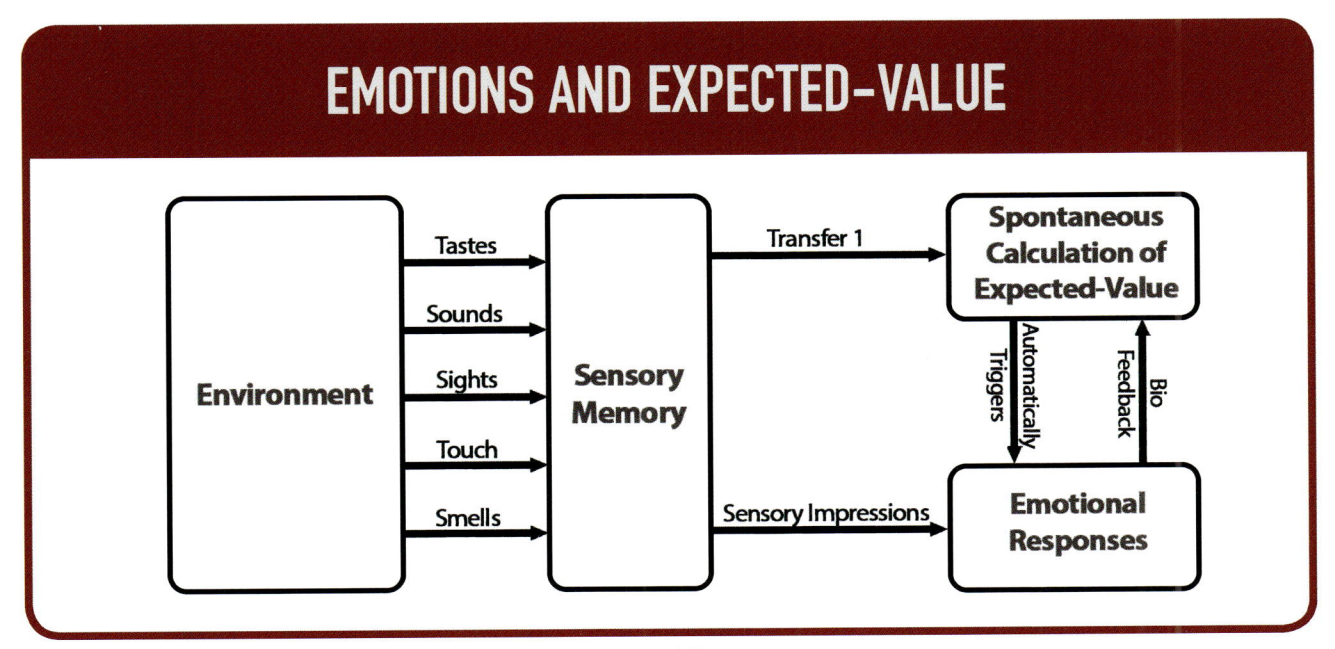

EMOTIONS AND EXPECTED-VALUE

Model 1

CONCLUSION

Emotions represent some of our oldest and most intense feeling states. They cause us to approach, avoid, or attack objects in our environmental space based on our body's chemical reactions to external objects and events. Because these affective responses developed in an uncivilized and dangerous world, many are related to safety, security, and tend to make modern humans defensive. Emotions can also have negative effects on the individual's health such as worrying excessively or modern stress syndrome. These outcomes are primarily due to the fact that our emotions were designed for an environment that no longer exists. Emotions also play a major role in the purchase and use of many products and services. Examples would include perfume, roller coasters, pets, honeymoons, vacations, marriage counseling, drugs and alcohol, extreme sports, pepper spray, home security, and many more. Understanding your key accounts emotional states and reacting appropriately to them is one of the keys to successful relationships (personal and professional). Understanding your own emotional states and reacting appropriately is another key to success but it can be very difficult to suppress or alter such strong feelings.

Mood states and affective tones, while less intense than emotions, tend to appear more frequently and thus influence a wide variety of behaviors. In marketing it is critical for salespeople to know when a prospective customer is in a bad mood and therefore, unreceptive to persuasion (especially discrepant information). Also, note that when consumers fall into a bad mood, treating themselves to commercial products (i.e., self-gifting) is a commonly attempted cure (e.g., shopping spree, ice cream, alcohol, etc.).

EXPERIMENT 14.1
EMOTIONAL PERSUASION

1. Find one print ad and one TV ad that uses **positive emotions** and one print and one TV ad that uses **negative emotions.** Project your ads in class and describe the emotions involved.

2. Pick an hour of TV and examine the commercials. What percent of the ads used emotional appeals? What were the most frequently used emotional appeals?

3. When are emotional appeals most effective and when they are likely to fail?

ELABORATION QUESTIONS

- How emotional are you compared to your friends?

- How defensive or you compared to your friends?

- Give three examples of consumer products you have purchased on an emotional basis.

- Give some examples of key accounts who are currently suffering from emotional stress regarding a consumer purchase.

- How moody are you compared to your friends?

- What is the best way to handle an emotional customer?

- How much stress is caused by people working at jobs they do not like?

- What can we do to increase our positive emotions?

- Can an event remain emotional even after the negative stimulus is removed from the immediate environment?

- What are some common emotional appeals that salespeople use to close a sale?

CHAPTER 15
FEELINGS III: ATTITUDES AND STEREOTYPES

INTRODUCTION	**15.1**
ATTITUDES	**15.1**
The Definition of Attitudes	15.1
The Function of Attitudes	15.1
Stereotypes – Attitude Generalization	15.2
ATTITUDE FORMATION	**15.3**
ATTITUDE MAINTENANCE AND PROTECTION	**15.4**
Reasons for Attitude Maintenance	15.4
Attitude Maintenance Makes Early Information More Important	15.4
Early Information Experiment	15.4
ATTITUDE CHANGE	**15.5**
Definition of Attitude Change	15.5
Attitude Change is Difficult to Accomplish	15.5
Accomplishing Attitude Change	15.7
SUMMARY OF FEELINGS	**15.8**
Subjectivity of Feelings	15.8
Conflict Between Feelings	15.9
Control of Feelings	15.10
CONCLUSION	**15.10**
**EXPERIMENT 15.1	ATTITUDE CHANGES - OTHERS**	**15.11**
**EXPERIMENT 15.2	ATTITUDE CHANGES - SELF**	**15.11**
ELABORATION QUESTIONS	**15.12**

GUIDING QUESTIONS

- » What are attitudes?
- » How are attitudes different from expected-value and affect?
- » What is the function of attitudes?
- » What are stereotypes?
- » How are stereotypes related to attitudes?
- » How are attitudes formed?
- » What is the anchor-and-adjust model?
- » How and why are attitudes maintained and protected?
- » Why are first impressions so important?
- » What is attitude change?
- » How easy is it to change an attitude?
- » What are the most effective attitude change strategies?
- » What are similarities of the three types of feelings?
- » What are the differences in the three types of feelings?
- » What happens when feelings are subjective?
- » What happens when feelings conflict?
- » What happens when feelings are uncontrolled?

INTRODUCTION

*As noted in a preceding chapter, the ability to calculate expected-value is a tremendously adaptive device. However, the attention (short-term memory capacity) required to compute expected-value is in great demand and short supply. As a result, optimal use of processing capacity requires the individual to "automate" many feelings while saving situation-specific analysis for novel, threatening, or otherwise important events. These **automated evaluations** are known as **attitudes** and represent an important contribution to the individual's selection of behaviors.*

ATTITUDES

THE DEFINITION OF ATTITUDES

Although there is no universally accepted definition of attitudes, most are very similar and many employ the same terminology. For the purpose of our discussion, the definition offered by two leading attitude researchers, Fishbein and Azjen (1975, p. 6), will be adopted:

> ". . . **(an) attitude** can be described as **a learned predisposition to respond in a consistently favorable or unfavorable manner with respect to a given object.**"

An attitude is composed of calculations of expected-value and/or affective responses that have been learned, summarized, and **automated** through repeated experience with the object. Thus the formula for an attitude for an object is:

THE FUNCTION OF ATTITUDES

Most people engage in detailed evaluation on a limited basis, and this is especially true when the object being evaluated is boring, unimportant, or well known to the individual. This tendency to limit active evaluation is referred to as the **principle of information-processing parsimony**. According to this principle, because of man's limited cognitive capacity, human decision-makers will adopt strategies that permit them to process as little data as is necessary in order to make rational decisions. In other words, it is a mental burden for people to evaluate numerous environmental objects. So, over time we construct an attitude toward the object and then use this

Notice that according to the definition, attitudes **must** mediate behavior toward an object since **consistent association** is the basis for determining their existence. Thus, when an individual has an attitude toward an object (or person), his/her behavior toward that object **must be similar or consistent over time.**

$$\text{ATTITUDE}_{\text{OBJECT}} = \text{EXPECTED-VALUE}_{\text{OBJECT}} + \text{AFFECT}_{\text{OBJECT}}$$

The key determinant of an attitude is that it comes from the **long-term memory** in an **automated fashion**. Indeed, the easiest way to keep the three feeling states separate is to identify their source: expected-value comes from the short-term memory; affect comes from body chemistry; and attitudes come from the long-term memory.

automated feeling to prejudge it. Doing so saves a lot of STM capacity that would otherwise have to compute expected-value.

For example, consider your favorite musicians. Over time you had many positive experiences with their music. When they put out a new song you will have a favorable pre-judgment of it (positive attitude) so that detailed evaluation before purchase is not necessary (saving you time and energy).

Musical Preference - Rock and Roll

STEREOTYPES – ATTITUDE GENERALIZATION

Once a person develops an attitude toward an object, the attitude can be **generalized** so that it ultimately forms a **stereotype**. Specifically, attitudes formed toward members of a category can be generalized to the entire group. The key difference between attitudes and stereotypes is that you **personally know** all the objects of your **attitudes**. In contrast, for a stereotype, you do not personally know the object, it just belongs to a group that contains things you like or dislike. So, you assume that you will like/dislike this object too (due to cognitive consistency).

Continuing the music example, most people will organize musicians into organized groups (Level II codes) to facilitate memory and evaluation. For example, most people have categories that include rock and roll, rhythm and blues, bluegrass, country, etc. Once these categories have been defined, a general evaluation (i.e., a stereotype) can be assigned to each one.

Assume you have a positive stereotype for rock and roll and a negative stereotype toward bluegrass. Notice that once you have identified these categories and learned a stereotyped toward each one, it becomes very easy to evaluate music-related objects, such as songs, artists, concerts, etc. For example, if you are told a new song is rock and roll, you will be **predisposed** to perform positive behaviors toward it (since your stereotype toward rock and roll is favorable). As a result, you will be likely to listen to the song and perhaps buy it or recommend it to a friend.

Similarly, suppose you are told that a new station is operating on a Bluegrass format. Since your stereotype toward bluegrass is unfavorable, you probably will not listen to the station (selective exposure). In both examples, stereotypes play an important "screening" role by **predisposing** your actions based upon generalizations from previously learned attitudes. This, in turn, reduces processing time requirements since new objects do not need detailed individual processing (expected-value) but can be conveniently judged by their membership in a broader (summarized) category. In this way, your stereotypes influence many of your interactions with the environment. This generalizing process seems especially likely for objects that are frequently encountered.

Thus, in an attempt to reduce evaluation, people consolidate, summarize and automate evaluations toward objects they know well (attitudes) and objects

THE ANCHOR AND ADJUST MODEL OF ATTITUDE FORMATION

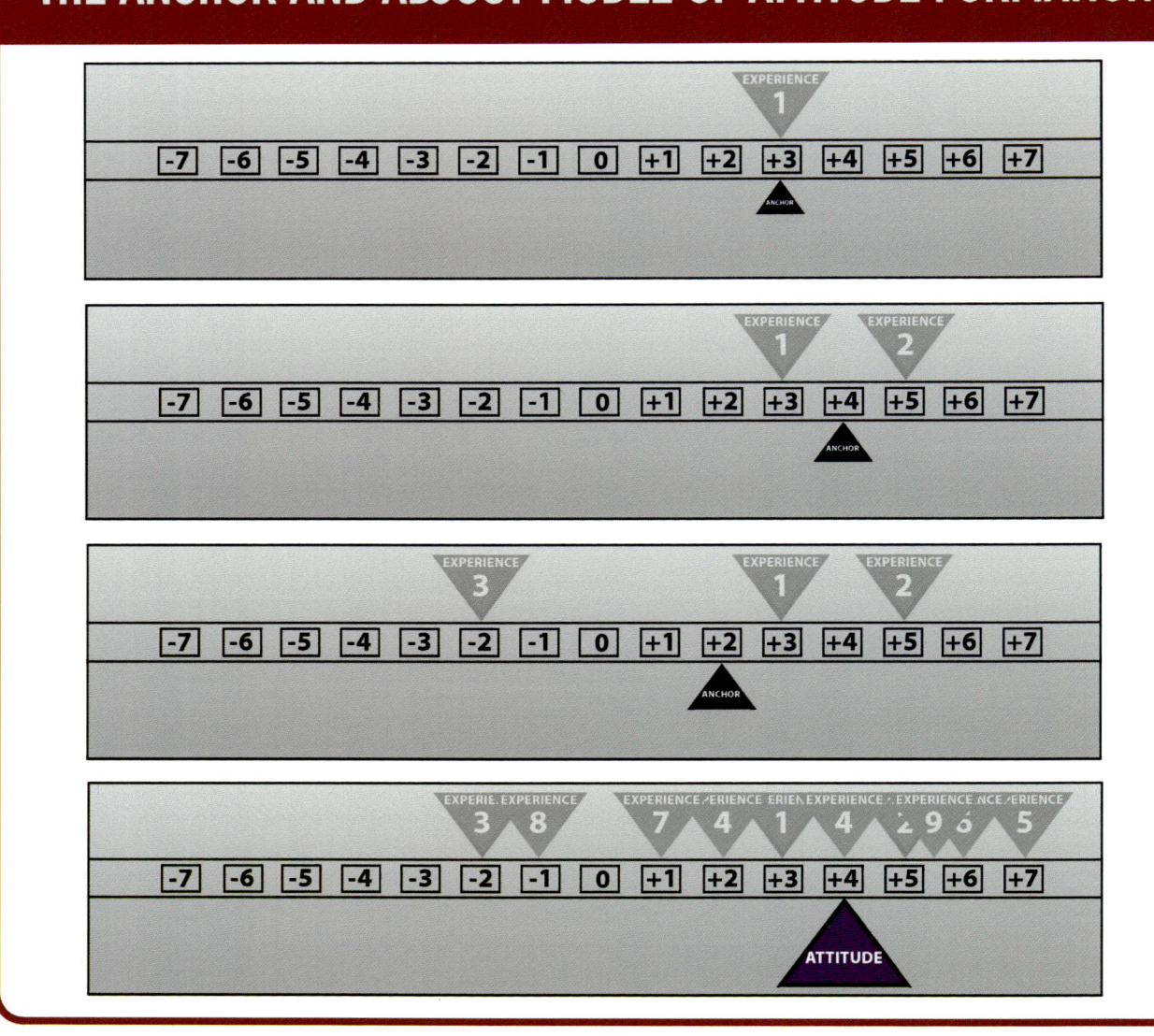

Model 1

they may have never experienced (stereotypes). Once constructed, attitudes and stereotypes serve as a quick and efficient referents for behavior.

ATTITUDE FORMATION

It is important to note that the process whereby emotions and/or expected-value is **learned** and **consolidated** into a summary label is typically an **extended learning process**. As an example, Wright (1976) states: "Attitude formation is a lengthy, continuous procedure in which a person repeatedly encounters new information about the product, integrates this into his/her existing global impressions, encounters another piece of data, reintegrates, etc. As it unfolds, it is a **leisurely process**." (emphasis added)

The attitude formation process is often illustrated using an **anchor and adjust** model as shown below. In this model, the gray triangles represent each experience with the attitude object and its degree of favorableness or unfavorableness and the attitude anchor is the black triangle on the bottom. The anchor position is originally set by the first experience with the

15.3

object so it is directly below the first experience. At this formative stage, the anchor position is usually weak and easily moved. The second experience is more positive which moves the anchor in that direction. Now the anchor position will locate around the average of the two experiences. Experience three is negative so the anchor moves in that direction. Over the series of experiences, the anchor position moves in the direction of the new experience, but each time the forming attitude gains more strength and becomes harder to move - as shown by its increasing size. At some point, the individual will have so much experience that the anchor position transforms into an attitude. At this point, the position becomes **automated** and extremely **hard to change**.

ATTITUDE MAINTENANCE AND PROTECTION

REASONS FOR ATTITUDE MAINTENANCE

Many researchers have concluded that once people expend the time and effort required to construct an attitude, they will be motivated to maintain or protect it. Obviously, our tendencies toward cognitive consistency and our selective defense mechanisms will operate to support existing attitudes. Reasons why people engage in attitude maintenance include the following:

1. Individuals find attitude discrepant information to be psychologically uncomfortable and therefore, are motivated to reduce incoming dissonant information (Festinger 1957).

2. Once an attitude is revealed through consistent **behavior** toward an object, discrepant information could be viewed as an indictment of this past behavior. Accordingly, since we have a vested interest in maintaining our self-esteem, we are motivated to protect the dispositions revealed by past behavior (Bem 1972).

3. It is normally easier for individuals to perceive, comprehend, and remember consistent information because it is more easily organized and integrated into the existing cognitive structure (Anderson 1975).

ATTITUDE MAINTENANCE MAKES EARLY INFORMATION MORE IMPORTANT

It is important to note that both the selective defense mechanisms and attitude maintenance processes operate to bias incoming information to be more consistent with already established beliefs, values, and attitudes. Because of this, relatively early information about an object or person is overly represented in the cognitive structure. This makes early information critical in the attitude formation process because **first impressions** set the **initial anchor position** during attitude formation. In this instance, the individual establishes several initial beliefs about an object and then interprets further information to be consistent with these initial beliefs, regardless of the actual content of the new information.

EARLY INFORMATION EXPERIMENT

The power of first impressions can be demonstrated in a study using a popular research design. Subjects are randomly assigned to one of two treatment groups. Each group reads two paragraphs one positive, one negative about a hypothetical person named Jim. The only difference between the two treatment groups is the order of the information. One group read the positive information first, followed by the negative information. This order is reversed in the second treatment group. Each respondent was then asked to evaluate Jim on four commonly used semantic differential scales. The descriptions of Jim and the evaluation scales used are shown by Figure 1.

Positive Information: "Jim is a very friendly, outgoing, and easy to get along with boy. He has many friends who he eats lunch with and walks to school with. He is very motivated and likes to organize games to play at recess. He enjoys having good times with the kids

EVALUATION SCALES

JIM IS

good	+4	+3	+2	+1	0	-1	-2	-3	-4	*bad*
unfavorable	-4	-3	-2	-1	0	+1	+2	+3	+4	*favorable*
pleasant	+4	+3	+2	+1	0	-1	-2	-3	-4	*unpleasant*
unsuccessful	-4	-3	-2	-1	0	+1	+2	+3	+4	*successful*

Figure 1

he is with and they enjoy being his friend. He is very popular around school and is the first person to meet any new kids."

Negative Information: "Jim is the class clown and gets into trouble a lot for talking and goofing off. He does not think it is necessary to learn anything but just to have a good time. Because of this, his grades are very low and he is constantly being sent down to the principal's office. Jim is very mischievous and loves to pull pranks and practical jokes on the other kids. While they are usually harmless, they are annoying to the teacher."

Evaluation Scales: Based upon what you just read, please mark your overall opinion of Jim on the scales in Figure 1.

For analysis purposes, the responses to the four scales were added together to provide an overall evaluation of Jim that could range from -16 to +16. The results showed dramatically the forceful impact of early information. Respondents (n = 62) who read the **positive paragraph first** had a rated Jim **+5.05**. For those receiving the **negative information first** (n = 63), the rating of Jim was **+0.92**. In other words, both groups read exactly the same information about Jim, but those who received the positive information first were significantly more favorable toward him. A graphic representation of this effect is shown in Figure 2.

ATTITUDE CHANGE

DEFINITION OF ATTITUDE CHANGE

Conceptually, attitude change can be defined as a **significant alteration in an individual's predisposition to respond to an object.** Because attitudes, by definition, direct overt behavior, attitude change must cause a change in behavior toward the object. In fact, since **attitudes must always be inferred from behavior**, there is no way to identify attitude change except through behavior change. In addition, the definition of attitudes requires that this change be demonstrated by **new** and **consistent** behaviors.

ATTITUDE CHANGE IS DIFFICULT TO ACCOMPLISH

Because attitudes are often based upon beliefs and values, a successful attempt to change them must involve providing the subject with **new** or **discrepant information** about the target object (Fishbein and Ajzen 1975, p. 388). Accordingly, there are three basic methods by which the expected-value component of attitudes can be changed:

1. Change a belief (b_i) element.
2. Change an evaluation (e_i) element.
3. Add a new belief-evaluation ($b_i e_i$) component to the individual's cognitive structure.

15.5

THE POWER OF FIRST IMPRESSIONS

FIRST IMPRESSION   SECOND IMPRESSION   CONCLUSION

JIM IS VERY FRIENDLY...   JIM GETS INTO TROUBLE A LOT

JIM GETS INTO TROUBLE A LOT... JIM IS VERY FRIENDLY

Figure 2

If we consider these alternatives, it is easy to see why attitudes are so resistant to change attempts. First, changing beliefs is difficult due to the operation of **selective defense mechanisms**, which systematically eliminate and/or distort discrepant information to make it more consistent with existing beliefs. Indeed, the essence of cognitive dissonance theory is that individuals are motivated to reduce discrepant cognitions (Festinger 1957). Also, since an attitude is generated from several or many beliefs, it seems unreasonable to expect significant dispositional changes to occur, unless **dramatic, new information is received and accepted.**

Second, changing a person's evaluation of attributes would require an alteration of the person's values and/or method of evaluation. By their very nature, values function to distinguish good from bad, and right from wrong. Accordingly, **values are often even more resistant to change than beliefs.**

Third, adding new (or contradictory) belief and value components is also limited by the operation of the selective defense processes. Moreover, because attitudes normally require several ($b_i e_i$) components to generate the required affective intensity, the **overall attitude** would probably change only slightly with the addition of a new b_ie_i component (depending on content and salience).

Finally, by definition, attitudes cannot be easily changed. Recall that attitudes require **consistent** behavior toward an object. To change an attitude would necessarily entail a significant change in object-related behaviors. Therefore, if attitude change were easily accomplished then the frequent behavioral changes would violate the definitional requirement of **consistent behavior** – people with real attitudes do not flip back and forth.

Thus, though certainly not impossible, attitude change is exceedingly difficult to accomplish. Normally, dramatic new information is required. This information would probably need to come from direct experience with the object (i.e., through descriptive beliefs). Based on the discussion above, we can conclude that true attitude change is very difficult to accomplish.

ACCOMPLISHING ATTITUDE CHANGE

Difficulty aside, people sometimes seek to change the attitudes of others. As we have seen, this involves giving the target person new or discrepant information. Several guidelines for inducing attitude change are:

1. Attitude change will be maximized to the extent that the new or discrepant information is **salient, important, or instrumental to the target person.** For example, changing a college student's attitude about being shy is easier if the student knows this trait is counterproductive to job interviewing success.

2. Attitude change will be maximized to the extent that the new or discrepant information is delivered by a **credible source.** Unknown or non-credible sources are too easily derogated to be very effective in triggering true attitude change.

3. Attitude change will be maximized to the extent that the new or discrepant information is delivered in a **dramatic or attention-getting** way. This helps to overcome the target person's tendencies toward selective exposure and attention.

4. Attitude change will be maximized to the extent that the new or discrepant information is **repeated frequently**. This helps to overcome peoples' tendencies toward selective comprehension and retention.

5. Attitude change will be maximized to the extent that the target person can be induced to **interact positively** with the object of the attitude change attempt. For example, offering

Repetition in Advertising

free samples to persons who normally do not buy the brand can change some attitudes.

6. Put the target person in a **curious** mind set (as opposed to a cognitively consistency mind set) by asking interesting Level III questions.

SUMMARY OF FEELINGS

We have now examined the major characteristics of the three types of feelings. At this point, it will be useful to compare these evaluations on several important dimensions: subjectivity, conflict, and control.

SUBJECTIVITY OF FEELINGS

In our terminology, feelings are subjective to the extent that they are inaccurate for the immediate environment, and thus result in punishment when freely expressed through behavior. Therefore, the subjectivity or objectivity of any particular feeling depends on the extent to which it produces a maladaptive or adaptive behavior.

In this light, we can see that **emotions** are subjective for two reasons. First, they were designed by natural selection to help our ancestors adapt to a predator-filled environment. Due to their physical nature, these feelings have not changed as fast as our environment has changed. The result is that we are emotionally prepared for an environment that no longer exists. This can cause problems and maladaptive behaviors, as for example, an angry outburst toward an employer or loved one. The second reason emotions are subjective is because they are nonverbal in nature. When other people expect us to act "logically" or "rationally," it means they look for us to carefully calculate expected-value. However, emotions cannot easily take verbal goals into account, and, therefore, often produce "irrational" actions.

Expected-value represents human feelings that are based on controlled calculations in the STM, but even here, problems can occur. This happens because the accuracy of the cost-benefit equation is directly determined by the accuracy of the beliefs and values used in the calculation. As we have seen, humans have powerful tendencies to form biased beliefs and values due to cognitive consistency. In these cases, the individual will select overt behaviors that promise the greatest instrumentality, only to find their expectations are inaccurate.

Emotional Outburst

Attitudes

Attitudes are subjective for several reasons. First, attitudes may be based on summarized and generalized expected-value (and or emotions), which makes them susceptible to some errors and omissions (i.e., they can be composed of erroneous beliefs and values). A second disadvantage to letting attitudes direct behavior is that as automated summary labels, they lose a great deal of detail and specificity. For example, if you have a negative stereotype toward a category of objects, you will be unlikely to perform positive behaviors toward the objects assigned to this category. Here, you will miss individual and specific opportunities to interact with valued members of the group.

Because emotions, expected-value, and attitudes are often subjective, they result in a deterioration of the individual's schedule of reinforcement if they are freely expressed through behavior. Most people are aware of this phenomenon – we all feel obliged to hide our true feelings in some situations. In these cases, we realize that expressing our feelings will lead to punishment so we simply hide them and misrepresent ourselves. Unfortunately, as we have seen, the technique of not acting the way we feel (to avoid immediate punishment) creates significant frustration.

CONFLICT BETWEEN FEELINGS

As we have seen, three different types of feelings contribute to a person's selection of behaviors. In many instances, feelings from these different categories will conflict. When conflict occurs, the individual needs a mechanism to weigh the importance of the various feelings. This mechanism is called **motivation** and is directly tied to the individual's current **need states.** Indeed, Maslow hypothesized that motivation to satisfy a particular need depends upon the priority of that need and its present level of satisfaction.

For example, survival needs such as food and safety take priority over love and self-esteem needs. If feelings related to love conflict with feelings related to safety, the individual could be predicted to comply with the most basic needs. Thus, you may have a positive attitude toward a loved one, but if you are undergoing negative emotional states (e.g., sickness, fatigue, intoxication), you may engage in negative actions toward him/her. Another example is when an individual suppresses sexual emotions due to the possibility of negative future consequences (i.e., expected-value).

Even though emotions, expected-value, and attitudes may conflict, the individual must still choose the best available behavior. This choice is usually made on the basis of the relative goal attainment (instrumentality) promised by the alternative behaviors, all things considered. Notice that when conflict exists, once a decision is made, some feelings will be repressed.

CONTROL OF FEELINGS

As detailed earlier, people are capable of both automatic and controlled information processing. Nowhere are these two types of processing more demonstrated than in the generation of feelings. As an example of how feelings can be consciously controlled, consider how you will evaluate your employment opportunities after college. Probably, you will carefully compare the alternatives on salient attributes like salary, type of work involved, geographic location, opportunity for advancement, etc. After this conscious and controlled process, you will select the alternative you feel best suits your needs (i.e., has the highest expected-benefits). In this instance, your feelings have been "controlled" through direct awareness.

Conversely, emotions are nonverbal and thus they are not under the control of your internal dialogue. These feelings are automatic, and frequently occur without conscious recognition. Similarly, attitudes are also automated, but they are feelings of a verbal nature. In both cases, the individual does not consciously control his/her feelings. Not surprisingly, behaviors engendered by uncontrolled feelings can often turn out to be maladaptive.

CONCLUSION

Human beings are designed by natural selection to perform overt behaviors that are feeling-expressive. Accordingly, people almost always act the way they feel. These feelings may be an emotion, a spontaneous calculation of expected-value, an attitude/stereotype, or any combination of the three. Frequently, conflict will occur among feelings and force the individual to choose the behavior that promises the greatest reward, all things considered.

A major problem with feelings is that they are often subjective. These inaccuracies cause maladaptive actions that are subsequently punished by the environment. Because people are normally unaware that their feelings are inaccurate, they are often puzzled and frustrated by these punishments, thereby causing more negative feelings. In addition, when automated feelings produce maladaptive behaviors, the individual cannot identify the true nature of the problem (i.e., his/her own feelings) because s/he cannot remember the feeling that triggered the action. Accordingly, they believe that the environment or other people are punishing them for no apparent reason. Thus, when examining human behavior from the scientific viewpoint, we see a need for people to control their feelings, yet the inability for them to do so.

Losing Control of Feelings

EXPERIMENT 15.1
ATTITUDE CHANGES – OTHERS

1. Identify on of your key accounts who has a strong attitude or stereotype that you would like to change.

2. Explore the origin of the attitude/stereotype and why it is so strongly held.

3. Develop a list of three possible attitude change strategies based on the material on page 15.10.

4. Try these strategies over time (not all at once) and record the success or failure of each.

5. Summarize your results, which strategies worked and which did not?

EXPERIMENT 15.2
ATTITUDE CHANGES – SELF

1. Identify one of your own attitudes or stereotypes that you would like to change.

2. Explore the origin of the attitude/stereotype and why it is so strongly held.

3. Develop a list of three possible attitude change strategies based on the material on page 15.10.

4. Try these strategies over time and record the success or failure of each - enlist the help of your key accounts if possible.

5. Summarize your results, which strategies worked and which did not?

ELABORATION QUESTIONS

- Give an example where you successfully changed another person's attitude. To what do you attribute your success?

- Give some examples of stereotypes that consumers have towards products and services.

- How long did it take for you to develop some of your current attitudes?

- What is the best way to recover from a bad first impression?

- How do you normally react when someone tries to change your attitude?

- Do people with low self-confidence change their attitudes more easily?

- What percentage of your behavior is determined by expected-value? Affect? Attitudes?

- When should we hide our feelings and when should we show them?

- Is stereotyping a bad thing if everyone does it?

- Can an attitude be formed based on informational beliefs (what someone else tells you) or are descriptive beliefs (personal experience) required?

- How is it that stereotypes change (at the societal level) over time?

CHAPTER 16
CONSUMER DECISION-MAKING

INTRODUCTION	**16.1**
DECISION-MAKING VERSUS NON-DECISION-MAKING	**16.2**
Decision-Making or Problem Solving	16.2
Non-Decision-Making	16.2
THE DECISION-MAKING PROCESS	**16.2**
STEP ONE: PROBLEM RECOGNITION	**16.3**
Definition	16.3
Causes	16.3
Triggering Problem Recognition in Others	16.4
STEP TWO: INFORMATION SEARCH	**16.4**
Establishing Salient Evaluative Criteria	16.4
Accessing Information on Salient Evaluative Criteria	16.4
STEP THREE: EVALUATION OF ALTERNATIVES	**16.5**
Attitude-Referral	16.5
Calculating Expected-Value	16.6
The Conjunctive Rule	16.6
The Disjunctive Rule	16.7
The Lexicographic Rule	16.7
Other Choice Rules	16.7
STEP FOUR: CHOICE	**16.8**
STEP FIVE: FEEDBACK	**16.8**
CONCLUSION	**16.8**
**EXPERIMENT 16.1	TRIGGERING PROBLEM RECOGNITION**	**16.8**
ELABORATION QUESTIONS	**16.9**

GUIDING QUESTIONS

- What is consumer decision-making?
- What is consumer non-decision-making?
- What are the major characteristics of decision-making and non-decision-making?
- What are the steps in the decision-making process?
- What is problem recognition?
- How is problem recognition triggered?
- How do consumers search for information?
- What are salient evaluative criteria?
- When do consumers search internally for product information?
- When do consumers search externally for product information?
- How do consumers compare alternative products?
- What is the attitude-referral decision rule?
- What is the calculation of expected-value decision rule?
- What is the conjunctive decision rule?
- What is the disjunctive decision rule?
- What is the lexicographic decision rule?
- What are hybrid decision rules?
- What is feedback and how does it affect future purchase behaviors?

INTRODUCTION

In previous chapters, we have examined the thoughts and feelings that direct behavior to positively evaluated alternatives. However, at the end of the last chapter we saw that people often have feelings that conflict with one another and that this causes serious problems for consumers. In this chapter, we will see how the cognitive and affective components of the internal model are used in consumer decision-making. Clearly, this is a central issue in consumer behavior because it is the final decision that leads to purchase and ultimately sales revenues for the marketer.

Making careful decisions, solving important problems, and choosing from an array of attractive products is a fundamental aspect of being a modern consumer. Indeed, most consumers are required to solve a variety of problems every day. However, we must remember that much of our problem-solving equipment was originally designed for solving survival-related problems. Today, many of these problems have been solved for us thanks to civilized rules and regulations. Unfortunately, some people have real difficulties trying to adjust their inherited equipment (especially emotions) to the types of problems they face today.

Another difficulty in decision-making is that people often become bored with a problem they have repeatedly solved (e.g., finding one's way home from work). In such cases, the amount of attention devoted to the problem tends to decrease over time. Ultimately, the individual may automate a solution path so that conscious effort is no longer required (e.g., s/he drives home but think about something else). In fact, because of the perceptual bottleneck, most people automate solutions to frequently encountered problems, thereby saving precious short-term memory capacity for the most important and/or interesting problems.

Thus, for each individual we see a fluctuating pattern of decision-making techniques. True problem solving which uses the short-term memory to carefully evaluate alternatives is used sparingly, and sometimes begrudgingly (due to the mental effort required). On the other hand, automated solutions are used to solve many of the small problems and a surprising number of important problems. In general, the degree of conscious effort that precedes a decision can be placed on a continuum as shown in Model 1.

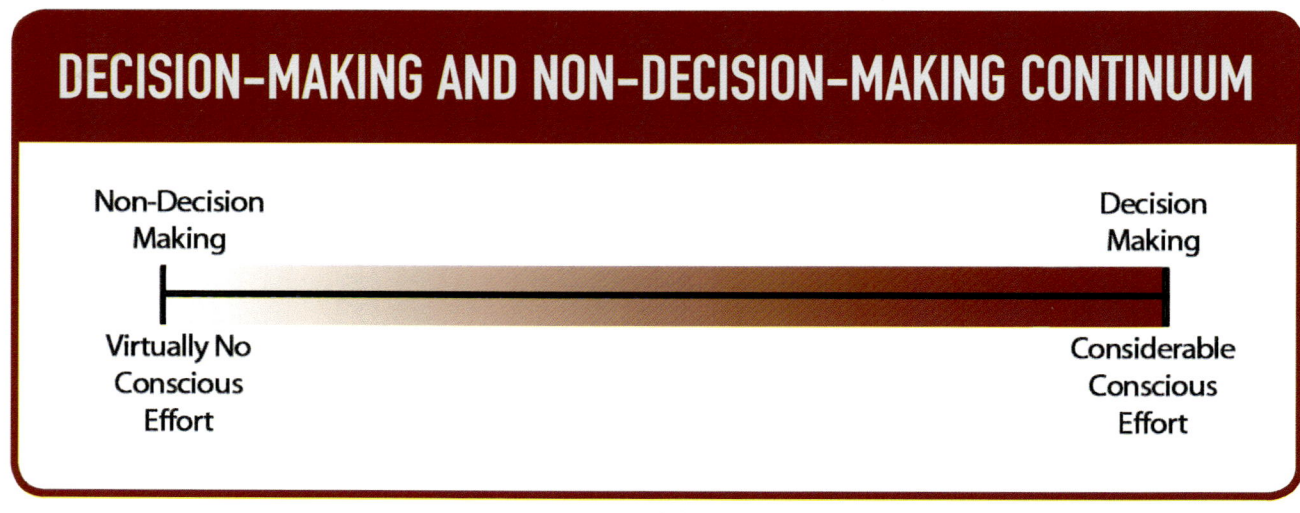

DECISION-MAKING AND NON-DECISION-MAKING CONTINUUM

Non-Decision Making — Decision Making

Virtually No Conscious Effort — Considerable Conscious Effort

Model 1

DECISION-MAKING VERSUS NON-DECISION-MAKING

DECISION-MAKING OR PROBLEM SOLVING

The terms "decision-making" and "problem solving" will be used interchangeably and refer to evaluation techniques that involve a large amount of **purposeful thinking.** Compared to non-decision-making processes, decision-making is usually controlled, effortful, objective, adaptive, and scarce.

Decision-Making is Controlled. The basic requirement for "controlled" evaluation is **direct awareness.** Therefore, controlled evaluations require the individual to use some of the limited capacity of the short-term memory (i.e., consciousness or attention). The awareness implicit in decision-making carries with it the advantages of careful and detailed evaluations. During this process the individual consciously searches for relevant information, thereby making the decision process relatively controlled.

Decision-Making is Effortful. Decision-making is relatively effortful for two reasons. First, cognitive effort must be expended to actively use the short-term memory in a controlled fashion. Second, people engage in decision-making for their more important decisions so they are more prone to actively search for objective data related to the choice. This also means that decision-making is usually based on more **recent** information than non-decision-making (which relies on old information due to its automated and semi-automated nature).

Decision-Making is Objective. We have already seen that evaluations are often subjective (especially emotions and attitudes), but some feelings are more adaptive than others. In general, **informed feelings** work best because they are based on a representative information sample. Of course, the representativeness of any individual's information sample is dependent upon the size of the sample and the **objectivity** with which it is drawn. Thus, decision-making is typified by controlled processes that tend to increase the amount and the objectivity of the object-related information that is considered during evaluation. As such, decision-making tends to be less error prone than non-decision-making.

Decision-Making is Adaptive. Because problem solving tends to be more controlled, objective, and sensitive, the behaviors it generates are among the most adaptive performed by the individual. This adaptiveness is rewarded by the individual receiving reinforcement.

Decision-Making is Scarce. By definition, decision-making requires the attention and awareness of the individual. However, the capacity and duration restrictions of the STM create a perceptual bottleneck for human beings. As a consequence, the amount of decision-making capacity available is severely limited.

NON-DECISION-MAKING

In contrast to decision-making, non-decision-making tends to be automatic, effortless, based on old information, analyzed subjectively, and often results in maladaptive behaviors which are punished. However, due to the restricted amount of decision-making space available in short-term memory, non-decision-making is abundant. This chapter will focus on decision-making while the major types of non-decision-making will be discussed in the next two chapters. A summary comparison between decision-making and non-decision-making is presented in Table 1.

THE DECISION-MAKING PROCESS

In earlier chapters we saw how human beings were genetically programmed to solve "primary" problems related to nourishment, protection, and reproduction. Thus, it is not an exaggeration to say that human beings are first and foremost problem solvers and decision-makers. As an example, if you were stranded in the middle of a forest what would you do first?

If you think about it, you should find that your answer to the question just posed is not very different from what you would do the first day on a new job. In both

DECISION-MAKING VERSUS NON-DECISION-MAKING

Decision-Making	Non-Decision-Making
1. Tends to be controlled (STM)	1. Tends to be automated (LTM)
2. Tends to be effortful	2. Tends to be effortless
3. Tends to be based on current information	3. Tends to be based on old information
4. Tends to be objective	4. Tends to be subjective
5. Tends to be adaptive and rewarded	5. Tends to be less adaptive and less rewarded
6. Is relatively scarce	6. Is relatively abundant

Table 1

cases, you would first attempt to satisfy your most pressing survival problem. In the forest, you would probably explore the immediate environment and look for secure territory and protection of various kinds (e.g., shelter, weapons, etc.). On a new job, you would probably explore the immediate environment which would be more complex, consisting of sub-environments including social, political, economic, etc. Then you would design various strategies for success, including protection of various kinds (e.g., checking with superiors, following orders, etc.).

The more we investigate human decision-making techniques, the more we find a specific pattern. Indeed, this process has been studied for some time and has been organized into five stages: problem recognition, information search, evaluation of alternatives, choice, and feedback.

STEP ONE: PROBLEM RECOGNITION

DEFINITION
The decision-making process begins with **problem recognition.** This stage is triggered whenever an individual recognizes, that there is a significant difference between the desired state of affairs and the actual state of affairs.

CAUSES
A major cause of problem recognition is the **rising and falling appetites** of the homeostatic needs. By definition, these needs can be satisfied only temporarily and inevitably begin to rise again. At some point, the needs state deviates too much from homeostasis and a problem (i.e., unsatisfied drive state) emerges.

Another major cause of problem recognition in marketing is the normal **consumption** and **depletion** of products and services on hand. As supplies are used up, consumers recognize that they must replace the items or some important need will go unsatisfied.

Another cause of problem recognition is consumer **growth** and **maturation.** As consumers age, they outgrow the need for some product categories (e.g., skate boards) and grow into the need for others (e.g., automobiles). Growth and development assure that consumers will face new problems and decisions throughout their lives

Another source of consumer problems are **unrealistic beliefs** and values that produce subjective expectations and feelings. When these components are erroneous (due to cognitive consistency or a biased information sample), the real world will be **unlikely** to conform to the individual's desires and expectations. In this instance, we can now see one price that people pay for subjective information-processing tendencies.

TRIGGERING PROBLEM RECOGNITION IN OTHERS

One of the most common persuasive techniques is to trigger problem recognition in other people, and then explain to them how your product will solve their problem. Advertising and personal selling in particular use this approach. Basically, this process can be triggered in two ways.

Identify your product as an ideal state. For example, advertisements stress that Budweiser is the "King of Beers," trying to establish it as the "ideal point" for domestic beers.

Identify inadequacies in the consumer's present state. Here, for example, an advertisement for a realtor could show a large family "suffering" in a small house.

It is important to note that problem recognition is almost always a highly personal process. As a result, promotions that seek to trigger problem recognition must be carefully designed. It is especially important to offer a *viable* (realistic) *solution* if you trigger problem recognition in others. Otherwise, you are likely to frustrate them into counterattack or withdrawal.

STEP TWO:
INFORMATION SEARCH

After a problem has been identified, most people will search for information on alternatives that may lead to a solution. The first step in this search process is to establish what types of information are relevant (or salient) to the problem at hand. Once such criteria are established, the individual can acquire relevant information.

ESTABLISHING SALIENT EVALUATIVE CRITERIA

Salient evaluative criteria are characteristics or features of a target object (or person) that are considered *important*. Thus, evaluative criteria are important attributes that are implicitly valued as good or bad. For an automobile, examples would include price, warranty terms, performance, perceived prestige, etc.

Obviously, these evaluative criteria differ in importance depending upon the individual's *current needs*. For example, when selecting a restaurant for lunch, the attribute "speed of service" will become increasingly important as the time available for lunch decreases.

Thus, evaluative criteria represent attributes that the individual can use to judge the object's value. The more important the criterion, the more weight it will carry in the overall evaluation of the object. The importance of a particular evaluative criterion can be expected to change when the decision maker's current needs and objectives change.

ACCESSING INFORMATION ON SALIENT EVALUATIVE CRITERIA

Once the individual establishes the evaluative criteria that are salient, s/he must then acquire information relevant to these criteria. This information is processed in the form of beliefs that represent the probability of association between the evaluative criteria and alternative objects. Suppose, for example, that a person is pressed for time and thus establishes a current objective of "eating lunch in a hurry." This represents a salient evaluative criterion to be applied to possible restaurants. To evaluate each restaurant, however, the individual will need to *recall* or *acquire* information relevant to the probability that each restaurant provides fast service.

Internal Search. Relevant information may be available as already established beliefs in memory. Here, the total effort required to solve the problem is significantly reduced. However, there is ample opportunity for error when we rely on our memory for important information. If the environmental contingencies have changed, the information from memory will be "old data" and can lead to a bad decision. Problems can also arise if the memory system has forgotten or distorted the salient information.

External Search. If insufficient information exists in memory, the individual will have to acquire relevant data from external sources, like surfing the web, asking friends, reading advertisements, talking to salespeople, etc. Notice that when external sources are needed,

Eating in a Hurry

some cost (in terms of overt effort expended) is incurred by the individual. How much effort a person is willing to expend to consult external information sources is determined by the usual cost-benefit analysis. When the perceived cost of further search is greater than the value of the information to be obtained, search will be terminated.

It is important to note that due to the perceptual bottleneck, tendencies toward selective retention, and the rapid pace of technology, we can predict that people often will need to consult external sources for expert (objective) information regarding many important choices. Therefore, the motivation to perform external search is one of the most adaptive skills in decision-making.

STEP THREE:
EVALUATION OF ALTERNATIVES

Once the individual has established salient evaluative criteria and acquired external information and/or remembered internally stored information, s/he can go on to evaluate alternative solution paths. In the decision-making mode, several types of "decision rules" are available to the individual. To continue with the restaurant example, suppose a consumer is deciding among four fast food restaurants for lunch (Arby's, McDonald's, Dairy Queen, Wendy's). Which one will be chosen often depends on the type of **decision rule** the individual selects.

ATTITUDE-REFERRAL

This is perhaps the easiest decision rule people can use to make a choice, since all the required information is conveniently stored in the memory system. As we learned earlier, attitudes are relatively strong, intense, feelings stored as summary labels in the LTM. If the individual has an attitude toward any or all of these restaurants, s/he can easily refer to the LTM to determine the one s/he **"likes best."** No new information is required, no effortful deliberations are needed, and the choice can be made very quickly.

Of course, people can only refer to attitudes if they have previously taken the time and effort to construct and learn (remember) them. Research has clearly established that strong object-related feelings (attitudes) do not exist for many consumer choices, especially when they are trivial (low-cost, low-risk) or infrequent. Instead, attitudes are most likely to exist (and thus be used) for objects that are frequently encountered or personally important.

Also note, that even if an individual has an attitude toward an object it will direct behavior only when the attitude-referral decision rule is used. We can all think of examples when we have performed counter-attitudinal behaviors because other factors caused us not to use the attitude-referral decision rule. As an example, if you were shopping with friends you might buy a more expensive brand of jeans than your favorite brand to impress your friends. In the final analysis, attitudes will direct behaviors only when: (1) they exist, and (2) the attitude-referral decision rule is used.

CALCULATING EXPECTED-VALUE

Use of this decision rule means that the individual takes the time and effort to spontaneously calculate the overall expected-value for each alternative. The information may come from memory or from external sources, but only salient criteria are evaluated. This is defined as a ***compensatory model***, meaning that the object's good features are balanced against the bad. In this way the good attributes "compensate" for the negative attributes, and the overall judgment is what counts. Choice is determined by comparing the calculations of EV for each alternative, and then selecting the alternative that promises the greatest benefits, all things considered.

THE CONJUNCTIVE RULE

Sometimes one or a few attributes are so important that they dominate the evaluation process. In these cases, the individual may use **non-compensatory** models (i.e., those that do not balance good features against bad features). One of these models is called the ***conjunctive rule*** where the evaluator sets up minimum requirements or cutoffs for salient evaluative criteria. If an alternative does not meet all cutoffs, it is rejected regardless of how well it scores on other attributes. Hence only those brands that pass all minimum acceptable values are considered. To continue with the restaurant example, suppose a consumer has an evaluative structure like Table 2.

EVALUATIVE STRUCTURE

Restaurant	Speed of Service	Price	Taste	Variety	Probability of Indigestion
Arby's	Slow	High	Very Good	Very Good	Low
McDonald's	Very Fast	Low	Moderate	Poor	High
Dairy Queen	Slow	Moderate	Good	Moderate	Moderate
Wendy's	Fast	Moderate	Good	Good	Moderate
Minimum Cutoffs	Fast	Moderate	Good	Good	Moderate
Acceptable Values	Very Fast	X	X	X	X

Table 2

An example of the conjunctive rule is provided by the row labeled ***minimum cutoffs.*** For this person, the minimum acceptable levels of the five evaluative criteria are: fast service, moderate price, good taste, good menu variety, and moderate probability of indigestion. Using this rule only Wendy's passes ***all*** cutoff values and thus represents the only acceptable restaurant. When more than one alternative passes all cutoffs, however, the final decision rule is unclear. Perhaps the evaluator will select the first alternative to pass all minimum values, or perhaps other rules will subsequently be applied.

THE DISJUNCTIVE RULE

The rationale for this non-compensatory rule is that an alternative may score high enough on one criterion to make it acceptable, regardless of its ratings on other criteria. An example of this rule is provided by the row labeled ***acceptable value.*** This row indicates that if a restaurant's speed of service is rated as very fast or higher, it is acceptable regardless of ratings on other attributes. According to this rule, McDonald's would qualify as the only acceptable restaurant. As in the case of the conjunctive rule, further decisions may be required if more than one alternative possesses the desired feature(s).

THE LEXICOGRAPHIC RULE

This rule assumes that evaluative criteria can be ranked in terms of importance. Alternatives are then compared on the most important criterion, and if one brand is preferred over other brands (on this criterion) it is chosen. If several alternatives are evaluated equally on the most important attribute, they are compared on the second most important criterion. This process is repeated until a selection is made. If speed is the most important criterion, it will be the first criterion considered. If two alternatives pass the cutoff of fast or very fast (e.g., Wendy's and McDonald's), then the next most important criterion will be considered.

OTHER CHOICE RULES

Research has shown that people are extremely adaptive in selecting choice rules. The five choice rules noted above are the most common, but depending on the situation, people can be quite creative in how they determine choice. Often, we combine several features of different rules to form ***hybrid decision rules.*** For example, we might use attitude-referral to generate a list of potential solutions, and then use the conjunctive model to chose from the "evoked set" of alternatives. It is often difficult to predict which choice rules will be applied in any given situation, though researchers are busy trying to answer this question.

Evaluating Alternatives

STEP FOUR: CHOICE

Choice represents the overt behavior of the decision maker. Normally, it entails the actual procurement of the alternative that was evaluated most favorably. If for any reason the selected alternative is unavailable, the individual must undertake further evaluation, though this may be as simple as choosing the alternative that was originally evaluated as the second best. In some cases more elaborate reevaluation is required; this is often the case when new information is received (e.g., price changes), or when the specifics of the choice situation differ significantly from those expected.

STEP FIVE: FEEDBACK

After choice has been implemented, the decision maker will gain direct experience with the selected alternative. If the choice performs according to expectations (or surpasses them), the consumer will be satisfied. If the choice performs below expectations, the consumer will identify a new problem **dissatisfaction** with choice. In this case, the consumer may engage in complaining behavior, return the product, or simply remember his/her dissatisfaction for subsequent purchase decisions. Whatever happens, direct experience with the choice usually has important consequences for future object-related actions because it forms descriptive beliefs.

It is important to note that feedback can be misinterpreted because it is influenced by tendencies toward cognitive consistency. For example, a consumer may misuse a product, resulting in its working poorly. In this case, many people would infer that the product was of poor quality because the alternative inference (that they themselves caused the problem) would not be consistent with their ego-support tendencies.

CONCLUSION

The decision-making process consists of five basic steps (problem recognition, information search, evaluation of alternatives, choice, and feedback). Fortunately, this process is easy to study and understand because, by definition, we are aware of our own decision-making experiences. Thus, decision-making occurs at a level that is relatively controlled, effortful, current, objective, and adaptive. The enormous advantages of this controlled processing are reflected in solved problems, adaptive behaviors, and environmental rewards. Unfortunately, decision-making requires attention and awareness which are in short supply but great demand. As a result, while almost everyone is capable of, and does accomplish some amount of problem solving, a great number of less important decisions are addressed by non-decision-making techniques.

EXPERIMENT 16.1
TRIGGERING PROBLEM RECOGNITION

1. Identify two key accounts who have problems but are unaware of them.

2. For each key account try to trigger problem recognition in a tactful and creative way.

3. Summarize your techniques and how successful they were.

4. Trigger recognition of one of your problems that you are unaware of - use key accounts if needed.

5. What is the best way to trigger problem recognition in other people?

ELABORATION QUESTIONS

- What portion of your consumer behaviors are prefaced by decision-making?

- What is the best sales approach if you have a customer who is going through the decision-making process?

- Give some examples of effective strategies to get consumers to recognize a problem with their existing products.

- What were your salient evaluative criteria when selecting a university? What decision rule did you use? Why?

- List five product categories where you do not need to search externally for information.

- Give one example of when you have used each of the following decision rules in the purchase of a product or service: attitude referral, expected-value, conjunctive, disjunctive, lexicographic.

- What are the major factors that determine if you are satisfied or dissatisfied with a product or service?

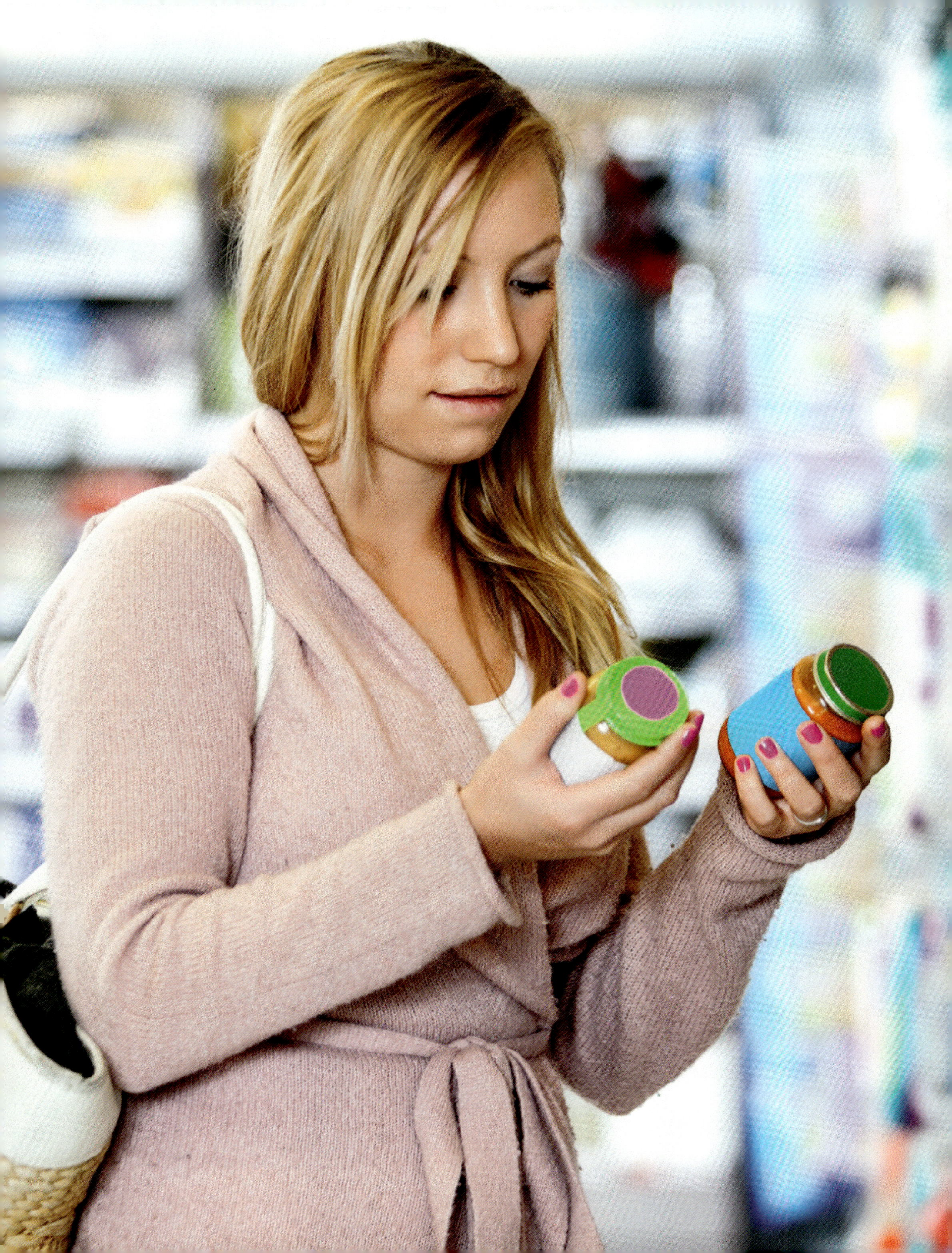

CHAPTER 17
NON-DECISION MAKING I: THINKING SHORTCUTS

INTRODUCTION 17.1
    Mental Shortcuts 17.1
    Motivation for Mental Shortcuts 17.1
    Attitudes 17.2
    Emotions 17.2
    Psychological Reactance 17.2

SHORTCUT CATEGORY #2: ACTING WITH MINIMAL THINKING 17.3
    Introduction 17.3
    Scripted Behaviors 17.4
    Impulsive Behaviors 17.6

SHORTCUT CATEGORY #3: ACTING WITHOUT THINKING 17.6
    Definition of Habits and Routines 17.6
    Acquisition of Habits - Learning With and Without Awareness 17.7
    Motivation for Forming Habits 17.8
    Consequences of Habits 17.8

CONCLUSION 17.8

EXPERIMENT 17.1 | PSYCHOLOGICAL REACTANCE 17.9

EXPERIMENT 17.2 | BREAKING SCRIPTS AND HABITS 17.9

ELABORATION QUESTIONS 17.10

GUIDING QUESTIONS

- What is the **THINK → FEEL → ACT** sequence?
- What are metal shortcuts?
- What is feeling without thinking?
- What is psychological reactance?
- How does reverse psychology work?
- What is the boomerang effect?
- When does psychological reactance occur?
- What is acting with minimal thinking?

- What are scripted behavior?
- Why do consumers use scripts?
- How are scripts formed?
- What is a causal script?
- What is a role script?
- What are impulsive behaviors?
- What are habits and routines?
- What is learning without awareness?
- Why do people form habits?
- What are the consequences of habits?

INTRODUCTION

In previous chapters, we learned that people undertake "reasoned behaviors" when they take the time and effort to think and feel before they act. Specifically, we have examined consumer thinking (i.e., attention, awareness, involvement, knowledge, beliefs, and memory), consumer feelings (i.e., expected-value, affect, and attitudes), and consumer choice (i.e., decision-making). This "reasoned" decision making sequence of behaviors is often abbreviated as: **THINK → FEEL → ACT.** *Note that when the consumer is engaged in the full decision-making process s/he actively participates in each of the three stages using relatively* **objective and controlled situation-specific analyses.**

Many models of human exchange behavior have focused on these controlled processes to explain how individuals transform environmental information into overt behavior. In general, these models hypothesize that people evaluate, infer, remember, or otherwise **think and feel before they act.** A great deal of research effort has been devoted to describing and explaining these decision-making processes with the implicit assumption that they are often operationalized by individuals before they act. Examples of such decision-making models include economic man, cognitive psychology, field theories, utility theory, and expectancy-value theory.

MENTAL SHORTCUTS

Many researchers have come to believe that the amount of careful decision-making that precedes behavior has been greatly over-estimated. The emphasis on problem-solving models is not really surprising for three major reasons. First, because decision-making represents the complete evaluation and choice process, it is naturally of great interest to marketers. Second, it is relatively easy to study and understand the decision-making process because, by definition, it is conscious and thus readily available to both researcher and consumer. Third, most of the problem solving models were conceived and developed by using the very decision-making processes (i.e., thinking) that were subsequently generalized to other people in different situations.

In summary, we have seen that when people are in the "reasoned behavior" mode, they follow a response sequence of **THINK → FEEL → ACT**. In this case, the environment is surveyed and carefully analyzed (thinking), then evaluated according to the existing value structure of the actor (feeling), and finally an appropriate behavior is performed (acting). Usually, though not always, this carefully deliberated response sequence will maximize the individual's subsequent schedule of reinforcement. Unfortunately, we now know that people do not precede all, most, or in some cases, even many actions with an informed and objective deliberation. It is more common for people to preface their behaviors with one of several abbreviated versions of the **THINK → FEEL → ACT** sequence.

MOTIVATION FOR MENTAL SHORTCUTS

We have already noted that the theory of **information-processing parsimony** suggests that people tend to be lazy with their mental efforts. This path of least resistance model is based on the premise that thinking and evaluating are mentally burdensome, and therefore, they are minimized on many (but not all) occasions. Indeed, many theories have been developed that describe specific variations of human behavior that are not prefaced by careful thought and evaluation. These theories can be organized into five major categories of mental shortcuts.

MENTAL SHORTCUTS

BEHAVIOR CATEGORY	RESPONSE SEQUENCE
I. Reasoned Behaviors	THINK → FEEL → ACT
II. Non-Reasoned Behaviors	
A. Thinking Shortcuts	
1. Feeling without Thinking	FEEL → ACT
2. Acting with Minimal Thinking	think → FEEL → ACT
3. Acting without Thinking	→ ACT
B. Feeling Shortcuts	
4. Acting without Feeling	THINK → ACT → FEEL
5. Impression Management	FEEL NEGATIVE → ACT POSITIVE

Figure 1

SHORTCUT CATEGORY #1
FEELING WITHOUT THINKING
(FEEL → ACT)

A common alternative for people unwilling to engage in careful deliberation is the **FEEL → ACT** response sequence. This represents a major shortcut, since spontaneous calculation in the short-term memory (i.e., Thinking) is not required, as it is in the decision-making sequence. There are three major examples of this thinking shortcut: (1) *attitudes* (i.e., prefabricated evaluations), (2) *emotions* (i.e., instinctual evaluations), and (3) *reactance* (discussed below). In each of these cases, the individual makes an implicit (and often unrecognized) decision to trade the detail of reasoning for the quickness and effortlessness of the **FEEL → ACT** sequence.

ATTITUDES

Attitudes have been defined as "automated feelings" because they are predispositions to respond in a consistently favorable or unfavorable manner with respect to an object, issue, or person. Attitudes are shortcuts because they eliminate the need for spontaneous calculation of expected-value. This saves us considerable mental effort each day, especially with frequently encountered objects. Of course, we also noted that attitudes are situationally insensitive and therefore, can produce maladaptive behaviors.

EMOTIONS

"Emotional" is a term frequently used to describe people who let their primary feelings (such as fear, anger, territoriality) direct large portions of their overt behavior. As we saw earlier, emotions are basically suited to an environment that no longer exists (for most of us). Emotions tend to be non-verbal, hard to suppress, and not forward thinking. When expressed in today's society, emotional responses can be punished, thus deteriorating the individual's schedule of reinforcement. This is the ultimate price for taking mental shortcuts and using "uninformed feelings" to direct behavior.

PSYCHOLOGICAL REACTANCE

Another type of behavior prefaced by a lack of awareness is described by reactance theory. The term *reactance* refers to the motivational state of a person who perceives that his/her freedom of choice has been threatened. Such threats often come in the form of an influence attempt that relies on coercion or high-pressure tactics. People who perceive a threat to their freedom of choice usually engage in behaviors that they think will reassert their freedom. Operationally, such reactance effects often take two major forms:

1. A person will become increasingly more interested in denied or forbidden behaviors. For example, if you tell people not to do something, they often become more interested in doing it. This is sometimes referred to as **reverse psychology.**

2. A person will become increasingly less interested in forced alternatives or behaviors. This is sometimes labeled the **boomerang effect,** as for example when a salesperson's hard sell becomes threatening and ultimately causes the customer to become reticent or to lose interest.

For a reactance effect to occur, two conditions must be met. First, there must be a **prior expectation of freedom** regarding the choice or behavior. Second, the perceived loss of freedom must relate to an issue or behavior that has some **consequence or importance** to the individual. When these two conditions hold, and an individual perceives a threat to freedom, reactance effects often occur.

Behaviors generated by reactance effects qualify as feeling without thinking because the individual does not carefully calculate the expected-value of the reactance behavior. Instead, the operational feelings are based on a perceived threat to freedom of choice, though it is important to remember that perception does not equal reality (i.e., the threat may be "imagined"). Notice, however, that in their attempt to reassert freedom of choice, people may perform behaviors that are counterproductive to their own interests (e.g., a consumer who is persuaded to buy a product that is not really needed, just because it was the last one left and others wanted it). Thus, when engaged in a reactance mode, people can easily adopt behaviors that are subjective and maladaptive.

Perceived Loss of Freedom

In a marketing context, Clee and Wicklund (1980) have identified several applications of reactance theory. First, hard sell promotional strategies must not appear excessively coercive, or the boomerang effect may occur. Second, product scarcity may increase the consumer's interest or desire by suggesting a potentially unavailable purchase behavior. Third, a reactance effect often occurs whenever the individual makes a major purchase decision. In this case, a "self-imposed" threat to freedom of choice occurs because after the actual selection is made, the freedom to chose among competing alternatives is no longer available. The resulting post-purchase increase in the desirability of non-chosen alternatives tends to magnify post-purchase cognitive dissonance.

SHORTCUT CATEGORY #2
ACTING WITH MINIMAL THINKING
(think → FEEL → ACT)

INTRODUCTION
A common shortcut of the **THINK → FEEL → ACT** response sequence occurs whenever people preface their actions with minimal thinking. There are two major examples of this thinking shortcut: (1) scripted behaviors, and (2) impulsive behaviors.

Scripted Behavior for Attracting Attention

SCRIPTED BEHAVIORS

Definition. In general, scripts represent ***prescribed*** behavior patterns that are enacted on cue. By observation and experience, individuals learn and then over-learn the behaviors associated with particular cues (e.g., how to attract attention from others). When appropriate cues are encountered (e.g., you go to a party and see someone you would like to meet), the actor accesses the appropriate script and plays the corresponding role (e.g., begins to perform his/her "attract that person's attention" script). This process often occurs at the subconscious level (i.e., without awareness) and thus, scripted behaviors are relatively automated or over-learned.

In these instances, a small amount of superficial environmental analysis is performed (think), after which the individual employs a mental subroutine or script, to guide his/ her overt behavior. Notice that scripted behaviors are likely to differ significantly from reasoned behaviors because scripted behaviors do not actively process the particulars of the situation, but instead represent a general behavior pattern.

Motivation for Using Scripts. Researchers have advanced the following reasons for the use of scripts:

1. Many behaviors are easily over-learned and do not require constant higher order processing. For example, driving the same route to and from work each day frequently becomes over-learned. It is not uncommon for drivers to experience moments of realization that they drove for a considerable distance without thinking about the actual driving. Also, using scripts can help us to multi-task.

2. Directing behavior by script frees the higher order processes to work on more important problems, plans, ideas, dreams, etc. In addition, using scripts represents an opportunity to let the mind "rest" or "relax."

3. Thinking is effortful and therefore, is less likely to be operationalized in situations where it is not needed. This resembles a "path of least resistance" motive (i.e., information processing parsimony).

Summarizing the results of a series of experiments, involving the use of scripts Langer (1978) notes:

> *"These studies seem to support the idea that much of the behavior we assume to be performed mindfully instead is enacted rather mindlessly; . . . people may process only a minimal amount of information to get them through their day."*

Formation of Scripts. Scripts are formed as careful evaluations, and then begin to lose detail and become summarized, consolidated, and automated over time and with repetition. Detailed processing generates reasoned or "thinking" behaviors where individuals actively process the specifics of the situation and refer to these specifics before acting. However, as these specific evaluations are transferred to long-term memory for future use, they are generalized, organized, and summarized. Some loss of detail comes from forgetting through decay, interference, and retrieval failure.

Over time, as the summary label is repeatedly activated, the original evaluation becomes **over-learned** through practice and therefore, strongly entrenched as a behavioral cue. In addition to being more easily accessed and operationalized, these summary labels are quick, easy, and efficient behavioral cues, consistent with information processing parsimony.

Examples of Scripts. As an example of a script, think about how you act at a restaurant. If you had a videotape of the last twenty restaurants you visited, you would likely see a great deal of similarity in your behavior. When you enter a restaurant you probably have a preformed script for behaviors which may look something like this:

1. Look for a hostess	5. Wait
2. Sit at a table	6. Eat
3. Observe menu	7. Pay check
4. Order food	8. Depart

Types of Scripts. One important type of script is a **causal script,** which we use to identify cause-effect relationships. We have already examined how people commonly make a large number of inferences and

Restaurant Script - Review Menu

assumptions about other people and events. In order to produce these inferences, the individual must have some causal scripts of how the world works. Causal scripts are frequently used to create inferences when the individual is required to fill in missing information with guesses and assumptions. For example, you may have automated a script that relates money to happiness (i.e., you automatically believe that having a lot of money would make you happy).

Another important type of script is a **role script.** These scripts associate certain general environmental cues to certain general over learned behaviors. Here, behavior is directed by reference to the appropriate script or role rather than by a detailed analysis of the situation. A housewife, for example, may purchase an expensive name brand rather than an inexpensive but virtually identical generic brand because she includes the script "Buy a good brand for the family" in her wife-mother role. Careful higher order processing might lead to the purchase of the generic brand, but the script may control purchase due to its ease of reference and its over-learned and automatic nature.

Thus, people are capable of both detailed "thinking" analysis and general "non-thinking" analysis as behavioral antecedents. In the case of scripts or **cognitive schemata**, actions are prefaced by minimal thinking. However, scripts are not the only example of minimal thinking.

IMPULSIVE BEHAVIORS

Basically, an impulsive behavior is one enacted without the benefit of careful problem definition or evaluation. In other words, impulsive behaviors tend to be made on the spur of the moment. They are not carefully thought out or planned. Upon closer inspection, however, it turns out that impulsive actions do follow the basic decision-making process (i.e., problem recognition, information search, evaluation of alternatives, and choice) as described earlier.

The difference is that here problem recognition often occurs quickly due to a situational cue or stimulus (e.g., feeling hungry and seeing a candy bar at a grocery store checkout station). Often such a spontaneously defined problem is resolved by selecting from a small set of alternatives (sometimes only one). The spur-of-the-moment nature of unplanned behaviors materially reduces the information search and evaluation of alternatives stages of the decision-making process. Not surprisingly, impulsive behaviors can turn out to be maladaptive in the long run.

Essentially, impulse behavior occurs when the entire decision-making process is collapsed into a short time span - often only seconds. Usually, however, some external stimulus is required to trigger problem recognition while simultaneously suggesting an immediate and convenient solution. Here, the minimal thinking prefacing behavior involves the evaluation of the triggering stimulus and the abbreviated decision-making process (shortened as it is).

SHORTCUT CATEGORY #3
ACTING WITHOUT THINKING
(→ ACT)

DEFINITION OF HABITS AND ROUTINES

For our purposes, a **habit** will be defined as an established behavior pattern that has been fully automated. Examples of habits would include smoking, eating three times a day, brushing teeth, using sarcastic humor, being shy, etc. A **routine** is the temporal program (i.e., timetable) for habits. Examples would include smoking after every meal; eating at 8:00 a.m., noon, and 6:00 p.m. every day; and brushing your teeth after every meal, working out at the gym every Monday and Wednesday, etc..

Virtually any verbal or overt behavior can become habitual, although complex behaviors (e.g., playing a piano, or shooting free throws) may require many trials before automation is achieved. Notice that a habit is similar to a script in that both are little "acts" that people perform. The difference is that scripted behaviors are activated by certain environmental cues. This process requires some thinking to identify the environmental cue. In contrast, a habit is so fully automated that environmental cues are not necessary to initiate the behaviors.

As an example, think of a person who smokes cigarettes when s/he is feeling nervous. This is a scripted behavior: cue = feeling nervous, response = smoke a cigarette. However, smoking is easily automated so the individual may start smoking habitually (i.e., even when s/he is not nervous). We can say that when the person smokes in response to being nervous s/he is engaged in a scripted behavior, and when s/he smokes without feeling nervous s/he is engaged in an automated (habitual) behavior.

ACQUISITION OF HABITS - LEARNING WITH AND WITHOUT AWARENESS

In general, we learn habits in two ways. The first is through conscious effort. For example, a basketball player may work long hours in an attempt to automate good free throw shooting form, or a pianist may work to automate a segment of a difficult piece of music. In both cases, the learner is aware of his/her efforts to learn the habit and can recollect the process by which s/he acquired it.

A second major way habits are learned is without awareness. Earlier, we discussed the concept of operant learning, whereby individuals acquire behaviors based upon a schedule of reinforcement. One of the examples used was the boy who was rewarded by his father for performing athletic behaviors and punished for "non-masculine" behaviors. Normally, such a child will acquire a host of athletic behaviors. Notice, however, that the child may be **too young** to understand fully what he is learning and why. In such a case, the child has learned athletic behaviors without an awareness of why or how. Even for adults, schedules of reinforcement are often **subtle** and **indirect**, making it difficult for them to be precisely aware of what or how they are learning. In summary, people learn many behaviors by a schedule of reinforcement. Often this process occurs without the explicit awareness of the learner. This is especially likely when:

1. The learner is young and incapable of identifying the schedule of reinforcement that "stamps in" the actions, or

2. The learner is any age but the schedule of reinforcement is subtle or indirect, or built in small increments over long periods of time.

Practicing Free Throws

MOTIVATION FOR FORMING HABITS

It should be noted that most behaviors that become habitualized once served an adaptive purpose in terms of expected-benefits. In the cigarette example, the individual began to smoke as a coping technique for releasing nervous energy. Although we know smoking is dangerous to health in the long run, the release of nervous energy is extremely instrumental to an anxious person in the short run. We can, therefore, predict that many young people will experiment with smoking to ease their nervousness. Unfortunately, the overt behaviors involved in smoking are easily learned, over-learned, and finally automated. Once this occurs, the individual will begin to smoke even when not nervous and ultimately acquire a smoking habit. It should also be noted that smoking has addictive (i.e., nicotine) as well as automated elements driving the behavior.

CONSEQUENCES OF HABITS

The good thing about habits is that no real thinking (not even minimal thinking) is required to perform them. In fact, the determining characteristic of habits is that they are performed without awareness (i.e., in non-thinking mode). In some cases, habits are useful and adaptive, like brushing your teeth after every meal. But in other cases, habits are detrimental to the adaptive mission of the individual (i.e., smoking or automatically criticizing everything new). In such instances, the individual pays a heavy price for automating maladaptive behaviors, which ultimately are punished by the environment. Even worse, due to the non-thinking nature of these actions, the individual rarely can identify them as problems since they are performed **without awareness.** As a result, it is common for people to attribute environmental punishments to incorrect sources when a habitualized behavior is the real cause.

A second major problem with habits and routines is that they can be expected to yield to the **law of diminishing returns** sooner or later. When the point of boredom is reached, the individual's perceived utility begins to decline, but the reason is obscured from conscious view. This can create a negative dynamic where people with many automated behaviors become bored, and ultimately depressed with their lack of positive reinforcement.

A third limitation of habits is that they tend to place the individual in a non-thinking mode of response. When the behaviors involved are simple (e.g., brushing teeth) or unimportant, routinization may benefit the individual. However, when the habitualized response is important or consequential (e.g., driving home from work), acting without thinking or evaluating can have severe consequences for the individual.

Thus, habitualization of some responses is a necessary by-product of our limited short-term memory. When easy or unimportant actions become automated, the individual's adaptiveness can be increased. When complex or consequential actions become routinized, however, the individual may be better off using decision-making processes.

CONCLUSION

In this chapter, we have examined a variety of shortcuts that reduce the amount of time people spend thinking before they act. At times, we cut thinking out of the response process altogether by feeling without thinking (attitudes, emotions, and reactance) and/or acting without thinking (habits and routines). At other times, the amount of thinking needed to respond is minimized by scripts, or impulsive decisions. While these non-reasoned behaviors save us time and mental effort, they also can cause us to act erroneously and to receive punishments. These thinking shortcuts are further complemented by a variety of feeling shortcuts discussed in the next chapter.

EXPERIMENT 17.1
PSYCHOLOGICAL REACTANCE

1. Find three ads or sales promotions that try to create the reactance effect. Project them in class and explain how they create a perceived loss of freedom for consumers.

2. Under what conditions is reactance most likely to influence consumer choice.

3. Give two examples of when you saw the reactance effect in a key account.

4. Try to create a reactance effect in one of your key accounts. Describe in class what you did and how successful it was.

EXPERIMENT 17.2
BREAKING SCRIPTS AND HABITS

1. Identify a major script or habit that you have developed that is maladaptive or limiting your growth.

2. Explain the origin of the script or habit.

3. Make an effort to eliminate the script/habit for a period of three days. Use your key accounts for feedback if necessary.

4. Summarize how well you did and the major difficulties you encountered.

ELABORATION QUESTIONS

- Give some examples of when you have engaged in the psychological reactance effect with a product or service.

- When is the best time or best situations to use the reactance effect in marketing?

- What are the major roles you play and what are the products you buy that are related to these roles?

- Give three examples of consumer scripts you use.

- Give three examples of impulsive purchase behaviors you have made and why you did not use decision-making.

- Give two examples of habits you have learned without awareness.

- What happens to consumer habits over time?

CHAPTER 18
NON-DECISION MAKING II: FEELING SHORTCUTS

INTRODUCTION 18.1
SHORTCUT CATEGORY #4: ACTING WITHOUT FEELING 18.1
    Low-Involvement Learning 18.1
    Trial Behaviors 18.2
    Self-Perception Theory 18.3
    Social Labeling 18.3
SHORTCUT CATEGORY #5: IMPRESSION MANAGEMENT 18.5
    Definition 18.5
    Personal Identity 18.6
    Expressive/Intrinsic Behaviors 18.6
    Coping/Extrinsic Behaviors 18.6
    Expressive vs Coping Behaviors 18.7
    The Coping Self 18.7
    The Hidden Self 18.7
    Ratio of Intrinsic to Extrinsic Behavior 18.8
    Identity Crisis 18.8
    Self-Esteem and Intrinsic/Extrinsic Behavior 18.8
    Social-Esteem versus Self-Esteem 18.9
RADICAL AND RATIONAL HONESTY 18.9
    Radical Honesty 18.9
    Rational Honesty 18.10
    The Extrinsic Society 18.10
    Importance of Marketing Yourself 18.10
    Consequences of Impression Management 18.10
SUMMARY OF NON-REASONED BEHAVIORS 18.10
EXPERIMENT 18.1 | PERSUASION BY SOCIAL LABELING 18.12
EXPERIMENT 18.2 | IMPRESSION MANAGEMENT 18.12

GUIDING QUESTIONS

- What are non-feeling behaviors (**THINK → ACT → FEEL**)?
- What is low involvement learning?
- How does advertising affect consumers who are not involved?
- Why is trial so important in marketing?
- What triggers trial purchase?
- What is self-perception theory?
- Which overt behaviors in a relationship require "love?"
- What is social labeling?
- When are consumers most receptive to suggestion?
- What factors determine whether a social label will be effective?
- What is impression management?
- When are people most likely to engage in impression management?
- How much of consumer behavior is prefaced by decision-making versus non-decision making?

INTRODUCTION

In Chapter 16 we examined the human problem-solving sequence of **THINK → FEEL → ACT.** *In Chapter 17 we learned that humans often take mental shortcuts in order to minimize the thinking component of the decision making sequence. In this chapter we will examine shortcuts that bypass the feeling or evaluation component of the decision-making process. Each of the theories discussed below was developed to explain situations where people do not act the way they feel (i.e., violate the Feel -> Act sequence).*

SHORTCUT CATEGORY #4: ACTING WITHOUT FEELING (THINK → ACT → FEEL)

LOW-INVOLVEMENT LEARNING

This theory was developed by Krugman (1965) to explain how repetitive television advertisements can affect viewers without their awareness. This theory is **restricted only to television (or radio) ads because unlike print ads** (which require active participation in the form of reading) broadcast media can work on "passive" viewers. Passive viewers are those who are not actively paying attention to the commercial. Instead, they may be thinking of the program, talking to a friend, or daydreaming, but they still see and/or hear parts of the ad message.

A second restriction to this theory is that it occurs only for **trivial or uninvolving products** (i.e., aluminum foil, tooth paste, etc.). In these cases, consumers have no reason to evaluate the product carefully, and therefore, they suspend their selective defense mechanisms. Since these screens are normally used to block out discrepant information, their suspension leaves the consumer in a vulnerable state. With these screens down, and over **massive repetition**, Krugman (1965) hypothesized that advertisements can rearrange beliefs in the viewer's internal model -- **without the viewer's awareness.**

As an example, consider the Ultra-Brite campaign that claimed the brand could "give your mouth sex appeal." This attribute (sex appeal) is normally not a major evaluative criteria for toothpastes. However, over massive repetition, the uninvolved consumer may come to associate sex appeal with toothpaste in the long-term memory.

EVALUATIVE CRITERIA FOR TOOTHPASTE

Before Advertising	During Advertising	After Advertising
1. Decay Prevention	1. Decay Prevention	1. Decay Prevention
2. Taste	2. Taste	2. **Sex Appeal**
3. Breath Freshening	3. Breath Freshening	3. Taste
4. Low Cost	4. Low Cost	4. Breath Freshening
5. Reliable Brand	5. **Sex Appeal**	5. Low Cost
	6. Reliable Brand	6. Reliable Brand

Table 1

As shown above, before advertising, the consumer does not include sex appeal as one of the evaluative criteria for toothpaste. However, during exposure to numerous TV ads that stress the "sex appeal" of Ultra-Brite, the consumer has learned (without awareness) to include sex appeal when evaluating toothpastes (as shown above). If the consumer is exposed to massive repetition over time, sex appeal can become more salient in the long-term memory as shown in the "after advertising" column above. At this point, the consumer may go shopping for toothpaste and subconsciously look for sex appeal. In addition, this consumer has developed a strong association between sex appeal and Ultra-Brite from exposure to the TV ads. As a result, the consumer may buy Ultra-Brite without knowing exactly why, since conscious evaluation did not precede choice. The consumer buys the brand on the basis of a vaguely held, subconscious, expectation of sex appeal.

The major problem with this theory is that it relies on shifts in **subconscious** beliefs to explain the **THINK → ACT → FEEL** sequence. This means the theory is very difficult to test scientifically, and it is therefore, very speculative. Nevertheless, the model's two major underlying principles (i.e., selective information processing and learning without awareness), have been empirically validated so many marketing researchers have accepted this theory, due to its "intuitive appeal." In summary, it is reasonable to expect that low-involvement learning might occur in the marketplace when all the conditions noted above are met.

TRIAL BEHAVIORS

A second occasion where consumers may purchase a product (or perform other target behaviors) without first forming feelings is known as "trial." Indeed, the major rationale for performing a trial behavior is to "find out if you like it." In these cases, we once again see the **THINK → ACT → FEEL** sequence, where product evaluation does not precede purchase.

A major reason for trial is that consumers are unsure of the product's attributes (i.e., they have lower order beliefs due to their lack of direct experience with the brand). For example, a consumer may read an advertisement for a new snack food item. The advertisement makes the snack sound good tasting, but due to the **vested interest** of the sponsor, the consumer may not "believe" the claims. Instead of "liking" the product based on the ad, the consumer may decide that the new snack item **might** be good. In this instance, an easy way to remove the uncertainty is to "trial purchase" the product and then base higher-order beliefs on the resulting direct experience. When implicitly evaluated, these strong beliefs will create strong feelings toward the product.

It is important to note that trial behaviors can be predicted only when the trial is relatively low in cost and risk. If the consequences from purchase are significant, few people will risk a trial that may create negative feelings. For example, people almost always test drive a car before purchase. In this case, a trial creates strong

Trying a New Snack Food

beliefs, which lead to strong feelings of expected-value and ultimately to a willingness to make a committed purchase.

Thus, **trial and error** is a major example of the **THINK ⟶ ACT ⟶ FEEL** response sequence. When the trial is low in cost and risk, the information value that creates higher order beliefs is easily obtained. Normally, this is a very useful and adaptive trade. However, if the trial behavior is high in cost or risk (e.g., drugs, marriage, durable and expensive goods, etc.), it is easy to perform maladaptively and pay a prolonged or expensive price for the lesson.

SELF-PERCEPTION THEORY

Self-perception theory was developed by Daryl Bem (1972) to describe a particular situation when people act without feeling. According to Bem, this can happen when a person's internal states (feelings) are "weakly cued." An internal state is said to be weakly cued or ambiguous when, during maturation, a child is not taught to adequately describe that feeling. While states such as hunger or pain may be easily taught to the developing child, less concrete or identifiable feelings (like romantic "love") may not be properly cued. In this case, the individual will not have a clear conception of what "love" is.

According to self-perception theory, people act without feeling and then observe their own behavior to determine how they feel. As an example, a list of behaviors that could evolve in a romantic relationship are presented in Figure 1.

In this hypothetical sequence of behaviors, there is probably a point at which you would say: "I would not do this unless I 'loved' the other person." However, people who are not sure of what love is have no easily cued internal states to direct their overt behavior. Indeed, teens are often told that what they think is "true love" is, in fact, just a "crush," an "infatuation," or "puppy love." No wonder so many people have such a difficult time knowing what love really is and how they are supposed to respond to it!

In these cases, people may observe their own behavior and then **infer** what their feelings must be in order to act that way. Thus, a young man who has a weak idea of love may decide that he is in love because he has performed certain overt behaviors (e.g., spent a lot of money, dated exclusively, etc.). This situation reflects the **THINK ⟶ ACT ⟶ FEEL** sequence since the overt behaviors were not prefaced by feelings.

SOCIAL LABELING

Social labeling occurs when a person is described as being a certain way, and then s/he begins to act in a manner similar to the description (i.e., label). As it turns out, under certain conditions, people are very suggestible, and thus, they can be influenced through social labeling.

POSSIBLE PROGRESSIVE BEHAVIORS IN A ROMANTIC RELATIONSHIP

1. Talking to each other
2. Smiling at each other
3. Talking/texting
4. Meeting out
5. Kissing
6. Sex
7. Dating
8. Dating regularly
9. Dating exclusively
10. Living together
11. Marrying
12. Having children

Figure 1

Inferring Love from Your Own Behavior

In general, social labeling refers to the practice of describing (labeling) another person as having a certain characteristic or feeling. If this description meets certain conditions, the labeled individual will engage in overt behaviors that are consistent with the label.

For example, a shopper may be casually looking at some watches, perhaps just "passing the time," while waiting for someone else. Suppose a salesperson labeled this customer as follows: "I can't blame you for being interested in that watch; it's interesting that you should like that particular one. Because you're interested in top value for your money it has a few features you would like to know about." Here, the labeled individual may begin to display overt behaviors like asking questions, listening to a sales talk, or actually buying the watch, based upon a description of his/her own feelings and "interests."

Actually, the basis for social labeling theory is found in self-perception theory. Recall that people sometimes infer their feelings by observing their own behavior. In social labeling, a description from an outside source is a strong cue to help the person identify how s/he feels. To be effective however, a label must conform to the following rules:

1. The target person must be **aware** of the label. As we saw earlier, one way to maximize attention value is to make the label positive (i.e., reinforcing) or consistent.

2. The target person must **accept** (believe) the label. In general, labels will be accepted when they:

    a. have rewarding or positive implications for the target person.

    b. are consistent with the target person's overt behaviors.

    c. do not contradict strongly held feelings.

    d. are delivered by a credible source.

    e. do not appear to have a manipulative intent.

3. The target person must comprehend the label. In order to minimize selective comprehension, the label should imply that the target person "is" a certain way, not that they **"should be"** a certain way.

To summarize social labeling, people often act in the way they are described by others. This technique can be used to conform other people's actions to your desires, if you can find an opportunity to reasonably label some of their overt behaviors. For example, if you live with messy roommates, you should avoid labeling them "slobs" since this will maximize the probability that they will be slobs around you. A better strategy is to look for an opportunity to label them as "neater" or "starting to be more tidy" and then consistently reinforce this positive label. In fact, if you practice this technique until you become an accomplished practitioner, you will probably be surprised at how suggestible people really are.

SHORTCUT CATEGORY #5: IMPRESSION MANAGEMENT
(FEEL NEGATIVE → ACT POSITIVE)

In the last chapter, we noted that people often activate roles or scripts instead of taking the time and effort to think out how they should act. **Impression management** is a specific type of role playing that can be defined as **giving an outward impression that is inconsistent with true inner feelings.** Almost everyone has experienced this phenomenon. Consider for example, an employee who actually dislikes his manager but "pretends" to like him while at work. In this case, true feelings of dislike for the manager are being overruled by the STM's calculation of expected-value (e.g., the value of the job's income, or the opportunity for advancement).

DEFINITION

Impression management also can be defined as the **deliberate bending of the truth in order to make a favorable impression**. In other words, impression management is a direct form of misrepresentation. The "whole truth" is not revealed for a good reason, doing so might endanger the immediate attainment of important goals. However, what people often fail to realize is that the suppression of strong feelings is harmful to body chemistry and creates substantial frustrated energy. For example, the employee who hates his boss but acts as if he likes him will have to vent the negative feelings somehow. Often, this outlet takes the form of talking negatively about the boss behind his back. Unfortunately, this shows other people that he is playing up to the boss which erodes his credibility.

Social Labelling

Impression Management

Thus, people who misrepresent their true feelings are engaged in the process of impression management. In this case the **THINK → FEEL → ACT** sequence is distorted to **THINK → FEEL NEGATIVE → ACT POSITIVE**. In these instances, the individual usually gains some short-term reward, but at the expense of his/her body chemistry and long-run external reinforcement. This is a poor trade in the long run, but one that human beings are often quite willing to make.

PERSONAL IDENTITY

This model starts with Maslow's Biological Intrinsic Self (BIS) which is who you were "born to be." Your BIS is your biological potentials based on the combination of genes that you were born with and includes all the unique talents and specific traits that separate you from others. Remember, humans show variation on every trait so your unique deviations (i.e., the times you are not in the middle of the distribution but at one of the extreme ends) play an important role in determining your identity.

EXPRESSIVE/INTRINSIC BEHAVIORS

As young people grow up, they continually express their biological intrinsic self. This "expressive" behavior is observed by parents, teachers, friends, and society and is punished or rewarded depending on environmental values. When the intrinsic self is rewarded the person continues to grow naturally and in a healthy fashion (i.e., the BIS is in harmony with environmental values).

COPING/EXTRINSIC BEHAVIORS

Normally, the BIS will include behaviors (e.g., risk taking) that conflict with parental/societal values and, therefore, are punished. When the intrinsic self is punished, the individual must make a difficult choice:

1. Continue to perform expressive behaviors (and receive intrinsic rewards like higher self-esteem) but be punished by others (and lose social-esteem), or,

2. Develop **coping behaviors** in order to obtain extrinsic rewards (but suffer intrinsic punishment and loss of self-esteem). Coping behaviors can be defined as actions that are not natural for your BIS but are rewarded by your key accounts and society.

EXPRESSIVE VS COPING BEHAVIORS

Most people can be expected to fluctuate between these two choices - sometimes staying true to the intrinsic self (expressive behaviors) and sometimes suppressing the intrinsic self to please others (coping behaviors). After practicing coping behaviors for a while, people begin to manage the impression they give to others by withholding parts of their BIS (sometimes important parts).

Note that the motivation for people to perform coping behaviors is very high because we need things that only other people can give us - especially when we are young. This gives adults extreme reinforcement power over children and allows them to (rather easily) suppress parts of the child's intrinsic self (i.e., curiosity, independence, etc.).

After practicing impression management for a number of years it starts to become a scripted behavior (semi-automated) and in some cases can become habitual (fully automated). In addition, many other people are also engaged in impression management so it almost seems natural (but it is not).

THE COPING SELF

After learning coping behaviors for a number of years, people reach a point where their personal identity no longer includes just intrinsic components. Over time they have acquired a new aspect of self – the "coping self." This represents the behaviors performed to please other people but that are not natural to the individual.

THE HIDDEN SELF

Assume that by the age of 20 a person has developed a personal identity that is composed of 50 percent intrinsic self and 50 percent coping self. This would mean that 50 percent of the individual's intrinsic self has been lost (replaced by coping behaviors). The individual is still aware of the intrinsic desires but must "hide" them from the view of others (to receive

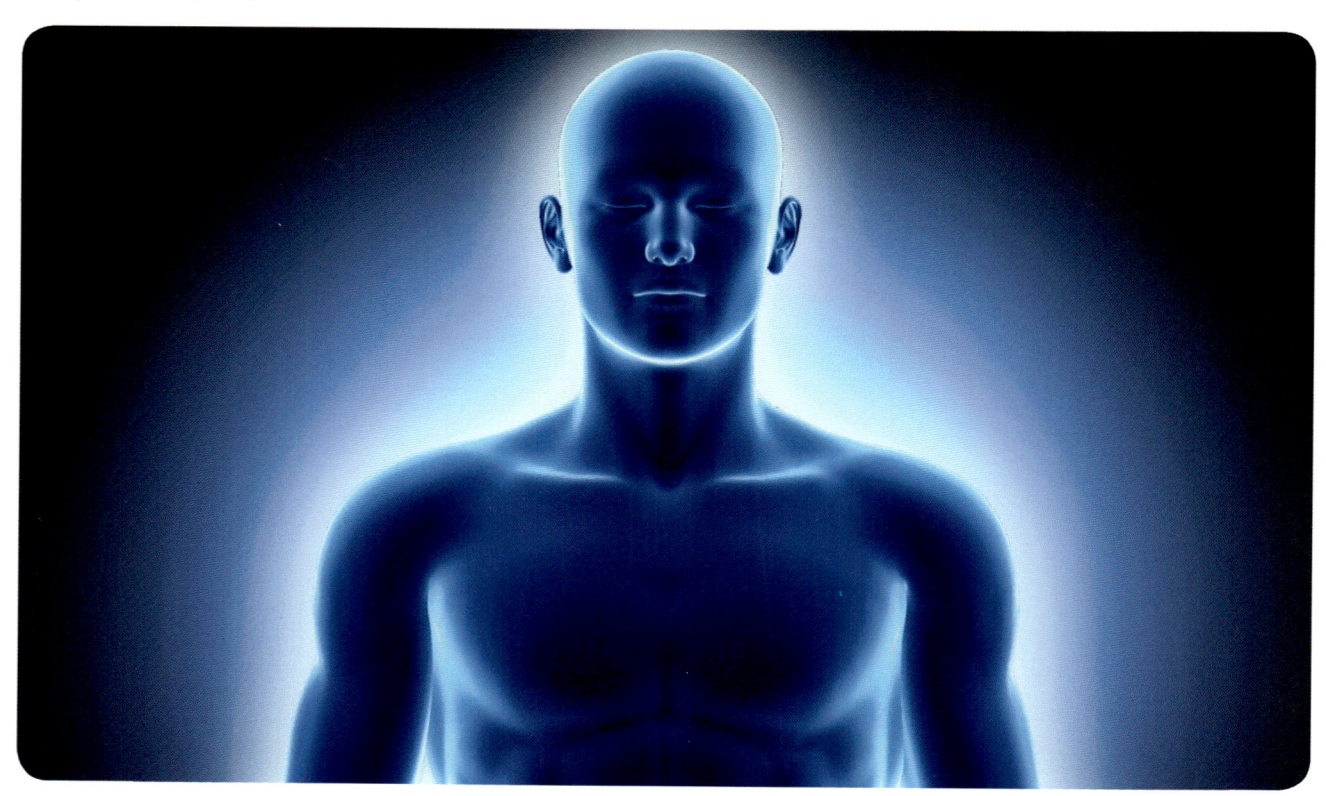

Biological Intrinsic Self

Coping Behavior

rewards and/or avoid punishments). Indeed, if the BIS is in serious conflict with parental/societal values the person will have to take on many coping behaviors and have a large "hidden self." Not surprisingly, having to hide significant components of the intrinsic self builds anger, guilt, and frustration while lowering self-esteem. Also, hiding important parts of who we are is a major way that we engage in impression management.

RATIO OF INTRINSIC TO EXTRINSIC BEHAVIOR

It seems clear that most people end up performing a significant amount of extrinsic behaviors in their jobs (and often in personal environments too). We know that as the percentage of extrinsic behavior increases, the frustration pool fills and ultimately reaches its maximum threshold at which point the person must vent (often using self-destructive "defense structures" which make the person sick). An important question is "how high can the ratio of extrinsic behaviors be before these negative effects set in?" At 80% intrinsic and 20% extrinsic the individual has a net of 60% = (80-20) intrinsic behavior – which seems acceptable.

At 60/40 the individual has a net of only 20% intrinsic – which seems unacceptable. At 50/50 there is 0% net intrinsic behavior. Anything below 50/50 will produce a net of **extrinsic** behavior and certainly at this point we would expect to see the negative consequences from frustration and low self-esteem.

IDENTITY CRISIS

In some cases, a person can be subjected to a schedule of reinforcement that stamps out much of the intrinsic self. In such cases, the individual has to violate many intrinsic personal values in order to please other people. While this creates short-term social reinforcement it also creates guilt and a continuing loss of self-esteem. Indeed, when people have lost much of their intrinsic self (50%?) they can be expected to undergo an **identity crisis** (e.g., "Who am I," or "What have I become?")

SELF-ESTEEM AND INTRINSIC/ EXTRINSIC BEHAVIOR

One way to look at self-esteem is by examining the amount of intrinsic/extrinsic behavior performed. From this perspective, self esteem is increased whenever we perform intrinsic acts and decreased whenever we have to cope or hide. Thus:

$$\text{SELF-ESTEEM} = [\text{INTRINSIC BEHAVIOR}] - [\text{EXTRINSIC BEHAVIOR}]$$

SOCIAL-ESTEEM VERSUS SELF-ESTEEM

It is important to note that self-esteem is much more difficult to achieve than social esteem. This is because social esteem (approval from others) can be achieved from either intrinsic behaviors or extrinsic behaviors. Other people usually do not care whether your behavior is expressive or coping as long as you do what they want (i.e., satisfy their needs). Thus:

and sometimes confrontational with key accounts. In this model, the goal is not to gain an extrinsic reward (e.g., keeping on good terms with a friend or staying married). Instead the only goal worthy of pursuit is telling the truth, the whole truth, and nothing but the truth. After that we let the chips fall where they may. The friends we have left will be those who like us for who we really are – not the impression we manage through coping behaviors. Thus, under the radical honesty model we are prepared to give up extrinsic social-esteem for intrinsic self-esteem.

$$\text{SOCIAL-ESTEEM} = [\text{INTRINSIC BEHAVIORS}] + [\text{EXTRINSIC BEHAVIORS}]$$

RADICAL AND RATIONAL HONESTY

RADICAL HONESTY

In **radical honesty** we seek 100% truthfulness (answering questions honestly) and 100% self expression (revealing our true feelings whether we are asked or not). To achieve this we need to be very direct

After discussing this idea with a lot of people it is my conclusion that 95% think it is unrealistic so the whole idea of becoming more self-expressive is dismissed. I often wonder what it would be like to live in a radically honest society where you expect others to give you the truth in a direct fashion and hear it often enough not to become defensive about it. I tend to think such a society would be much healthier in the long run (after a difficult adjustment period).

Radical Honesty

RATIONAL HONESTY

The concept of rational honesty tries to strike a more attainable balance between the number of extrinsic behaviors and the number of intrinsic behaviors we perform. Here, instead of seeking full (100%) truthfulness and expressiveness, we settle for what most people think is a more reasonable: 95% truthfulness and 80% self expression. The motivation for rational honesty is the realization that the consequences of coping and impression management are disastrous to self esteem, growth, and quality of life. Rational honesty means we make a **serious** and **creative** attempt to communicate our true feelings to our key accounts. However:

1. We must make sure that the feelings we are expressing are as **informed** and as **objective** as possible rather than being based on emotions, attitudes, or stereotypes.

2. Next, we find a **creative** way to express our feelings that will not provoke a defensive reaction from our key accounts. The best way to do this is often to ask **interesting and illuminating questions** or phrasing things non-combatively (e.g., "what else might you wear" instead of "I hate that").

3. Also, sometimes we will have to **wait** for a good time to reveal the truth (e.g., when they are in a good mood).

These activities will require withholding the truth on occasion – at least temporarily. The pay-off is that our key accounts (who often are not used to hearing the truth) will be better able to handle our self-expression when it occurs.

THE EXTRINSIC SOCIETY

Note that if we live in a society that punishes self-expression and rewards impression management we would expect many people have lost much of their intrinsic self. These people would have to take on many coping behaviors and as a result we should expect the general population to have relatively low self-esteem, become sick over time, and have strong needs for self-help.

IMPORTANCE OF MARKETING YOURSELF

Note that this theory suggests why marketing yourself is so important. First, you must be yourself - if your intrinsic self is suppressed you become sick. However you must also market your intrinsic self in a sophisticated fashion to make sure it receives maximum rewards and minimum punishment.

CONSEQUENCES OF IMPRESSION MANAGEMENT

There are a variety of negative consequences associated with impression management. These include:

1. High levels of frustration and negative body chemistry.

2. The use of self-destructive and/or anti-social coping techniques.

3. Weakened immune system.

4. Loss of credibility over time.

5. Loss of self-identity and self-esteem.

6. Low potential for growth and self-actualization.

SUMMARY OF NON-REASONED BEHAVIORS

NON-THINKING BEHAVIORS

In many situations, people act rather automatically after minimal thinking. The minimal thinking in these circumstances usually includes (1) a general or superficial evaluation of the situation, and (2) the quick and easy reference to an attitude, emotion, script, or impulse. Behaviors prefaced by minimal thinking often depart widely from the most adaptive action, thereby deteriorating the individual's schedule of reinforcement.

In addition, these thinking shortcuts occur in virtually every environmental domain and this definitely includes marketing. Based upon our knowledge of the limited capacity of the short-term memory, it is not really surprising to find so many behaviors prefaced by

...king. Indeed, virtually everyone is forced ... some responses, and on occasion, these ...ay increase the individual's adaptiveness. ... is also not surprising to find that behaviors generated by automatic processing are typically among the individual's most subjective and maladaptive.

Such behaviors engender a schedule of reinforcement that is likely to contain considerable punishment. In addition, due to the "non-thinking" nature of these behaviors, it is often difficult or impossible for the individual to consciously recognize the origin of these environmental punishments. Typically, when we feel we have been arbitrarily punished, we feel depressed and often perform further self-destructive actions.

NON-FEELING BEHAVIORS

In this chapter, we examined a second category of behavioral shortcuts. These non-feeling behaviors can occur in a variety of circumstances, often without conscious recognition by the internal model. In such cases, humans act without feeling, or against feelings. Like thinking shortcuts, feeling shortcuts save time and mental effort in the short run. They also tend to deteriorate the individual's schedule of reinforcement, as many people have discovered. For example, what do you think the probability of success is for couples who get married because they wanted to "try it out," or because they had self-perceptions that they were in love, or because they were labeled as a perfect couple? No doubt these non-feeling behaviors have contributed significantly to keeping the divorce rate high.

Together, non-thinking and non-feeling behaviors account for an important portion of most people's behavioral repertoire. These behavioral categories are summarized in Figure 2.

SUMMARY OF NON-REASONED BEHAVIORS

THINKING SHORTCUTS

1. **Feeling without Thinking (FEEL → ACT)**
   a. Attitudes
   b. Emotions
   c. Reactance

2. **Acting with Minimal Thinking (think → FEEL → ACT)**
   a. Scripted Behavior
   b. Impulse Behavior

3. **Acting with No Thinking (→ ACT)**
   a. Habits
   b. Routines

FEELING SHORTCUTS

4. **Acting without Feeling (THINK → ACT → FEEL)**
   a. Low-Involvement Learning
   b. Trial Behaviors
   c. Self Perception
   d. Social Labeling

5. **Acting Against Feelings (THINK → FEEL NEGATIVE → ACT POSITIVE)**
   a. Impression Management

Figure 2

EXPERIMENT 18.1
PERSUASION BY SOCIAL LABELING

1. Identify two key accounts that have behaviors you would like to see change (e.g., sarcasm, negative attitude toward another friend, messy, etc.).

2. Use the social labeling persuasion technique being sure to record:

    a. the label and why it would be accepted, and

    b. the circumstances under which it was applied (e.g., what behavior approached the label).

3. Record how many labels were applied and with what effect.

4. Summarize what you learned about the social labeling technique.

EXPERIMENT 18.2
IMPRESSION MANAGEMENT

1. Identify a key account relationship where you engage in a lot of impression management. Over a period of three days, make a serious and creative effort to be more self-expressive.

    a. Summarize the major episodes where you reveal your true feelings,

    b. Summarize how the other person reacted, and

    c. Summarize how you felt afterwards.

2. Based on your experience what are some ideas to help others achieve rational honesty?

ELABORATION QUESTIONS

- Can you think of any products you have purchased based on massive exposure to TV advertising?
- What types of products are you most likely to try out before you buy?
- Has trial ever lead you to maladaptive behaviors?
- What is your definition of romantic love? What is it based on?
- Have you ever been in a relationship based on self-perceived love?
- Give three examples of how a salesperson could use social labeling.
- What have been the major consequences from your impression management?
- Compute your ratio of intrinsic/extrinsic behaviors when:
  - You were a baby
  - You were 7 years old
  - You were 14 years old
  - Today
- What is the most intrinsic job you have had and what was the ratio of intrinsic/extrinsic behaviors?
- At what point in the intrinsic/extrinsic ratio do you think a person starts to become sick?
- What happens to people who are really good at impression management?
- What are reasonable alternatives to impression management?

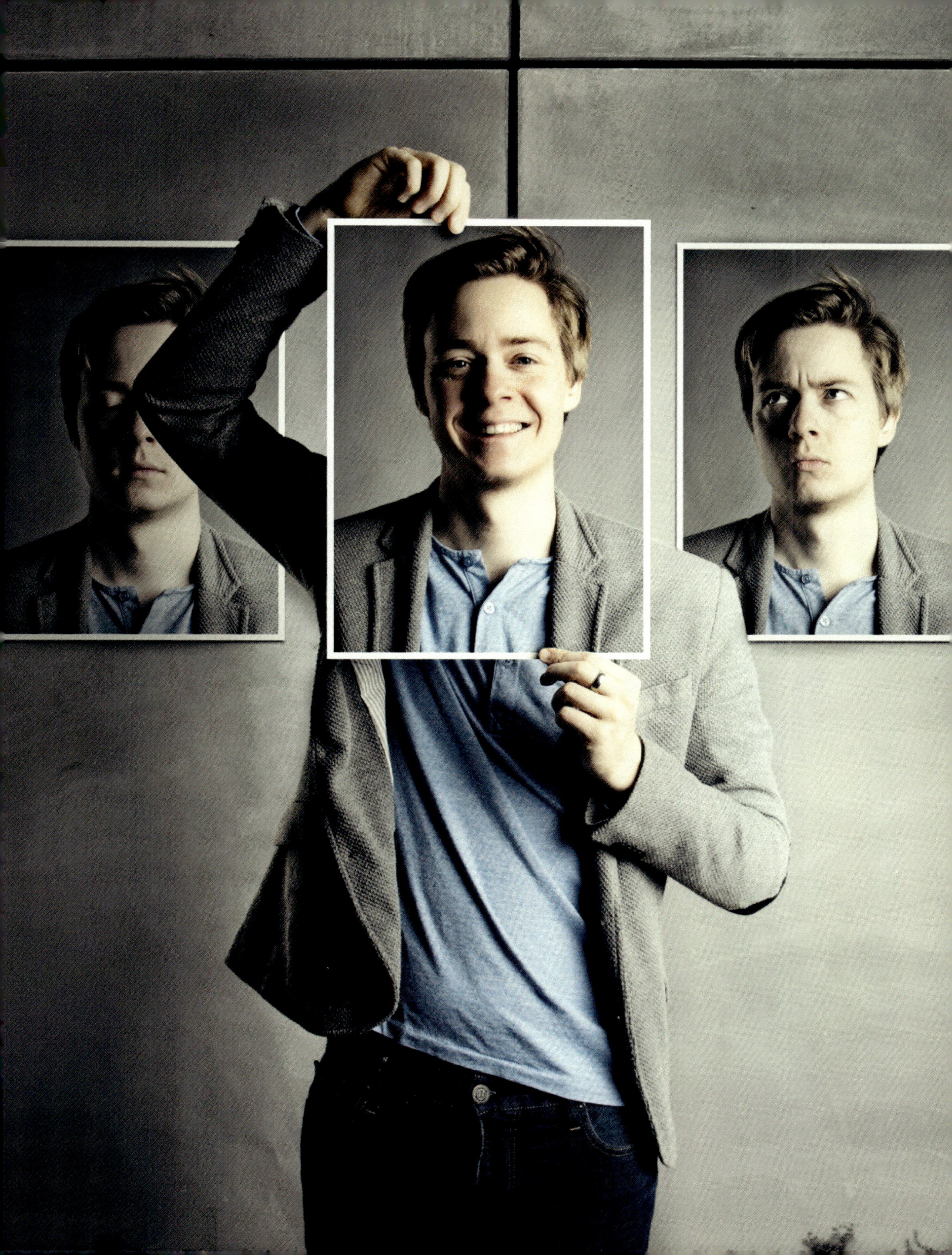

CHAPTER 19
RELATIONSHIP MARKETING

RELATIONSHIP MARKETING	**19.1**
Transaction Marketing	19.1
Relationship Marketing	19.1
Relationship Marketing and Key Accounts	19.1
Technology and Relationship Marketing	19.2
Types of Commercial Relationships	19.3
THREATS TO RELATIONSHIPS	**19.3**
Dissatisfaction	19.4
Change and Growth Over Time	19.4
Increased Opportunity for Competition	19.4
Automation of Exchange	19.4
Frustration and Use of Defense Structures	19.4
Self-Importance	19.4
CONFLICT	**19.4**
Degree of Conflict	19.4
Conflict and Argumentation	19.5
AVOIDING CONFLICT	**19.6**
RESOLVING CONFLICT	**19.6**
One Person Solutions	19.6
Two Person Solutions	19.7
Three Person Solution	19.8
LIVING WITH CONFLICT	**19.8**
TERMINATE THE RELATIONSHIP?	**19.8**
SUMMARY	**19.9**
CONCLUSION	**19.9**
**EXPERIMENT 19.1	CONFLICT RESOLUTION**	**19.9**
ELABORATION QUESTIONS	**19.10**

GUIDING QUESTIONS

- » What is transaction marketing?
- » What is relationship marketing?
- » Which type of marketing is best for key accounts?
- » How is technology related to relationship marketing?
- » How have data bases and the internet changed marketing?
- » What are the different types of commercial relationships?
- » How is dissatisfaction a threat to relationships?
- » How is growth a threat to relationships?
- » How is competition a threat to relationships?
- » How is automation a threat to relationships?
- » How is frustration a threat to relationships?
- » How is self-importance a threat to relationships?
- » What determines the degree of conflict in a relationship?
- » When is conflict resolvable and when is it unresolvable?
- » What are the best techniques for handling unresolvable conflict?
- » What are the best techniques for handling resolvable conflict?
- » How do you resolve conflict?

RELATIONSHIP MARKETING

Marketing can be seen from two different perspectives: (1) the transaction marketing approach, or (2) the relationship marketing approach.

TRANSACTION MARKETING

According to this perspective, the focus of marketing should be the **sale**. This is because sales revenues are the lifeblood of any firm. This orientation causes us to focus on a single transaction. Our interest in the consumer declines after the sale is made as we target new and different consumers. Historically, marketing has emphasized *"the sale is the end of the process"* approach.

RELATIONSHIP MARKETING

According to this perspective, the focus of marketing should be more on the **customer** than on the sale. Actually, consumer oriented focus is even more important after the sale because repeat purchase is also a key to a firm's long-term success. *"The sale is the beginning of the process"* approach is currently being stressed as more is learned about how devastating customer defection can be to a firm's profits. The key aspect of this approach is that a firm must strive for continuing exchanges of value. That is, businesses need a good relationship with consumers because that maximizes the probability of brand loyalty and repeat purchase of their brand.

RELATIONSHIP MARKETING AND KEY ACCOUNTS

It costs a lot more to engage in relationship marketing than transaction marketing in terms of both expenses and personnel. For this reason, it is important to determine when it makes sense to follow the relationship marketing model. Some exchanges do not lend themselves to **consumer commitment** and repeat purchase (e.g., inexpensive/low risk products) so the transaction model can be applied effectively to many of these situations. Conversely, relationship marketing, which focuses on the **life-time value** of the customer, is well designed for key account relationships (both professional and personal).

Transaction Marketing

Relationship Marketing

TECHNOLOGY AND RELATIONSHIP MARKETING

It is worthwhile noting that the focus on relationship marketing has occurred during the modern technological age. There are two major reasons for this. First, is the availability of ***modern customer databases.*** These databases allow marketers to access enormous amounts of information on any of their customers. Moreover, this information is available almost instantaneously and can be sorted and manipulated in a variety of useful ways. For example, marketers can keep track of their customers' birthdays and send them a card or small gift on the appropriate day. Similarly, bookstores can track the purchase patterns of their customers and recommend additional books or magazines that correspond to the consumers' reading interests. Note that this would add value to the customer's relationship with the bookstore and, no doubt, increase the sales of books.

The second technological advance that has facilitated relationship marketing is ***the Internet***. The Web represents tremendous opportunities for information exchange with customers and therefore, can be a great benefit to relationship marketing efforts. Examples here would include marketers who list answers to frequently asked questions on their web site. This allows for an ***interactive information exchange***

Interactive Information Exchange

that is directed by the consumer (and is low cost to the marketer). As a result, consumers can find out information about specific products, get the latest price information, investigate product availability, determine delivery dates, etc. Without question, the availability of this technology makes relationship marketing more realistic, especially for small businesses.

TYPES OF COMMERCIAL RELATIONSHIPS

In the complex marketplace of today there are many different types of commercial relationships. On the continuum of commercial relationships shown in Model 1, transaction marketing and relationship marketing represent the end points. In the extreme, transaction marketing involves only a single exchange. Most often, these are durable and long-lasting products that may not require replacement over a consumer's lifetime (e.g., house, power washer, tools, garden tractor, etc). At the other of the continuum, would be a continuing relationship between the customer and the provider of products and services (e.g., your family doctor).

However, there are various forms of relationships that fall in between the extremes. For example, **serial transactions** occur when a customer patronizes a business – but not for relationship reasons. For example, the business may be conveniently located on the customer's route home. In this case, the consumer's product needs are being satisfied with the least effort but there is no meaningful relationship between the business and the customer. We can expect such a relationship to terminate quickly if the situation changes (e.g., the consumer moves to a new location).

Periodic relationships are those that do have strong ties between the consumer and marketer but tend to be temporary. For example, a consumer may decide to restore an old sports car and develop a relationship with a parts supplier. During the restoration period (six months to years) there will probably be a serious relationship between the company and the consumer because automobiles often reflect our self-identity. However, once the car is restored, the commercial relationship will decline (at least until the consumer decides to restore another car).

Thus, commercial relationships adopt many different forms and it is important to keep this in mind as we develop the relationship marketing model. Ultimately, the key element in defining a commercial relationship is the level of personal **commitment** and **involvement** shown by both parties to the exchange. In developing our model, we will focus on continuing exchanges which usually benefit the most from relationship marketing.

THREATS TO RELATIONSHIPS

The key element that differentiates continuing exchanges (that benefit from relationship marketing) from short-term exchanges (that benefit from transaction marketing) is the **time frame** involved. In relationship marketing we seek **customers for life.** In many ways this is like a "commercial marriage" between the firm and its customers. A major reason for this is that customer **defections** are extremely expensive to the firm. Unfortunately, as time periods lengthen, many stresses are brought to bear on the

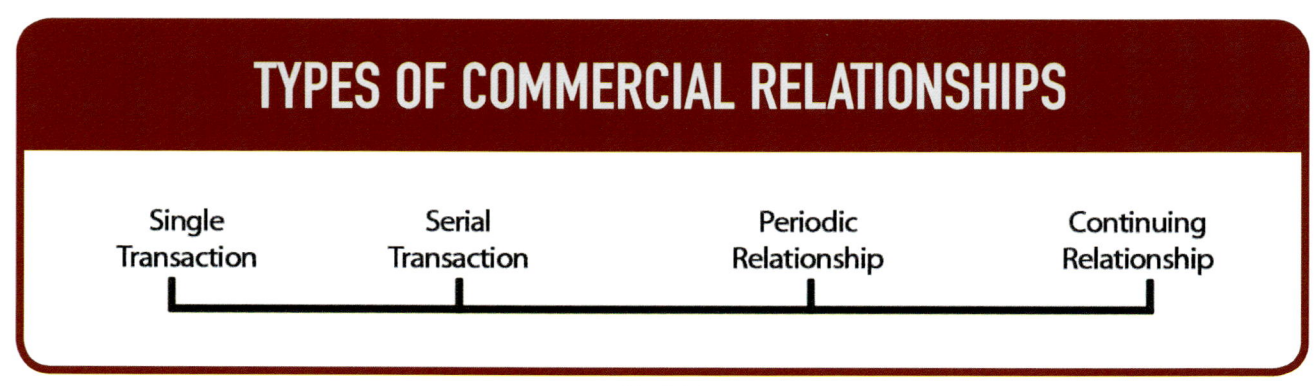

TYPES OF COMMERCIAL RELATIONSHIPS

Single Transaction — Serial Transaction — Periodic Relationship — Continuing Relationship

Model 1

relationship that ultimately cause conflict and may lead to termination.

DISSATISFACTION

To motivate consumers to repurchase our products and services, we must achieve consumer satisfaction. If consumers are dissatisfied with the product they lose motivation to buy it again. As we will see later, achieving satisfaction repeatedly over a long period of time can be very difficult in today's marketplace.

CHANGE AND GROWTH OVER TIME

When exchanges take place over long periods of time there are ample opportunities for changes to occur on both sides of the exchange. The consumer's needs and motives will change as they mature, and the company will change some of its personnel as well as elements of its product offering. Thus, even small changes can accumulate into big changes over time. When the two parties to exchange grow in different directions, it can place great stress on the relationship.

INCREASED OPPORTUNITY FOR COMPETITION

In marketing, we expect our competitors to try to alienate our best customers – its part of their job. However, as we extend the time frame to many years, we can expect many serious attempts to cause our customers to defect. In relationship marketing, we must be very sensitive to any efforts by competitors to create **disloyalty** in our customers and be ready to counter them effectively.

AUTOMATION OF EXCHANGE

Life cycles of involvement suggest that high involvement leads to familiarity which, in turn, can lead to automation of the exchange and a decline in value over time. This has a negative effect on the value of the relationship and often causes it to terminate. As an example, in advertising, when a team has worked on an account for a long time, they tend to get bored and stale. When the client notices this they often take their business to a different ad agency where they get more attention.

FRUSTRATION AND USE OF DEFENSE STRUCTURES

As noted earlier, many people have high levels of frustration in their internal model. When this happens they often use defense structures to vent the frustration. Key accounts often are at the receiving end of these anti-social coping techniques. It does not take too long for this type of behavior to erode the basis of an exchange of value.

SELF-IMPORTANCE

Perhaps the greatest of all threats to continuing exchanges, selfishness is a formidable obstacle that intrudes on most relationships over time. The key issues involved in self-importance and self-worth are complex and discussed in detail in a later chapter.

CONFLICT

We have already seen that when two people have similar values about an issue, they agree and mutually reinforce each other (e.g., they both like the same types of movies, the same type of food, etc.). Conversely, when two parties have different values, and they interact in that area, they disagree and conflict occurs. Because no two internal models have identical values, conflict occurs in all exchange relationships over time. This can be demonstrated using Venn diagrams as shown below. In Diagram A, there is a large amount of value overlap – the two people agree on many issues and can interact over a wide range of topics (e.g., religion, politics, etc.) without causing conflict. Thus, these two individuals are highly compatible.

In Diagram B, there is a small amount of value overlap – the two people disagree on many issues and will experience a lot of conflict in their relationship when these issues arise. Because of the factors noted above, the amount of conflict in continuing exchanges is often high and increases over time. Indeed, one of the best predictors of how long a relationship will last is the amount of conflict that occurs and how it is, or is not, resolved.

VALUE OVERLAP AND AMOUNT OF CONFLICT

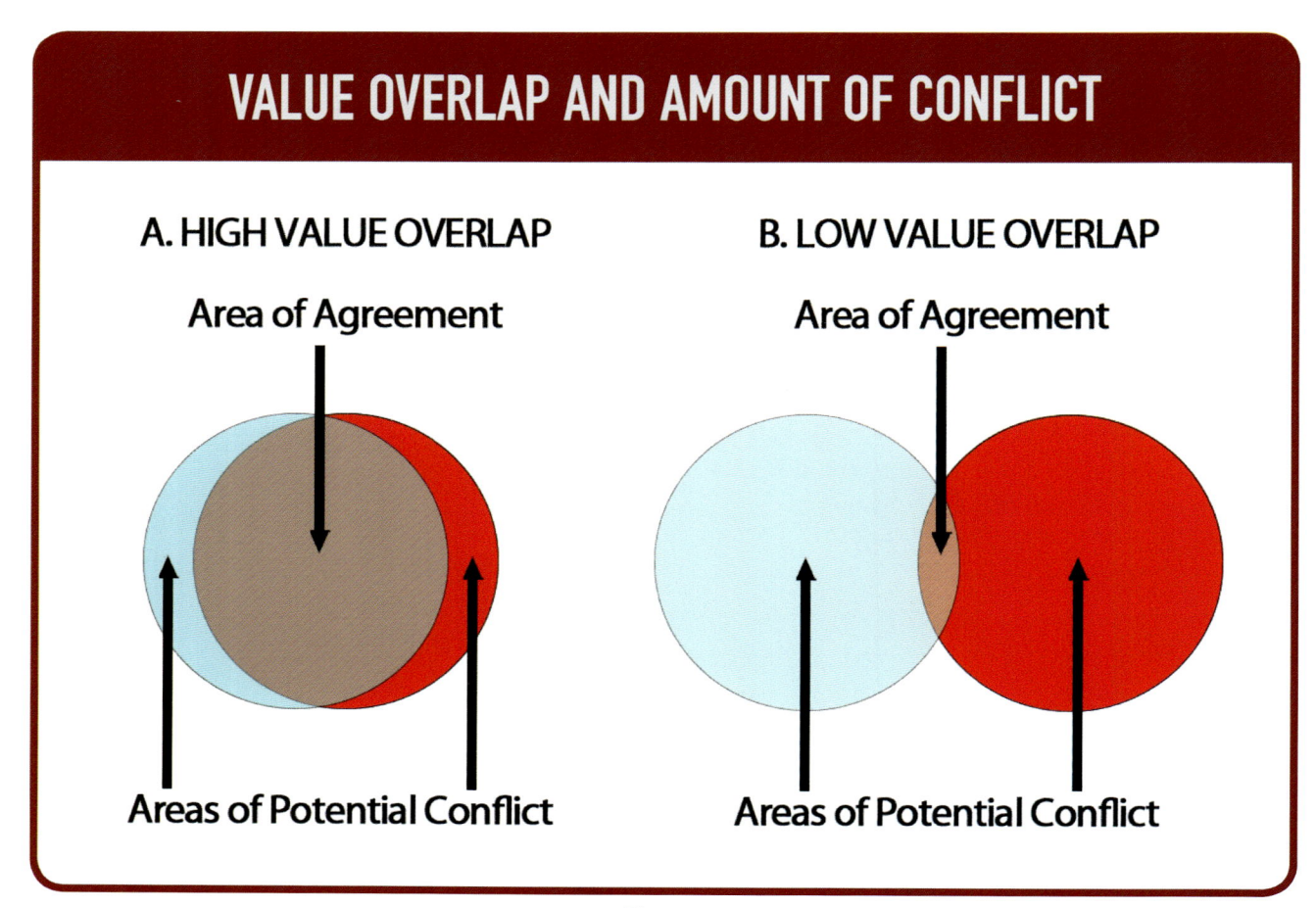

A. HIGH VALUE OVERLAP

Area of Agreement

Areas of Potential Conflict

B. LOW VALUE OVERLAP

Area of Agreement

Areas of Potential Conflict

Figure 1

DEGREE OF CONFLICT

Severity: Minor/Major. Conflict can be minor or major. Minor differences (e.g., what restaurant to eat at, which TV program to watch, etc.) are relatively easy to resolve (though over time they can accumulate into serious conflict). However, when the values that conflict are strongly held or central to the individual's self concept, the degree of conflict becomes serious. In these cases, it can be very difficult to resolve the conflict in a successful manner.

Frequency: Seldom/Often. Conflict can occur frequently or rarely. Thus, when conflict is rare and minor, the relationship can be considered strong (because some conflict is inevitable). However, when conflict escalates and becomes frequent and major, the relationship is in jeopardy of failure - unless the conflict can be avoided or resolved.

CONFLICT AND ARGUMENTATION

When people realize that conflict exists, an argument often occurs. Here we try to persuade the other party to adopt a value or belief similar to ours. Unfortunately, as we have seen, it can be very difficult to change another person's internal model – especially if the target value is central or strongly held. These persuasion attempts often turn into arguments where each person defends (and thus strengthens) their original value. As the argument continues, one or both parties feel threatened and often produce an emotional threat reaction (e.g., defensive posture, increase in voice levels, attacks not related to the original issue, etc.). Once emotions come into play, the situation frequently deteriorates into a negative exchange and the relationship is weakened. Also note that as each person defends his/her original value (usually by recalling from memory the reasons they hold it), the value is strengthened, assuring more conflict in the future.

Silent Treatment

If arguments become common, people often begin to use defensive structures to cope (e.g., sarcasm, silent treatment, avoidance, etc.). Over time and repetition, these maladaptive coping techniques become semi-automated and then fully automated (e.g., bickering couple). As a result, argumentation is rarely a successful way to resolve conflicts but instead signals that the relationship is losing value over time.

AVOIDING CONFLICT

The parties to exchange may decide to avoid the issue that causes conflict as much as possible. If discussing a certain topic (e.g., politics, religion, etc.) creates conflict and there is little chance of changing the other person's mind, then there is little point in discussing it because the resulting conflict will lessen the value of the relationship. Unfortunately, many important issues cannot be avoided very long, for example, where to live after graduating, when to start a family, what religion to train the children in, etc.

Ultimately, avoiding the issue means we must avoid the other person, thereby increasing psychological distance and lessening the value of the relationship. Or, not expressing our opinions when the other party is present. Of course, this builds frustration until the threshold is surpassed, triggering venting or coping techniques. As noted earlier, these techniques can be defensive like using the "silent treatment," eating for pleasure, arguments, etc.

RESOLVING CONFLICT

If conflict cannot be avoided (and often this is the case), we must confront the areas of disagreement and attempt to resolve the conflict. There are a variety of techniques to resolve conflict and they can be organized by how many parties are involved.

ONE PERSON SOLUTIONS

Acquiescence. In this case, one of the two people does not change the target value but lets the other person have his/her way. This may happen when one person has a weak value and does not care as much as the other. This technique can be effective for infrequent and/or weak value conflict but usually causes repressed feelings which attack the strength of the relationship at the subconscious level (i.e., the accumulation of frustrated energy).

Creativity. Another way to resolve conflict is for one party to use creativity to change the situation. For example, if you are angry that your room mate does not take out the trash you will become frustrated until you surpass your threshold and then vent or cope. Often, defensive structures are used to release this negative energy, thereby damaging the relationship. An easy alternative is to take the trash out yourself - of course this will only work if you frame the task creatively as a striving opportunity. You will usually find that the energy it takes to be angry at a key account is much higher (and more negative) than the energy required to take out the trash yourself.

Growth Experiments. Another option for solving conflict is to conduct some of the growth experiments available in this text and at strive4growth.com. These experiments usually require you to see things from another's point of view, or expand your level of tolerance for people who are not like you.

TWO PERSON SOLUTIONS

Negotiation and Compromise. Here the two parties explain their views without trying to change the other person's values. Ultimately, one or both parties will have to make a compromise if the negotiation process is to be successful. The motivation to make a compromise is equal to [Expected Value- Expected Costs] so we can expect people to make more compromises at the beginning of a relationship when benefits are high and costs are low. However, over time the relationship's value often decreases (while costs increase) so the motivation to make compromises goes down. The result is argumentation and bickering which further lessen the relationship's value. People who can negotiate their differences and find successful middle ground between their positions can maintain good relationships for extended periods of time.

Negotiation

Mediation

THREE PERSON SOLUTION

Mediation or Adjudication. Here, a third party is called in to provide an "objective" perspective on the conflict. The mediator makes recommendations to ease or resolve the conflict (e.g., a married couple seek counseling to resolve recurring conflict). In "binding" arbitration the entire decision is left up to the third party and both sides agree to accept whatever decision is handed down. Legal resolution through the justice system is also a common example of this approach to conflict resolution and is called adjudication.

LIVING WITH CONFLICT

If the conflict cannot be avoided nor resolved, the only choice for maintaining the relationship is to live with (i.e., tolerate) the conflict. This option seems most useful when conflict is minor and infrequent.

Agree to Disagree. Here, the two parties work to understand and respect the other person's values. Neither party has to change his/her values in this resolution technique, but both must accept the other's view. This can be an effective technique but can also be very difficult for a cognitively consistent internal model. It seems to work best when there is more value than conflict in the relationship and when the conflict that does occur involves central values that cannot be changed easily.

TERMINATE THE RELATIONSHIP?

If the above techniques cannot be used to resolve conflict or lessen it to acceptable levels, the relationship is in jeopardy. We have already examined the strong tendencies for humans to become adapted to their exchange partners. As a result, relationship value is often highest at the beginning and then starts to drop. It is at this point (i.e., "the honeymoon is over"), when conflict escalates from minor to major and from infrequent to more frequent. As relationship value declines and relationship costs increase (due to unresolved conflict) a point is reached where the relationship involves more conflict than value. When this happens, motivation to continue the relationship is lost so termination is a common way to resolve the differences.

Indeed, it is for this reason that most exchange relationships do not last longer – termination is a common conflict resolution strategy. As an example, in advertising the relationship between the client and the agency is crucial and can be terminated by either party. Clients often grow tired of the same approach and request more resources (e.g., top creative and production people) be allocated to their account. If the client is unhappy with the personnel assigned to the account they will frequently end the relationship and change agencies. Conversely, if the client's demands become unreasonable, and the account is not producing much profit, the agency can "resign" the account and ask the client to find a new agency. Indeed, it is these dynamics that help to make advertising a volatile industry.

Coming to terms with the idea that most relationships are temporary is easy for some and extremely difficult for others. If true, it means that most of us will go through many relationship life cycles in our time. Accordingly, "breaking-up," plays a significant role in our lives and should be better studied and understood. Having a philosophy of breaking up could be a great advantage for many of us. For example, any relationship that you have experienced but ultimately failed can be seen as motivation to develop our conflict resolution skills - to prevent future failures. From Maslow's model we could see this as real personal growth and any relationship we grow from is, in all, a positive experience.

SUMMARY

You can expect to encounter conflict in all of your exchange relationships – personal and professional. The techniques you use to resolve this conflict will play a major role in determining the level of success you achieve in your relationships. Note that the longer a relationship lasts, the more opportunity there is for conflict to occur. Because of this, it is important to have effective conflict resolution techniques to be successful at relationship marketing. Indeed, most firms have a customer service policy to help minimize the conflict between customers and the firm.

CONCLUSION

Traditionally, relationship marketing has been reserved for high end (wealthy) customers buying expensive products. In today's marketplace however, relationship marketing has taken on new prominence. This is because customer defection has been shown to be very expensive (it can cost 20 times more to get a new customer than to retain an old one). At the same time, rapid developments in technology allow marketers to achieve personal communications with more customers than ever before and store relevant information in an easy to use format. Accordingly, the focus on relationship marketing will likely increase in the future.

EXPERIMENT 19.1
CONFLICT RESOLUTION

1. Identify a key account relationship you have that has excessive conflict in it. Explain the relationship and the source of conflict.

2. When did serious conflict first begin in this relationship?

3. Use the negotiate and compromise technique to see if you can come up with creative ways to resolve the conflict.

4. How successful were you and why?

5. Provide suggestions for effectively handling conflict in personal and professional environments.

ELABORATION QUESTIONS

- What are the best conflict resolution strategies to use when you are forced to interact with another individual who has different values (for example at work or with in-laws)?

- Which techniques do you see people using that do not work.

- Are there are any advantages to dealing with conflict before it escalates? What are the best ways to do this?

- When are the extra costs of relationship marketing not worth it?

- At what point is the level of conflict in a relationship so high that termination is the best alternative?

- Is conflict healthy in any way?

- Would you prefer to work for a company that focuses on relationship marketing or one that focuses on transaction marketing?

- What are your most common conflict resolution techniques?

- Can a positive chemical bath prevent conflict? Does conflict produced a negative chemical bath?

- Looking at the threats to relationships, which of these factors have most often intruded into your romances? Which factors have most often intruded into your jobs?

CHAPTER 20
SELF-IMPORTANCE AND SELF-WORTH

SELF-IMPORTANCE AND SELF-WORTH — 20.1
   Definition of Self-Importance — 20.1
   Definition of Self-Worth — 20.1
   Effects of Self-Importance and Self-Worth on Exchange Relationships — 20.1
   Self-Importance/Self-Worth Ratio — 20.1

SOURCES OF SELF-IMPORTANCE — 20.2
   Genetic Self-Importance — 20.2
   Lengthy Dependency Period — 20.3
   Social Rewards and Social Competition — 20.3
   Perceptual Self-Centeredness — 20.3
   Neurotic Need States — 20.4
   Modeling Other Peoples' Self-Importance — 20.4
   Success — 20.4

DISTRIBUTION OF SELF-IMPORTANCE — 20.4
CONSEQUENCES OF SELF-IMPORTANCE — 20.5
SELF-IMPORTANCE AND META-MOTIVATION — 20.9
LOSING SELF-IMPORTANCE — 20.9
   When to Lose Self-Importance — 20.9
   Short-Run Versus Long-Run Orientation — 20.9

GAINING SELF-WORTH — 20.10
CONCLUSION — 20.10
EXPERIMENT 20.1 | LOSING SELF-IMPORTANCE — 20.11
EXPERIMENT 20.2 | GAINING SELF-WORTH — 20.12
ELABORATION QUESTIONS — 20.13

GUIDING QUESTIONS

- » What is self-importance?
- » What is self-worth?
- » What is the self-importance/self-worth ratio?
- » What are the main sources of self-importance?
- » How is self-importance distributed among people?
- » What are the consequences of self-importance?
- » How does biased accounting influence relationship success?
- » How is self-importance a threat to others?
- » Why is it hard to see self-importance in ourselves?
- » How is self-importance related to self-esteem?
- » How difficult is it to change self-important behaviors?
- » When should we lose self-importance?
- » How can we lose self-importance?
- » What prevents us from losing self-importance?
- » How is self-importance related to meta-motivation and growth?
- » How can we gain self worth?
- » How are self-importance and self-worth related to relationship marketing?

SELF-IMPORTANCE AND SELF-WORTH

DEFINITION OF SELF-IMPORTANCE

Self-importance is defined as a person's belief that s/he is a highly important (i.e., significant or consequential) individual in the environment. This belief causes self-important people to **put their own needs ahead of the needs of others.** As such, someone who is self-important is likely to be described as "egotistical," "conceited," or "self-centered." Self-importance is the motivating force behind many maladaptive behaviors including selfishness, greed, deceit, procrastination, double standards, etc. Despite these detrimental effects, the forces that nourish self-importance are often too powerful to overcome. It should be noted that by this definition some people are, in fact, important (e.g., the President of the United States, the Pope, etc.). However, as used here, self-importance is the average person's tendency toward **exaggerated** feelings of importance.

DEFINITION OF SELF-WORTH

Self-worth is basically the opposite of self-importance. Those who are self-worthy **put other people's needs ahead of their own.** Also, self-worth causes people to focus on their own **higher needs** as opposed to lower needs. This normally has a positive influence on relationships and represents a movement toward personal growth and self-actualization. Often, self-worth is based on **prosocial accomplishments** (like helping others or contributing to charity), and/or **individual accomplishments** (like staying on a healthy diet or earning high grades). Notice that self-worth does not come from external sources (e.g., compliments from others) but from within. Self-worth also has a positive effect on internal body chemistry (i.e., positive emotions).

EFFECTS OF SELF-IMPORTANCE AND SELF-WORTH ON EXCHANGE RELATIONSHIPS

Exchange relationships always involve the **give and take** of value. The value may be money, products, professional services, or personal services. The effects of self-importance on exchange relationships can be summarized as follows:

1. Self-importance causes us to **take** or demand things from others, with little or no gratitude. It also causes us to **discount the value** of what we **get**.

2. Self-importance causes us to **give** things to others **reluctantly**, and when we do give, it causes us to keep track of who owes us what in return. It also causes us to **over-value** what we **give**.

Conversely, the effects of self-worth on exchange relationships can be summarized as follows:

1. Self-worth causes us to **take** things from others **with appreciation**, recognizing the effort involved. It also causes us to **over-value** what we **get**.

2. Self-worth causes us to **give** to others **freely**, without keeping an inventory of who owes us what. It also causes us to **under-value** what we **give**.

SELF-IMPORTANCE/SELF-WORTH RATIO

Based on the above definitions, we can conclude that each person will have a fluctuating pattern of giving and taking. For example, suppose person A puts his needs above others' needs 80% of the time and puts others' needs ahead of his own 20% of the time. This

First Date

person would have a self-importance/self-worth (SI/SW) ratio of 80/20 and be considered high in self-importance and low in self-worth. Suppose person B puts his needs above others' needs only 20% of the time and puts others' needs ahead of his own 80% of the time. This person would have a SI/SW ratio of 20/80 and be low in self-importance and high in self-worth. An SI/SW ratio of 50/50 would represent the break-even position which many believe is the most effective ratio for partners in continuing exchanges (i.e., they give and take equally).

Note that there are a variety of factors that can affect the SI/SW ratio exhibited by an individual. For example, neurotic need states and bad moods shifts the ratio upward toward higher self-importance. Conversely, good moods and situations where we are consciously trying to make a good impression (e.g., job interview or first date) tend to lower the SI/SW ratio – at least temporarily. Thus people can be expected to have a fluctuating pattern of SI/SW not a fixed ratio. The overall average of the SI/SW ratio is the single best determinant of the individual's level of self-importance.

SOURCES OF SELF-IMPORTANCE

GENETIC SELF-IMPORTANCE

To our genes, there is nothing more important than ourselves. The fundamental genetic goals of survival and reproduction demand that humans live long enough to repopulate the species. Not surprisingly, this gives significant survival value to self-importance. When it comes down to what is best for society versus what is best for the individual, the self-serving genes will almost always opt for the latter. As Watson (1979) notes:

> *"Deception, even within a species, is a biological fact. Whenever the interests of the genes are at stake, there will be lies and deceit: children will deceive their parents, husbands will cheat on wives, and brother will lie to brother. For in the final analysis, it is the individual that matters to the genes."*

LENGTHY DEPENDENCY PERIOD

In addition to genetic factors, the lengthy dependency stage for human offspring tends to increase our self-importance. During the first part of their lives, babies are totally incapable of surviving on their own. They need, and usually get, a lot of attention from parents, siblings, and society at large. In this environment, it is not surprising that some of the earliest learned beliefs of the developing and impressionable internal model should be related to self-importance. Remember, early information is overly represented in the belief structure due to the protective nature of the selective defense mechanisms. Thus, children often seek attention from others as a major goal and this tends to inflate self-importance.

SOCIAL REWARDS AND SOCIAL COMPETITION

Society also contributes to the developing child's consolidation of his/her self-importance. In the long-run it is important for society to have some mechanism to compel individual behavior to conform to group norms. One way is to make the individual **dependent** upon social rewards. To accomplish this goal, society exposes the developing child to a bewildering array of groups and organizations at an early age. Social reinforcements, such as special recognition in the group, assignment to leadership roles, etc., are then distributed to individuals conforming most closely to group norms and goals.

Because this social recognition operates by elevating the individual's status in the group, it can easily accentuate self-importance. Indeed, pedestrian usage of the term "ego" usually refers to individuals who are constantly seeking social recognition for their personal performance. Since only other people can give "social rewards," egotistical people are ultimately dependent on society for the recognition they have been trained to need. We are all like that, to one extent or another.

Competition for social rewards also can accentuate self-importance. Social competition is often strong because (1) many people are seeking social recognition according to Maslow's hierarchy of needs and motives, (2) some cultures value competition as a good thing and thus reinforce it, and (3) people are rewarded for winning both externally and internally (e.g., the thrill of victory). Note that the tendency for people to "show off" is driven by social competition coupled with self-importance.

PERCEPTUAL SELF-CENTEREDNESS

Another factor accentuating self-importance is the fact that each person's perception of the world is self-oriented. Because the environment is internally deciphered, each of us really is at the "center of the world." Each calculation of expected-value is computed by an actor with definite vested interests. As in any biased judging situation, there is little chance of even-

Obsessed with Oneself

handedness when it comes down to what is best for us versus what may be good for someone else. Accordingly, it seems only natural that our perceptual and decision-making equipment would be given a protected and elevated status in its own interpretation of the importance of things. This dynamic does not mean people are always self-important but it does imply that we usually favor our ideas and our decisions over others.

NEUROTIC NEED STATES

Neurotic need states can develop during childhood which later show up as self-importance. Specific sources of self-importance would include (1) deficiency needs not met, (2) affluence, (3) selfish character traits developed from solving deficiency needs, (4) parental misfortune (i.e., bad parents), etc.

MODELING OTHER PEOPLES' SELF-IMPORTANCE

Due to the factors listed above, many humans have high self-importance. As a result, we learn to be that way ourselves by imitating the behavior of others. For example, parents and friends often seek advantages, so we do it too, usually without thinking about it. Self-importance rubs off on others.

SUCCESS

When humans are successful, and get rewarded, it is in our nature to develop a little (or a lot) of egotism. Boasting and bragging are classic examples of this tendency.

DISTRIBUTION OF SELF-IMPORTANCE

Many people possess excessive amounts of self-importance as a consequence of the reasons listed above. In addition, once established, self-importance is protected by our tendencies toward **cognitive consistency** as implemented by the selective defense mechanisms. Therefore, while many human traits are "normally distributed" (i.e., a bell-shaped curve), self-importance is skewed toward people developing too much, as shown in Model 1.

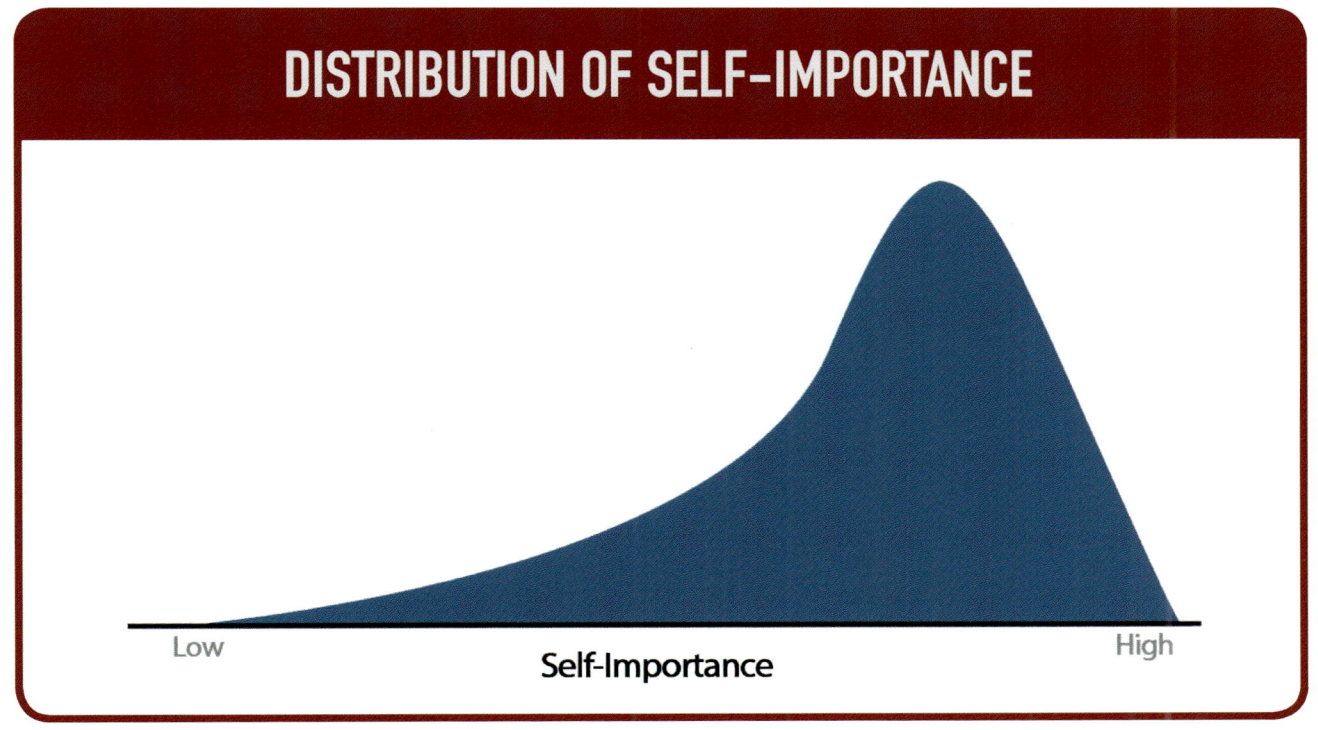

DISTRIBUTION OF SELF-IMPORTANCE

Self-Importance (Low to High)

Model 1

CONSEQUENCES OF SELF-IMPORTANCE

SELF-IMPORTANCE AND BIASED ACCOUNTING

Self-importance has dramatic implications for human exchange behavior. First, self-importance causes problems in human exchange behavior by distorting the calculation of expected-value. Since all exchanges are **give-and-take** by definition, it is important that people believe they are getting value from the exchange that is at least equal to the amount they are giving. In the most successful exchange relationships, both parties feel they are better off (i.e., have higher value) after the exchange than before it. Such relationships are easy to maintain because both people benefit simultaneously. For example, you can probably think of the early stages of a friendship or romance where you and the other person were highly motivated to interact and both felt better off for the time spent together.

In this example, we see that for each exchange a person makes, there is a corresponding **"psychological T-account"** where what is gained (credit) and what is given (debit) are mentally registered. The balance of the T-account is the expected-value (or loss) of the relationship and determines the **motivation to continue the exchange.** Notice what happens to the T-accounts for self-important people. First, since self-importance causes us to under-value what others give, it reduces the perceived credit we enter in the mental ledger. In addition, since self-importance causes us to over-value what we give to others, it increases the perceived debit we enter into the account. This combination quickly causes the T-account to be out of balance (in our own view) and means that we will: (1) attempt to **give less** and **take more** from the relationship, or (2) **lose motivation** to continue it.

To illustrate biased accounting, assume Murphy and Ramesh are college roommates and that both are self-important. They are watching Monday Night Football, but Murphy has to be at work at 9 pm to tend bar. Unfortunately, Murphy's car will not start so he asks Ramesh for a ride to work. Ramesh is annoyed because his favorite team is playing football on TV. However, he reluctantly agrees, leaves the game, and gives Murphy a ride to work. At this point the psychological T-accounts of both people are shown in Model 2.

Let's assume that a ride to work is actually worth $10. Notice that because each person has high self-importance, Murphy has **underestimated** the value of what he received and credited Ramesh's account only $5. Similarly, Ramesh is self-important and therefore, has **overestimated** the value of what he gave in the exchange by debiting Murphy's account $15.

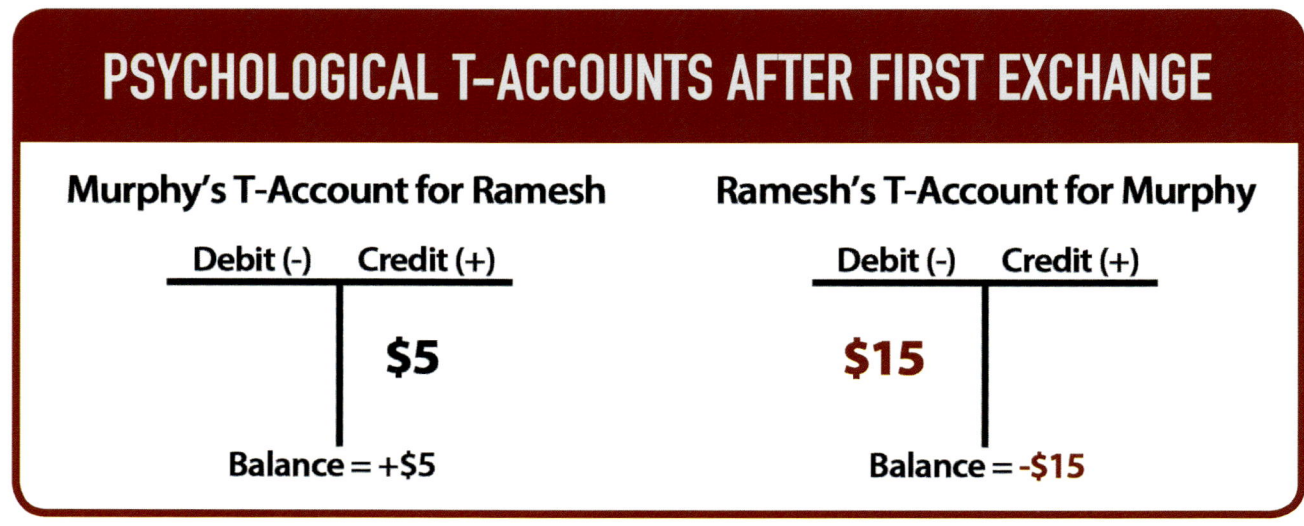

PSYCHOLOGICAL T-ACCOUNTS AFTER FIRST EXCHANGE

Murphy's T-Account for Ramesh

Debit (-)	Credit (+)
	$5

Balance = +$5

Ramesh's T-Account for Murphy

Debit (-)	Credit (+)
$15	

Balance = -$15

Model 2

PSYCHOLOGICAL T-ACCOUNTS AFTER SECOND EXCHANGE

Murphy's T-Account for Ramesh

Debit (-)	Credit (+)
$15	$5

Balance = -$10

Ramesh's T-Account for Murphy

Debit (-)	Credit (+)
$15	$5

Balance = -$10

Model 3

Now, let's assume the situation is exactly reversed and Ramesh needs a ride to work from Murphy. This time Murphy has to leave a MNF football game and give Ramesh a ride to work. Following the same logic as above, after this exchange, the psychological T-accounts will look something like Model 3.

Notice that both accounts have debit balances. In other words, both Murphy and Ramesh expect the other person to do them a favor to even out the account. The next day at lunch they may argue about who should pick up the tab. Ramesh thinks Murphy owes him $10 so Murphy should buy lunch. Similarly, Murphy thinks Ramesh owes him $10 so Ramesh should buy lunch. At this point the relationship will encounter problems in the form of both people trying to ***take more*** and ***give less*** (in order to even out the T-account). This is because both parties believe they are being taken advantage of. Because of this, each person refuses to buy lunch for the other. Ultimately, the T-accounts will become so uneven (due to continued biased accounting) that one or both parties will lose the motivation to continue the exchange.

Finally, it should be noted that the degree of discrepancy between the actual value of a ride to work (e.g., $10 in this example) and a self-important individual's estimate of the value ***given*** (e.g., $15 for a ride to work) or estimate of the value ***gained*** (e.g., $5 for a ride to work) depends entirely on the ***SI/SW ratio*** of the individuals. If the two parties are only slightly self-important, only small differences will be registered. However, even small discrepancies can accumulate into serious conflict over time.

It is important to note that the opposite effect occurs if the people in the exchange are self-worthy. Here, by definition, both people will exaggerate what they ***receive*** from the other party while underestimating what they have ***given*** to the exchange. This is because self-worth causes us to appreciate the value of what others give, which, in turn, allows us to give more freely. In this case, the two parties may also argue over who should buy lunch but this time, both parties will be trying to pay. This scenario is much less common (due to the small number of self-worthy people) and does not have the same level of negative effects on the relationship.

Based on this analysis the prognosis for a successful long term exchange relationship is (1) ***very good*** when both parties are self-worthy, (2) ***moderate*** when one is self-worthy and one is self-important, and (3) ***very poor*** when both are self-important. Because many people are highly self-important we can see that many human exchange relationships have a poor chance of success (in the long run). Also, note that due to intense competition in the business world (that accentuates self-importance) the same effects are expected in exchanges with professional key accounts.

SELF-IMPORTANCE AS A THREAT TO OTHERS

Another result of the skewed distribution of self-importance is that many (self-important) people must compete for limited rewards (e.g., the attention of the group). The person who "wins" is likely to be resented by the people who "lose" – if the losers are high in self-importance. Indeed, the level of resentment will be directly proportional to the individual's level of self-importance. Therefore, when a person achieves success, s/he can become threatening to other people who have high self-importance.

For example, suppose you get the highest grade on an exam and brag about the achievement to your friends and classmates. You have performed at a high level, but your friends and classmates look "bad" by comparison. Not surprisingly, this comparison threatens their self-importance and they are likely to engage in counterattack and withdrawal behaviors toward you (if they have high self-importance). For example, they might make a sarcastic remark like "where did you hide the crib sheet" (counterattack) or "who cares I didn't even study for that test," (withdrawal). If you took the time to carefully inspect your schedule of reinforcement you would likely find that many punishments and withdrawals result from your tendencies to demonstrate self-importance.

In the business world, where many self-important people actively compete for success it is easy to fall prey to these dynamics. Thus, many people make mistakes when trying to "promote" themselves (or a product) because of the way self-important behaviors are received by others. For example, if people boast and brag about themselves it can be received as a threat to others (who sometimes conspire to bring the braggart down (i.e., "office politics")). Conversely, self-worthy people are more likely to give **legitimate** compliments to others and ask them interesting **Level III** questions. These behaviors make others feel appreciated and important. Thus, one way to engage in successful relationship marketing is to make key accounts look good by using self-worth to direct your behaviors.

Office Gossip

SELF-IMPORTANCE AND SATISFACTION

Self-worth and self-importance also have an effect on the components used in the ***disconfirmation model*** to calculate consumer satisfaction and dissatisfaction. The disconfirmation model states that people compare what they actually get in exchanges to what they expected to get. When the actual value significantly exceeds the expected-value (positive disconfirmation) people are satisfied (a positive emotional state). When the actual value is significantly less than the expected value (negative disconfirmation), people are dissatisfied (a negative emotional state).

Note that by definition self-worthy people (1) give freely and do not expect each giving behavior to be immediately repaid, and (2) appreciate what is given to them by others. These dynamics cause self-worthy people (1) to have lower expectations of others in exchanges, and (2) to highly value what they actually receive in exchanges. This means the chances for positive disconfirmation go up significantly as self-worth rises. Conversely, the exact opposite effects occur as self-importance rises -- expectations of others are high and the value received is often discounted -- leading to frequent negative disconfirmation and dissatisfaction. It is an irony of life that self-important people are doomed to a life filled with significant dissatisfaction – mainly because nothing is ever good enough (i.e., negative disconfirmation).

SELF-IMPORTANCE IS SELF-CLOAKING

Surprisingly, people who are self-important usually are not aware that they possess this characteristic. There appear to be several reasons for this. First, by the time you are an adult, self-importance is almost completely automated -- it occurs without your own awareness. Second, because self-importance wants to interpret its own behavior in a favorable light, it is unlikely to notice itself. Indeed, it is often true that the more self-importance a person has, the less likely s/he is to admit it. On the other hand, people who are self-worthy tend to be more willing and able to find fault with their own behaviors. Thus, there is a negative correlation between self-importance and awareness of it.

As an example, when people are asked to rate their own level of self-importance, many find it hard to think of examples (because they have justified their past actions). Conversely, when other people act in a self-importance manner, it is easy for us to notice it. When students are asked to rate their roommates' level of self-importance, they can usually think of many examples when their friends have acted that way.

SELF-WORTH AND SELF-ESTEEM

There is a direct relationship between self-worth and self-esteem. One way to model self-esteem is:

> **SELF-ESTEEM = (SELF-CONFIDENCE + SELF-WORTH + SELF-IMAGE)**

Self-confidence reflects your ability to satisfy your own needs while self-worth reflects your ability to satisfy the needs of your key accounts. The higher your self-worth, the more giving you are, and the more giving you are, the more you can satisfy the needs of your key accounts (and the more willing you are to put their needs ahead of your own). Conversely, people with high self-importance have lower self-worth and therefore, lower self-esteem. Indeed, high self-importance represents a major reason that many humans have low self-esteem.

SELF-IMPORTANCE BECOMES AUTOMATED AND HARD TO CHANGE

Once tendencies toward self-importance become established (usually at an early age), they usually direct behavior in an automated manner (i.e., without awareness). This means the vast majority of self-important behaviors go unnoticed by the actor. This makes it very difficult to suppress or alter self-important behaviors so lowering this trait usually is difficult and requires numerous trials over extended periods of time.

SELF-IMPORTANCE AND META-MOTIVATION

Maslow often wondered why so few people reached the self-actualization stage. It seems likely that the SI/SW ratio plays a significant role in the attainment of both deficiency needs and growth needs. Specifically, the lower needs like safety and security can be well satisfied through self-important behaviors (e.g., hungry lions at a kill). By the time one gets to affiliation and social esteem needs, there is already a large degree of self-importance that has been learned without awareness, automated, and thus, has become a major part of the individual's character. However, the social needs, self-esteem needs, and growth needs are better satisfied through self-worth which is often in short supply by the time one is able to focus on higher needs. Ultimately, it may be that our self-importance (e.g., hedonism, procrastination, deception, etc.) prevents us from reaching the self-esteem needs and thus prevents meta-motivation. In this view, reaching meta-motivation requires a progressive loss of self-importance while at the same time there is a progressive increase in self-worth.

LOSING SELF-IMPORTANCE

> *"You take yourself too seriously," he said slowly. "You are too damn important in your own mind. That must be changed! You are so damn important that you feel justified to be annoyed with everything. You're so damn important that you can afford to leave if things don't go your way. I suppose you think that shows you have character. That's nonsense! You're weak and conceited!"*
> (**Castaneda** 1972, p. 40)

The concept of losing self-importance means that we purposefully decide to lessen our self-importance and/or raise our self-worth in a specific exchange relationship. This maneuver must be done **consciously** and strategically at first, and on a trial basis. To lose self-importance, perform Experiment 20.1 at the end of this chapter. This experiment basically requires that you put a key account's needs ahead of your own on a few selected occasions. Then, analyze how your key account reacts to your behaviors and your internal and external schedule of reinforcement.

WHEN TO LOSE SELF-IMPORTANCE

Losing self-importance usually requires a great deal of psychic energy and can produce considerable frustration, especially in the short run. Accordingly, losing self-importance makes the most sense when it involves a continuing and important exchange relationship. People find it easier to accomplish if the exchange relationship involves family, spouses, in-laws, children, clients, co-workers, superiors, or subordinates.

Also note that the ability to lose self-importance can be influenced by **mood states.** When people are in a bad mood it is very unlikely they will be able to lose self-importance effectively.

SHORT-RUN VERSUS LONG-RUN ORIENTATION

Losing self-importance is most beneficial when the exchange is long-term. In the short-run, an individual can often gain more by acting self-importantly. Because many people have a short-run perspective

Losing Self-Importance by Showing Gratitude

when making decisions, the degree of self-importance is often high. For example, if you actively listen to others and ask Level III questions, they will often return your behavior (if they have sufficiently high self-worth). When people lose self-importance, they usually see concrete returns on investment over the long term. In addition, the Return-On-Investment is normally **extremely high.** However, in the short run, losing self-importance can cause two opposite feelings.

In one case, the individual finds it very difficult to actually lose self-importance. For example, withholding your opinions from a conversation is extremely difficult for many people. This result seems to occur when the individual's level of self-importance is high, or the value being withheld is central and strongly held. In these cases, significant inner tension and frustrated energy can be produced from losing self-importance.

In contrast, some people find losing self-importance produces satisfaction in the short run. Often this occurs when people help others or perform a giving behavior that results in a sense of accomplishment. The degree to which the other person is characterized by high self-worth also seems to play a role -- people find it easier to lose self-importance for a person they consider to be self-worthy.

GAINING SELF-WORTH

> *"As long as you feel that you are the most important thing in the world you cannot really appreciate the world around you. You are like a horse with blinders, all you see is yourself apart from everything else."* (**Castaneda** 1972, p. 42)

Our automated tendencies toward self-importance make it easy for us to forget to thank people for their help. You can probably think of occasions when you have helped a friend or family member, without receiving any acknowledgment for your efforts. Likewise, we often fail to express our thanks to others in a meaningful fashion.

One way to overcome this maladaptive tendency is to write a letter of power periodically. A letter of power is designed to express sincere gratitude for help received. Therefore, the letter should increase the self-worth of the person who receives it and the person who sends it. It must, therefore, be absolutely credible, never exaggerating or giving insincere praise. A letter of power is carefully thought out and outlined -- considerable effort must go into its planning and writing. Use specific examples of how the person most helped you and what it meant to you. If the letter succeeds in **raising the self-worth of the receiver, it also has the effect of raising the sender's self worth.** This double reinforcement is a powerful and positive effect. To gain self worth complete Experiment 20.2 at the end of this chapter.

CONCLUSION

Relationship marketing seeks to produce **customers for life** in an attempt to maximize long-run profits. This goal can be achieved only if the company's representatives have a continuing exchange of value with the customers. Unfortunately, **continuing exchanges** are difficult to maintain due to human self-importance – especially biased accounting. Indeed in a world where most people have a SI/SW ratio well over 50/50, successful long-term relationships can be few in number.

Understanding this problem is the first step toward minimizing the effects of self-importance in your own exchange behaviors. However, this is very difficult for most people because self-importance is automated and therefore, hidden from conscious view most of the time. Fortunately, the losing self-importance experiment and gaining self-worth experiment can be performed repeatedly, each time increasing your self-worth or lowering your self-importance. Over time this will shift your SI/SW ratio in a positive direction.

This lowering of self-importance is an important goal because people with high self-worth can satisfy their social needs more effectively and thus move on to a focus on growth. Self-worth is also directly related to self-esteem and ultimately, to concepts like **love, intimacy, and tolerance** which are crucial to understanding successful relationship marketing as discussed in the next chapter.

EXPERIMENT 20.1
LOSING SELF-IMPORTANCE

Identify two different key account relationships where you act in a self-important manner to the extent that it detracts from the value in the relationship.

1. For key account # 1:

    a. What are the self-important behaviors?

    b. How did you develop the self-important behaviors?

    c. Explain how they detract from your exchange relationship.

    d. Identify two specific behaviors you could perform to eliminate or significantly reduce the level of your self-importance with this key account. Be sure that one of these involves some type of effortful overt behavior (i.e., physical activity).

    e. Perform the behaviors. Then, **explain in detail** what you did, giving specific examples. Make sure you do not use past behaviors – you must perform new behaviors for this experiment.

    f. Describe the effect these behaviors had on your **internal** schedule of reinforcement.

    g. Describe the effect these behaviors had on your **external** schedule of reinforcement. Consider both the short run, and expected long run results in your analysis.

2. Repeat steps a - g above for key account # 2.

3. Summarize what you learned from this experiment.

Popular Choices for the Losing Self-Importance Experiment

- Practice Active listening
- Focus on another
- Take interest in another
- Withhold your opinions
- Eliminate sarcasm and negativity
- Clean apartment/house
- Help a friend study
- Give others decision-making power
- Give legitimate compliments
- Help charity
- Drive friendly
- Host a parent at Level III
- Give sincere thanks

EXPERIMENT 20.2
GAINING SELF-WORTH

Select a person (or persons) who has helped you make it to or through college (e.g., parents, counselors, friend, etc.). If you are doing this experiment for class credit, **do not** chose a current or former boyfriend/girlfriend.

1. Explain in a few sentences why you selected this person(s).

2. Carefully plan and write a letter of power to this person.

    a. Think at Level III about specific examples of when the target person(s) helped you and how you benefitted. Include at least five specific examples.

    b. Carefully and eloquently express your gratitude in the letter. Your advanced level of education MUST show through in the letter.

    c. The letter must contain your absolute highest quality of work (e.g., no misspelled words, typos, improper grammar, etc). Have a friend carefully proofread the letter to eliminate mistakes. Any mistakes, shortcuts, or poor production quality in the letter will reduce your grade.

    d. The letter must reflect a considerable effort. The body should be at least one page long (single spaced) -- but can be longer.

    e. The letter must have creative elements to it - e.g., high quality paper, colorful photos scanned in, line art, favorite poems, quotes, song lyrics, etc. The more creativity you put in the letter, the higher grade you get.

    f. The letter must be laser printed - no hand written letter for this assignment.

3. Mail your letter **1 week** before the assignment due date to allow time to record reactions from the recipient's.

4. Turn in a copy of your letter on the paper you used. You may cross out any lines that you feel are too personal.

5. In ~ 300 words, describe the effects that writing the letter had on:

    a. Your internal schedule of reinforcement

    b. Your external schedule of reinforcement (if used a proofreader)

    c. The response/expected response from the recipient's.

ELABORATION QUESTIONS

- What is the highest SI/SW ratio that can be successful in a long-term relationship?

- When is it better to be self-important than to be self-worthy?

- What are the main sources of self-worth?

- What is your overall average SI/SW ratio? Compare your estimate with people who know you well.

- Do self-worthy people get "used?"

- How would you rate yourself on the determinants of self-importance?

- How are deprivation and affluence of deficiency needs related to the SI/SW ratio?

- How many of your key accounts owe you a favor? How many of your key accounts do you owe a favor to?

- Does self-worth "rub-off" on others?

- If one person has a SI/SW ratio of 80/20 and his/her girlfriend/boyfriend has a SI/SW ratio of 20/80 will the relationship work out in the long-run? Why or why not?

- When are you most likely to resent the success of others?

- Are you frequently disappointed by other people? By products? By services?

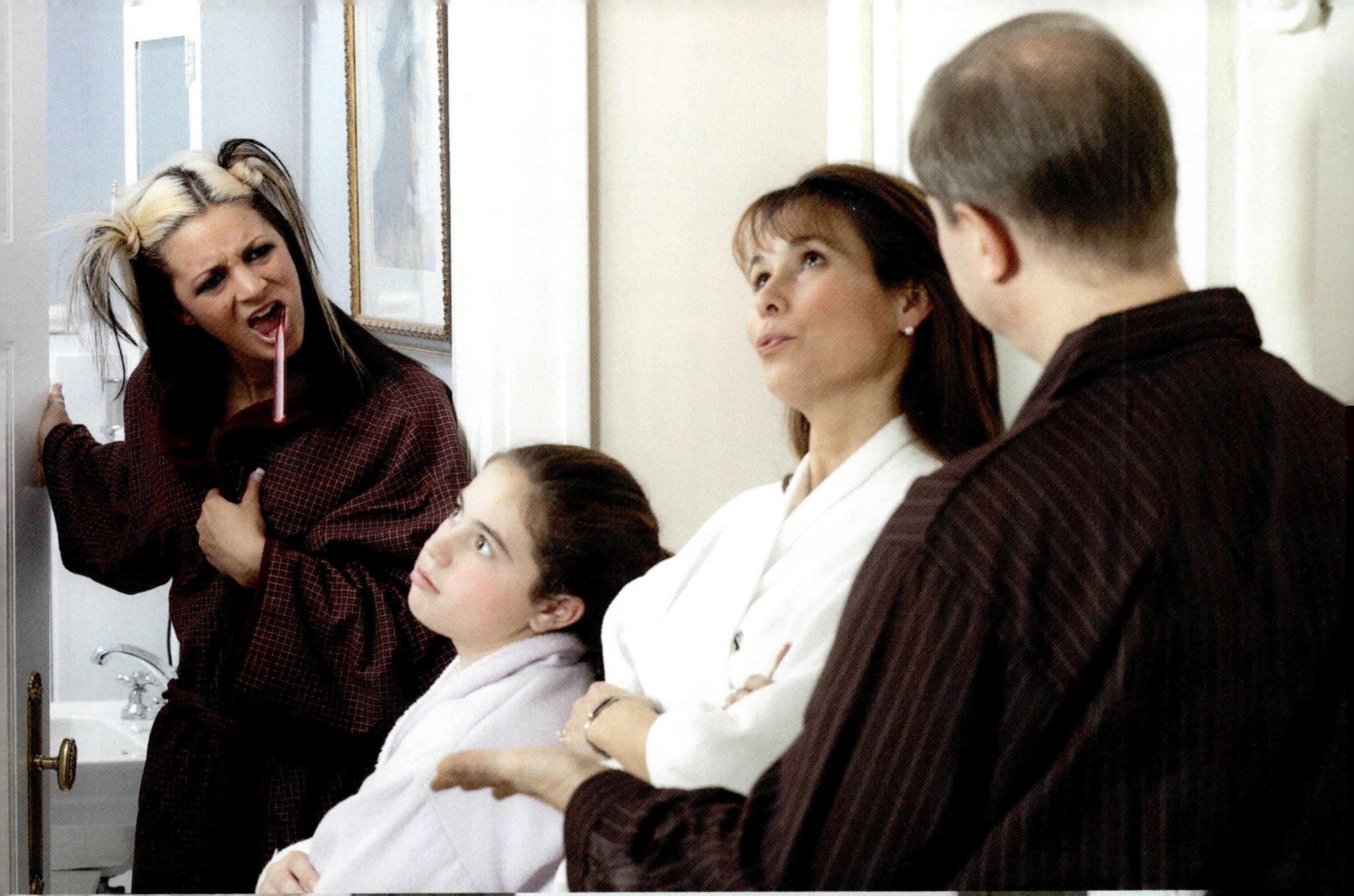

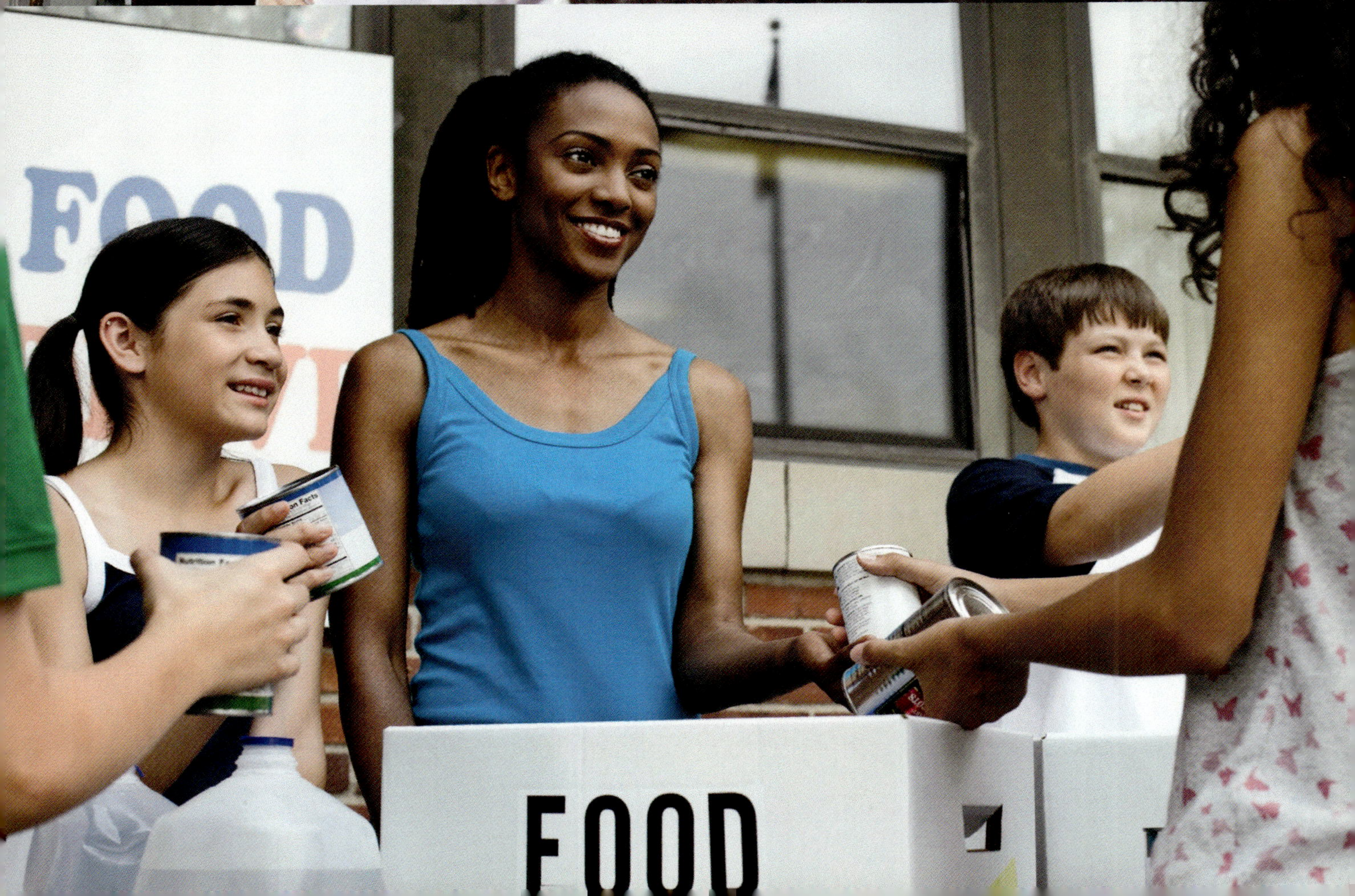
FOOD
FOOD

CHAPTER 21
LOVE & RELATIONSHIP MARKETING

LOVE & RELATIONSHIP MARKETING — 21.1
INTIMACY THEORY — 21.1
    Definition of Intimacy — 21.1
    Indirect Intimacy — 21.3
    Importance of Intimacy — 21.3
    The Intimacy Audit — 21.3
    Antisocial or Damaged BIS — 21.3
    Negative Response to Intimacy — 21.3
TYPES OF INTIMACY — 21.4
LOSS OF INTIMACY — 21.5
    Totality of Self-Expression — 21.6
    Lack of Self-Expression — 21.6
    Intimacy over Time — 21.7
LOVE AND THE EXCHANGE OF VALUE — 21.7
    Love Defined — 21.7
    Five Bridge Theory — 21.7
    Combinations of Intimacy — 21.8
TOLERANCE THEORY — 21.8
    The Need for Tolerance — 21.8
    The Value of Diversity — 21.8
    Intolerance and Loss of Self-Expression — 21.9
    Reasons for Intolerance — 21.9
    Tolerance and Marketing — 21.9
CONCLUSION — 21.9
EXPERIMENT 21.1 | INTIMACY, LOVE, AND TOLERANCE — 21.10
EXPERIMENT 21.2 | SELF-DESTRUCTIVE BEHAVIORS — 21.10
ELABORATION QUESTIONS — 21.11

GUIDING QUESTIONS

- How is love related to relationship marketing?
- What is intimacy and how is it achieved?
- How is the Biological Intrinsic Self related to self-esteem?
- Why is telling the truth so difficult at times?
- What happens when people reject who we are?
- What is indirect intimacy and how much value does it produce?
- Why is intimacy important in exchange relationships?
- What happens when two people do not want the same level of intimacy of their relationship?
- What are the different types of intimacy?
- What factors caused a loss of intimacy over time?
- Why is it important to achieve full disclosure of the intrinsic self?
- What is the definition of love (from an exchange relationship point of view)?
- What is five bridge theory?
- Why is love so complex?
- Why do we need tolerance?
- How does intolerance cause a loss of self-expression?
- Should we tolerate self-destructive tendencies in other people?
- What are the major reasons for intolerance?
- Why is tolerance important in marketing?

LOVE & RELATIONSHIP MARKETING

From a relationship perspective, marketing is viewed as an continuing exchange of value between two parties. While **money** is often the focus of commercial exchanges, it has **no intrinsic value**. Instead, people value money because of the things it can buy. Intrinsically, humans value anything that:

1. Facilitates the five preconditions (i.e., striving opportunities, freedom, curiosity, need to know, and self-expression)

2. Allows deficiency need gratification (i.e., food, sleep, activity, sex, sensory pleasure, physical safety, psychological security, belongingness, *love*, esteem from others, and self-esteem)

3. Allows neurotic or subconscious need gratification,

4. Allows growth need gratification (achieving the meta-motives through creativity)

Indeed, Maslow (1970) concluded that all relationships (personal and professional) succeed or fail based on the amount of **need gratification exchanged**. Any relationship that fails to satisfy the evolving needs of the parties to exchange will decline over time. It is important to note that Maslow (1970) also concluded that humans need **love and affection** all through their life and that deprivation of the love needs causes serious problems for adults. While it may seem a bit strange to discuss love in a consumer behavior text (most other marketing texts avoid the subject all together) there is much to learn about successful long-term relationships by examining this construct (and its correlates, intimacy and tolerance). Indeed, consumers "love" at least some of the products and services they purchase (e.g., pets, cars, vacations, food, etc.). Thus, understanding the determinants of love and intimacy can help you add value to your exchange relationships – both personal and professional.

The main problem with studying this topic is that, as we saw in an earlier chapter, many people have a **weakly cued** idea of what love is. This means there will be major differences among people as to how to define this need state. Keep in mind that this discussion is ultimately designed to help you understand how to **add value to continuing relationships** rather than a model of romantic love (although that topic is included in the model). Finally, the model developed here is based on Maslow's (1971) concept of "being" love.

INTIMACY THEORY

DEFINITION OF INTIMACY

Intimacy can be defined as **shared truth** about one's **Biological Intrinsic Self (BIS)**. The BIS is basically defined as who you were born to be - your true inner (intrinsic) nature. Sharing the truth in an exchange relationship involves **reciprocity** or a two-stage process.

Stage 1 — Revealing the BIS. Intimacy begins when one person reveals part of his/her Biological Intrinsic Self to another person. The more important the exchange relationship, the more important it is to be self-expressive (in order to achieve need gratification - especially the higher needs). Note also that because the BIS is our real self it is directly tied to self-esteem. Specifically, if the BIS is accepted self-esteem increases and if the BIS is rejected self/social-esteem decreases Thus there is significant risk involved in revealing the truth because one takes the chance of being embarrassed or rejected by the other party. Because of this risk of losing social-esteem or self-esteem, one

Revealing Your Biological Intrinsic Self

could hypothesize that intimacy normally builds slowly until mutual trust is established. However, revealing the BIS is not, by itself, sufficient to achieve intimacy. It is also necessary that the other party responds in an appropriate way to the revelation.

Stage 2 — Feedback from Key Account. When a person has revealed part of his/her BIS to another, a number of reactions are possible:

1. **Reward.** In this case the BIS is revealed to a key account, and the key account responds positively. This reward makes the person feel loved, adds significantly to esteem, and increases the probability of further intimacy.

2. **Acceptance.** Here, the BIS is expressed to a key account, but the response is acceptance rather than reward. In this case, the key account may not approve of, or agree with, your BIS but nevertheless accepts you for who you are. This response makes the person feel somewhat accepted, adds somewhat to self/social-esteem, and slightly increases the probability of further intimacy.

3. **Constructive Criticism.** In this case the BIS is expressed to a key account but the response is constructive criticism (e.g., "tough love"). This response makes the person feel challenged and may activate meta-motives. If growth occurs, it adds significantly to self-esteem and increases the probability of further intimacy. If growth does not occur, the probability of further intimacy declines.

4. **Rejection.** In this case the BIS is expressed to a key account, but the response is negative. This rejection is felt punishment and lowers self/social-esteem thereby decreasing the probability of further intimacy. Rejection, therefore, is expected to degrade the intrinsic value of the relationship.

5. **Attack.** Sometimes, when a divergent BIS is revealed, it may be attacked verbally (e.g., sarcasm, threats, etc.) or physically (e.g., spanking, fights, etc.). This is the ultimate form of rejection and significantly lowers social/self-esteem and decreases the probability of further intimacy. Attack is expected to quickly degrade the intrinsic value of the relationship.

From this analysis, it is clear that responses 1 - 3 above are the best way to build a relationship over time. During the chemical bath stage, these responses are easy to achieve. However, intimacy often decline as the involvement life cycle unfolds, and during the decline stage, intimacy is probably very difficult to achieve. Indeed, one could reasonably hypothesize that the (current) level of intimacy in a relationship is a good predictor of the level of involvement.

INDIRECT INTIMACY

A second type of intimacy involves a **one-way relationship** rather than a two-way (reciprocal) exchange of value. In the case of "indirect intimacy," the BIS is expressed to another person (or object) that does not or cannot respond. An example of this would be a teenage girl who is in "love" with a music pop star and spends hours talking to a picture of him. Or, in the movie "Castaway" the volleyball became "Wilson," which allowed Tom Hanks to express his BIS. Indeed, many people are familiar with the practice of talking to inanimate objects or non-verbal life forms (e.g., pet fish) in order to express parts of the BIS. In these cases, there is a real need to express strong intrinsic feelings, even if the feelings cannot be returned (there may be "imagined" responses, however). A major advantage here is that the **probability of rejection is low.**

It would be interesting to compare the long-term value of reciprocal relationships versus one-way relationships. Certainly, positive intimacy is superior to indirect intimacy in terms of intrinsic value. However, reciprocal relationships are very dynamic and subject to change, decline, and termination. In contrast, indirect relationships often continue to return significant value over many years because there is less chance of receiving rejection. Cherished objects from childhood, memorabilia, fan clubs, hero worship, etc. are common examples of this type of relationship.

IMPORTANCE OF INTIMACY

According to Maslow's model, one of the most diagnostic traits of any exchange relationship is the degree of intimacy involved. This is because self-expression is essential to achieving need gratification. As noted, Maslow believed that **all** relationships succeed or fail

Wilson from Castaway

based on the amount of need gratification exchanged. Accordingly, understanding intimacy will allow you to add value to your continuing exchanges.

THE INTIMACY AUDIT

Theoretically, one could conduct an intimacy audit on any relationship. The maximum level of intimacy that can exist is 100 % which would signify that the entire intrinsic self has been revealed to, and accepted by, a key account. An intimacy level of 50 % would indicate that only half of the intrinsic self has been revealed to, and/or accepted by a key account. In general, positive intimacy adds value while rejection and conflict cause a decrease in the level of intimacy.

ANTISOCIAL OR DAMAGED BIS

What happens when the Biological Intrinsic Self is (1) antisocial by nature, or (2) damaged through rejection or attack by others? In these cases, the BIS must be suppressed for the good of society. However, a major question is how many antisocial people have a maladaptive BIS (bad by nature) and how many are reflecting violent repressions of their intrinsic self by others (neurotic needs developed due to rejection and attack)?

NEGATIVE RESPONSE TO INTIMACY

Another difficult issue is when to reward intimacy and when to punish it. Even though responding negatively to another's personal revelation reduces intimacy, there may be reasons to do so.

First, both parties to the exchange may not desire the same level of intimacy. If one person "gets too close," the other may withdraw or provide negative feedback to keep a desired distance.

Second, a personal revelation may violate "species values" or human nature. If the person has lied, cheated, physically hurt others, etc., a negative response is appropriate. In this case, further intimacy requires the person who violated species values to admit wrong doing and correct the behavior (i.e., positive growth). If growth is achieved, self-esteem increases and intimacy is advanced. If growth is refused (i.e., the person refuses to admit wrong-doing and/or to correct the unacceptable behavior) the level of intimacy will decline.

TYPES OF INTIMACY

Based on the previous definitions, five different types of intimacy can be identified:

GENETIC INTIMACY

Genetic intimacy occurs when two parties to exchange are genetically related. Relationships included here are parents and children, siblings, and relatives. Note that when a couple has a child they form a **secondary-genetic bond** because each contributes half of the child's DNA.

EMOTIONAL INTIMACY

Emotional intimacy occurs when the parties to exchange have shared experiences which trigger strong body chemistry. Emotional intimacy may be based on positive or negative experiences. Positive experiences would include the chemical bath, the thrill of discovery, the thrill of victory, etc. Negative experiences would be tragedy bonds (getting through hardships together), helping one another through difficult times, nursing one another through sickness, etc.

PSYCHOLOGICAL INTIMACY

Psychological intimacy occurs when parties to the exchange share beliefs and values. For example, this would include two people who agree on political issues and therefore have discussions where they reinforce

Genetic Intimacy - Mother and Child

Decline in Intimacy

each other's views. This can also include shared intellectual challenges such as competing in contests or shared creativity were people work together to produce a divergent but relevant product.

SPIRITUAL INTIMACY

Spiritual intimacy occurs when parties to the exchange share strong beliefs that are **not verifiable.** These beliefs must be accepted on "faith" so reasonable people have significant differences on spiritual matters. Examples here or would include people who share religious beliefs, or people who believe that aliens are visiting Earth in UFO's.

PHYSICAL INTIMACY

Physical intimacy occurs when the parties to the exchange share physical touch. The nature of the touching varies widely depending on the relationship.

Non-Sexual Physical Intimacy. Although people normally associate physical intimacy with sex, most touching is not sexual in nature. Examples include shaking hands, "high-fiving," chest bumping, pats on the back, hugs, kisses on the cheek, etc. Thus, most intimate relationships involve physical touching and the amount of physical contact between the two parties is almost always a good indication of the ***psychological distance*** between them. As intimacy levels increase, from any of the other sources (genetic, emotional, psychological, or spiritual), the level of physical contact normally increases.

Sexual Physical Intimacy. Because sex is the closest physical behavior two people can perform, it involves a high degree of intimacy by definition. Often, sexual intimacy occurs after other forms of intimacy have been achieved. This suggests that sex will be one of the first behaviors to be lessened or removed from a relationship if other intimacy levels decline.

One reason sexual intimacy is difficult to understand is that sex can satisfy a variety of human needs states. For example, a "one-night stand" can be seen as gratifying the lower physiological needs while "relationship sex" can gratify lower needs as well as affiliation, love, social esteem, and self-esteem needs.

LOSS OF INTIMACY

Intimacy is hard to maintain and can decline over time for a number of reasons:

1. **Truth Can Be Difficult.** Intimacy requires truth to reveal the biological intrinsic self. Truth is difficult for most people - even the suggestion of "radical honesty" (being totally honest with all key accounts) panics many people.

2. **Impression Management.** Impression management is learned early in life and accounts for a considerable part of most people's behavioral repertoire. Over time people lose awareness that they are even engaged in impression management. The automated nature of these behaviors makes them almost impossible to suppress. As people start playing roles, parts of the BIS are hidden, and intimacy declines.

3. **Natural Variations in BIS.** Many people's BIS may not be well adapted to long-term relationships (like marriage or staying at the same job for many years). Examples would include those who define love as the chemical bath (which fades with familiarity), those with a high need for variety, those with a fear of commitment, or those who are still young.

4. **Self-Importance and Need for Dominance.** Need for dominance, competition, and self-importance often increase over time as parties to the exchange become adapted to one another. At the same time, submissiveness, cooperation, and self-worth decrease, placing a great strain on intimacy.

5. **Unresolved Conflict.** Unresolved conflict often leads to withdrawal (e.g., the "silent" treatment) which is a clear indication that psychological distance is increasing and intimacy is decreasing.

6. **Low Self-Esteem.** Low self-esteem causes many people to withhold important parts of the BIS from the other party, thereby decreasing intimacy.

7. **Life Cycle of Love.** During the beginning of the relationship when the chemical bath is strong the parties to exchange do not need to work at intimacy. However, when the chemical bath dissipates conflict occurs and tension is the result. At this point intimacy often begins to decline.

8. **Changes in BIS.** The BIS changes and grows as the individual ages, causing people to move in different directions, grow apart, and lose intimacy.

9. **Repressed BIS.** If one or both party to the exchange has a repressed BIS, s/he may not be able to achieve intimacy in these areas (i.e., s/he cannot reveal their BIS because s/he does not know what it is).

10. **Guilt.** If one party has high *guilt* from past behaviors s/he may avoid intimacy so s/he does not have to face the guilt or because s/he (reasonably) expects rejection from other people. In either case, self-esteem will be too low for full intimacy to be achieved.

TOTALITY OF SELF-EXPRESSION

We could hypothesize that a key to self-esteem is to achieve **full disclosure** of the Biological Intrinsic Self. It does not really matter if you have one person to whom you can reveal the entire self or whether you reveal the entire self over a series of key account relationships. The important thing is that the full biological self is disclosed - and accepted. Note that this assumes each of us is familiar with our BIS. If the BIS has been repressed the person will not be able to express his/her real self to others. This implies a need for self-awareness in humans that may help explain the ever growing "self-help" industry.

LACK OF SELF-EXPRESSION

Although self-expression is a precondition to need gratification, it can be disenfranchised to satisfy deficiency needs. For example, people often misrepresent their true feelings in an effort to avoid hurting someone's feelings or trying to avoid confrontation or an argument. Indeed, "living a lie," suggests that a person covers up major parts of the Biological Intrinsic Self to achieve other, lower, goals. While such behavior may be successful in achieving safety and security needs, it also tends to build frustration over time and make the person "sick." Indeed, many people in modern society build significant frustration while gratifying their safety and security needs (e.g., work at a boring job, engage in impression management, stay in bad relationships, etc.). Another common example of this **down-leveling** is when people stay in a relationship even though intimacy levels are low because they want to avoid loneliness.

INTIMACY OVER TIME

It is important to note that most people have a continuing need for intimacy. This is because as the Biological Intrinsic Self grows and evolves to reach its final potential. As these changes occur, they must be expressed to our key accounts. As a result, intimacy needs tend to be high throughout a person's lifetime.

LOVE AND THE EXCHANGE OF VALUE

In Maslow's model, love plays a central role in need gratification because each human needs love and affection all through life. Indeed, the lack of love is a key factor in many neurotic and/or psychotic behaviors. Thus, it is critical for humans to achieve the needed levels of love in their value exchanges. Surprisingly, "love" and the love needs have received almost no systematic development in the marketing literature. While this may not be surprising given the past focus on transaction marketing, intimacy and love will need to play a central role as more relationship marketing models are developed.

LOVE DEFINED

From Maslow's perspective, love can be defined as a subjective, internal feeling state, based on a pattern of intimacy (i.e., shared truth) over time. In other words, intimacy is the primary determinant of love. Therefore, the people you love should know you the best. For example, your loved ones should know who you really are, they should know your secret goals and desires, they should know what you plan to do in the future, etc. "Being love" occurs when a person loves you for your true self (i.e., your biological intrinsic self) not because you do things for them or because you arouse them. This can only be achieved through intimacy.

To test this proposition, think of your current and past love relationships. First, identify the level of intimacy that does or did exist in each relationship (be sure to consider all five bridges identified below). Next, identify the level of love you felt toward this person. According to the model, there should be a high correlation between the two.

FIVE BRIDGE THEORY

Using the *five types of intimacy* previously defined, we can propose a model of five intimacy bridges that can connect people. These are: genetic, emotional,

Love

physical, psychological, and spiritual intimacy bridges. When all five bridges are present in a relationship it should have maximum intimacy, high value, and high involvement. **Maximum love** is hypothesized to exist when all five bridges connect the exchange partners at Level III. For this reason, **romantic** and **family** relationships can be expected to play a prominent role in gratifying our love needs.

Note that almost all societies have a taboo against having sex with close genetic relatives. Therefore, it can be concluded that romantic relationships can have only four bridges until children are born (which represents a strong bond based on "secondary genetic bonds," but not shared genes).

Most professional relationships and friendships have neither sexual nor genetic intimacy involved. Thus, the maximum level of intimacy is four bridges: emotional, psychological, non-sexual physical, and spiritual intimacy bridges. Note that a good friendship with three or four bridges at Level III can provide more love than a romantic or family relationship that has declining or missing intimacy bridges.

COMBINATIONS OF INTIMACY

A major reason **love is complex** is that we can have different combinations of intimacy with different people. For example, you may have Level III spiritual intimacy with a person but no sexual intimacy. Or you may have sexual intimacy with no psychological intimacy (e.g., a one-night stand). Note that non-sexual relationships can provide great value and love (if real intimacy is achieved) without the entanglements that often go with sexual exchanges (e.g., territoriality, diminishing returns, etc.). Perhaps this is why the Greek Hedonists concluded that the best source of pleasure is friendship.

TOLERANCE THEORY

THE NEED FOR TOLERANCE

The need for tolerance theory is based on the idea that self-expression is a major precondition to need gratification. This means that all humans should be able to express their Biological Intrinsic Self, or else they will not be able to achieve need satisfaction. If they are unable to achieve need satisfaction, they are likely to become antisocial and/or self-destructive. Therefore, it is the best interests of the society to allow all biological intrinsic selves to be expressed -- **as long as they do not violate species values** (e.g., physically harming others, stealing, etc).

THE VALUE OF DIVERSITY

Human beings show variation on every trait and this is a major reason why exchange partners are interesting and relationships are dynamic. These differences are due to random gene combination, as well as differences in acculturation, maturation, and growth. A major issue is what variation human beings are willing to tolerate in one another. For example, people are quite willing to tolerate some differences. We allow virtually any variation regarding food intake. There is no law against over-eating, eating a bad diet, or under-eating. This variation is acceptable to us even though obesity has become the nation's number one health problem. Indeed, the idea of making over-eating illegal seems preposterous.

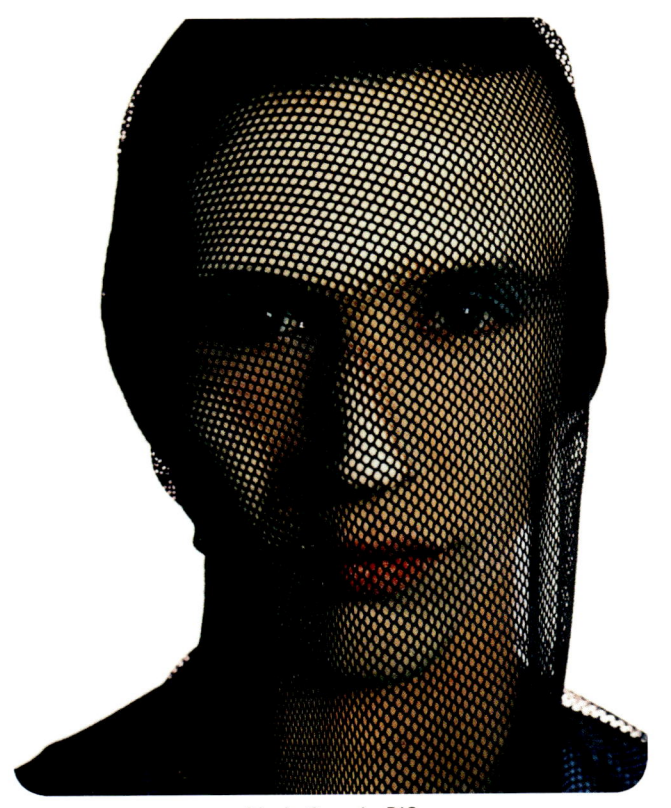

Variations in BIS

We also allow variation in alcohol consumption - after the person is old enough to make an informed choice - even though alcohol is a very dangerous (and toxic) drug. Similarly, we allow adults to smoke cigarettes even though almost a half million Americans die each year from the effects of tobacco consumption.

In contrast, we do not allow variation in the consumption for a number of other products and services. These include certain drugs, prostitution, riding motorcycles without a helmet (in some states), etc.

INTOLERANCE AND LOSS OF SELF-EXPRESSION

However, we must examine how intolerance and inability of consumers to express their BIS affects behavior. For example, homosexuals, for many years, were not allowed to express who they really were for fear of punishment, attack, or criminal prosecution. This created high frustration and, no doubt, many negative behaviors from the repressed group. Enlightened modern thought realizes that people's sexual orientation should not influence their ability to contribute to society.

Similar progress has been made with gambling. For many years gambling was illegal in the USA. As a result, the demand for this service was unregulated and illegal markets prospered (offering criminal gangs an incredible profit opportunity). Then, gambling was legalized in Nevada and slowly other states began not only to legalize it but sponsor it actively in state lotteries (including advertising in mass media to stimulate the amount of gambling that occurs). Currently, Nevada is the only state that has legalized prostitution which makes for interesting speculation about the future.

The prohibition of alcohol in the 1920s and 1930s demonstrated to many people that the evils of prohibiting a product (that is in great demand) can be greater than the evils of the product itself. Because of this, prohibition of alcohol was finally repealed.

Violence (physical harm to other people), is one of the greatest dangers to society but usually was seen by Maslow as a reaction against the suppression of the Biological Intrinsic Self rather than an evil BIS. This suggests societies that refuse to tolerate variations on human traits almost ensure a suffering and violent segment in their society.

REASONS FOR INTOLERANCE

There are a variety of reasons why people are intolerant of variations in the behavior of others. **Self-importance** is surely a major cause of intolerance – especially when combined with tendencies **toward cognitive consistency.** These two forces make it easy to become judgmental and intolerant. Another major reason for intolerance are the **dominance needs** which include the desire to impose our values on other people. **Fear** and **frustration** must also be considered as contributors to intolerance, at least in some situations. **Hardening of values** (especially non-verifiable values) also contributes to intolerance.

TOLERANCE AND MARKETING

The reason this discussion is relevant to consumer behavior is that marketing is the human interface of the firm. Indeed, the firm's very existence depends on **sales** so it is our job to find customers and add to their value any way we can. In this scenario, intolerance will lead to failed relationships, customer defections, a smaller market share, and lower profits. Moreover, in today's international business environment consumers with widely different cultural values are of interest to the firm. It is part of marketing's job to make these customers feel welcomed and well served. Indeed, if we are engaged in relationship marketing we will need tolerance in order to establish intimacy (which adds Level III value) with key accounts from different cultures.

CONCLUSION

One of the most common themes in the history of art, music, film, and theater is the need for love and lack thereof. From an exchange-based perspective of love, intimacy, and tolerance, we can understand why there is so little love. Real love requires intimacy – getting to know another person's Biological Intrinsic Self and accepting it. In the natural world, there is tremendous variation in the BIS on every dimension of being human (e.g., height, strength, sense of humor, sexual orientation, intelligence, etc.). In addition, more variations are introduced through cultural values which change dramatically from one country to another. The end result is that each human being is a unique combination of strengths and weaknesses reflected in the BIS. For love to exist we must be tolerant of these differences rather than attacking them. Unfortunately, due to our innate and powerful tendencies toward cognitive consistency, selective defense, need for dominance, etc., we can find it very difficult to achieve tolerance. When this happens with professional key accounts, our relationships fail and our customers defect. The only way to prevent this is to keep the consumer satisfied (next chapter).

EXPERIMENT 21.1
INTIMACY, LOVE, AND TOLERANCE

1. Conduct an "intimacy audit" for five of your key accounts.
   a. How much of you do they know? (percentage)
   b. How much of them do you know? (percentage)

2. Explain the relationship you find between intimacy and "love."

3. What is the connection between intimacy and tolerance in these relationships

4. What is the best way to achieve "being love" in your life?.

EXPERIMENT 21.2
SELF-DESTRUCTIVE BEHAVIORS

1. Interview two people you know who have self-destructive behaviors (e.g., binge drinking, drug abuse or addiction, eating disorders, risk-taking activities, etc.).

2. How did the self-destructive behaviors begin? What needs do they satisfy?

3. Categorize the self-destructive behaviors and discuss any differences that are important.

4. In your opinion, what would be the best course of action to lessen or eliminate these self-destructive behaviors?

ELABORATION QUESTIONS

- Give three examples of products or services that you "love."

- Is it important to "love" your job?

- Is there a hierarchy to the five types of intimacy that can exist in a relationship? re some more important than others?

- How would you compare genders in terms of the five intimacy bridges and the importance of each?

- How do neurotic needs influence a person's ability to achieve love, intimacy, and tolerance?

- How does five bridge theory explain the fact that sometimes opposites attract?

- How does lack of genetic intimacy affect the other four bridges?

- Is rejection of the BIS ever good?

- Can indirect intimacy be unhealthy?

- What is the best cure for self-destructive behavior?

- What are reasonable limits for tolerance?

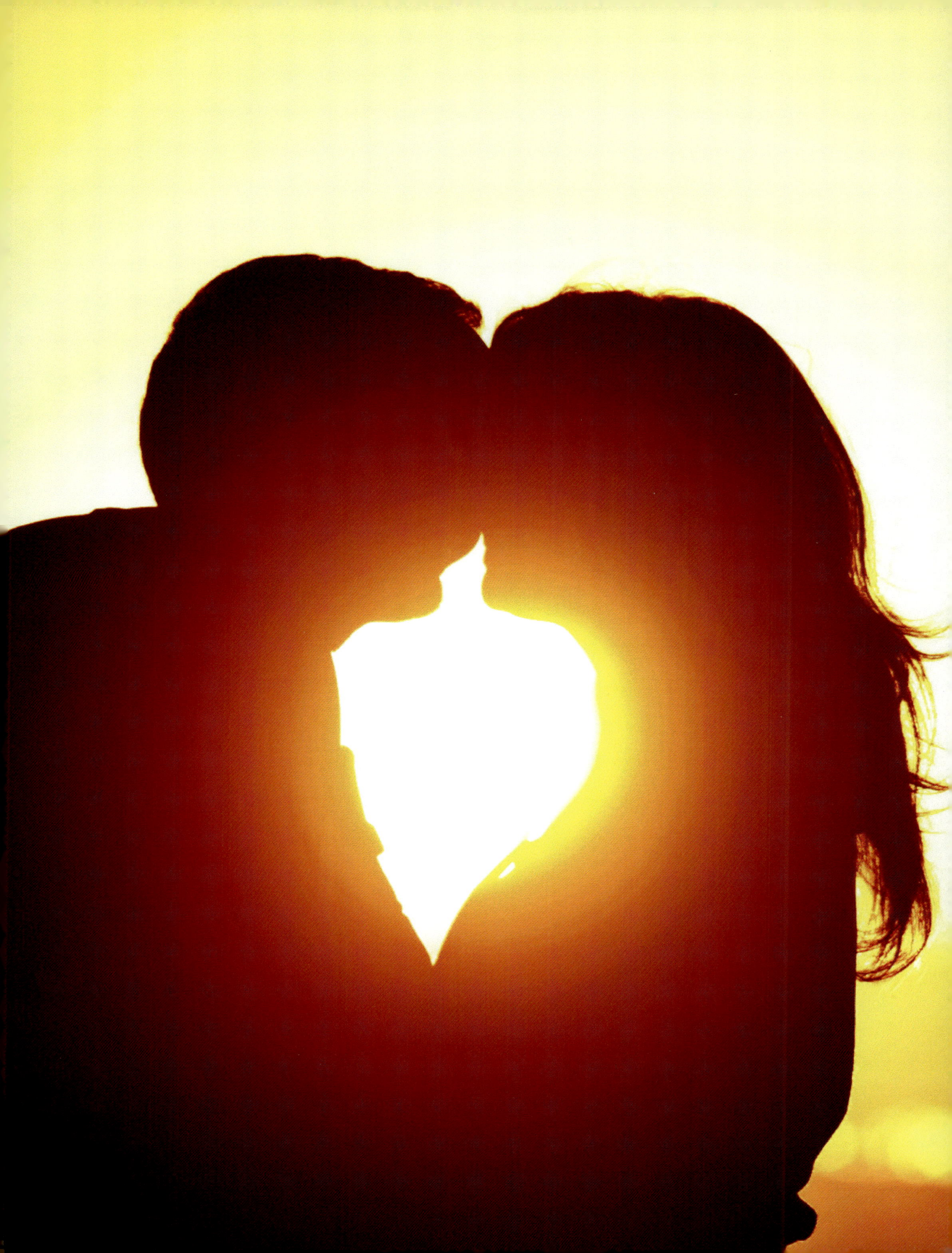

CHAPTER 22
CONSUMER SATISFACTION, DISSATISFACTION, AND QUALITY OF LIFE

INTRODUCTION	22.1
CONSUMER SATISFACTION AND DISSATISFACTION	22.1
THE DISCONFIRMATION MODEL	22.2
THE PRODUCT PERFORMANCE MODEL OF SATISFACTION	22.3
Product Performance	22.3
Product Performance and Primary Affect	22.3
AFFECT AS SATISFACTION MODEL	22.4
COMMON SOURCES OF DISSATISFACTION	22.5
Unrealistic Expectations	22.5
The Law of Diminishing Returns	22.6
Grumbling Theory	22.6
PREVENTING DISSATISFACTION	22.7
Preventing Personal Dissatisfaction	22.7
Preventing Consumer Dissatisfaction	22.7
EXPRESSING CONSUMER DISSATISFACTION	22.7
THE PARADOX OF PERSUASION	22.8
Brand Management Exercise	22.8
CONSUMER SATISFACTION AND QUALITY OF LIFE	22.8
Satisfaction from Lower Need Gratification	22.8
Satisfaction from Higher Need Gratification	22.9
**EXPERIMENT 22.1	SATISFACTION AND THE ELEMENT OF SURPRISE**	22.10
Implications	22.10
CONCLUSION	22.10
ELABORATION QUESTIONS	22.11

GUIDING QUESTIONS

- » What is consumer satisfaction?
- » What is consumer dissatisfaction?
- » What is net satisfaction?
- » What is the disconfirmation model of consumer satisfaction?
- » What happens when consumer expectations are confirmed?
- » What happens when consumer expectations are positively disconfirmed?
- » What happens when consumer expectations are negatively disconfirmed?
- » What is the product performance model of consumer satisfaction?
- » When will product performance be more important than disconfirmation?
- » What is the affect model of consumer satisfaction?
- » What is the desire-congruency model of consumer satisfaction?
- » What are the common sources of consumer dissatisfaction?
- » What is grumbling theory?
- » What is the best way to prevent personal dissatisfaction?
- » What is the best way to prevent consumer dissatisfaction?
- » What is the relationship between consumer satisfaction and quality of life?
- » What is meta-satisfaction?
- » To what extent do the consumption of products and services create human satisfaction?

INTRODUCTION

Consumer satisfaction is viewed as a central construct in marketing because it influences a variety of important variables including: brand attitude, consumer loyalty, complaining behavior, other dissatisfaction responses, perceived company performance, and quality of life. Indeed, consumer satisfaction has been an important and productive area in marketing research for many years. After numerous empirical studies much is known about satisfaction as well as its antecedents and consequences.

CONSUMER SATISFACTION AND DISSATISFACTION

SATISFACTION
Satisfaction is a **positive emotional reaction** that a consumer has after using a product or service. It is a meaningful, although temporary, affective state.

DISSATISFACTION
Dissatisfaction is a **negative emotional reaction** that a consumer has after using a product or service.

NET SATISFACTION
A major issue in marketing is whether satisfaction and dissatisfaction are opposite ends of the same continuum or completely different states. Many researchers argue that they should be regarded as **separate constructs** (Aaker and Day 1971; Czepiel and Rosenberg 1977; Oliver 1993; Omodei and Wearing 1990; Patti and Aaker 2002). For example, Maddox (1981) notes that satisfaction and dissatisfaction are different constructs so one's level of satisfaction is independent of the level of dissatisfaction. If true, this suggests that consumers can have a level of satisfaction and a level of dissatisfaction with a brand. For example, you may be satisfied with your favorite ice cream's taste and cost but be dissatisfied with it's packaging (e.g., it only comes in gallon containers which causes a lot of wasted product).

We will define **Net Satisfaction** as the consumer's overall judgment of the product after combining both satisfaction and dissatisfaction (i.e., **net satisfaction = satisfaction + dissatisfaction**). This suggests that marketing managers seeking to maximize consumers' satisfaction should pursue a dual strategy: (1) to maximize satisfaction, **and** (2) to minimize dissatisfaction.

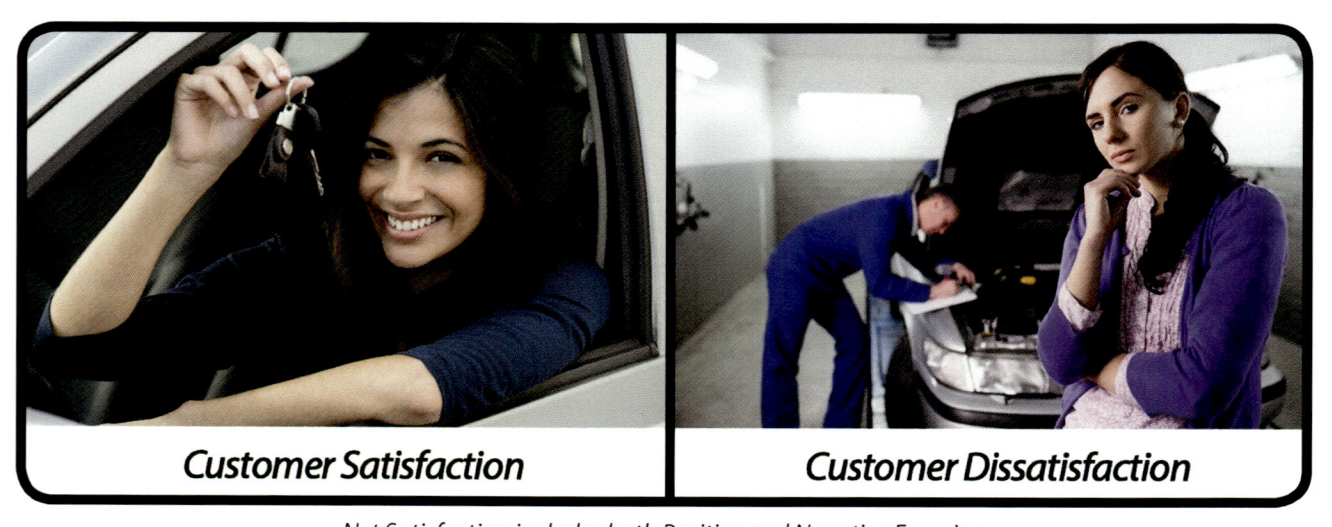

| Customer Satisfaction | Customer Dissatisfaction |

Net Satisfaction includes both Positive and Negative Experiences

22.1

CONTINUUM OF NET SATISFACTION AND DISSATISFACTION

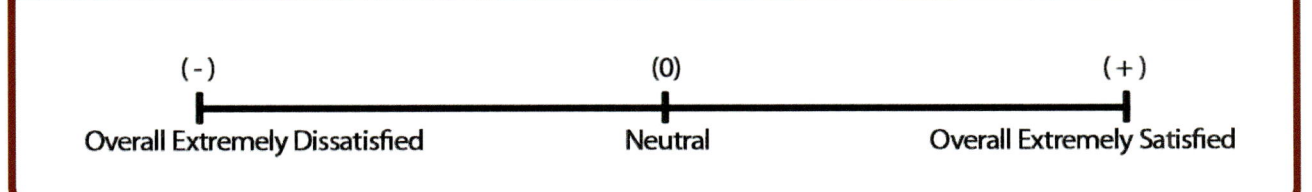

(−) Overall Extremely Dissatisfied — (0) Neutral — (+) Overall Extremely Satisfied

Model 1

THE DISCONFIRMATION MODEL

The disconfirmation model is the most widely recognized theory of consumer satisfaction. This is a **cognitive model** applicable in situations where consumers carefully evaluate the brand and compare it to their pre-purchase expectations.

EXPECTATIONS

As we have seen, consumers normally have expected-value (EV) for the products and services they buy. This EV may be spontaneously calculated in short-term memory or drawn with little awareness from long-term memory. In either case, consumers normally will not part with their money unless they expect more value than they are giving up.

PRODUCT PERFORMANCE

After purchase, the consumer uses the product and experiences it's performance. This normally produces **descriptive beliefs** which allow the consumer to confidently evaluate the product's performance.

COMPARISON PROCESS

Next, the consumer undergoes a cognitive comparison process whereby perceived brand performance is compared to pre-purchase expectations. The motivation for this comparison is that behavior is goal directed and people desire feedback regarding goal achievement. However, this comparison may not occur if the product is unimportant or the consumer has automated product use.

COMPARISON NORMS

Research has identified a variety of different norms that consumers can use during the comparison process. These include comparing the brand's performance to: what was expected, what was deserved, the minimum tolerable performance, cultural standards, similar brands, the best brand, the ideal product, or specific desires.

CONFIRMATION

In this case, the product's performance is approximately **equal** to expectations so the expectations are said to be "confirmed." Here, performance is within the **zone of indifference,** which often goes unnoticed by consumers. In these cases, confirmation simply reinforces the consumer's prior attitude. Thus, confirmation indicates there is **no surprise** so the effects of disconfirmation (i.e., satisfaction or dissatisfaction) do not occur.

POSITIVE DISCONFIRMATION

In this case, the product's performance is noticeably **above** expectations (or other comparison norm), so the expectations are **disconfirmed** but in a positive way (i.e., the consumer gets **more** than expected). According to the disconfirmation model, when expectations are positively disconfirmed, consumers are satisfied and have positive emotions.

NEGATIVE DISCONFIRMATION

In this case, the product's performance is noticeably **below** expectations, so the expectations are **disconfirmed** but in a negative way (i.e., the consumer gets *less* than s/he expected). According to the disconfirmation model, when expectations are negatively disconfirmed they trigger a desire to understand what went wrong (i.e., attributional processes) before assigning blame.

ATTRIBUTIONS

Consumers seek to understand the reason why negative disconfirmation occurred. If the consumer attributes the cause to the product or manufacturer, then dissatisfaction with the brand occurs. If the consumer attributes the cause of the negative disconfirmation to himself or other uncontrollable factors, dissatisfaction will not be directed toward the brand or manufacturer (Folkes 1984; Oliver 1989). Thus, when negative disconfirmation occurs and consumers attribute the cause of the problem to the brand/manufacturer the result is dissatisfaction with the brand.

SUMMARY

A graphic summary of the disconfirmation model of consumer satisfaction is presented in Model 2.

THE PRODUCT PERFORMANCE MODEL OF SATISFACTION

PRODUCT PERFORMANCE

Some marketing researchers have questioned whether disconfirmation of expectations is the major source of consumer satisfaction. In an influential article, Churchill and Suprenant (1982), noted that in the disconfirmation model the product's performance is used only as a standard of comparison by which to assess the degree of disconfirmation. This represents a major problem because the product's **performance** should produce the majority of satisfaction by directly gratifying the consumer's needs and desires. Essentially, the disconfirmation (surprise) component of satisfaction can be expected play a smaller role in many situations.

PRODUCT PERFORMANCE AND PRIMARY AFFECT

During use, the salient attributes of the product should satisfy the consumer's needs and desires that originally started the purchase process. If the product satisfies the consumer's needs and desires, direct positive affect is produced and is associated with the brand. This is called **primary affect** and represents

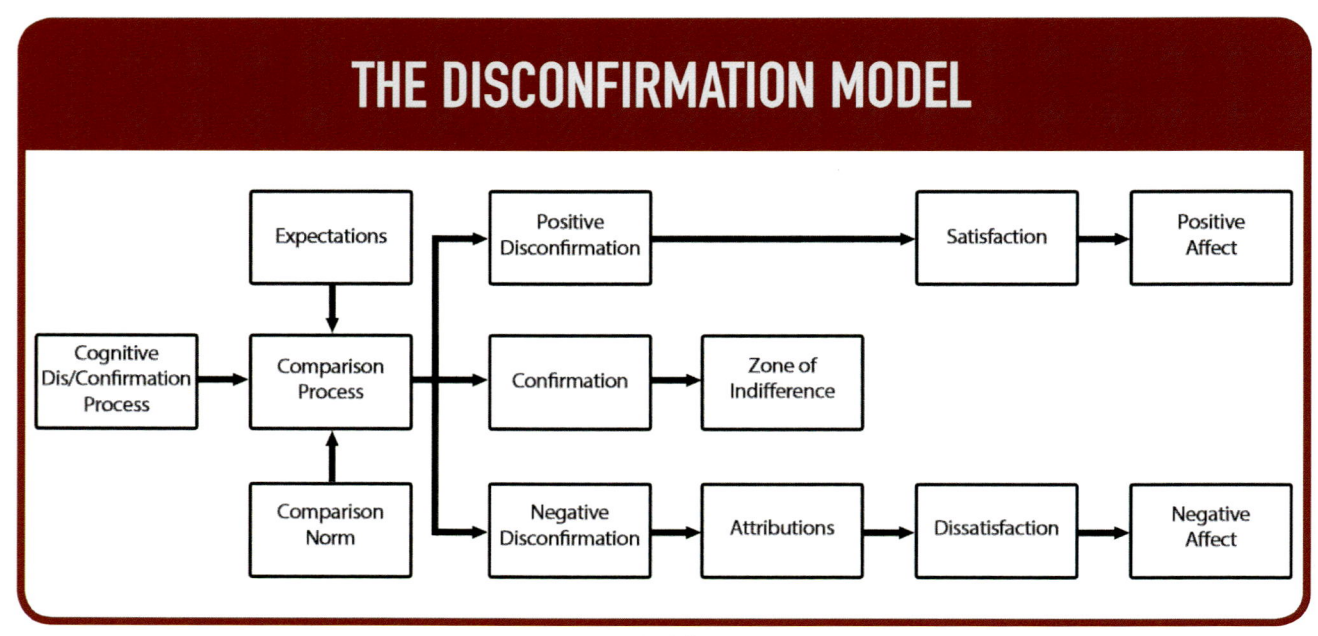

THE DISCONFIRMATION MODEL

Model 2

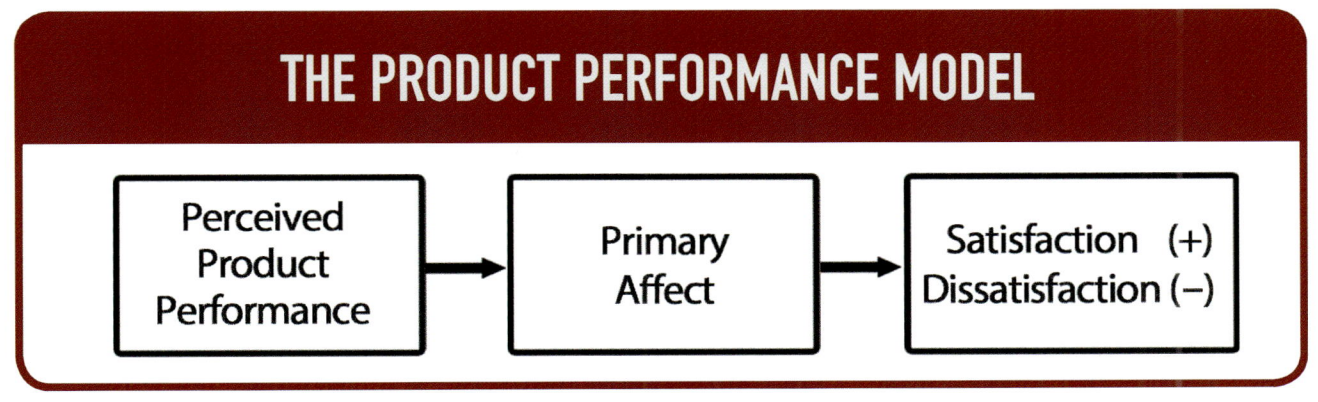

THE PRODUCT PERFORMANCE MODEL

Perceived Product Performance → Primary Affect → Satisfaction (+) Dissatisfaction (−)

Model 3

the consumer's immediate response to whether the product has satisfied the original needs and desires.

To illustrate the difference between these two sources of satisfaction, think about a consumer who uses a discount coupon to buy a pizza. Assume the consumer eats some of the pizza and is satisfied. Would you expect most of the satisfaction to come from the good taste and gratification of hunger (i.e., the product's performance) or the fact that it cost less than expected (i.e., positive disconfirmation of cost)? While both will probably participate in net satisfaction judgments, often the satisfaction from the product's performance will play a bigger role than disconfirmation of expectations.

Empirical research (Churchill and Suprenant 1982), tested different levels of expectations and different levels of performance across durable and non-durable products. They discovered that satisfaction for the durable product was determined solely by product performance and that satisfaction for the nondurable product was determined by both disconfirmation and product performance.

AFFECT AS SATISFACTION MODEL

A third major model of consumer satisfaction is the ***affect model.*** Here, consumers can be satisfied with a product's performance even if it only meets (instead of exceeds) expectations. Specifically, each consumer has some products that produce favorable emotional responses regardless of the level of expected-value. As an example, you probably have some favorite foods (e.g., ice cream) that you enjoy even though you expect it to taste good. Accordingly, whenever consumers have positive emotions after product use satisfaction is said to exist. Conversely, some experiences can produce negative emotions even if expectations are low. As an example, if you go to a job interview (with low expectations for your performance) and do poorly, you will probably still be dissatisfied with your performance. A graphic representation of the affect as satisfaction model is shown in Model 4.

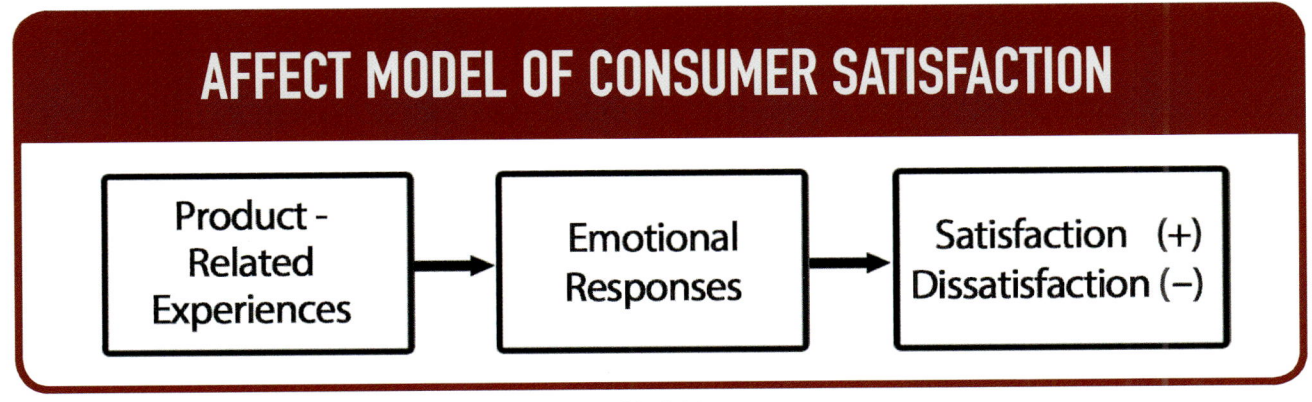

AFFECT MODEL OF CONSUMER SATISFACTION

Product-Related Experiences → Emotional Responses → Satisfaction (+) Dissatisfaction (−)

Model 4

COMMON SOURCES OF DISSATISFACTION

UNREALISTIC EXPECTATIONS

Expected value is determined by beliefs and values. As noted earlier, the perceptual bottleneck combines with cognitive consistency to create and maintain biased beliefs and values. We can now see the price of these tendencies toward cognitive consistency, since biased beliefs and values produce expectations that are unlikely to be realized. When the actual environment is encountered, the inaccurate expectations are rarely achieved, thus causing dissatisfaction for the individual.

For example, one reason why many people do not like to watch (or read) news reports is that they are filled with "bad news." To avoid unpleasant information we simply screen out the bad news through selective exposure. This screening has a direct impact on the internal model's view of the world. If we miss unpleasant but accurate news reports, it will be difficult for the internal model to generate accurate expectations.

Our examination of the internal model has identified numerous reasons why human beings generate unrealistic expectations. These would include the following.

1. We forget the low correlation between people's verbal and overt behavior.
2. We forget that people often engage in impression management.
3. We attribute high credibility to people who do not deserve it.
4. We often make inferences and assumptions that are unrealistic.
5. Normative training early in life (which stresses how the world should be) creates many unrealistic beliefs and values (e.g., Santa Claus).
6. We are often guided by our self-importance to believe others should place our interests above their own.

Notice that even though these problems can cause serious frustration, they also can be prevented by careful editing of the internal model.

Unrealistic Expectations

Grumbling Orientation

THE LAW OF DIMINISHING RETURNS

The law of diminishing returns states that as people obtain an increasing amount of a commodity, they will reach a point where additional units of that commodity generate less utility or value than the preceding unit. In other words, people tend to become bored with things they possess in large quantities. As a result, consumers can experience less value than they expected when dealing with products **over time**. This scenario is guaranteed to produce some dissatisfaction.

GRUMBLING THEORY

Maslow (1970) also developed what he called "grumbling theory" – the idea that satisfaction is only temporary and ultimately leads to "higher discontent." Grumbling theory has two major causes. First, when a consumer's need is gratified there will be a period of satisfaction (increase in positive affect) and/or tension reduction (decrease in negative affect). However, this feeling is normally ***fleeting and quickly replaced by the next striving cycle.*** The reason for this is multiple motivation: consumers have a variety of needs active at any time so gratifying one may produce satisfaction but the striving orientation of humans quickly redirects our attention to the next ungratified need. This suggests that the period of satisfaction for many needs (especially lower needs) may be much shorter than what has been indicated in the consumer satisfaction literature (where satisfaction is expected to have long lasting consequences in terms of brand attitude and repeat purchase behaviors).

The second reason for a grumbling orientation is that people **inherently need more and more to make them satisfied.** As basic needs (e.g., hunger) are satisfied over and over, the source of reinforcement grows tiring (e.g., eating the same breakfast every day).

> *"After a period of happiness, excitement, and fulfillment, comes the inevitable taking it all for granted, and becoming restless and discontented again for more!"* (**Maslow** 1970, p. xiv)

Thus, consumers can be expected to have a grumbling orientation much of the time. Satisfaction is often more ephemeral and shorter-lived than marketing models indicate – especially when consumers have many pressing needs and/or declining utility. Thus, grumbling theory can be used to explain a significant portion of consumer dissatisfaction.

PREVENTING DISSATISFACTION

PREVENTING PERSONAL DISSATISFACTION

Upon careful inspection it is clear that the only legitimate way to minimize our own personal dissatisfaction (based on the disconfirmation model) is to carefully edit the internal model so that our beliefs and values are ***realistic***. Obviously, completing this task would involve considerable cognitive dissonance and require maximum flexibility.

Over-Estimating Value. Instead, some people use the internal model in a way that maximizes the probability of dissatisfaction by being ***unrealistically optimistic.*** Because the internal model is free to infer any expectations it wants to, we often imagine the ***best case scenario*** to please ourselves in the short run. This is immediately gratifying to the internal model, and can produce positive body chemistry. However, these are reactions to a possible future that may not eventuate. If the best case scenario does not develop (and it often does not), we end up paying for our optimism through long-term dissatisfaction and negative body chemistry. Disconfirmed expectations also tend to make us moody, pessimistic, and cynical.

Under-Estimating Value. Alternatively, some people are ***unrealistically pessimistic*** and "low ball" their expectations by thinking of possible negative consequences. Note that this will keep expectations low so the chance of negative disconfirmation (and dissatisfaction) is significantly reduced. However, there are disadvantages to this approach too. As an example, when our expectations (i.e., E) are too low, our expected-value (i.e., EV) also will be low so our resulting ***motivation*** will be too low as well. For example, if we have an interview for a job that is hard to get, we may keep our expectations low (e.g., "I probably won't get this job") to prevent future negative disconfirmation. However, by doing so we have lowered our motivation to try hard to get the job (e.g., "why should I go to a lot of effort if I am unlikely to get the job").

In summary, if our expectations are unrealistically low we lack sufficient motivation to give our best effort. On the other hand, if our expectations are unrealistically high we encounter negative disconfirmation and dissatisfaction. Given these options the best choice is to keep expectations as realistic as possible – for both ourselves and our customers.

PREVENTING CONSUMER DISSATISFACTION

In most cases, marketing managers are especially sensitive to consumer dissatisfaction and seek to minimize it. To achieve this goal managers need to control the ***quality of the products*** that reach the market because few things create more negative disconfirmation than poor performance. In addition, the manager must carefully control the ***claims made in advertising*** and promotional efforts. While some "puffery" is allowable, creating unrealistically high consumer expectations is bound to lead to negative disconfirmation and consumer dissatisfaction. Finally, marketing managers must have an effective ***customer service policy*** so that when consumers are dissatisfied they are handled in a way that eliminates the negative feelings.

EXPRESSING CONSUMER DISSATISFACTION

When consumers are dissatisfied with a product or service they can undertake a variety of complaining behaviors. These include:

1. Do nothing (if minor)
2. Verbal complaint to company
3. Written complaint to company
4. Avoid future purchase and use
5. Engage in negative word-of-mouth
6. Sue the company
7. Organize a boycott
8. Contact government agencies (BBB, etc.)
9. Start a competing company

Obviously, such behaviors cause serious problems for the brand so most companies will go to great lengths to prevent consumer dissatisfaction from reaching the level that triggers them.

THE PARADOX OF PERSUASION

Using the disconfirmation model as a guide can reveal an interesting dilemma for marketers. Ultimately, the goal is to get people to buy the brand and then be satisfied with it. Of course, the best way to maximize satisfaction is for consumers to have low expectations for the brand and then experience positive disconfirmation. However, if consumers have low expected-value before purchase, they are unlikely to buy the brand at all. Because of this, some marketers try to maximize the consumer's expected-value by **overselling** the brand (i.e., exaggerating claims). While this will maximize short-term sales, these consumers are likely to experience negative disconfirmation (if the brand does not live up to the promises made) and become dissatisfied.

Therefore, it is very difficult to specify the level of expectations that should be set in promotions. Ultimately, the best approach (according to the disconfirmation model) is to raise consumer expectations high enough to create short term sales but also to retain sufficient value to surprise the consumer after purchase (thereby creating positive disconfirmation and satisfaction).

BRAND MANAGEMENT EXERCISE

As an example of the paradox of persuasion assume that you are the brand manager for a tire company. You have a new tire that the research and development department tells you will last 40,000 miles with average driving. The price of the tire is $75. Most other manufacturers also have a 40,000 mile tire that costs $75.

1. To stimulate demand, your advertising agency wants to advertise the tire as getting 50,000 miles – how would you respond?

2. The legal department wants you to advertise the tire as getting 30,000 miles to avoid future lawsuits – how would you respond?

3. Ultimately what is the best way to maximize near-term sales and also produce maximum positive disconfirmation after purchase?

CONSUMER SATISFACTION AND QUALITY OF LIFE

SATISFACTION FROM LOWER NEED GRATIFICATION

An important an interesting question is: "to what extent does satisfaction from products and services determine a person's overall satisfaction or **quality of life**?" Certainly, products and services satisfy a significant number of lower need states by reducing tension and/or adding pleasure. Few people would doubt that people living in prosperous countries have a higher quality of life than people living in economically deprived countries. However, economically advanced countries have been criticized for being overly materialistic and wasteful. While these criticisms may be true, the root of these problems are neurotic need states (which are hard to satisfy and thus can stimulate over-consumption and conspicuous consumption). In this case, the major source of the problem is not free enterprise or capitalism but the deprivation and affluence that produces neurotic needs. In any event, there is no question that much of a person's quality of life is determined by the products and services s/he buys to satisfy the lower needs.

SATISFACTION FROM HIGHER NEED GRATIFICATION

In Maslow's (1970) model, the highest satisfaction comes from satisfying growth needs via **peak experiences** (i.e., moments of ecstasy which usually include an element of attainment and surprise). Such experiences provide extreme satisfaction and alter the character of the individual in a positive way. In marketing, a peak experience has been defined as "a transformational experience and one that surpasses the usual level of intensity, meaningfulness, and richness" (Dodson 1996). For example, if a consumer has a peak experience while mountain biking it should cause the bike to be incorporated into the consumer's **extended self.** The bike may also become a symbol that acts to identify the person socially with the characteristics of the chosen activity.

Thus, gratifying growth needs produces **meta-satisfaction** which yields higher and more enduring levels of personal satisfaction. Products and services that help consumers become more aware of, aspire to, and

Peak Experience

ultimately satisfy their growth needs, can provide them with a more intense, longer lasting, and healthier kind of satisfaction. Examples of products and services that could accomplish this include: educational services, extreme sports (e.g., parachuting, mountain climbing, river rafting), restoring a classic car, eco-tourism, etc. Indeed, meta-satisfaction is so valued by consumers that Yalch and Brunel (1996, p. 410) conclude: "price evaluations might be higher when the product's advertising focuses on higher order needs." Ultimately, meta-satisfaction may be required for consumers to achieve maximum loyalty to a brand.

The satisfaction produced by gratifying higher needs is not just directed toward a specific product or consumption experience. In addition, meta-satisfaction can be integrated into consumers' judgments about their quality of life and therefore impact longitudinal well-being. Fournier and Mick (1999) note that satisfaction toward the product is sometimes accompanied by fulfillment of motivations central to life, notably: self-esteem, self-efficacy, and self-actualization. Therefore, **growth-based consumption experiences** can play a significant role in enhancing consumer growth and increasing overall quality of life.

IMPLICATIONS

There is an important link between consumer behavior and quality of life. Products and services are commonly used to gratify lower needs and thus create much human satisfaction. In addition, products and services that facilitate, encourage, or engender growth also will be significantly correlated to quality of life and play an important role in consumer self-identity. While marketing is often criticized for perpetuating material desires and over-consumption it can also be an essential part of consumer growth, well-being, and quality of life.

CONCLUSION

Marketing has been defined as the "delivery of a standard of living." In Maslow's (1970) model, marketing institutions will produce maximum satisfaction when they deliver products and services that stimulate consumer growth and creativity. In this regard, the Self-Help industry (understanding and satisfying deficiency and neurotic needs) should ultimately give way to the Self-Growth industry (products and services that stimulate personal growth and creativity). Maslow (1970) ultimately concludes that the purpose of human life is to strive for growth. Marketing and consumer behavior have a vital role to play in this objective.

EXPERIMENT 22.1
SATISFACTION AND THE ELEMENT OF SURPRISE

1. In the disconfirmation model, satisfaction occurs when consumers experience a positive surprise. The surprise element is crucial to understanding and using this model effectively. As long as there is a surprise, positive satisfaction should result.

2. To experiment with this model, think of two current key accounts of yours.

3. Next, think of a small gift (under $5) that these people would like and that would be a **surprise**.

4. Give the key accounts the gifts and observe their reaction.

5. Did you notice a **positive emotional state** after giving the gift. Note that to create satisfaction the gift does not have to cost a lot of money it only has to **surprise the recipient**.

ELABORATION QUESTIONS

- Give three examples of products you use whose performance falls into the **zone of indifference** and thus does not really register satisfaction or dissatisfaction.

- Give two examples where you have encountered positive disconfirmation and two examples were you have encountered negative disconfirmation after purchasing a product or service.

- Give two examples of products where disconfirmation plays a greater role in satisfaction than the product's performance.

- What percent of the time do your friends and family spend grumbling?

- Does grumbling theory mean that consumers will complain no matter what?

- When are you most likely to **overestimate** the value of a product or service?

- When are you most likely to **underestimate** the value of a product or service?

- What is the most dissatisfied you have ever been with a product or service and how did you express this feeling?

- What percentage of your satisfaction in life comes from products and services that you purchase?

- Give three examples of products or services that satisfy growth needs.

- Give one example when you have experienced meta-satisfaction.

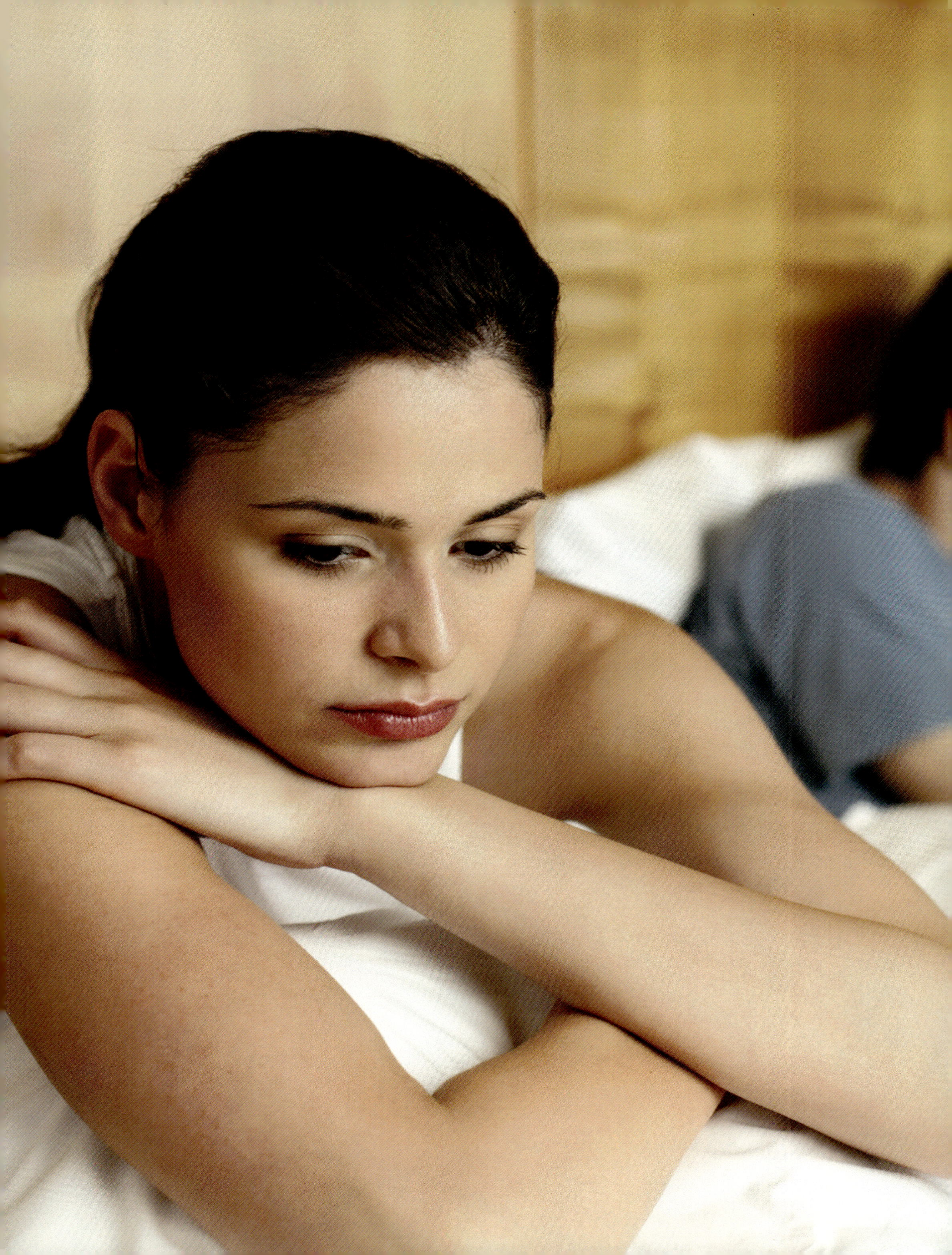

CHAPTER 23
CONSUMER LOYALTY AND DISLOYALTY

INTRODUCTION 23.1
CONSUMER LOYALTY 23.1
    Traditional Definition of Brand Loyalty 23.1
    Importance of Loyalty 23.1
    Obstacles to Loyalty 23.1
OLIVER'S LOYALTY MODEL 23.2
    Personal Allegiance 23.2
    Social Support 23.2
    Types of Loyalty 23.3
    The Relationship Between Satisfaction and Loyalty 23.4
    Dissatisfaction Strategies 23.4
    Summary of Oliver's Model 23.5
A NEED-BASED MODEL OF CONSUMER LOYALTY 23.5
    Need-Based Definition of Loyalty 23.5
    Loyalty Requires History 23.6
    Loyalty Requires Alternatives 23.6
    Sub-Optimal Choices 23.6
    Motivation for Consumer Loyalty 23.7
    Temporary Loyalty 23.8
    The Loyalty Quotient 23.8
    The Life Cycle of Loyalty 23.8
    Meta-Loyalty 23.8
CONSUMER DISLOYALTY 23.9
CONCLUSION 23.9
EXPERIMENT 23.1 | CUSTOMER LOYALTY STRATEGIES 23.9
ELABORATION QUESTIONS 23.10

GUIDING QUESTIONS

- What is the traditional definition of consumer loyalty?
- Why is consumer loyalty important?
- What are the obstacles to consumer loyalty?
- What is consumer defection?
- What is multiple loyalty?
- What are switching incentives?
- How is personal allegiance related to loyalty?
- How is social reinforcement related to loyalty?
- What are the different types of loyalty?
- What is weak loyalty?
- What is village loyalty?
- What is love loyalty?
- What is full loyalty?
- What is a relationship between loyalty and satisfaction?
- What are dissatisfaction strategies?
- What is the need-based model of consumer loyalty?
- Does loyalty require sacrifice?
- What is the difference between consumer patronage and consumer loyalty?
- What are sub-optimal choices?
- Why our consumers loyal?
- What is the loyalty quotient?
- How often are humans loyal over time?
- What is meta-loyalty?

INTRODUCTION

*Loyalty is a major issue in any model of relationship marketing. Indeed, it is ultimately the goal of marketing efforts to build as much consumer loyalty as possible. In addition, consumer loyalty is a significant part of **brand equity**. Accordingly, understanding consumer loyalty is a major goal of marketers. In addition, loyalty is an important issue with our personal key accounts and represents a good reflection of how much value both parties see in the exchange.*

CONSUMER LOYALTY

TRADITIONAL DEFINITION OF BRAND LOYALTY

Traditionally, customer loyalty has been described as having two major requirements. First, the consumer must have a ***favorable attitude*** toward the brand (i.e., s/he likes the brand). Second, the consumer must ***purchase the product frequently*** (not 100% of the time but a high percentage, say 80%). When these conditions hold, the consumer is said to be ***"brand loyal."***

IMPORTANCE OF LOYALTY

Attaining customer loyalty is one of the most common goals of any business due to its positive effects on profits. It is commonly agreed that the cost of ***customer retention*** is significantly less than the cost of acquiring new customers and in some cases this difference is very large. In addition, the net present value increase in profit that results from a 5% increase in customer retention varies from 25% to 95% in 14 major industries. Also, having loyal customers reflects favorably on the brand, company, and management.

OBSTACLES TO LOYALTY

Achieving customer loyalty can be very difficult for a number of reasons including the following.

Consumer Defection. Consumer defection rates are usually high and vary from 65% to 95% for consumers who claim they were ***satisfied*** with their last purchase. In the auto industry (where 90% of buyers are satisfied with their last purchase) defection rates are 60% to 70% (Oliver 1999).

Multiple Loyalty. Consumers can be loyal to more than one brand in a product category. For example, most consumers who eat at fast food restaurants get

Loyal Customer

bored eating at the same place and thus have three or four different restaurants that they patronize. This is called **multiple loyalty** and does not meet the traditional definition because 80% of their purchases will not come from one brand. In addition, true loyalty tends to be a rare trait among many consumers and thus may be difficult or impossible for a marketer to achieve.

Switching Incentives. Competitors are constantly trying to get consumers to **defect** by offering a wide array of switching incentives. Indeed, some argue it is **irrational** for customers to be loyal in this environment.

Variety Drive. Humans are known to like variety in many products and services in order to prevent boredom. The natural drive for variety makes loyalty difficult to achieve.

OLIVER'S LOYALTY MODEL

Oliver (1999) has gone beyond the traditional definition of brand loyalty (i.e., a positive attitude and frequent purchase) by defining loyalty as a deeply held commitment to repatronize a preferred product despite any situational influences and/or competitor promotions that have the potential to cause brand switching. In this model, customer loyalty is determined by two major factors, personal allegiance and social support.

PERSONAL ALLEGIANCE

Personal allegiance reflects the consumer's intrinsic commitment to the brand. At the extreme, consumers can **love** the brand (this is one of the few marketing models to actually define and use "love"). Allegiance determines how **attentive** a customer is to **alternative products** or vendors. When personal allegiance is high the consumer will not be attracted to alternative brands and will avoid or disregard persuasion attempts. Because consumers pay no attention to competing brands they are considered to be loyal.

SOCIAL SUPPORT

This factor represents how much **social reinforcement** (from key accounts) a consumer gets for buying a specific brand. If all your friends are buying a certain

Harley Owner's Club

Affective Loyalty

brand of jeans you will tend to buy them too (if you want to fit in with your peer group). In this case, the consumer may have no personal allegiance to the brand but buy it because of the social rewards that significant others will provide. For example, if you want to be friends with the people in the local Harley-Davidson motorcycle club, you better consider buying a Harley.

TYPES OF LOYALTY

By cross classifying personal allegiance and social support, Oliver (1999) develops four categories of consumer loyalty as shown in Table 1.

Weak Loyalty. When **personal allegiance is low** and **social support is low,** weak loyalty is said to exist. Oliver (1999) identifies four types of loyalty within this quadrant.

1. **Cognitive Loyalty.** Here the consumer is **loyal to the best product.** The best product is determined by the calculation of expected-value. This is the weakest form of loyalty because consumers are attentive to information from competing brands and can quickly change their preference depending on market developments. The consumer's loyalty is susceptible to counter argumentation or any information suggesting a new or improved brand is now superior.

2. **Affective Loyalty.** Consumers are loyal to brands that have consistently produced **satisfaction or pleasure.** This is a stronger type of loyalty because these feelings are not susceptible to counter argumentation.

3. **Conative Loyalty.** Consumers are more loyal and definitely **intend to repurchase** their preferred brand. However, situational influences (e.g., big price discount on alternative brand, preferred brand out-of-stock, etc.) may cause some defections.

TYPES OF LOYALTY

		Social Support Low	Social Support High
Personal Allegiance	Low	Weak Loyalty	Village Loyalty
	High	Love Loyalty	Full Loyalty

Table 1

4. **Action Loyalty.** Consumers buy the brand in an *automated fashion.* This is a strong type of loyalty because consumers intend to buy the brand and are relatively insensitive to situational influences and relatively inattentive to alternative brand information.

Village Loyalty. When **personal allegiances is low** but **social support is high,** village loyalty is said to exist. In this case, consumers are loyal in order to achieve social reinforcement and camaraderie with their peer groups. Social affiliation and esteem are important motivators and group membership often requires the acceptance and use of certain products and services (e.g., Harley Owner Groups, Tattoo's, retirement villages, fraternities, sororities).

Love Loyalty. When **personal allegiance is high** and **social support is low,** love loyalty is said to exist. In Oliver's (1999) model, the extreme end of the personal allegiance continuum represents love. To reach this state, three requirements are needed.

1. **Sensual Reinforcement:** Here, *positive emotions* are created through product use (e.g., music, travel, pets, food, etc).
2. **Adoration:** The consumer *will not consider alternatives* to the "loved" object. Conversely, "there is no better predictor of relationship failure than high attentiveness to alternatives." (Oliver 1999, p. 38)
3. **Unfailing commitment:** The consumer has made a *psychological pledge* to continue the relationship with the brand. This is similar to a mental "wedding vow."

Full Loyalty. When **personal allegiances is high** and **social support is high**, full loyalty is said to exist. In this case, consumers are loyal to achieve personal **and** social goals. The product is "a part of me" and "an extension of me." Examples include, Trekkies, fan clubs, Cheeseheads (a.k.a. Packer fans), skiers, religious sects, cults, and RVer's.

THE RELATIONSHIP BETWEEN SATISFACTION AND LOYALTY

Traditionally, product satisfaction was seen as leading to a strong favorable attitude toward the brand which, in turn, caused the consumer to repeat buy. Satisfied consumers were loyal consumers. However, the high defection rates for satisfied consumers suggests that this historical model is not always accurate.

In the new model, satisfaction is seen as a necessary but insufficient condition for loyalty to occur. As Oliver (1999, p. 42) notes: "satisfaction does not transform into loyalty as much as it is a seed that requires nurturance." When satisfaction is coupled with personal allegiance and social support, it grows into loyalty which can resist all alternative brands.

DISSATISFACTION STRATEGIES

While satisfaction does not guarantee loyalty, dissatisfaction will usually cause disloyalty in the form of **brand switching.** Therefore, if a company can help create dissatisfaction with a competitor's product there is a high probability that those consumers will switch brands. This suggests that some part of the marketing budget should be spent on developing strategies to *alienate the affections* of the customers of our rivals. Can you think of any marketing strategies that try to accomplish this effect?

Sensual Reinforcement

SUMMARY OF OLIVER'S MODEL

True loyalty is difficult to achieve and hard to maintain. There must be consistent satisfaction from product use and the development of personal allegiance and social reinforcement to achieve "full loyalty." Note that according to this model, full loyalty is beyond the reach of marketers in many product categories that do not lend themselves to automation, adoration, or social endorsement.

A NEED-BASED MODEL OF CONSUMER LOYALTY

While previous definitions of loyalty suggest that it is based on satisfaction, Oliver's model suggests that loyalty also has a **need basis.** Specifically, Oliver (1999) shows that maximum loyalty will exist when the consumer's **love needs** and **social needs** are satisfied through product purchase and use. Thus, the relationship between consumer need satisfaction and loyalty is an important area for future research and consideration.

NEED-BASED DEFINITION OF LOYALTY

Loyalty occurs when a person **voluntarily** makes a **sub-optimal choice.** In this context, "sub-optimal" means that there is some type of **sacrifice** on the part of the consumer. The epitome of loyalty is a soldier who will march into battle knowing there is a high probability of death. In this example, the sacrifice is obvious and total. In marketing, loyalty exists when a consumer makes a sacrifice by purchasing a brand that is **known to be inferior** to competing brands in some respect. For example, if you are shopping for cola and notice that Coke is on sale, but you purchase Pepsi as usual, you are making a small sacrifice (i.e., paying more) and thus, showing some loyalty.

This is related to need-satisfaction because "sub-optimal" means that the consumer's needs are **undersatisfied** in some important way. This suggests that loyalty over time (i.e., **longitudinal loyalty**) is relatively hard to achieve because as deprivation grows, consumers will reach their **switching point**

Loyalty to Older Cell Phone

where they change brands rather than suffer more deprivation. Indeed, true loyalty comes with high, and often rising, opportunity costs. Thus, loyalty involves continued patronage even though need deprivation occurs (and the greater the sacrifice, the greater the loyalty). This is a more dynamic model because the nature of loyalty will be determined by variables like: type of needs under satisfied, degree of deprivation, duration of deprivation, etc. Note that if the decision is not sub-optimal, loyalty is not needed because preference will rest on product performance, or other expected-value from the brand.

In Oliver's (1999) model, maximum loyalty occurs when the consumer is inattentive to alternative products. However, an even stronger form is when the customer is knowledgeable about alternatives, knows that his favored brand is sub-optimal, yet purchases it anyway. Based on this definition a consumer's degree of loyalty to a brand is reflected by the **number of sub-optimal choices** made, and/or the **extremity of the sacrifice** involved. In the extreme form, if the favored brand was not available the consumer would forego need satisfaction altogether and this would be the greatest level of sub-optimal choice (i.e., no substitution).

Thus the need-based model, makes a distinction between **consumer loyalty and consumer patronage.** Patronage occurs whenever a consumer repeatedly buys a brand. The motivation for this may be because it is the best brand available, or because it has become an automated purchase. In any event, the consumer is not making a sub-optimal choice, or at least, is not aware that s/he is making a sub-optimal choice (e.g., automated purchase). Consumer loyalty begins to occur as soon as sacrifices start to be required. In the need-based model, **weak loyalty** refers to **small sacrifices** being made and **strong loyalty** refers to **big sacrifices** being made. The relationship between consumer patronage and consumer loyalty is shown in Model 1.

An excellent example of consumer loyalty, are the customers who bought Harley-Davidson motorcycles during the AMF ownership years. The build quality of the motorcycles was notoriously low (they leaked oil on showroom floors!) but loyal consumers waited in queues to purchase the bikes at a high price which was clearly a sub-optimal choice in terms of performance. Indeed, these consumers dutifully improved the bikes at their own expense with aftermarket equipment and up-grades.

LOYALTY REQUIRES HISTORY

In a need base model, an exchange relationship has value to either party in direct relation to the need satisfaction that occurs. In continuing relationships, a series of exchanges takes place and, overall, the parties must be better off after the exchange (profit) or else motivation to continue the exchange will decline. At times in the relationship, one party may have to make a choice that is personally sub-optimal (e.g., be tolerant of others' mistakes, place other's needs ahead of your own, place yourself at risk, pick up the tab, etc.). In marketing, sub-optimal choices include: waiting a long time to take possession, paying premium prices, accepting lower performance than competing brands, etc. As the exchange unfolds over time, opportunities for loyalty will occur and a pattern of **sub-optimal choices develops.** In any event, loyalty requires some type of meaningful history between the two parties - you can be nice to a stranger but you cannot be loyal to a stranger.

LOYALTY REQUIRES ALTERNATIVES

It is important to note that loyalty requires that more attractive alternatives are available to the consumer. If there are **no better** alternatives it is not consumer loyalty that exists but consumer patronage. Also, if there is no alternative, loyalty cannot exist. For example, would a consumer who keeps using old (sub-optimal) software because he cannot afford a new computer be considered loyal to the software? The answer according to the need-based loyalty model is "no" because there really is no viable alternative. If the consumer suddenly got enough money to buy a new computer with any software then there would be a true test of loyalty.

SUB-OPTIMAL CHOICES

We know almost nothing about sub-optimal choices in marketing so this is an area that will have to be aggressively researched if consumer loyalty is to be better understood. Indeed, loyalty can be defined as a

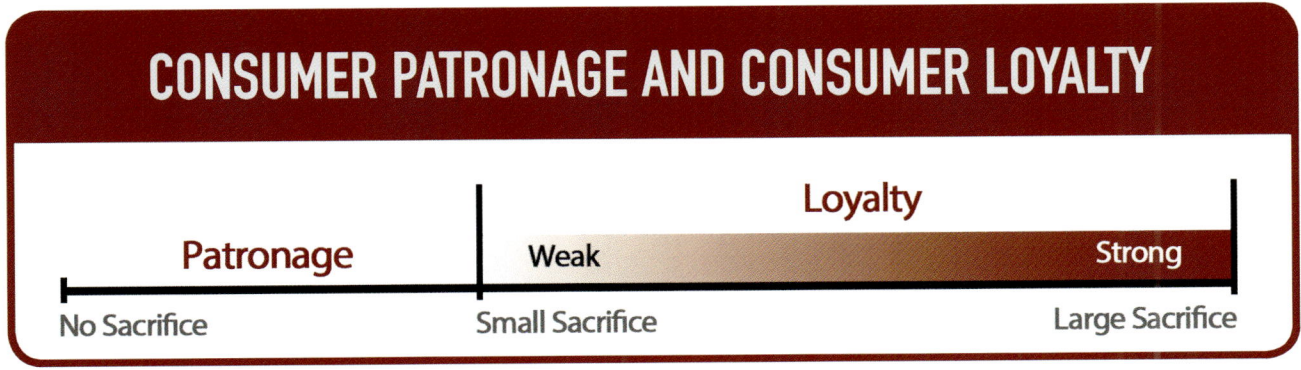

CONSUMER PATRONAGE AND CONSUMER LOYALTY

Patronage	Loyalty	
	Weak	Strong
No Sacrifice	Small Sacrifice	Large Sacrifice

Model 1

pattern of sub-optimal choices over time. The nature, characteristics, antecedents, and consequences of sub-optimal choice are important future research areas. For example, major questions in need of answers include:

1. What are the major forms of sub-optimal choice?

2. How many sub-optimal choices are required before loyalty exists?

3. How can managers develop strategies that are coordinated to the type of sub-optimal behavior needed?

4. Loyalty is a voluntary sub-optimal choice, what happens when consumers are **forced** to accept sub-optimal choices either by fear or unavailability?

5. What happens when consumers become aware that they are being "forced" into sub-optimal choices? With the internet and other modern communications, the "have-nots" can easily see what they are missing. This can lead to **consumer humiliation, consumer envy,** and **consumer jealously** all of which have major public policy implications for marketing, quality of life in the world, and peace on earth.

MOTIVATION FOR CONSUMER LOYALTY

Perhaps the most intriguing question in consumer loyalty research is **why** are consumers loyal? Marketing managers who understand the answer to this question would be able to develop effective strategies to maximize consumer loyalty behaviors. In Oliver's (1999) model, consumers are loyal because: 1) they have received repeated pleasure from the product, 2) they buy the product automatically without considering alternatives, 3) the product satisfies social needs, 4) the product satisfies love needs. However, in the need-based model, the underlying causes of loyalty are different, and include the following.

Justice. Loyalty is often motivated by **meta-needs** particularly **justice.** As an example, if friends take care of you when you are sick (and thereby performed sub-optimal behaviors (given the high opportunity costs of nursing a friend)), you would be loyal if you returned the sub-optimal behaviors and took care of them when they were sick (or performed some other sub-optimal behavior). The underlying motive here is justice or "I should treat others as they treat me." Similarly, when a brand satisfies a consumer repeatedly the consumer should be willing to accept some sub-optimal elements, at least for a short period of time. However, the types of sub-optimal requirements can vary greatly (e.g., moderate wait times versus low performance) as can the marketplace (e.g., number of competing brands).

In this light, developing **brand equity** can be seen as building **latent loyalty.** The higher the equity the more likely the consumer will be to make sub-optimal choices for the brand.

Thus, a major source of consumer loyalty comes through attempts to achieve the meta-motive of justice. Guilt-based loyalty also seems to be based on perceived justice. Similarly, people will be loyal to products, services, and people who embody universals like truth, freedom, beauty, and other meta-needs.

Personal or Social Identity. Loyalty also can be motivated by **personal or social identity.** An example is fans of Star Trek who, after many years, still can get satisfaction from watching the

Star Trek Fans

original episodes even though they know every word and plot twist by heart. In this case, the loyalty comes from the fact that Star Trek represents the consumer's identity in important ways (e.g., being future oriented, having an integrated crew, helping those in trouble). These "species values" are "archetypes" shared by all humankind and represent latent growth needs that can be triggered by products and services. The previous example of Harley-Davidson motorcycle buyer's loyalty rested largely on personal and social identity because the bikes are an extension of the bikers. This loyalty may be the strongest in many consumer situations including being loyal to products you used as a child or products that your parents used.

Satisfaction-Based Loyalty. This is similar to affective loyalty in Oliver's model. Over time some brands become favorites because they repeatedly bring us pleasure. This history of satisfaction with the brand is stored in memory as a positive attitude and can trigger purchase even if the brand is no longer optimal. In this case the consumer is loyal (i.e., making a sacrifice) as long as the favorable attitude is strong enough to offset the sacrifice required. It would be interesting to know what ultimately causes satisfied consumers to switch brands and what types of satisfaction resist switching the longest.

TEMPORARY LOYALTY

In this case the consumer believes that the sub-optimal characteristic is only temporary and will return to full value in the future. In this case, consumers are willing to put up with a sub-optimal choice for a limited period of time perhaps due to inertia (i.e., to avoid switching costs). With rapid technological development this can be an important form of loyalty for manufactures of computers, software, electronics, etc. Basically the strategy here is to stay loyal until your favored brand can put out a new and improved model making it no longer sub-optimal.

THE LOYALTY QUOTIENT

Overtime in any exchange relationship we can calculate the loyalty quotient of the parties involved. The loyalty quotient and would be defined as:

$$\text{LOYALTY QUOTIENT} = \frac{\text{NUMBER OF SUB-OPTIMAL CHOICES MADE}}{\text{NUMBER OF SUB-OPTIMAL CHOICES POSSIBLE}}$$

Thus, a person who makes a sub-optimal choice at every opportunity has a loyalty quotient equal to 100%.

THE LIFE CYCLE OF LOYALTY

If loyalty is tied to consumer need states it must be a more dynamic construct that previous models suggest. According to **grumbling theory,** loyalty leads to commitment and repeated use, which leads to familiarity, which leads to boredom, which leads to switching tendencies, which leads to **consumer promiscuity.** In this light, loyalty can be seen as a dynamic variable which may have a predictable life-cycle where high loyalty exists for only a short period of time (i.e., after satisfaction but before boredom). Thus, consumer loyalty over a long time (longitudinal loyalty) must be considered to be a relatively rare and special case according to grumbling theory. In the need-based model, loyalty is seen as a dynamic concept rather than a trait that you do or do not possess. This also makes loyalty more interesting and helps explain why loyalty is hard to find and why it may not correlate to satisfaction.

META-LOYALTY

According to Maslow, satisfaction is maximized when the higher needs are gratified. Thus, "meta-loyalty" would occur when a person or product helps an individual achieve any of the meta-motives. Notice that this loyalty is based on growth through creativity (which is the purpose of life according to Malsow). Also, notice that intimacy, love, and tolerance are preconditions to the meta-motives as they allow the BIS to emerge and provide a safe haven from which to explore the growth process. Thus, the strongest and most enduring type of loyalty is meta-loyalty. In this case, the loyalty bond is based on intimacy, love and tolerance which provide a platform to reach the meta-motives. As growth occurs, and the meta-motives are gratified the relationship reaches the highest levels, provides the maximum rewards, and, in turn, creates the most powerful loyalty bonds.

CONSUMER DISLOYALTY

Disloyalty occurs when a person will not voluntarily make a sub-optimal choice for a product or person. Examples would be an old friend who refuses to lend you $10 for lunch, or a friend who would not help you move because he had better things to do. In marketing, disloyalty is equivalent to switching behavior and **consumer promiscuity.** While loyalty typically has a positive connotation and disloyalty a negative connotation there are powerful reason why disloyalty is common (especially in the market place).

In addition to the three barriers to loyalty in Oliver's model (consumer defection, multiple loyalties, and switching incentives), the need-based model highlights at least six other barriers to loyalty.

1. The striving nature of many consumers motivates them to shop and compare to find the best deals and this will not lead to loyalty.

2. Freedom of choice requires alternatives but loyalty removes alternatives.

3. Curiosity and need to know reflect drives that are the opposite of being inattentive to alternatives.

4. As consumers grow, self-expression requires new and different product mixes which again works against brand loyalty.

5. Grumbling theory suggests that loyalty will be relatively rare because consumers reach a point of declining utility, which leads to boredom, and then, escalating needs for alternatives.

6. Satisfying growth needs often requires creativity, divergence, and change – all of these work against loyalty over time (i.e., growth-based disloyalty).

CONCLUSION

In the need-based model, loyalty occurs when sacrifices are made. Consumers are willing to make these sacrifices for reasons of justice, self-identity, and accumulated satisfaction. Because sacrifice means that some needs go unsatisfied, loyalty is difficult to achieve and reflects a strong commitment to the relationship. Based on this model, understanding consumer loyalty involves understanding the types of sacrifices expected from the consumers. For example, strong consumer loyalty over a long time requires significant sacrifice and therefore, is probably rare (and difficult for many marketers to achieve in the competitive marketplace).

EXPERIMENT 23.1
CUSTOMER LOYALTY STRATEGIES

1. Interview and observe your key accounts to see which people and products they are most loyal to and which they are least loyal to.

2. List the major characteristics that produce high and low loyalty.

3. Generate a general customer loyalty policy (i.e., a list of steps you would recommend to keep customers loyal).

4. How important is meta-satisfaction to loyalty?

ELABORATION QUESTIONS

- What are your loyalty quotients for each of your roommates?
- In what ways is loyalty to people different from loyalty to products?
- Is loyalty actually good for consumers?
- Give two examples of advertising campaigns that try to increase consumer allegiance and two examples that try to increase social support for consumers of their brand.
- What products have you been loyal to the longest? Why?
- Is there a relationship between age and loyalty?
- Would you rather have personal allegiance or personal identity from your consumers?
- As a consumer, when are you most promiscuous?
- Give a product category where you have multiple loyalty.
- What do you think of Oliver's definition of love?
- When are you most likely to make a sub-optimal choice
- Give an example of meta-loyalty.
- Using a product example, give an example of consumer patronage and an example of consumer loyalty.

REFERENCES

A

Aaker, Jennifer L. (1999), "The Malleable Self: The Role of Self-Expression in Persuasion," *Journal of Marketing Research*, 36 (1), 45-57.

Aaker, David A., Richard P. Bagozzi, James M. Carman, and James M. MacLachlan (1980), "On Using Response Latency to Measure Preferences," *Journal of Marketing Research*, 17 (May), 237 244.

Aaker, David A., and John G. Myers (1975), *Advertising Management*, Englewood Cliffs, NJ: Prentice Hall.

Abelson, Robert P. (1976), "Script Processing in Attitude Formation and Decision Making," in J. S. Carroll and J. W. Payne, eds., *Cognition and Social Behavior*, Potomac, MD: Lawrence Erlbaum.

_____ (1981), "Psychological Status of the Script Concept," *American Psychologist*, 36, No. 7 (July), 715 729.

Abrams, Jack (1966), "An Evaluation of Alternative Rating Devices for Consumer Research," *Journal of Marketing Research*, 3 (May), 189 193.

Ahtola, Olli T. (1975), "The Vector Model of Preferences: An Alternative to the Fishbein Model," *Journal of Marketing Research*, 11 (February), 52 59.

Ainscough, Thomas L. and Michael G. Luckett (1996), "The Internet for the Rest of Us: Marketing on the World Wide Web," *Journal of Consumer Marketing*, 13 (September), 36-47.

Alba, Joseph W. and Wesley J. Hutchinson (2000), "Knowledge Calibration: What Consumers Know and What They Think They Know," *Journal of Consumer Research*, 27 (2), 123-156.

Alba, Joseph W., John Lynch, Barton Weitz, Chris Janiszewski, Richard Lutz, Alan G. Sawyer, and Stacy Wood (1997), (Interactive Home Shopping: Consumer, Retailer, and Manufacturer Incentives to Participate in Electronic Marketplaces," *Journal of Marketing*, 61 (July), 38-53.

Alimo-Metcalfe, B. (2001), "Maslow -- A Different View," *Psychologist*, 14 (4), 179-180.

Allport, G. W. (1954), "The Historical Background of Modern Social Psychology," in *Handbook of Social Psychology*, vol. 1, G. Lindzey, ed., Cambridge, MA: Addison Wesley.

Anderson, Barry F. (1975), *Cognitive Psychology: The Study of Knowing, Learning, and Thinking*, New York: Academic Press.

Anderson, James C. and James A. Narus (1990), "A Model of Distributor Firm and Manufacturer Firm Working Partnerships," *Journal of Marketing*, 54 (1), 42-58.

Andrews, Jonlee and Daniel C. Smith (1996), "In Search of the Marketing Imagination: Factors Affecting the Creativity of Marketing Programs for Mature Products," *Journal of Marketing Research*, 33 (2), 174-187.

Ariely, Dan (2000), "Controlling Information Flow: On the Importance of Control in Decision-Making and the Value of Information," *Journal of Consumer Research*.

Assael, Henry and George S. Day (1974), "Attitudes and Awareness as Predictors of Market Share," *Journal of Advertising Research*, 8 (4), 3 10.

Atkinson, J. W. (1964), *An Introduction to Motivation*, New York: Van Nostrand.

Atkinson, R. C. and R. M. Shiffrin (1968), "Human Memory: A Proposed System and its Control Processes," in *The Psychology of Learning and Motivation: Advances in Research and Theory*, vol. 2, K. W. Spence and J. T. Spence, eds., New York: Academic Press, 89 195.

Babin, Barry J., James S. Boles, and Donald P. Robin (2000), "Representing the Perceived Ethical Work Climate Among Marketing Employees," *Journal of the Academy of Marketing Science*, 28 (3), 345-358.

B

Bagozzi, Richard P., Alice M. Tybout, C. Samuel Craig, and Brian Sternthal (1979), "The Construct Validity of the Tipartite Classification of Attitudes," *Journal of Marketing Research*, 16 (February), 88 95.

Bagozzi, Richard P., and Robert E. Burnkrant (1979), "Attitude Organization and the Attitude- Behavior Relationship," *Journal of Personality and Social Psychology*, 37, (6), 913 929.

Bagozzi, Richard P., Mahesh Gopinath, and Prashant U. Nyer (1999), "The Role of Emotions in Marketing," *Journal of the Academy of Marketing Science*, 27 (2), 184-206.

Bagozzi, Richard P., Richard P. and Utpal Dholakia (1999), "Goal Setting and Goal Striving in Consumer Behavior," *Journal of Marketing*, 63 (4),19-32.

Barker, Roger G. (1975), "Commentaries on Belk, `Situational Variables and Consumer Behavior'," *Journal of Consumer Research*, 2 (December).

(1974), "The Theory of Stochastic Preference and Brand Switching," *Journal of Marketing Research*, 11, (February), 1 20.

Bass, Frank M. and William L. Wilkie (1973), "A Comparative Analysis of Attitudinal Predictions of Brand Preference," *Journal of Marketing Research*, 10 (August), 262 269.

Bauer, Raymond (1958), "The Limits of Persuasion," *Harvard Business Review*, (September October), 105 110.

_____ (1964), "The Obstinate Audience," *American Psychologist*, 19, 319 328.

Bauer, Raymond and A. H. Bauer (1960), "America, Mass Society and Mass Media," *The Journal of Social Issues*, 16, 3 66.

Baumeister, Roy F. and David G. Mick (2002), "Yielding to Temptation: Self-Control Failure, Impulsive Purchasing, and Consumer Behavior," *Journal of Consumer Research*, 28 (4), 670-676.

Bazerman, Max H. (2001), "Consumer Research for Consumers," *Journal of Consumer Research*, 27 (4), 499-504.

Beach, Lee R. and James A. Wise (1969), "Subjective Probability Estimates and Confidence Ratings," *Journal of Experimental Psychology*, 79 (3), 438 444.

Bechtel, Gordon G. and P. J. O'Connor (1979), "Testing Micro preference Structures," *Journal of Marketing Research*, 16 (May), 247 257.

Beckwith, Neil E. and Donald R. Lehmann (1975), "The Importance of Halo Effects in Multi Attribute Attitude Models," *Journal of Marketing Research*, 12 (August), 265 275.

Belch, George E. (1981), "An Examination of Comparative and Noncomparative Television Commercials: The Effects of Claim Variation and Repetition on Cognitive Response and Message Acceptance," *Journal of Marketing Research*, 18 (August), 333 349.

_____ (1982), "The Effects of Television Commercial Repetition on Cognitive Response and Message Acceptance," *Journal of Consumer Research*, 9, 56 65.

Belk, Russell W. (1975), "Situational Variables and Consumer Research," *Journal of Consumer Research*, 2 (December), 157 164.

_____, (1988), "Possessions and the Extended Self," *Journal of Consumer Research*, 15 (2), 139-168.

Belk, Russell W., George E. and Michael Belk (1990), *Introduction to Advertising and Promotion Management*, Homewood IL: Richard D. Irwin, Inc.

Bem, D. J. (1972), "Self Perception Theory," in *Advances in Experimental Social Psychology*, vol. 6, L. Berkowitz, ed., New York: Academic Press, 1 62.

Bem, D. J. and Andrea Allen (1974), "On Predicting Some of the People Some of the Time: The Search for Cross Situational Consistencies in Behavior," *Psychological Review*, 81, (6), 506 520.

Bennett, Peter D. and Gilbert D. Harrell (1975), "The Role of Confidence in Understanding and Predicting Buyers' Attitudes and Purchase Intentions," *Journal of Consumer Research*, 2 (September), 110 117.

Berkman, Harold W. and Christopher C. Gilson (1978), *Consumer Behavior*, Encino CA: Dickenson.

Berthon, Pierre, Leyland F. Pitt, Richard T. Watson (1996), "Marketing Communication and the World Wide Web," *Business Horizons*, 39 (September-October), 24-32.

Berger, Ida E., and Andrew A. Mitchell (1989), "The Effects of Advertising on Attitude Accessibility, Attitude Confidence, and the Attitude-Behavior Relationship," *Journal of Consumer Research*, 16 (December), 269-279.

Berscheid, Ellen, William Graziano, Thomas Monson, and Marshall Dermer (1976), "Outcome Dependency: Attention, Attribution, and Attraction," *Journal of Personality and Social Psychology*, 34, (3), 978 989.

Bettman, James R. (1974), "A Threshold Model of Attribute Satisfaction Decisions," *Journal of Consumer Research*, 1 (September), 30 35.

_____ (1979), *An Information Processing Theory of Consumer Choice*, Reading, MA: Addison Wesley.

_____ (1981), "A Functional Analysis of the Role of Overall Evaluation of Alternatives in the Choice Process," in *Advances in Consumer Research*, vol. 9, Andrew A. Mitchell, ed., Ann Arbor, MI: Association for Consumer Research, 87 93.

Bettman, James R., Noel Capon, and Richard J. Lutz (1975a), "Multi attribute Measurement Models and Multiattribute Attitude Theory: A Test of Construct Validity," *Journal of Consumer Research*, 1 (March), 1 14.

Bettman, James R., Noel Capon, and Richard J. Lutz (1975b), "Cognitive Algebra in Multi Attribute Attitude Models," *Journal of Marketing Research*, 12 (May), 151 164.

Bettman, James R., and Michel Z. Zins (1979), "Information Format and Choice Task Effects in Decision Making," *Journal of Consumer Research*, 6 (September), 141 153.

Bloch, Peter H. and Grady D. Bruce (1984), "Product Involvement as Leisure Behavior," *Advances in Consumer Research*, 11 (1), 197-202.

Blodgett, Jeffrey G., Donald H. Granbois, and Rockney G. Walters (1993), "The Effects of Perceived Justice on Complainants' Negative Word-of-Mouth Behavior and Repatronage Intentions," *Journal of Retailing*, 69 (4), 399-428.

Blodgett, Jeffrey G. and Donna J. Hill (1997), "The Effects of Distributive, Procedural, and Interactional Justice on Postcomplaint Behavior," *Journal of Retailing*, 73 (2), 185-210.

Bohrnstedt, George W. (1970), "Reliability and Validity Assessment in Attitude Measurement," in *Attitude Measurement*, Gene F. Summers, ed., Chicago: Rand McNally, 80 99.

Bonfield, E. H. (1974), "Attitude, Social Influence, Personal Norm, and Intention Interactions as Related to Brand Purchase Behavior," *Journal of Marketing Research*, 11 (November), 379 389.

Bostrom, R., J. Vlandis, and M. Rosenbaum (1961), "Grades as Reinforcing Contingencies and Attitude Change," *Journal of Educational Psychology*, 52, 112 115.

Bowers, William J. (1968), "Normative Constraints on Deviant Behavior in the College Context," *Sociometry*, 31 (December), 370 85.

Bridge, Gary R., Leo G. Reeder, David Kanouse, Donald R. Kinder, Vivian Tong Nagy, and Charles M. Judd (1977), "Interviewing Changes Attitudes - Sometimes," *Public Opinion Quarterly*, 41, 56 64.

Brim, Orville G., Jr. (1955), "Attitude Content Intensity and Probability Expectations," *American Sociological Review*, 20 (February), 66 76.

Brooker, George (1976), "The Self-Actualizing Socially Conscious Consumer," *Journal of Consumer Research*, 3 (2), 107-114.

Bruno, Albert V. and Albert R. Wildt (1975), "Toward Understanding Attitude Structure: A Study of the Complementarity of Multi Attribute Attitude Models," *Journal of Consumer Research*, 2 (September), 137 145.

Buchholz, Laura M. and Robert E. Smith (1991), "The Role of Consumer Involvement in Determining Cognitive Response to Broadcast Advertising," *Journal of Advertising*, 20, (1), 4-17.

Burke, Raymond R. (1996), "Virtual Shopping: Breakthrough in Marketing Research," *Harvard Business Review*, 74 (March-April), 120-31.

_____ (1997), "Do You See What I See? The Future of Virtual Shopping," *Journal of the Academy of Marketing Science*, 25 (4).

Burnkrant, Robert E. (1974), "Attribution Theory in Marketing Research: Problems and Prospects," *Advances in Consumer Research*, vol. 2, M. J. Schlinger, ed., 465 469.

C

Campbell, Donald T. (1963), "Social Attitudes and Other Acquired Behavioral Dispositions," in S. Koch, ed., *Psychology: A Study of a Science*, Vol. 6, New York: McGraw Hill.

_____ (1975), "On the Conflicts Between Biological and Social Evolution and Between Psychology and Moral Tradition," *American Psychologist*, 36 (December), 1103 1126.

Campbell, Donald T and Donald W. Fiske (1970), "Convergent and Discriminant Validation by the Multitrait Multimethod Matrix," in *Attitude Measurement*, Gene F. Summers, ed., Chicago: Rand McNally, 100 124.

Cantril, Hadley (1946), "The Intensity of an Attitude," *Journal of Abnormal Social Psychology*, 41, 129 135.

Castaneda, Carlos (1968), *The Teachings of Don Juan: A Yaqui Way of Knowledge*, New York: Touchstone.

_____ (1971), *A Separate Reality*, New York: Touchstone.

_____ (1972), *Journey to Ixtlan*, New York: Touchstone.

_____ (1974), *Tales of Power*, New York: Touchstone.

_____ (1977), *The Second Ring of Power*, New York: Touchstone.

Cattell, R. B. (1957), *Personality and Motivation Structure and Measurement*, NY: Harcourt, Brace, & World.

Chattopadhyay, Amitava and Prakash Negundati (1992), "Does Attitude Toward the Ad Endure? The Moderating Effects of Attention and Decay," *Journal of Consumer Research*, 19 (June), 26-33.

Chintagunta, Pradeep K. (1999), "Variety Seeking, Purchase Timing, and the Lightning Bolt Brand Choice Model," *Management Science*, 45 (4), 486-498.

Clancy, Kevin J. and Robert Garsen (1970), "Why Some Scales Predict Better," *Journal of Advertising Research*, 10 (October), 33 38.

Clee, Mona A. and Robert A. Wicklund (1980), "Consumer Behavior and Psychological Reactance," *Journal of Consumer Research*, 6 (March), 389 405.

Cohen, A. R. (1964), *Attitude Change and Social Influence*, New York: Basic Books.

Cohen, Jacob and Patricia Cohen (1975), *Applied Multiple Regression/Correlation Analysis for the Behavioral Sciences*, Hillsdale, NJ: Lawrence Erlbaum.

Colley, R. (1961), *Defining Advertising Goals for Measured Advertising Results*, New York: Association of National Advertisers.

Converse, Philip E. (1970), "Attitudes and Nonattitudes: Continuation of a Dialogue," in *The Quantitative Analysis of Social Problems*, Edward R. Tufte, ed., Reading, MA: Addison Wesley.

Cook, Stuart W. and Claire Selltiz (1970), "A Multiple Indicator Approach to Attitude Measurement," in *Attitude Measurement*, Gene F. Summers, ed., Chicago: Rand McNally and Co., 23 41.

Cooper, Peter and Rupert Tower (1992), "Inside the Consumer Mind: Consumer Attitudes to the Arts," *Journal of the Market Research Society*, 34 (4), 299-311.

Copland, Brian (1963), "An Evaluation of Conceptual Frameworks for Measuring Advertising Results," *Proceedings, 9th Annual Conference*, The Advertising Research Foundation.

Cotte, June and S. Ratneshwar (1998), "Consumer Decisions on Discretionary Time: A Sociocognitive Perspective," *Advances in Consumer Research*, 25 (1), 268-275.

Cowles, Deborah and Lawrence A. Crosby (1986), "Measure Validation in Consumer Research: A Confirmatory Factor Analysis of the Voluntary Simplicity Lifestyle Scale," *Advances in Consumer Research*, 13 (1), 392-397.

Cox, David F., ed. (1967), *Risk Taking and Information Handling in Consumer Behavior*, Boston: Harvard University.

Craik, Fergus and Robert Lockhart (1972), "Levels of Processing: A Framework for Memory Research," *Journal of Verbal Learning and Verbal Behavior*, 11, 671 684.

Cronbach, Lee J. (1951), "Coefficient Alpha and the Internal Structure of Tests," *Psychometrika*, 16, (No. 3), September, 297 334.

Crow, Lowell, Richard W. Olshavsky, and John O. Summers (1980), "Industrial Buyer's Choice Strategies: A Protocol Analysis," *Journal of Marketing Research*, 17, 34 44.

Culbertson, F. M. (1957), "Modification of an Emotionally Held Attitude Through Role Playing," *Journal of Abnormal and Social Psychology*, 54, 230 233.

Cummings, W. H. and M. Venkatesan (1976), "Cognitive Dissonance and Consumer Behavior: A Review of the Evidence," *Journal of Marketing Research*, 13 (August), 303 308.

Cunningham, Scott M. (1966), "Perceived Risk as a Factor in Diffusion of New Product Information," in *Science, Technology and Marketing, Fall Conference Proceedings of the American Marketing Association*, Raymond M. Haas, ed., 698 721.

Darley, William K. and Robert E. Smith (1993), "Advertising Claim Objectivity: Antecedents and Effects," *Journal of Marketing*, Volume 57, Number 4, (October), pp. 100-113.

_____, and Robert E. Smith (1995), "Gender Differences in Information Processing Strategies: An Empirical Test of the Selectivity Model in Advertising Response," *Journal of Advertising*, Volume 24, Number 1, (Spring), pp. 41-56.

Dawkins, Richard (1976), *The Selfish Gene*, New York: Oxford University Press.

Day, George S. (1970), *Buyer Attitudes and Brand Choice Behavior*, New York: Free Press.

_____ (1972), "Evaluating Models of Attitude Structure," *Journal of Marketing Research*, 9 (August), 279 286.

Deighton, John (1984), "The Interaction of Advertising and Evidence," *Journal of Consumer Research*, 11 (December), 763-770.

deMille, Richard (1978), *Castaneda's Journey*, Santa Barbara, CA: Capra Press.

deRopp, Robert S. (1979), *Warrior's Way*, 2nd ed., New York: Dell Publishing Co., Inc.

Delozier, M. Wayne (1976), *The Marketing Communications Process*, New York: McGraw Hill Book Company.

Deutsch, Morton and Robert M. Krauss (1965), *Theories in Social Psychology*, New York: Basic Books Inc.

Dickson, Peter R. and Paul W. Miniard (1978), "A Further Examination of Two Laboratory Tests of the Extended Fishbein Attitude Model," *Journal of Consumer Research*, 4 (March), 261 266.

Dixon, N. F. (1971), *Subliminal Perception: The Nature of a Controversy*, London: McGraw Hill.

Dodson K.J. (1996), "Peak Experiences and Mountain Biking: Incorporating the Bike into the Extended Self," *Advances in Consumer Research*, 23, 317-322.

Domzal, Teresa J. and Jerome B. Kernan (1993), "Variations and the Pursuit of Beauty: Toward a Corporal Theory of the Body," *Psychology & Marketing*, 10 (6), 495-511.

Dover, Philip A. and Jerry C. Olson (1977), "Dynamic Changes in an Expectancy Value Attitude Model as a Function of Multiple Exposures to Product Information," in *Contemporary Marketing Thought*, Barnett A. Greenberg and Danny N. Bellenger, eds., Chicago: American Marketing Association, 455 459.

Downs, Roger M. and David Stea (1977), *Maps in Minds*, New York: Harper and Row.

Duke, Lisa (2002), "Get Real!: Cultural Relevance and Resistance to the Mediated Feminine Ideal," *Psychology & Marketing*, 19 (2), 211-233.

Dunfee, Thomas W., N. C. Smith, and W.T. Ross Jr. (1999), "Social Contracts and Marketing Ethics," *Journal of Marketing*, 63 (3), 14-32.

E

Eagly, Alice H., Wendy Wood, and Shelly Chaiken (1978), "Causal Inferences About Communicators and Their Effect on Opinion Change," *Journal of Personality and Social Psychology*, 36 (No. 4), 424 435.

Ehrenberg, Andrews S. C. (1974), "Repetitive Advertising and the Consumer," *Journal of Advertising Research*, 14, (No. 2), 25 34.

Ellis, Albert and Robert A. Harper (1975), *A New Guide to Rational Living*, North Hollywood, CA: Wilshire Book Co.

Engel, James F., Roger D. Blackwell, and David T. Kollat, *Consumer Behavior*, 3rd ed., Hinsdale, IL: The Dryden Press.

_____, Hugh G. Wales, Martin R. Warshaw (1975), *Promotional Strategy*, 3rd ed., Homewood, IL: Richard D. Irwin, Inc.

_____, Martin R. Warshaw, and Thomas C. Kinnear (1979), *Promotional Strategy: Managing the Marketing Communications Process*, 4th ed., Homewood, IL: Richard D. Irwin.

Ericsson, K. A. and H. A. Simon (1980), "Verbal Reports as Data," *Psychological Review*, 87 (No. 3), 215 251.

Etter, William (1975), "Attitude Theory and Decision Theory: Where is the Common Ground," *Journal of Marketing Research*, 12 (November), 481 483.

Faison, Edmund W. J. (1977), "The Neglected Variety Drive: A Useful Concept for Consumer Behavior," *Journal of Consumer Research*, 4, 172 175.

Farley, John U., Jerrold Katz, and Donald R. Lehmann (1978), "Impact of Different Comparison Sets on Evaluation of a New Subcompact Car Brand," *Journal of Consumer Research*, 5 (September), 138 142.

Fazio, Russell H., Jeaw mei Chen, Elizabeth C. McDonel, and Steven J. Sherman (1982), "Attitude Accessibility, Attitude Behavior Consistency, and the Strength of the Object Evaluation Association," *Journal of Experimental Social Psychology* (in press).

_____ and Mark P. Zanna (1981), "Direct Experience and Attitude Behavior Consistency," in *Advances in Experimental Social Psychology*, 14, L. Berkowitz, ed., 161 202.

_____, Martha C. Powell, and Carol J. Williams (1989), "The Role of Attitude Accessibility in the Attitude-to-Behavior Process," *Journal of Consumer Research*, 16 (December), 280-288.

Festinger, Leon (1957), *A Theory of Cognitive Dissonance*, Evanston, IL: Row, Peterson.

_____ and N. Maccoby (1964), "On Resistance to Persuasive Communication," *Journal of Abnormal and Social Psychology*, 68, (No. 4), 359 366.

Fischoff, Baruch, Paul Slovic, and Sarah Lichtenstein (1980), "Knowing What You Want: Measuring Labile Values," in *Cognitive Processes in Choice and Decision Behavior*, Thomas S. Wallsten, ed., Hillsdale, NJ: Lawrence Erlbaum Assoc., 117 141.

Fishbein, Martin ed., (1967), *Readings in Attitude Theory and Measurement*, New York: Wiley.

Fournier, Susan and David G. Mick (1999), "Rediscovering Satisfaction," *Journal of Marketing*, 63 (4), 5-23.

Frick, W.B. (2000), "Remembering Maslow: Reflections on a 1968 Interview," *Journal of Humanistic Psychology*, 40 (2), 128-147.

Friedmann, Roberto and , Parker V. Lessig (1986), "A Framework of Psychological Meaning of Products," *Advances in Consumer Research*, 13 (1), 338-342.

_____ and Icek Ajzen (1975), *Belief, Attitude, Intention and Behavior: An Introduction to Theory and Research*, Reading, MA: Addison Wesley.

Freud, Sigmund (1938), "Three Contributions to the Theory of Sex," in *The Basic Writings of Sigmund Freud*, A. A. Brill, ed., New York: Random House, Inc., 553 629.

_____ (1938), "The History of the Psychoanalytic Movement," in *The Basic Writings of Sigmund Freud*, A. A. Brill, ed., New York: Random House, Inc., 933 977.

_____ (1938), "The Interpretation of Dreams," in *The Basic Writings of Sigmund Freud*, A. A. Brill, ed., New York: Random House, Inc., 181 549.

_____ (1938), "Psychopathology of Everyday Life," in *The Basic Writings of Sigmund Freud*, A. A. Brill, ed., New York: Random House, Inc., 35 178.

_____ (1938), "Totem and Taboo," in *The Basic Writings of Sigmund Freud*, A. A. Brill, ed., New York: Random House, Inc., 807 930.

G

Ganesan, Shankar (1994), "Determinants of Long-Term Orientation in Buyer-Seller Relationships," *Journal of Marketing*, 58 (2), 1-19.

Garbarino, Ellen C. and Julie A. Edell, (1997), "Cognitive Effort, Affect, and Choice," *Journal of Consumer Research*, 24 (September), 147-158.

Garbarino, Ellen (1999), "The Different Roles of Satisfaction, Trust, and Commitment in Customer Relationships," *Journal of Marketing*, 63 (2), 70-87.

Ginter, James L. (1974), "An Experimental Investigation of Attitude Change and Choice of a New Brand," *Journal of Marketing Research*, 11 (February), 30 40.

Graham, William and Joe Balloun (1973), "An Empirical Test of Maslow's Need Hierarchy Theory," *Journal of Humanistic Psychology*, 13 (1), 97-108.

Granbois, Donald H. (1979), "Why Don't Consumers Search for More Information? An Overview," *Association for Consumer Research Conference Proceedings*, Chicago, IL.

Green, B. F. (1954), "Attitude Measurement," in *Handbook of Social Psychology*, G. Lindzey, ed., 1, Reading, MA: Addison Wesley.

Greenwald, Anthony G. (1968), "Cognitive Learning, Cognitive Responses to Persuasion, and Attitude Change," in *Psychological Foundations of Attitudes*, A. G. Greenwald, T. C. Brock, and T. M. Ostrum, eds., New York: Academic Press, 147 170.

_____ and Clark Leavitt (1984), "Audience Involvement in Advertising: Four Levels," *Journal of Consumer Research*, 11 (June), 581 592.

Grey Matter (1968), Vol. 39 (November).

Guthrie, E. R. (1935), *The Psychology of Learning*, New York: Harper.

Guttman, Louis (1944), "A Basis for Scaling Qualitative Data," *American Sociological Review*, 9, 139 150.

Hackman, Richard J. and Lynn R. Anderson (1968), "The Strength, Relevance, and Source of Beliefs About an Object in Fishbein's Attitude Theory," *Journal of Social Psychology*, 76, 55 67.

Hagerty, Michael (1999), "Testing Maslow's Hierarchy of Needs: National Quality-Of-Life across Time," *Social Indicators Research*, 46 (3), 249-271.

Haley, Russell I. and Peter B. Case (1979), "Testing Thirteen Attitude Scales for Agreement and Brand Discrimination," *Journal of Marketing*, 43, (Fall), 20 32.

Harlow, Harry F. (1959),"Love in Infant Monkeys," *Scientific American Psychologist*, 17, 1-9.

Harlow, Harry F. (1971), *Learning to Love*, San Francisco: Albion

Hartley, E. L. (1946), *Problems in Prejudice*, New York: Kings Crown Press.

Harvey, O. J. and G. Beverly, (1961), "Some Personality Correlates of Concept Change Through Role Playing," *Journal of Abnormal and Social Psychology*, 63, 125 130.

Havlena, William J. and Morris B. Holbrook (1980), "The Varieties of Consumption Experience: Comparing Two Typologies of Emotion in Consumer Behavior," *Journal of Consumer Research*, 13 (December), 394-404.

Haskins, J. B. (1964), "Factual Recall As A Measure of Advertising Effectiveness," *Journal of Advertising Research*, 2, 2 28.

Heise, David R. (1970), "The Semantic Differential and Attitude Research," in *Attitude Measurement*, Gene F. Summers, ed., Chicago: Rand McNally and Co., 235 253.

Heslin, Richard, Brian Blake, and James Rotton (1972), "Information Search As A Function of Stimulus Uncertainty and The Importance of the Response," *Journal of Personality and Social Psychology*, 23, (No. 3), 333 339.

Hauser, John R. and Glen L. Urban (1979), "Assessment of Attitude Importances and Consumer Utility Functions: Von Newman Morgenstern Theory Applied to Consumer Behavior," *Journal of Consumer Research*, 5 (March), 251 262.

Hawes, Douglass K. (1979), "Leisure and Consumer Behavior," *Journal of the Academy of Marketing Science*, 7 (4), 391-403.

Heeler, R. M. (1972), "The Effects of Mixed Media, Multiple Copy, Repetition, and Competition in Advertising: A Laboratory Investigation," Ph.D. Dissertation, Stanford University, Graduate School of Business.

Heeler, Roger M., Michael J. Kearney, and Bruce J. Mehaffey (1973), "Modeling Supermarket Product Selection," *Journal of Marketing Research*, 10 (February), 34 37.

Heider, Fritz (1927), "Thing and Medium," *Symposium*, 1, 109 158.

Hendrick, Clyde and B. A. Seyfried (1974), "Assessing the Validity of Laboratory Produced Attitude Change," *Journal of Personality and Social Psychology*, 29, 865 870.

Heylighen, F. (1992), "A Cognitive-Systemic Reconstruction of Maslow's Theory of Self-Actualization," *Behavioral Science*, 37 (1), 39-58.

Hirschman, Elizabeth C. and Morris B. Holbrook (1982), "Hedonic Consumption: Emerging Concepts, Methods and Propositions," *Journal of Marketing*, 46 (3), 92-101.

Hoch, Stephen J. and John Deighton (1989), "Managing What Consumers Learn from Experience," *Journal of Marketing*, 53 (April), 1-20.

_____, Stephen J. and Young-Won Ha (1986), "Consumer Learning: Advertising and the Ambiguity of Product Experience," *Journal of Consumer Research*, 13 (September), 221-233.

_____, Stephen J. and George F. Loewenstein (1991), "Time-inconsistent Preferences and Consumer Self-Control," *Journal of Consumer Research*, 17 (4), 492-507.

Hoffman, Donna L. and Thomas P. Novak (1996), "Marketing in Hypermedia Computer-Mediated Environments: Conceptual Foundations," *Journal of Marketing*, 60 (July), 50-68.

Holbrook, Morris B. (1977), "Comparing Multiattribute Attitude Models by Optimal Scaling," *Journal of Consumer Research*, 4, 165 171.

_____ (1978), "Beyond Attitude Structure: Toward the Informational Determinants of Attitudes," *Journal of Marketing Research*, 15 (November), 545 556.

_____ and Joel Huber (1979), "Separating Perceptual Dimensions from Affective Overtones: An Application to Consumer Aesthetics," *Journal of Consumer Research*, 5 (March), 272 283.

_____, Morris B., Robert W. Chestnut, Terence A. Oliva, and Eric A. Greenleaf (1984), "Play as a Consumption Experience: The Roles of Emotions, Performance, and Personality in the Enjoyment of Games," *Journal of Consumer Research*, 11 (2), 728-739.

Hopkinson, Gillian C. and Davashish Pujari (1999), "A Factor Analytic Study of the Sources of Meaning in Hedonic Consumption," *European Journal of Marketing*, 33 (3/4), 273-290.

Houston, Michael J. (1979), "Consumer Evaluations of Product Information Sources," *Current Issues and Research in Advertising*, 135 144.

_____ and Michael L. Rothschild (1977), "A Paradigm for Research on Consumer Involvement" working paper, University of Wisconsin.

_____, Michael J., Terry L. Childers, and Susan E. Heckler (1987), "Picture-Word Consistency and Elaborative Processing of Advertisements," *Journal of Marketing Research*, 24 (4), 359-369.

Hovland, C. I., I. L. Janis, and H. H. Kelley (1953), *Communication and Persuasion*, New Haven: Yale University Press.

_____ and Walter Weiss (1952), "The Influence of Source Credibility on Communication Effectiveness," *Public Opinion Quarterly* (Winter), 635 650.

_____, et al. (1957), *The Order of Presentation in Persuasion*, New Haven: Yale University Press.

Howard, John A. and Jagdish N. Sheth (1969), *The Theory of Buyer Behavior*, New York: John Wiley and Sons, Inc.

Hoffman, Donna L. and Thomas P. Novak (1996), "Marketing in Hypermedia Computer-Mediated Environments: Conceptual Foundations," *Journal of Marketing*, 60 (July), 50-68.

Hunt, J, V. (1963), "Motivation Inherent in Information Processing and Action," in *Motivational and Social Interaction - Cognitive Determinants*, ed. O. J. Harvey, NY: Ronald Press, 35-94.

Hunt, Shelby D. (1976a), *Marketing Theory: Conceptual Foundations of Research in Marketing*, Columbus, OH: Grid, Inc.

_____ (1976b), "The Nature and Scope of Marketing," *Journal of Marketing*, 40 (July), 17 28.

_____, Shelby D., Van R. Wood, and Lawrence B. Chonko (1989), "Corporate Ethical Values and Organizational Commitment in Marketing," *Journal of Marketing*, 53, (3), 79-90.

Hyde, Thomas S. and James J. Jenkins (1973), "Recall for Words as a Function of Semantic, Graphic, and Syntatic Orienting Tasks," *Journal of Verbal Learning and Verbal Behavior*, 12, 471 480.

Insko, Chester A. and John Schopler (l967), "Triadic Consistency: A Statement of Affective Cognitive Conative Consistency," *Psychological Review*, 74, (No. 5), 361 376.

Jacoby, Jacob, Robert W. Chestnut, and William Silberman (1977), "Consumer Use and Comprehension of Nutritional Information," *Journal of Consumer Research*, 4, (No. 2), 119 128.

_____ and Wayne D. Hoyer (l982), "Viewer Miscomprehension of Televised Communication: Selected Findings," *Journal of Marketing*, 46 (Fall), 12 16.

Janis, I. L. and B. T. King (1954), "The Influence of Role Playing on Opinion Change," *Journal of Abnormal and Social Psychology*, 49, 211 218.

Jastrow, Robert (1977), *Until the Sun Dies*, New York: W. W. Norton & Co. Inc.

Jolibert, Alain and Gary Baumgartner (1997), "Values, Motivations, and Personal Goals: Revisited," *Psychology & Marketing*, 14 (7), 675-688.

Jones, Edward E. and Keith E. Davis (1965), "From Acts to Dispositions," in *Advances in Experimental Psychology*, Leonard Berkowitz, ed., New York: Academic Press, 219 266.

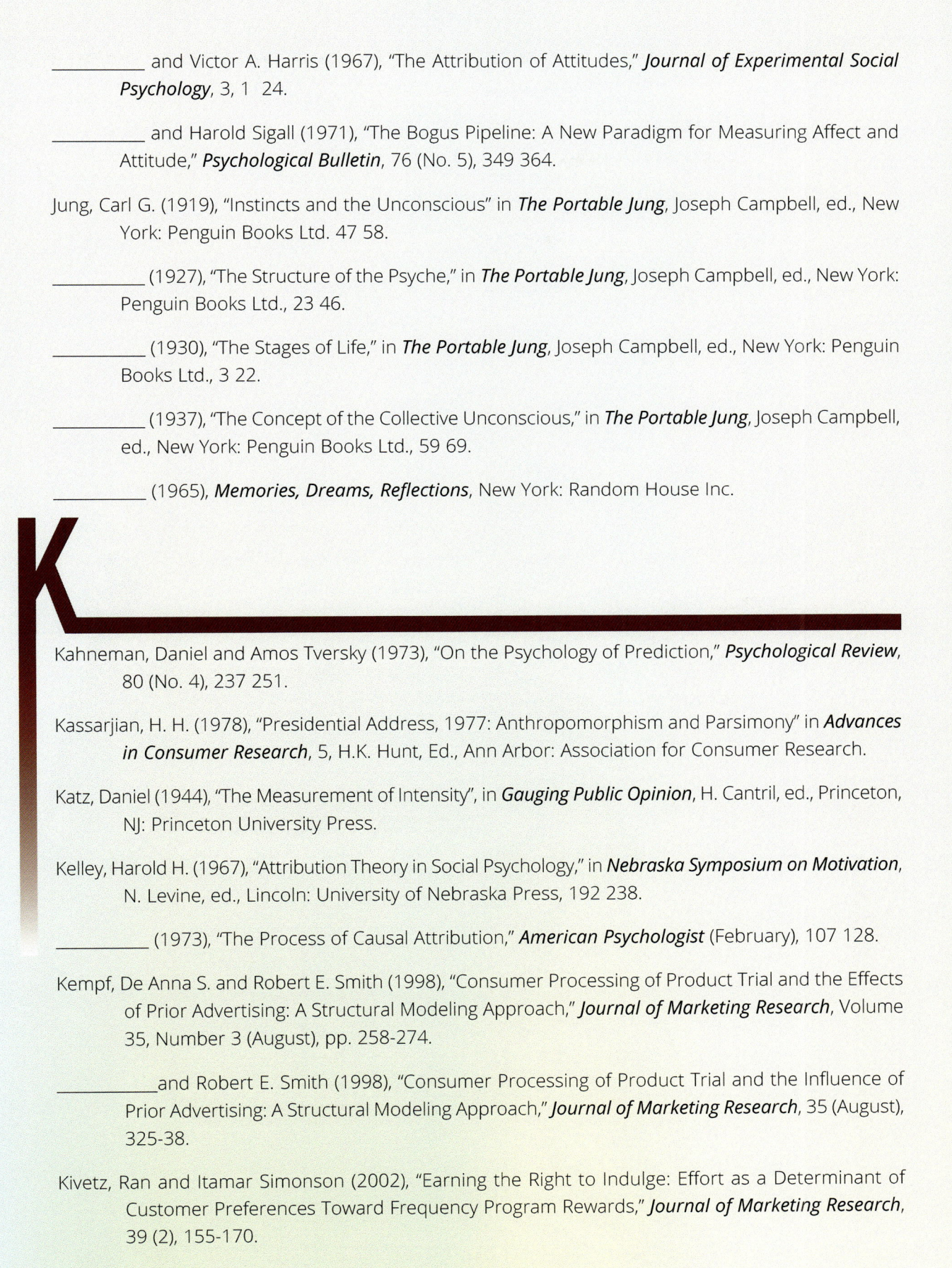

_____ and Victor A. Harris (1967), "The Attribution of Attitudes," *Journal of Experimental Social Psychology*, 3, 1 24.

_____ and Harold Sigall (1971), "The Bogus Pipeline: A New Paradigm for Measuring Affect and Attitude," *Psychological Bulletin*, 76 (No. 5), 349 364.

Jung, Carl G. (1919), "Instincts and the Unconscious" in *The Portable Jung*, Joseph Campbell, ed., New York: Penguin Books Ltd. 47 58.

_____ (1927), "The Structure of the Psyche," in *The Portable Jung*, Joseph Campbell, ed., New York: Penguin Books Ltd., 23 46.

_____ (1930), "The Stages of Life," in *The Portable Jung*, Joseph Campbell, ed., New York: Penguin Books Ltd., 3 22.

_____ (1937), "The Concept of the Collective Unconscious," in *The Portable Jung*, Joseph Campbell, ed., New York: Penguin Books Ltd., 59 69.

_____ (1965), *Memories, Dreams, Reflections*, New York: Random House Inc.

K

Kahneman, Daniel and Amos Tversky (1973), "On the Psychology of Prediction," *Psychological Review*, 80 (No. 4), 237 251.

Kassarjian, H. H. (1978), "Presidential Address, 1977: Anthropomorphism and Parsimony" in *Advances in Consumer Research*, 5, H.K. Hunt, Ed., Ann Arbor: Association for Consumer Research.

Katz, Daniel (1944), "The Measurement of Intensity", in *Gauging Public Opinion*, H. Cantril, ed., Princeton, NJ: Princeton University Press.

Kelley, Harold H. (1967), "Attribution Theory in Social Psychology," in *Nebraska Symposium on Motivation*, N. Levine, ed., Lincoln: University of Nebraska Press, 192 238.

_____ (1973), "The Process of Causal Attribution," *American Psychologist* (February), 107 128.

Kempf, De Anna S. and Robert E. Smith (1998), "Consumer Processing of Product Trial and the Effects of Prior Advertising: A Structural Modeling Approach," *Journal of Marketing Research*, Volume 35, Number 3 (August), pp. 258-274.

_____and Robert E. Smith (1998), "Consumer Processing of Product Trial and the Influence of Prior Advertising: A Structural Modeling Approach," *Journal of Marketing Research*, 35 (August), 325-38.

Kivetz, Ran and Itamar Simonson (2002), "Earning the Right to Indulge: Effort as a Determinant of Customer Preferences Toward Frequency Program Rewards," *Journal of Marketing Research*, 39 (2), 155-170.

Klein, Lisa R. (1998), "Evaluating the Potential of Interactive Media Through a New Lens: Search versus Experience Goods," *Journal of Business Research*, 41, 195-203.

Klink, Richard R. and Daniel C. Smith (2001), "Threats to External Validity of Brand Extension Research," *Journal of Marketing Research*, 38 (3), 326-335.

Kotler, Philip (1988), *Marketing Management*, Englewood Cliffs, NJ: Prentice-Hall.

Kover, Arthur J. (2001), "Advertising and Freedom and the Complex Market," *Journal of Advertising Research*, 41 (6), 5.

Kozinets, Robert V. (2002), "Can Consumers Escape the Market? Emancipatory Illuminations from Burning Man," *Journal of Consumer Research*, 29 (1), 20-38.

Krishnan, H. Shanker and Robert E. Smith (1998), "The Relative Endurance of Attitudes, Confidence and Attitude-Behavior Consistency: The Role of Information Source and Delay," *Journal of Consumer Psychology*, Volume 7 (3), pp. 273-298.

Kiesler, Charles A. and Paul A. Munson (1975), "Attitudes and Opinions," *Annual Review in Psychology*, 415 456.

King, B. T. and I. L. Janis (1956), "Comparison of the Effectiveness of Improvised Versus Nonimprovised Role Playing in Producing Opinion Changes," *Human Relations*, 9, 177 186.

Klapper, Joseph (1960), *The Effects of Mass Media*, Glencoe, IL: Free Press.

Klonglan, G.E. and E.W. Coward (1970), "The Concept of Symbolic Adoption: A Suggested Interpretation," *Rural Sociology*, 35 (March), 77 83.

Korzybski, Alfred (1933), *Science and Sanity*, Lancaster, PA: Lancaster Press.

Krugman, Herbert E. (1965), "The Impact of Television Advertising: Learning Without Involvement," *Public Opinion Quarterly*, 29, 349 356.

_____ (1971), "Brain Wave Measures of Media Involvement," *Journal of Advertising Research*, 11 (February), 3 9.

Lampert, Shlomo I. (1979), "The Attitude Pollimeter: A New Attitude Scaling Device," *Journal of Marketing Research*, 16 (November), 578 582.

Langer, Ellen J. (1978), "Rethinking the Role of Thought in Social Interactions," in *New Directions in Attribution Research*, 2, Lawrence Erlbaum Associates, Harvey, Ickes, and Kidd eds., Potomac, MD.

Lacher, Kathleen T. and Richard Mizerski (1994), "An Exploratory Study of the Responses and Relationships Involved in the Evaluation of, and in the Intention to Purchase New Rock Music," *Journal of Consumer Research*, 21 (2), 366-380.

Langrehr, Frederick W. (1991), "Retail Shopping Mall Semiotics and Hedonic Consumption," *Advances in Consumer Research*, 18 (1), 428-433.

LaPiere, R.T. (1934), "Attitudes vs Action," *Social Forces*, 13, 230 237.

Lavidge, Robert J. and Gary A. Steiner (1961), "A Model For Predictive Measurements of Advertising Effectiveness," *Journal of Marketing*, 25 (October), 59 62.

Leakey, Richard E. (1981), *The Making of Mankind*, New York: E.P. Dutton.

Lemon, N.F. (1968), "A Model of the Extremity, Confidence and Salience of an Opinion," *British Journal of Sociology and Clinical Psychology*, 7, 106 114.

Leclerc G., R. Lefrancois, M. Dube, R. Hebert, and P. Gaulin (1998), "The Self-Actualization Concept: A Content Validation," *Journal of Social Behavior and Personality*, 13 (1): 69-84.

Lester, David (1990), "Maslow's Hierarchy of Needs and Personality," *Personality and Individual Differences*, 11 (11), 1187-1188.

Lewin, Kurt (1938), "The Conceptual Representation and Measurement of Psychological Forces," *Contributions to Psychological Theory*, 1, (No. 4).

_____, Tamar Dembo, Less Festinger, and Pauline S. Sears (1944), "Level of Aspiration," in *Personality and the Behavior Disorders*, J. McV. Hunt, ed., New York: Donald Press, 333 378.

Lewis, Gareth and Sven Svebak (1978), "The Psychophysiology of Metamotivation," in *Motivational Styles in Everyday Life: A Guide to Reversal Theory*, American Psychological Association, 97-115.

Likert, Rensis (1932), "A Technique for the Measurement of Attitudes," *Archives of Psychology*, No. 140.

Locander, William B. and Peter W. Hermann (1979), "The Effect of Self Confidence and Anxiety on Information Seeking in Consumer Risk Reduction," *Journal of Marketing Research*, 16 (May), 268 274.

_____ and W. Austin Spivey (1978), "A Functional Approach to Attitude Measurement," *Journal of Marketing Research*, 15 (November), 576 587.

Lussier, Dennis A. and Richard W. Olshavsky (1979), "Task Complexity and Contingent Processing in Brand Choice," *Journal of Consumer Research*, 6, 154 165.

Lutz, Richard J. (1975), "Changing Brand Attitudes Through Modification of Cognitive Structure," *Journal of Consumer Research*, 1 (March), 49 58.

_____ (1977), "An Experimental Investigation of Causal Relations Among Cognitions, Affect, and Behavioral Intentions," *Journal of Consumer Research*, 3 (March), 107 197.

_____ and Jack Swasy (1977), "Integrating Cognitive Structure and Cognitive Response Approaches to Monitoring Communications Effects," in *Advances in Consumer Research*, 4, William D. Perreault, ed., Atlanta: Association for Consumer Research, 363 71.

M

MacKenzie, Lutz and Belch (1986), "The Role of Attitude Toward the Ad as a Mediator of Advertising Effectiveness: a Test of Competing Explanations," *Journal of Marketing Research*, 23 (May), 130-143.

MacLachlan, James, John Czepiel, and Priscilla La Barbera (1979), "Implementation of Response Latency Measures," *Journal of Marketing Research*, 16 (November), 573 577.

MacLean, Paul D. (1973), *A Trione Concept, Concept of the Brain and Behavior*, Toronto: University of Toronto Press.

Marks, L. J. and M. A. Kamins (1988), "The Use of Product Sampling and Advertising: Effects of Sequence of Exposure and Degree of Advertising Claim Exaggeration on Consumers' Belief Strength, Belief Confidence, and Attitudes," *Journal of Marketing Research*, 25 (August), 266-82.

Markus, Hazel (1977), "Self Schemata and Processing Information About the Self," *Journal of Personality and Social Psychology*, 35, No. 2.

Maslow, Abraham H. (1962), "Lessons Learned from the Peak Experiences," *Journal of Humanistic Psychology*, 2, 9 18.

_____ (1970), *Motivation and Personality*, 2nd ed., New York: Harper.

_____, Abraham H, (1967), "Theory of Metamotivation: The Biological Rooting of the Value-Life," *Journal of Humanistic Psychology*, 7 (2), 93-127

_____, Abraham H. (1936a),"A Theory of Sexual Behavior of Infrahuman Primates," *Journal of Genetic Psychology*, 48, 310-338.

_____, Abraham H. (1936b),"The Role of Dominance in the Social and Sexual Behavior of Infrahuman Primates, I: Observations at Vilas Park Zoo," *Journal of Genetic Psychology*, 48, 261-277.

_____, Abraham H. (1942),"Self-esteem (Dominance-feeling) and Sexuality in Women," *Journal of Social Psychology*, 16, 259-294.

_____, Abraham H. (1954), *Motivation and Personality*, New York, New York: Harper.

_____, Abraham H. (1967),"Neuroses as a Failure of Personal Growth," Humanitas, 3, 153-170.

_____, Abraham (1968), *Toward a Psychology of Being*, New York: Van Nostrum

_____, Abraham H. (1971), *The Farther Reaches of Human Nature*, New York, New York: Penguin Books.

Mazis, Michael B., Olli T. Ahtola, and R. Eugene Klippel (1975) "A Comparison of Four Multi Attribute Models in the Prediction of Consumer Attitudes," *Journal of Consumer Research*, 2 (June), 38 52.

McLuhan, Marshall and Quentin Fiore (1967), *The Medium is the Massage*, New York: Bantam Books Inc.

Mead, George H. (1934), *Mind, Self, and Society*, Chicago: University of Chicago Press.

Mehrabian, Albert and James A. Russell (1974), *An Approach to Environmental Psychology*, Cambridge, MA: M.I.T. Press.

Menon, Anil, et al. (1999), "Antecedents and Consequences of Marketing Strategy Making: A Model and a Test," *Journal of Marketing*, 63 (2), 18-40.

Meyer, Robert J. (1981), "A Model of Multiattribute Judgements Under Attribute Uncertainty and Informational Constraint," *Journal of Marketing Research*, 18 (November), 428 41.

Meyer-Levy, Joan, and Alice M. Tybout (1989), "Schema Congruity as a Basis for Product Evaluation," *Journal of Consumer Research*, 16 (June), 39-54.

Miller, Kenneth E. and James L. Ginter (1979), "An Investigation of Situational Variation in Brand Choice Behavior and Attitude," *Journal of Marketing Research*, 16 (February), 111 123.

Miniard, Paul W. and Joel B. Cohen (1979), "Isolating Attitudinal and Normative Influences in Behavioral Intentions Models," *Journal of Marketing Research*, 16 (February), 102 110.

Mizerski, Richard W., Linda L. Golden, and Jerome B. Kernan (1979), "The Attribution Process in Consumer Decision Making," *Journal of Consumer Research*, 6 (September), 123 140.

Mohr, Lois A. and Mary J. Bitner (1995), "The Role of Employee Effort in Satisfaction with Service Transactions," *Journal of Business Research*, 32 (3), 239-252.

Monroe, Robert A. (1977), *Journeys Out of the Body*, Garden City, NY: Anclia Press.

Moorman, Christine and Gerald Zaltman (1992), "Relationships Between Providers and Users of Market Research: The Dynamics of Trust Within and Between Organizations," *Journal of Marketing Research*, 29 (3), 314-328.

Morgan, Robert M. and Shelby D. Hunt (1994), "The Commitment-Trust Theory of Relationship Marketing," *Journal of Marketing*, 58 (3), 20-38.

N

Newcomb, Theodore M. (1950), *Social Psychology*, New York: The Dryden Press.

_____, Ralph H. Turner, and Philip E. Converse (1965), *Social Psychology*, New York: Holt, Rinehart and Winston.

Newell, A. and H. Simon (1972), *Human Problem Solving*, Englewood Cliffs, NJ: Prentice Hall.

Newman, Joseph W. and Bradley D. Lockeman (1975), "Measuring Prepurchase Information Seeking," *Journal of Consumer Research*, 2 (December), 216 222.

Nickels, William G. (1976), *Marketing Communications and Promotion*, Columbus, OH: Grid, Inc.

Nisbett, Richard E. and Timothy DeCamp Wilson (1977), "Telling More Than We Can Know: Verbal Reports on Mental Processes," *Psychological Review*, 84 (May), 231 259.

Nissen, Henry W. (1951) Phylogenetic Comparison, Handbook of Experimental Psychology, ed. S. S. Stevens, NY: John Wiley & Sons.

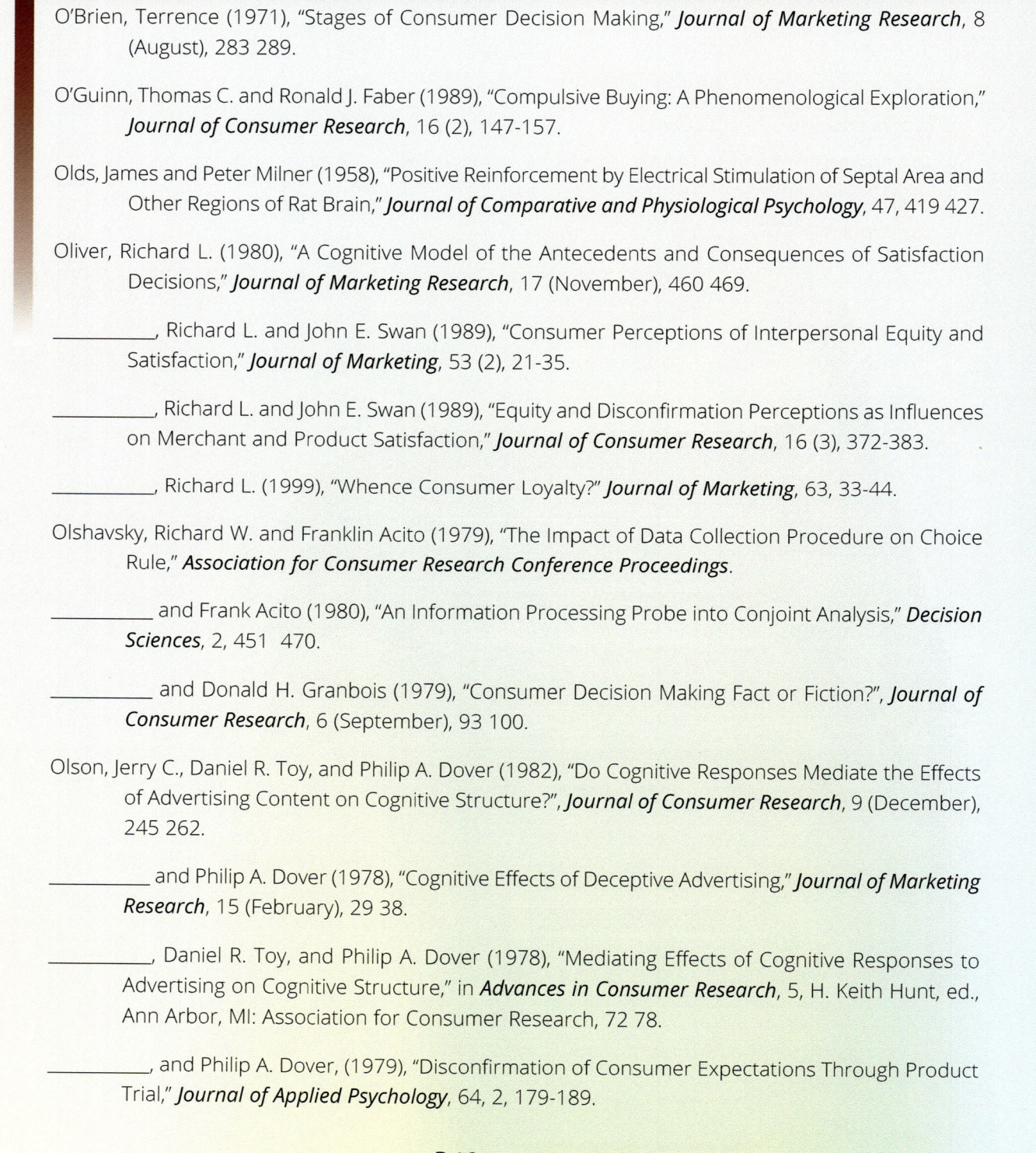

O'Brien, Terrence (1971), "Stages of Consumer Decision Making," *Journal of Marketing Research*, 8 (August), 283 289.

O'Guinn, Thomas C. and Ronald J. Faber (1989), "Compulsive Buying: A Phenomenological Exploration," *Journal of Consumer Research*, 16 (2), 147-157.

Olds, James and Peter Milner (1958), "Positive Reinforcement by Electrical Stimulation of Septal Area and Other Regions of Rat Brain," *Journal of Comparative and Physiological Psychology*, 47, 419 427.

Oliver, Richard L. (1980), "A Cognitive Model of the Antecedents and Consequences of Satisfaction Decisions," *Journal of Marketing Research*, 17 (November), 460 469.

_____, Richard L. and John E. Swan (1989), "Consumer Perceptions of Interpersonal Equity and Satisfaction," *Journal of Marketing*, 53 (2), 21-35.

_____, Richard L. and John E. Swan (1989), "Equity and Disconfirmation Perceptions as Influences on Merchant and Product Satisfaction," *Journal of Consumer Research*, 16 (3), 372-383.

_____, Richard L. (1999), "Whence Consumer Loyalty?" *Journal of Marketing*, 63, 33-44.

Olshavsky, Richard W. and Franklin Acito (1979), "The Impact of Data Collection Procedure on Choice Rule," *Association for Consumer Research Conference Proceedings*.

_____ and Frank Acito (1980), "An Information Processing Probe into Conjoint Analysis," *Decision Sciences*, 2, 451 470.

_____ and Donald H. Granbois (1979), "Consumer Decision Making Fact or Fiction?", *Journal of Consumer Research*, 6 (September), 93 100.

Olson, Jerry C., Daniel R. Toy, and Philip A. Dover (1982), "Do Cognitive Responses Mediate the Effects of Advertising Content on Cognitive Structure?", *Journal of Consumer Research*, 9 (December), 245 262.

_____ and Philip A. Dover (1978), "Cognitive Effects of Deceptive Advertising," *Journal of Marketing Research*, 15 (February), 29 38.

_____, Daniel R. Toy, and Philip A. Dover (1978), "Mediating Effects of Cognitive Responses to Advertising on Cognitive Structure," in *Advances in Consumer Research*, 5, H. Keith Hunt, ed., Ann Arbor, MI: Association for Consumer Research, 72 78.

_____, and Philip A. Dover, (1979), "Disconfirmation of Consumer Expectations Through Product Trial," *Journal of Applied Psychology*, 64, 2, 179-189.

Orne, M. T. (1962), "On the Social Psychology of the Psychological Experiment: With Particular Reference to Demand Characteristics and Their Implications," *American Psychologist*, 17, 776 783.

Ornstein, Peter A., Tom Trabasso, and Philip N. Johnson Laird (1974), "To Organize is to Remember," *Journal of Experimental Psychology*, 103, (No. 5), 1014 1018.

Osgood, C. E., G. J. Suci, and P. H. Tannenbaum (1957), *The Measurement of Meaning*, Urbana: University of Illinois Press.

Osselaer, Stijn M.J. Avn and Joseph W. Alba (2000), "Consumer Learning and Brand Equity," *Journal of Consumer Research*, 27 (1), 1-16.

Osterhus, Thomas L. (1997), "Pro-Social Consumer Influence Strategies: When and how do they Work?" *Journal of Marketing*, 61 (4), 16-29.

P

Packard, Vance (1958), *The Hidden Persuaders*, New York: Pocket Books Inc.

Page, Monte M. (1974), "Demand Characteristics and the Classical Conditioning of Attitudes Experiment," *Journal of Personality and Social Psychology*, 30, (No. 4), 468 476.

Palda, Kristian S. (1966), "The Hypothesis of a Hierarchy of Effects: A Partial Evaluation," *Journal of Marketing Research*, 3 (February), 13 24.

Park, Whan C. (1978), "A Few Questions on Consumer Information Processing: Two Product Cases, Coffee and Toothpaste," *Journal of Marketing Research*, 15 (May), 243 249.

Park, C. Whan and David L. Mothersbaugh (1994), "Consumer Knowledge Assessment," *Journal of Consumer Research*, 21 (1), 71-82.

Payne, John W. (1976), "Task Complexity and Contingent Processing in Decision Making: An Informational Search and Protocol Analysis," *Organizational Behavior and Human Performance*, 16, 366 387.

_____, Myron L. Braunstein, and John S. Carroll (1978), "Exploring Predecisional Behavior: An Alternative Approach to Decision Research," *Organizational Behavior and Human Performance*, 22, 17 44.

Penaloza, Lisa (2000), "The Commodification of the American West: Marketers' Production of Cultural Meanings at the Trade Show," *Journal of Marketing*, 64 (4), 82-110.

Pepitone, Albert (1976), "Toward a Normative and Comparative Biocultural Social Psychology," *Journal of Personality and Social Psychology*, 34, (No. 4), 641 653.

Pettijohn, T.F. (1996), "Perceived Happiness of College Students Measured by Maslow's Hierarchy of Needs," *Psychological Reports*, 79 (3), 759-762.

Puri, Radhika. (1996), "Measuring and Modifying Consumer Impulsiveness: A Cost-Benefit Accessibility Framework," *Journal of Consumer Psychology*, 5 (2), 87-113.

Perry, Ronald W., David F. Gillespie and Roy E. Lotz (1976), "Attitudinal Variables as Estimates of Behavior: A Theoretical Examination of the Attitude Action Controversy," *European Journal of Social Psychology*, 6 (No. 2), 227 243.

Peter, J. Paul (1981), "Construct Validity: A Review of Basic Issues and Marketing Practices," *Journal of Marketing Research*, 18 (May), 133 145.

Peter, J. Paul and Jerry C. Olson (1996), *Consumer Behavior and Marketing Strategy*, Homewood IL: Richard D. Irwin Inc.

_____ and Jerry C. Olson (1983), "Is Science Marketing?", *Journal of Marketing*, 47 (Fall), 111 125.

_____ and Michael J. Ryan (1976), "An Investigation of Perceived Risk at the Brand Level," *Journal of Marketing Research*, 13 (May), 184 188.

_____ and Lawrence X. Tarpey, Sr. (1975), "A Comparative Analysis of Three Consumer Decision Strategies," *Journal of Consumer Research*, 2 (June), 29 37.

Petersen, Karen K. and Jeffrey E. Dutton (1975), "Centrality, Extremity, Intensity Neglected Variables in Research on Attitude Behavior Consistency," *Social Forces*, 54 (No. 2), December, 393 414.

Petty, Richard E., John T. Cacioppo, and David Schumann (1983), "Central and Peripheral Routes to Advertising Effectiveness: The Moderating Role of Involvement," *Journal of Consumer Research*, 10 (September), 135 146.

Pierce, John C. (1975), "The Relationship Between Linkage Salience and Linkage Organization in Mass Belief Systems," *Public Opinion Quarterly*, 39, (No. 1), Spring, 102 110.

Plutchik, Robert (1980), "A Language for the Emotions," *Psychology Today*, (February) 68 78.

Pras, Bernard and John Summers (1975), "A Comparison of Linear and Nonlinear Evaluation Process Models," *Journal of Marketing Research*, 12 (August), 276 281.

_____ and John O. Summers (1978), "Perceived Risk and Compositional Models for Multiattribute Decisions," *Journal of Marketing Research*, 15 (August) 429 437.

R

Rapoport, Anatol (1953), *Operational Philosophy*, New York: John Wiley and Sons.

Ratchford, Brian T. (2001), "The Economics of Consumer Knowledge," *Journal of Consumer Research*, 27 (4), 397-411.

Ray, Michael L. (1973), "Marketing Communications and the Hierarchy of Effects," in *New Models for Mass Communication Research*, P. Clarke, ed., Beverly Hills: Sage Publishing, 147 176.

_____ and Alan G. Sawyer (1971), "Repetition in Media Models: A Laboratory Technique," *Journal of Marketing Research*, 8 (February), 29.

Regan, D. T. and R. H. Fazio (1977), "On the Consistency Between Attitudes and Behavior: Look to the Method of Attitude Formation," *Journal of Experimental Social Psychology*, 13, 38 45.

Reibstein, David J., Christopher H. Lovelock, and Ricardo De P. Dobson (1980), "The Direction of Causality Between Perceptions, Affect, and Behavior: An Application to Travel Behavior," *Journal of Consumer Research*, 6 (March), 370 376.

Reingen, Peter H. (1978), "On Inducing Compliance with Requests," *Journal of Consumer Research*, 5 (September), 96 102.

_____ and Jerome B. Kernan (1979), "More Evidence on Interpersonal Yielding," *Journal of Marketing Research*, 16 (November), 588 593.

Robertson, Thomas S. (1976), "Low Commitment Consumer Behavior," *Journal of Advertising Research*, 16 (No. 2), April, 19 27.

_____ and John R. Rossiter (1974), "Children and Commercial Persuasion: An Attribution Theory Analysis," *Journal of Consumer Research*, 1 (June), 13 20.

Rogers, Everett M. and F. Floyd Shoemaker (1971), *Communications in Innovation*, New York: The Free Press.

Rogers, Hudson P., C.M. Kochunny, and Alphonso Ogbuehi (1993), "Ethical Inclinations of Tomorrow's Marketers," *Journal of Marketing Education*, 15 (1), 11-19.

Rokeach, Milton (1968), *Beliefs, Attitudes and Values*, San Francisco: Jossey Bass, Inc.

Rolfsen, Kathy (1979), "Importance of Early Versus Late Information," unpublished paper based upon Reitz, *Behavior in Organizations*, 1977, 135 13.

Roselius, Ted (1971), "Consumer Rankings of Risk Reduction Methods," *Journal of Marketing*, 35 (January), 56 61.

Rosen, Benson and S. S. Lomorita (1971), "Attitude and Action: The Effects of Behavior Intent and Perceived Effectiveness of Acts," *Journal of Personality*, 39, 189 203.

Rosenberg, Milton J. (1960), "A Structural Theory of Attitude Dynamics," *Public Opinion Quarterly*, 24 (Summer), 319 40.

Rothschild, Michael L. (1974), "The Effects of Political Advertising on the Voting Behavior of a Low Involvement Electorate," unpublished Ph.D. dissertation, Stanford University.

_____ (1979), "Behavioral Learning Theory and Marketing," unpublished working paper, University of Wisconsin Madison.

Rowan, J. (1998), "Maslow Amended," *Journal of Humanistic Psychology*, 38 (1): 81-92.

Rowan, John (1999), "Ascent and Descent in Maslow's Theory," *Journal of Humanistic Psychology*, 39 (3), 125-131.

Rudner, Richard S. (1966), *Philosophy of Social Science*, Englewood Cliffs, NJ: Prentice Hall, Inc.

Russo, J. Edward and Eric J. Johnson (1980), "What Do Consumers Know About Familiar Products?" in *Advances in Consumer Research*, 7, Jerry C. Olson, ed., Ann Arbor: Association for Consumer Research, 417 423.

Rust, Roland T. and Richard L. Oliver (2000), "Should We Delight the Customer?" *Journal of the Academy of Marketing Science*, 28 (1), 86-94.

Ryan, Michael J. and E. H. Bonfield (1975), "The Fishbein Extended Model and Consumer Behavior," *Journal of Consumer Research*, 2 (September), 118 134.

S

Sagan, Carl (1977), *The Dragons of Eden*, New York: Ballantine Books.

Samu, Sridhar, H. Shanker Krishnan, and Robert E. Smith (1999), "Using Advertising Alliances for New Product Introduction: Interactions Between Product Complementarity and Promotional Strategies," *Journal of Marketing*, Volume 63, Number 1, (January).

Sawyer, A. G. (1971), "A Laboratory Experimental Investigation of the Effects of Repetition in Advertising," Ph.D. Dissertation, Graduate School of Business, Stanford University.

_____ (1973), "The Effects of Repetition of Refutational and Supportive Advertising Appeals," *Journal of Marketing Research*, 10, 23 33.

Scammon, Debra (1978), "Information Load' and Consumers," *Journal of Consumer Research*, 5, 148 155.

Schau, Hope J. (2000), "Consumer Imagination, Identity and Self-expression," *Advances in Consumer Research*, 27 (1), 50-56.

Schmidt, Jeffrey B. and Richard A. Spreng (1996), "A Proposed Model of External Consumer Information Search," *Journal of the Academy of Marketing Science*, 24 (3), 246-256.

Schneider, Benjamin and David E. Bowen (1999), "Understanding Customer Delight and Outrage," *Sloan Management Review*, 41 (1), 35-45.

Schneider, Walter and Richard M. Shiffrin (1977), "Controlled and Automatic Human Information Processing: I. Detection, Search, and Attention," *Psychological Review*, 84 (January), 1 66.

Schuman, Howard and Michael P. Johnson (1976), "Attitudes and Behavior," *Annual Review of Sociology*, 2, 161 207.

Scott, W. A. (1968), "Attitude Measurement," in *Handbook of Social Psychology*, 2nd ed., 2, G. Lindzey and E. Aronson, eds., Reading, MA: Addison Wesley.

Sechrest, Lee (1969), "Nonreactive Assessment of Attitudes," in *Naturalistic Viewpoints in Psychological Research*, Willems and Rausch, (eds.), Holt, Rinehart and Winston, 147 161.

Sense and Nonsense in Creative Research (1972), Grey Advertising, New York.

Settle, Robert B. and Linda L. Golden (1974), "Attribution Theory and Advertiser Credibility," *Journal of Marketing Research*, 11 (May), 181 185.

Sethi, Rajesh, Daniel C. Smith, and Whan C. Park (2001), "Cross-Functional Product Development Teams, Creativity, and the Innovativeness of New Consumer Products," *Journal of Marketing Research*, 38 (1), 73-85.

Shaw, Allen N. and Herbert A. Simm (1958), "Elements of a Theory of Human Problem Solving," *Psychological Review*, 65 (No. 3), 151 166.

Shaw, Deirdre and Terry Newholm (2002), "Voluntary Simplicity and the Ethics of Consumption," *Psychology & Marketing*, 19 (2), 167-185.

Sheluga, David A., James Jaccard, and Jacob Jacoby (1979), "Preference, Search, and Choice: An Integrative Approach," *Journal of Consumer Research*, 6 (September), 166 176.

Sherman, Steven J. (1980), "On the Self Erasing Nature of Errors of Prediction," *Journal of Personality and Social Psychology*, 39, (No. 2), 211 221.

Shiffrin, Richard M. and Walter Schneider (1977), "Controlled and Automatic Human Information Processing: II. Perceptual Learning, Automatic Attending and A General Theory," *Psychological Review*, 84 (March), 127 190.

Shocker, Allan D. and V. Srinivasan (1979), "Multiattribute Approaches for Product Concept Evaluation and Generation: A Critical Review," *Journal of Marketing Research*, 16 (May), 159 180.

Shoemaker, Robert W. and F. Robert Shoaf (1975), "Behavioral Changes in the Trial of New Products," *Journal of Consumer Research*, 2 (September), 104 109.

Shugan, Steven M. (1980), "The Cost of Thinking," *Journal of Consumer Research*, 7 (September), 99 111.

Simon, Herbert A. (1969), *The Sciences of the Artificial*, Cambridge, MA: MIT Press.

Simonson, Itamar and Stephen M. Nowlis (2000), "The Role of Explanations and Need for Uniqueness in Consumer Decision Making: Unconventional Choices Based on Reasons," *Journal of Consumer Research*, 27 (1), 49-68.

Singh, Jasbinder (2000), "Making Business Sense of Environmental Compliance," *Sloan Management Review*, 41 (3), 91-100.

Sirdeshmukh, Deepak, Jagdip Singh, Barry Sabol (2002), "Consumer Trust, Value, and Loyalty in Relational Exchanges," *Journal of Marketing*, 66 (1), 15-37.

Skinner, B. F. (1971), *Beyond Freedom and Dignity*, New York: Bantam Books.

Slovic, Paul, Baruch Fischoff, and Sara Lichtenstein (1977), "Behavioral Decision Theory," *Annual Review of Psychology*, 28, 1 39.

Smead, Raymond J. (1977), "Confidence in Judgment and Choice As A Function of Information Load and Integrative Complexity", unpublished doctoral dissertation, Indiana University.

Smith, Robert E. (1979), "Childrens' Advertising: Issues and Implications," in *Macro Marketing New Steps on the Learning Curve*, George Fisk and Robert W. Nason, eds., Boulder: Business Research Division, University of Colorado, 219 235.

_____ (1980), "Demand Effects in Evaluation Research," *Proceedings, American Institute for Decision Sciences*, National Conference (November 5), p. 319.

_____ and Shelby D. Hunt (1978a), "Attributional Processes and Effects in Promotional Situations," *Journal of Consumer Research*, 5 (No. 3), 149 158.

_____ and Shelby D. Hunt (1978b), "The Effectiveness of Personal Selling Over Advertising: An Attributional Analysis," in *Research Frontiers in Marketing: Dialogue and Directions*, Subhash C. Jain, ed., Chicago: American Marketing Association Combined Proceedings, 158 163.

_____ and Robert F. Lusch (1976), "How Advertising Can Position a Brand," *Journal of Advertising Research*, 16 (No. 1), February, 37 43.

_____ and Tiffany S. Meyer (1978), "Attorney Attitudes Toward Professional Advertising," in *Research Frontiers in Marketing: Dialogue and Directions*, Subhash C. Jain, ed., Chicago: American Marketing Association Combined Proceedings, 288 291.

_____ and Tiffany S. Meyer (1979), "Attorney Advertising: Bates and a Beginning," *Arizona Law Review*, 20, (No. 2), 427 483.

_____ and Tiffany S. Meyer (1980), "Attorney Advertising: A Consumer Perspective," *Journal of Marketing*, 44 (No. 2), Spring, 56 64.

_____ and William R. Swinyard (1980), "Involvement and the Hierarchy of Effects: An Integrated Framework," in *Attitude Research: A Look Back, A Look Ahead*, George B. Hafer, ed., Chicago: American Marketing Association, 86 98.

_____ and William R. Swinyard (1982), "Information Response Models: An Integrated Approach," *Journal of Marketing*, 46 (Winter), 81 93.

_____ and William R. Swinyard (1983a), "Attitude Behavior Consistency: The Impact of Product Trial Versus Advertising," *Journal of Marketing Research*, 20 (August), 257 267.

_____ and William R. Swinyard (1983b), "Cognitive Response to Advertising and Trial," working paper, Indiana University.

_____ and Laura M. Buchholz (1991), "Multiple Resource Theory and Consumer Processing of Broadcast Advertisements: An Involvement Perspective," *Journal of Advertising*, Volume 20, Number 3, (September), pp. 1-8.

_____ and William R. Swinyard (1988), "Cognitive Response to Advertising and Trial: Belief Strength, Belief Confidence and Product Curiosity," *Journal of Advertising*, Volume 17, Number 3, pp. 3-14.

_____ (1993), "Integrating Information From Advertising and Trial: Processes and Effects on Consumer Response to Product Information," *Journal of Marketing Research*, Volume 30, Number 2, (May), pp. 204-219.

_____ and Christine A. Vogt (1995), "The Effects of Integrating Advertising and Negative Word of Mouth Communications on Message Processing and Response," *Journal of Consumer Psychology*, Volume 4, Issue 2, pp. 133-152.

Soper, Barlow and Gary E. Milford (1995), "Belief When Evidence Does Not Support Theory," *Psychology and Marketing*, 12 (5), 415-422.

Sparkman, Richard M. Jr. and William Locander (1980), "Attribution Theory and Advertising Effectiveness," *Journal of Consumer Research*, 7 (December), 219 224.

Sparks, John R. and Shelby D. Hunt (1998), "Marketing researcher ethical sensitivity: Conceptualization, Measurement, and Exploratory Investigation," *Journal of Marketing*, 62 (2), 92-109.

Spreng, Richard A. and Scott B. MacKenzie (1996), "A Reexamination of the Determinants of Consumer Satisfaction," *Journal of Marketing*, 60 (3), 15-32.

Staats, A. W. and C. K. Staats (1958), "Attitudes Established by Classical Conditioning," *Journal of Abnormal and Social Psychology*, 57, 37 40.

Stanley, J. C. and H. J. Klausmeier (1957), "Opinion Constancy After Formal Role Playing," *Journal of Social Psychology*, 46, 11 18.

Steenkamp, Jan-Benedict, E.M., et al. (1999), "A Cross-National Investigation into the Individual and National Cultural Antecedents of Consumer Innovativeness," *Journal of Marketing*, 63 (2), 55-69.

Sternthal, Brian, Ruby Dholakia, and Clark Leavitt (1978), "The Persuasive Effect of Source Credibility: Tests of Cognitive Response," *Journal of Consumer Research*, 4 (March), 252 260.

Strong, E. C. (1972), "The Effects of Repetition in Advertising: A Field Experiment," Ph.D. Dissertation, Graduate School of Business, Stanford University.

Sumerlin J.R. and C.M. Bundrick (1996), "Brief Index of Self-Actualization: A Measure of Maslow's Model," *Journal of Social Behavior and Personality*, 11 (2), 253-271.

Summers, Gene F. ed. (1970), *Attitude Measurement*, Chicago: Rand McNally.

Swinyard, William R. (1980), "The Impact of Social Labeling on Buyer Seller Interactions: A Preliminary View," in *Theoretical and Empirical Research on Buyer Seller Interactions*, Chicago: American Marketing Association.

_____ (1981), "The Interaction Between Comparative Advertising and Copy Claim Variation," *Journal of Marketing Research*, 18 (May), 175 186.

_____ and Kenneth A. Coney (1978), "Promotional Effects on a High Versus Low Involvement Electorate," *Journal of Consumer Research*, 5, (No. 1), June, 41 48.

_____ and Charles H. Patti (1979), "The Communications Hierarchy Framework for Evaluating Copy Testing Techniques," *Journal of Advertising*, 8, (No. 3), Summer, 29 36.

_____ and Michael L. Ray (1977), "Advertising Selling Interaction: An Attribution Theory Experiment," *Journal of Marketing Research*, 14, (No. 4), November.

Taylor, James W. (1974), "The Role of Risk in Consumer Behavior," *Journal of Marketing*, 38 (April), 54 60.

Tax, Stephen S. and Stephen W. Brown, et al. (1998), "Customer Evaluations of Service Complaint Experiences: Implications for Relationship Marketing," *Journal of Marketing*, 62 (2), 60-76.

Thurstone, L. L. (1928), "Attitudes Can Be Measured," *American Journal of Sociology*, 33, 529 554.

Tischler, Len (1999), "The Growing Interest in Spirituality in Business," *Journal of Organizational Change Management*, 12 (4), 273-281.

Toy, Daniel R. (1982), "Monitoring Communication Effects: A Cognitive Structure/Cognitive Response Approach," *Journal of Consumer Research*, 9, 66 76.

Troutman, C. Michael and James Shanteau (1976), "Do Consumers Evaluate Products by Adding or Averaging Attribute Information?" *Journal of Consumer Research*, 3 (September), 101 106.

Tuten, Tracy L and Rachel A. August (1998), "Understanding Consumer Satisfaction in Services Settings: A Bideminsional Model of Service Strategies," *Journal of Social Behavior & Personality*, 13 (3), 553-564.

Tuzzolino, Frank and Barry R. Armandi (1981), "A Need-Hierarchy Framework for Assessing Corporate Social Responsibility," *Academy of Management Review*, 6 (1), 21-29.

Tybout, Alice M. and Richard F. Yalch (1980), "The Effect of Experience: A Matter of Salience?", *Journal of Consumer Research*, 6 (March), 406 413.

Tyebjee, Tyzoon T. (1979), "Response Time Conflict, and Involvement in Brand Choice," *Journal of Consumer Research*, 6 (December), 295 304.

Upshaw, Harry S. (1978), "Social Influence on Attitudes and on Anchoring of Congeneric Attitude Scales," *Journal of Experimental Social Psychology*, 14, 327 339.

V

Vinson, Donald E., Jerome E. Scott, and Lawrence M. Lamont (1977), "The Role of Personal Values in Marketing and Consumer Behavior," *Journal of Marketing*, 44 (April).

W

Waddock, Sandra and Neil Smith (2000), "Corporate Responsibility Audits: Doing Well by Doing Good," *Sloan Management Review*, 41 (2), 75-83.

Wakefield, Kirk L. and James H. Barnes (1996), "Retailing Hedonic Consumption: A Model of Sales Promotion of a Leisure Service", *Journal of Retailing*, 72 (4), 409-427.

Wallendorf, Melanie, Russell Belk, and Deborah Heisley (1988), "Deep Meaning in Possessions: The Paper," *Advances in Consumer Research*, 15 (1), 528-530.

Warland, Rex H. and John Sample (1973), "Response Certainty as a Moderator Variable in Attitude Measurement," *Rural Sociology*, 38 (Summer), 174 186.

Warshaw, Paul R. (1980), "A New Model for Predicting Behavioral Intentions: An Alternative to Fishbein," *Journal of Marketing Research*, 17 (May), 153 172.

Watson, J. B. (1919), *Psychology from the Standpoint of a Behavioralist*, Philadelphia: J. B. Lippincott.

Watson, Lyall (1979), *Lifetide*, New York: Bantam Books, Inc.

Weick, K. L. (1967), "Dissonance and Task Enhancement: A Problem for Compensation Theory?", *Organizational Behavior and Human Performance*, 2, 175 216.

Wicker, A. W. (1969), "Attitudes vs. Action: The Relationship of Verbal and Overt Behavioral Responses to Attitude Objects," *Journal of Social Issues*, 25, 41 78.

_____ (1975), "Commentaries on Belk,' Situational Variables and Consumer Behavior," *Journal of Consumer Research*, 2 (December), 165 167.

Wicker, F.W., G. Brown, J.A. Wiehe, A.S. Hagen, and J.L. Reed (1993), "On Reconsidering Maslow - an Examination of the Deprivation Domination Proposition," *Journal of Research in Personality*, 27 (2), 118-133.

Wilkie, William L. and Edgar A. Pessemier (1973), "Issues in Marketing's Use of Multi Attribute Attitude Models," *Journal of Marketing Research*, 10 (November), 428 441.

Wilke, William L. (1994), *Consumer Behavior*, Third Edition, New York: John Wiley & Sons.

Williams, Dale E. and Monte M. Page (1989), "A Multi-Dimensional Measure of Maslow's Hierarchy of Needs," *Journal of Research in Personality*, 23 (2), 192-213.

Wilson, David T., H. Lee Mathews, and James W. Harvey (1975), "An Empirical Test of the Fishbein Behavioral Intention Model," *Journal of Consumer Research*, 1 (March), 39 48.

Winter, Fredrick W. (1973), "A Laboratory Experiment of Individual Attitude Response to Advertising Exposure," *Journal of Marketing Research*, 10 (May), 130 140.

Woodruff, Robert B. (1972), "Measurement of Consumer's Prior Brand Information," *Journal of Marketing Research*, 9 (August), 258 263.

Wright, John S., Daniel S. Warner, Willis L. Winter, Jr., and Sherilyn K. Zeigler (1977), *Advertising*, New York: McGraw Hill Book Company.

Wright, Peter (1973), "The Cognitive Processes Mediating Acceptance of Advertising," *Journal of Marketing Research*, 10, 53 62.

_____ (1974), "Analyzing Media Effects on Advertising Responses," *Public Opinion Quarterly*, 38 (No. 2), 192 205.

_____ (1975), "Factors Affecting Cognitive Resistance to Advertising," *Journal of Consumer Research*, 2 (June), 1 9.

_____ (1976), "An Adaptive Consumer's View of Attitudes and Other Choice Mechanisms, As Viewed by an Equally Adaptive Advertiser," in *Attitude Research at Bay*, Debra Johusa and William D. Wells, eds., Chicago: American Marketing Association, 113 131.

_____ (1980), "Message Evoked Thoughts: Persuasion Research Using Thought Verbalizations," *Journal of Consumer Research*, 7 (September), 151 175.

_____ and Peter D. Rip (1980), "Product Class Advertising Effects on First Time Buyers' Decision Strategies," *Journal of Consumer Research*, 7 (September), 176 188.

Wright, Peter and David G. Mick (2002), "Marketplace Metacognition and Social Intelligence," *Journal of Consumer Research*, 28 (4), 677-682.

Wyer, Robert S. Jr. (1973), "Category Ratings as `Subjective Expected Values': Implications for Attitude Formation and Change," *Psychological Review*, 80 (No. 6), 446 467.

Yalch R. and F. Brunel (1996), "Need Hierarchies in Consumer Judgments of Product Designs: Is it Time to Reconsider Maslow's Theory?" *Advances in Consumer Research*, 23, 405-410.

Young-Won Ha, and Stephen J. Hoch (1989), "Ambiguity, Processing Strategy, and Advertising-Evidence Interactions," *Journal of Consumer Research*, 16 (December), 354-360.

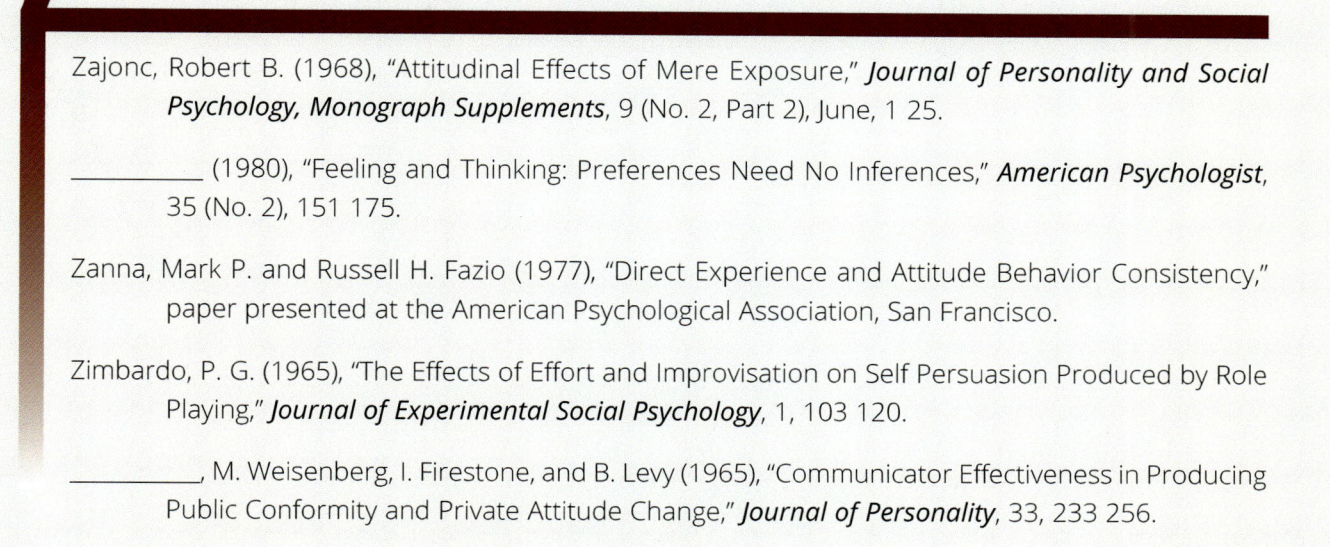

Zajonc, Robert B. (1968), "Attitudinal Effects of Mere Exposure," *Journal of Personality and Social Psychology, Monograph Supplements*, 9 (No. 2, Part 2), June, 1 25.

_____ (1980), "Feeling and Thinking: Preferences Need No Inferences," *American Psychologist*, 35 (No. 2), 151 175.

Zanna, Mark P. and Russell H. Fazio (1977), "Direct Experience and Attitude Behavior Consistency," paper presented at the American Psychological Association, San Francisco.

Zimbardo, P. G. (1965), "The Effects of Effort and Improvisation on Self Persuasion Produced by Role Playing," *Journal of Experimental Social Psychology*, 1, 103 120.

_____, M. Weisenberg, I. Firestone, and B. Levy (1965), "Communicator Effectiveness in Producing Public Conformity and Private Attitude Change," *Journal of Personality*, 33, 233 256.